ANDERSON'S
Law School Publications

Administrative Law Anthology
Thomas O. Sargentich

Administrative Law: Cases and Materials
Daniel J. Gifford

An Admiralty Law Anthology
Robert M. Jarvis

Alternative Dispute Resolution: Strategies for Law and Business
E. Wendy Trachte-Huber and Stephen K. Huber

The American Constitutional Order: History, Cases, and Philosophy
Douglas W. Kmiec and Stephen B. Presser

American Legal Systems: A Resource and Reference Guide
Toni M. Fine

Analytic Jurisprudence Anthology
Anthony D'Amato

An Antitrust Anthology
Andrew I. Gavil

Appellate Advocacy: Principles and Practice, Third Edition
Ursula Bentele and Eve Cary

Arbitration: Cases and Materials
Stephen K. Huber and E. Wendy Trachte-Huber

Basic Accounting Principles for Lawyers: With Present Value and Expected Value
C. Steven Bradford and Gary A. Ames

A Capital Punishment Anthology (and Electronic Caselaw Appendix)
Victor L. Streib

Cases and Materials on Corporations
Thomas R. Hurst and William A. Gregory

Cases and Problems in Criminal Law, Fourth Edition
Myron Moskovitz

The Citation Workbook: How to Beat the Citation Blues, Second Edition
Maria L. Ciampi, Rivka Widerman, and Vicki Lutz

Civil Procedure Anthology
David I. Levine, Donald L. Doernberg, and Melissa L. Nelken

Civil Procedure: Cases, Materials, and Questions, Second Edition
Richard D. Freer and Wendy Collins Perdue

Clinical Anthology: Readings for Live-Client Clinics
Alex J. Hurder, Frank S. Bloch, Susan L. Brooks, and Susan L. Kay

Commercial Transactions Series: Problems and Materials
Louis F. Del Duca, Egon Guttman, Alphonse M. Squillante, Fred H. Miller,
  Linda Rusch, and Peter Winship
    Vol. 1: Secured Transactions Under the UCC
    Vol. 2: Sales Under the UCC and the CISG
    Vol. 3: Negotiable Instruments Under the UCC and the CIBN

Communications Law: Media, Entertainment, and Regulation
Donald E. Lively, Allen S. Hammond, Blake D. Morant, and Russell L. Weaver

A Conflict-of-Laws Anthology
Gene R. Shreve

Constitutional Conflicts
Derrick A. Bell, Jr.

A Constitutional Law Anthology, Second Edition
Michael J. Glennon, Donald E. Lively, Phoebe A. Haddon, Dorothy E. Roberts, and Russell L. Weaver

Constitutional Law: Cases, History, and Dialogues
Donald E. Lively, Phoebe A. Haddon, Dorothy E. Roberts, and Russell L. Weaver

The Constitutional Law of the European Union
James D. Dinnage and John F. Murphy

The Constitutional Law of the European Union: Documentary Supplement
James D. Dinnage and John F. Murphy

Constitutional Torts
Sheldon H. Nahmod, Michael L. Wells, and Thomas A. Eaton

A Contracts Anthology, Second Edition
Peter Linzer

Contracts: Contemporary Cases, Comments, and Problems
Michael L. Closen, Richard M. Perlmutter, and Jeffrey D. Wittenberg

Contract Law and Practice
Gerald E. Berendt, Michael L. Closen, Doris Estelle Long, Marie A. Monahan, Robert J. Nye, and John H. Scheid

A Copyright Anthology: The Technology Frontier
Richard H. Chused

Corporate Law Anthology
Franklin A. Gevurtz

Corporate and White Collar Crime: An Anthology
Leonard Orland

A Criminal Law Anthology
Arnold H. Loewy

Criminal Law: Cases and Materials
Arnold H. Loewy

A Criminal Procedure Anthology
Silas J. Wasserstrom and Christie L. Snyder

Criminal Procedure: Arrest and Investigation
Arnold H. Loewy and Arthur B. LaFrance

Criminal Procedure: Trial and Sentencing
Arthur B. LaFrance and Arnold H. Loewy

Economic Regulation: Cases and Materials
Richard J. Pierce, Jr.

Elements of Law
Eva H. Hanks, Michael E. Herz, and Steven S. Nemerson

Ending It: Dispute Resolution in America
   Descriptions, Examples, Cases and Questions
Susan M. Leeson and Bryan M. Johnston

An Environmental Law Anthology
Robert L. Fischman, Maxine I. Lipeles, and Mark S. Squillace

Environmental Law Series
Jackson B. Battle, Robert L. Fischman, Maxine I. Lipeles, and Mark S. Squillace
   Vol. 1: Environmental Decisionmaking: NEPA and the Endangered Species Act,
      Second Edition
   Vol. 2: Water Pollution, Third Edition
   Vol. 3: Air Pollution, Third Edition
   Vol. 4: Hazardous Waste, Third Edition

Environmental Protection and Justice
   Readings and Commentary on Environmental Law and Practice
Kenneth A. Manaster

European Union Law Anthology
Karen V. Kole and Anthony D'Amato

An Evidence Anthology
Edward J. Imwinkelried and Glen Weissenberger

Federal Antitrust Law: Cases and Materials
Daniel J. Gifford and Leo J. Raskind

Federal Income Tax Anthology
Paul L. Caron, Karen C. Burke, and Grayson M.P. McCouch

Federal Rules of Civil Procedure, 1998-99 Edition
Publisher's Staff

Federal Rules of Evidence Handbook, 1998-99 Edition
Publisher's Staff

Federal Rules of Evidence: Rules, Legislative History, Commentary and Authority
   1998-99 Edition
Glen Weissenberger

Federal Wealth Transfer Tax Anthology
Paul L. Caron, Grayson M.P. McCouch, Karen C. Burke

First Amendment Anthology
Donald E. Lively, Dorothy E. Roberts, and Russell L. Weaver

The History, Philosophy, and Structure of the American Constitution
Douglas W. Kmiec and Stephen B. Presser

Individual Rights and the American Constitution
Douglas W. Kmiec and Stephen B. Presser

International Environmental Law Anthology
Anthony D'Amato and Kirsten Engel

International Human Rights: Law, Policy, and Process, Second Edition
Frank C. Newman and David Weissbrodt

Selected International Human Rights Instruments and
   Bibliography For Research on International Human Rights Law, Second Edition
Frank C. Newman and David Weissbrodt

International Intellectual Property Anthology
Anthony D'Amato and Doris Estelle Long

International Law Anthology
Anthony D'Amato

International Law Coursebook
Anthony D'Amato

International Taxation: Cases, Materials, and Problems
Philip F. Postlewaite

Introduction to the Study of Law: Cases and Materials
John Makdisi

Judicial Externships: The Clinic Inside the Courthouse, Second Edition
Rebecca A. Cochran

A Land Use Anthology
Jon W. Bruce

Law and Economics Anthology
Kenneth G. Dau-Schmidt and Thomas S. Ulen

The Law of Disability Discrimination, Second Edition
Ruth Colker and Bonnie Poitras Tucker

The Law of Disability Discrimination Handbook: Statutes and Regulatory Guidance Second Edition
Ruth Colker and Bonnie Poitras Tucker

Lawyers and Fundamental Moral Responsibility
Daniel R. Coquillette

Mediation and Negotiation: Reaching Agreement in Law and Business
E. Wendy Trachte-Huber and Stephen K. Huber

Microeconomic Predicates to Law and Economics
Mark Seidenfeld

Natural Resources: Cases and Materials
Barlow Burke

Patients, Psychiatrists and Lawyers: Law and the Mental Health System, Second Edition
Raymond L. Spring, Roy B. Lacoursiere, and Glen Weissenberger

Preventive Law: Materials on a Non Adversarial Legal Process
Robert M. Hardaway

Principles of Evidence, Third Edition
Irving Younger, Michael Goldsmith, and David A. Sonenshein

Problems and Simulations in Evidence, Second Edition
Thomas F. Guernsey

A Products Liability Anthology
Anita Bernstein

Professional Responsibility Anthology
Thomas B. Metzloff

A Property Anthology, Second Edition
Richard H. Chused

Public Choice and Public Law: Readings and Commentary
Maxwell L. Stearns

Readings in Criminal Law
Russell L. Weaver, John M. Burkoff, Catherine Hancock, Alan Reed, and Peter J. Seago

Science in Evidence
D.H. Kaye

A Section 1983 Civil Rights Anthology
Sheldon H. Nahmod

Sports Law: Cases and Materials, Third Edition
Ray L. Yasser, James R. McCurdy, and C. Peter Goplerud

A Torts Anthology, Second Edition
Julie A. Davies, Lawrence C. Levine, and Edward J. Kionka

Trial Practice
Lawrence A. Dubin and Thomas F. Guernsey

Unincorporated Business Entities
Larry E. Ribstein

FORTHCOMING PUBLICATIONS

Cases and Materials on the Law Governing Lawyers
James E. Moliterno

Cases and Problems in California Criminal Law
Myron Moskovitz

Elder Law: Readings and Materials
Thomas P. Gallanis, A. Kimberley Dayton, and Molly M. Wood

Family Law in Action: A Reader
Margaret F. Brinig, Carl E. Schneider, and Lee E. Teitelbaum

International Civil Procedure Anthology
David S. Clark and Anthony D'Amato

The Question Presented: Model Appellate Briefs
Maria L. Ciampi and William H. Manz

Resolution of Private International Disputes
David D. Caron

INTERNATIONAL TAXATION
CASES, MATERIALS, AND PROBLEMS

INTERNATIONAL TAXATION
CASES, MATERIALS, AND PROBLEMS

PHILIP F. POSTLEWAITE
Professor of Law
Northwestern University
School of Law

ANDERSON PUBLISHING CO.
CINCINNATI, OHIO

INTERNATIONAL TAXATION: CASES, MATERIALS, AND PROBLEMS
PHILIP F. POSTLEWAITE

© 1999 by Anderson Publishing Co.

All rights reserved. No part of this book may be reproduced in any form or by any electronic or mechanical means including information storage and retrieval systems without written permission from the publisher.

Anderson Publishing Co.
2035 Reading Road / Cincinnati, Ohio 45202
800-582-7295 / e-mail andpubco@aol.com / Fax 513-562-5430
World Wide Web http://www.andersonpublishing.com

ISBN: 0-87084-363-X

Dedication

In my class you will learn to think for yourselves again. You will learn to savor words and language. No matter what anybody tells you, words and ideas can change the world. . . . We are members of the human race, and the human race is filled with passion. Medicine, law, business, engineering, these are noble pursuits and necessary to sustain life. But poetry, beauty, romance, love, these are what we stay alive for. To quote from Whitman ". . . That you are here and life exists. An identity. That the powerful play goes on and you may contribute a verse." What will your verse be?

Dead Poets Society
(The Movie)

To my verse: Ruth, Jennifer, Jessalyn, and Matthew!

Table of Contents

Preface and Acknowledgments.. xxi

Chapter 1: Residency 1
§ 1.01 Overview of Taxing Structure for Individuals 1
           Cook v. Tait, 265 U.S. 47 (1924)................................. 2
§ 1.02 Overview of Taxing Structure for Domestic and Foreign Corporations.. 3
§ 1.03 The Residency Scheme—In General 4
§ 1.04 Citizenship.. 5
§ 1.05 Residency 5
§ 1.06 The Green Card Test 6
§ 1.07 The Substantial Presence Test 6
§ 1.08 The 30-Day De Minimis Rule 7
§ 1.09 The Tax-Home Exception... 8
           Weible v. United States, 244 F.2d 158 (9th Cir. 1957).. 9
§ 1.10 Exempt and Other Special Categories of Alien Individuals 12
§ 1.11 Residency Commencement and Termination 14
           Problem 1 15

Chapter 2: Source Rules 17
§ 2.01 Introduction 17
§ 2.02 Source Rules for Interest 20
§ 2.03 Exceptions to the Interest Source Rule...................... 21
§ 2.04 Source Rules for Dividends—Generally...................... 21
§ 2.05 Dividends from United States Corporations............... 22
§ 2.06 Dividends from Foreign Corporations......................... 22
§ 2.07 Source Rules for Personal Services Compensation 22
           Revenue Ruling 87-38, 1987-1 C.B. 176....................... 24
§ 2.08 Source Rules for Rents and Royalties 26
           Boulez v. Commissioner, 83 T.C. 584 (1984) 27
§ 2.09 Source Rules for Dispositions of United States Real Property Interests.. 30
§ 2.10 Source Rules for Sales of Personal Property............... 31
§ 2.11 Sales of Inventory Property... 31
§ 2.12 Sales of Noninventory Property 32
§ 2.13 Section 862—Income from Sources Without the United States 35

§ 2.14	Source Rules for Other Income	35
	Revenue Ruling 89-67, 1989-1 C.B. 233	36
	Problem 2	38

Chapter 3: Section 911 Exclusion — 41

§ 3.01	Taxation of Americans Abroad—Introduction	41
§ 3.02	Eligibility for the § 911 Exclusion	42
§ 3.03	The Tax Home Standard	43
§ 3.04	Bona Fide Residence Test	44
	Jones v. Commissioner, 927 F.2d 849 (5th Cir. 1991)	47
§ 3.05	Physical Presence Test	53
	Gelhar v. Commissioner, T.C. Memo 1992-162	55
§ 3.06	The Foreign Source Earned Income Limitation: § 911(b) Generally	57
	Revenue Ruling 80-254, 1980-2 C.B. 222	58
§ 3.07	Deferred Payments	58
§ 3.08	Amounts Received from a Sole Proprietorship or Partnership	59
§ 3.09	Limitation on the Amount of the Exclusion	60
§ 3.10	Employer-Provided Housing Exclusion	60
§ 3.11	Self-Provided Housing	62
§ 3.12	Computing the Foreign Earned Income Exclusion	62
	Problem 3	65

Chapter 4: Foreign Tax Credit — 67

§ 4.01	Introduction	68
§ 4.02	Credit Versus Deduction	68
§ 4.03	Persons Eligible to Take the Credit	69
§ 4.04	Creditable Taxes—General Principles	69
§ 4.05	Requirements for Credit	70
	Nissho Iwai American Corp. v. Commissioner, 89 T.C. 765 (1987)	71
	Revenue Ruling 90-107, 1990-2 C.B. 178	72
§ 4.06	Taxes on Business Income	73
§ 4.07	Taxes on Dividends, Interest, Other Passive Income, and Compensation	75
§ 4.08	Taxes "In Lieu Of" Income Taxes: § 903	75
§ 4.09	The § 904 Limitation upon the Amount of Taxes Which May Be Credited—In General	76
§ 4.10	The Separate Computations of the Overall § 904 Limitation	77
§ 4.11	Carryback and Carryover of Excess Taxes Paid: § 904(c)	80

§ 4.12	Corporations Eligible to Utilize the Foreign Tax Credit—Domestic Stockholders in Foreign Corporations: § 902	81
	First Chicago Corp. v. Commissioner, 96 T.C. 421 (1991)	82
§ 4.13	Calculating the Taxes Deemed Paid by Domestic Corporations	86
§ 4.14	The § 78 Gross-Up	87
§ 4.15	Two Variations on the § 904 Limitation: Capital Gains and Losses	87
§ 4.16	Recapture of Foreign Losses: § 904(f)	89
	Problem 4	91

Chapter 5: Tax Treaties—An Overview 93

§ 5.01	Overview	93
§ 5.02	Negotiation of Treaties	94
§ 5.03	Ratification of Treaties	94
§ 5.04	Interpretive and Supplementary Materials	95
§ 5.05	Relationship of Tax Treaties to United States Federal Law	96
§ 5.06	Tax Treaties and Double Taxation	97
§ 5.07	Persons Eligible for Treaty Benefits	97
§ 5.08	Saving Clauses	98
§ 5.09	Anti-Treaty Shopping Clauses	99
§ 5.10	Nondiscrimination Clauses	100
	Revenue Ruling 91-58, 1991-2 C.B. 340	101
§ 5.11	Competent Authority Procedures	102
	United States-Canada Income Tax Treaty	103
	United States-Canada Protocol to the Income Tax Treaty—1995	111
	Technical Explanation of United States Model Income Tax Treaty	115
	United States Model Income Tax Treaty	117
	Problem 5	127

Chapter 6: Tax Treaties and Passive Income 129

§ 6.01	Introduction	129
§ 6.02	Dividends	129
§ 6.03	Interest	130
§ 6.04	Royalties	131
§ 6.05	Gains from the Disposition of Property	131
§ 6.06	Income from Real Property	132
§ 6.07	Residual Income Clauses	132

Technical Explanation of United States-Canada
  Income Tax Treaty 132
Technical Explanation of the Protocol to the United
  States-Canada Income Tax Treaty—1995 143
Problem 6 155

Chapter 7: Tax Treaties and Business Income 157
§ 7.01 The Taxation of Business Profits—Generally 158
§ 7.02 Carrying on a United States Business 158
       Revenue Ruling 58-63, 1958-1 C.B. 624 159
§ 7.03 Fixed Place of Business 160
       Unger v. Commissioner, 936 F.2d 1316
       (D.C. Cir. 1991) 162
§ 7.04 Duration of Permanent Establishment 164
§ 7.05 Use of Another's Fixed Place of Business 165
§ 7.06 Use of Agents 165
§ 7.07 Dependent Agents 166
       Revenue Ruling 90-80, 1990-2 C.B. 170 167
§ 7.08 Agents Versus Purchasers 168
       Revenue Ruling 76-322, 1976-2 C.B. 487 168
§ 7.09 Agents Versus Lessees 170
§ 7.10 Scope of Business Profits Article 170
       Revenue Ruling 86-156, 1986-2 C.B. 297 171
§ 7.11 Business Profits Attributable to a Permanent
       Establishment 173
§ 7.12 Determination of Income Attributable to a
       Permanent Establishment 174
§ 7.13 Allocation and Apportionment of Expenses to a
       Permanent Establishment 177
§ 7.14 Dependent Personal Services—Employees 178
       Revenue Ruling 86-145, 1986-2 C.B. 297 180
§ 7.15 Independent Personal Services—Independent
       Contractors 181
§ 7.16 Computation of United States Tax Liability Under
       a Tax Treaty 182
§ 7.17 Disclosure of Treaty-Based Return Positions 183
       Technical Explanation of United States-Canada
       Income Tax Treaty 184
       Problem 7 189

Chapter 8: Nontreaty Persons—Investment Income 191
§ 8.01 General Taxing Pattern Applicable to Foreign Persons 191
§ 8.02 Taxation of Nonresident Individuals............................ 191
§ 8.03 Taxation of Foreign Corporations.................................. 193
§ 8.04 Income Described in §§ 871(a) and 881(a)—In General 194
§ 8.05 Withholding of 30 Percent Tax at Source..................... 195
§ 8.06 The Portfolio Interest Exception 195
Problem 8 197

Chapter 9: Nontreaty Persons—Existence of a Trade or Business... 199
§ 9.01 Trade or Business Status—Generally........................... 199
Revenue Ruling 88-3, 1988-1 C.B. 268......................... 201
Revenue Ruling 58-63, 1958-1 C.B. 624....................... 202
§ 9.02 Performance of Services... 202
Johansson v. United States, 336 F.2d 809 (5th Cir. 1964)... 203
§ 9.03 De Minimis Exception for Nominal Services 204
§ 9.04 Real Property.. 204
§ 9.05 Election to Be Taxed on a Net Basis 205
Revenue Ruling 92-74, 1992-2 C.B. 156....................... 206
§ 9.06 Dispositions of United States Real Property Interests 208
§ 9.07 Sales Activity 209
§ 9.08 Purchasing Activity 210
§ 9.09 Representative Office Activity 211
§ 9.10 Partnerships 211
§ 9.11 Use of Dependent and Independent Agents................. 212
§ 9.12 Licensees and Lessees.. 212
Problem 9 213

Chapter 10: Nontreaty Persons—Trade or Business Income 215
§ 10.01 Overview of the Taxation of Effectively Connected Income... 215
§ 10.02 Determination of Effectively Connected Income—In General 217
§ 10.03 Fixed or Determinable Income and Certain Other United States Source Income.. 217
§ 10.04 The Asset Use Test 218
§ 10.05 The Material Factor Test 219

§ 10.06	All Other United States Source Income	220
§ 10.07	Effectively Connected Foreign Source Income	221
	Revenue Ruling 75-253, 1975-1 C.B. 203	223
§ 10.08	Foreign Source Income Attributable to a Domestic Office or Place of Business	224
§ 10.09	United States Office or Other Fixed Place of Business	226
§ 10.10	Real Property Income Deemed Effectively Connected	227
§ 10.11	Allocation and Apportionment of Expenses—In General	227
§ 10.12	The Allocation Process	229
§ 10.13	The Apportionment Process	230
	Stemkowski v. Commissioner, 690 F.2d 40 (2d Cir. 1982)	231
	Problem 10	234

Chapter 11: Nontreaty Persons—Inventory Income; Branch Profits Tax ... 237

§ 11.01	Sales of Inventory Property	237
§ 11.02	Section 863(b)—Source Rules for Taxable Income	239
§ 11.03	Production and Sale of Inventory Property Involving a Foreign Jurisdiction	240
§ 11.04	Branch Profits Tax—In General	241
§ 11.05	Branch Profits Tax on the Dividend Equivalent Amount	241
§ 11.06	Special Rules for Year of Termination of United States Trade or Business	243
§ 11.07	Secondary Withholding Tax and Branch Profits Tax	244
	Problem 11	245

Chapter 12: Nontreaty Persons—United States Real Property Interests ... 247

§ 12.01	Background	247
§ 12.02	Tax Consequences of Treating Income as Effectively Connected to a United States Trade or Business	248
	Revenue Ruling 90-37, 1990-1 C.B. 141	249
§ 12.03	Direct Investment in United States Real Property	250
§ 12.04	United States Real Property Interests	250
§ 12.05	Dispositions	252

§ 12.06	Indirect Investment—Interests Held Through Domestic Corporations	253
§ 12.07	United States Real Property Holding Companies	253
§ 12.08	Indirect Investment—Interests Held Through Foreign Corporations	256
§ 12.09	Coordination of § 897 with Nonrecognition Rules	257
	Revenue Ruling 84-160, 1984-2 C.B. 125	258
	Problem 12	260

Chapter 13: Foreign Personal Holding Companies 263

§ 13.01	Foreign Personal Holding Companies	263
§ 13.02	The Gross Income Test	264
§ 13.03	Foreign Personal Holding Company Income	265
§ 13.04	Stock Ownership Test	266
§ 13.05	Deemed Dividend of Undistributed Foreign Personal Holding Company Income	268
§ 13.06	Undistributed Foreign Personal Holding Company Income	270
§ 13.07	The Dividends-Paid Deduction	270
§ 13.08	Deemed Dividends and the Indirect Foreign Tax Credit	271
	Revenue Ruling 74-59, 1974-1 C.B. 183	272
§ 13.09	Shareholders Required to Include the Deemed Dividend in Income	274
	Problem 13	275

Chapter 14: Controlled Foreign Corporations 277

§ 14.01	The Advantages of Tax Deferral	278
§ 14.02	The Intent Behind, and Overview of, the Controlled Foreign Corporation Provisions	278
§ 14.03	The United States Ownership Standard for Purposes of Controlled Foreign Corporation Status	280
§ 14.04	Amount of Imputed Income; Determining Ownership for Purposes of Income Inclusion	281
§ 14.05	Section 951 Inclusion and Computation: Subpart F Income and Earnings Invested in United States Property	283
§ 14.06	Subpart F Income; Foreign Base Company Income	284
§ 14.07	Foreign Personal Holding Company Income	284
	Revenue Ruling 82-209, 1982-2 C.B. 157	285
§ 14.08	Foreign Base Company Sales Income—In General	288
§ 14.09	Exempted Manufacturing and Same-Country Activities	288

§ 14.10	Foreign Base Company Services Income	290
§ 14.11	Allocation of Deductions to Base Company Income: Rules and Limitations	290
§ 14.12	Special Exceptions to Foreign Base Company Income	291
§ 14.13	Basis Adjustments	292
§ 14.14	Exclusions from Gross Income—Previously Taxed Earnings and Profits	292
§ 14.15	Controlled Foreign Corporation Interaction with the Foreign Tax Credit—§ 902 Implications	293
§ 14.16	Disposal of Stock of Controlled Foreign Corporations—§ 1248	294
§ 14.17	Shareholders and Transactions Subject to § 1248	295
§ 14.18	General Limitation on Amount of Gain Recaptured	295
	Problem 14	297

Chapter 15: International Taxation and Tax Policy 299

§ 15.01	Report of Treasury Department, Selected Tax Policy Implications of Global Electronic Commerce (November 21, 1996)	299

Preface and Acknowledgments

This text focuses on the major concepts of international taxation and their underlying policies. It stresses a problem-solving approach through the use of numerous, short problems interspersed among the relevant materials. This problem-solving approach parallels a "real world" experience and thus helps to develop legal and analytic skills.

The text is organized around three fundamental regimes of international taxation by the United States: (1) the basic rules of the United States with regard to taxing its domestic persons (i.e., citizens, residents, and domestic corporations) on their foreign activities; (2) the basic rules of the United States with regard to taxing nondomestic persons (i.e., nonresidents and foreign corporations) on their domestic activities; and (3) the safeguard rules employed by the United States in curbing the use by its domestic persons of foreign persons to conduct foreign activities.

The material in this text and accompanying teacher's manual, both of which are current through August 13, 1998, reflect the valuable assistance of a variety of people to whom the author expresses his thanks. Initially, the author wishes to thank the fine staff of Northwestern University School of Law. Many have been helpful and cooperative, in particular Cheri Zweig. Without their assistance, the project would still be in its embryonic stage. Further thanks are extended to Eric McElwain and Keith Pershall, Directors of the McGeorge University School of Law Summer Law Programs at Salzburg, Austria in 1996 and 1997, who allowed me to teach with these materials. Particular credit goes to the members of the Summer 1997 International Taxation class: Robert Arim, Anna Brislane, Larry Brown, Phyllis Coffin, Pete Fowler, John Genova, Stephanie Pearce, and Mick Walker on whom a draft of this text was inflicted. That usage, accompanied by student comments and reactions to the materials, permitted a far better refinement of the product than would have been attained operating in a vacuum. Special thanks go to my research assistants extraordinaire: Tamara Busch and Ann Chavie.

In order to ease the reading of the cases, some citations have been omitted without the use of ellipses, and in some instances footnotes in cases and other quoted material have been eliminated without indication. Any footnotes that were not edited retain their original numbers.

In this text, the word "section" or a section symbol (§) refers to sections of the Internal Revenue Code and the Regulations promulgated thereunder; Regulation or Reg., Proposed Regulations or Prop. Reg. refers to Treasury Department Regulations; Revenue Ruling or Rev. Rul. refers to Rulings published by the Internal Revenue Service; and Revenue Procedure or Rev. Proc. refers to Service-published Procedures.

Carolina Academic Press has granted permission to use portions of the work which originally appeared in its publication: Postlewaite, *International Taxation: Corporate and Individual, Third Edition* 1998.

Approach and Purpose

It is the author's intention to provide the student of international taxation with a basic introduction to the complicated world of corporate and individual international taxation from the perspective of the United States. These materials are intended for an introductory international taxation class, typically a two-hour class (but they could be expanded for a three-hour course) in which the sole prerequisite is a course in introductory Federal Income Taxation.

The area of international taxation is most complex, and the more difficult provisions within that area have been similarly described:

> In keeping with the high level of complexity, one has come to expect as a matter of course in the foreign tax area, the . . . provisions quickly reach, and rarely leave, a plateau of statutory intricacy seldom rivaled in other sections of the Code, thus, the provisions easily qualify as a "four star" example of Byzantine architecture in a statute not noted for its economy of line.[1]

Given the extensive and rapid developments occurring over the past decade, this comment aptly describes the field. As markets continue to globalize, international tax considerations multiply proportion-

---

[1] B. BITTKER & J. EUSTICE, FEDERAL INCOME TAXATION OF CORPORATIONS AND SHAREHOLDERS, ¶ 17.14 (4th ed 1979).

ately, if not geometrically. Moreover, the Treasury is concentrating an ever-increasing level of resources and attention on such issues and cross-border transactions. In light of these developments, it is increasingly important that one possess a working knowledge of the international tax provisions. However, given this complexity, the purpose of this work is to present the fundamental concepts of international taxation, hoping that the student who successfully journeys through them will have a working knowledge of these basic concepts. More advanced knowledge will require an additional course confronting more complex material and, possibly, frequent reference to a treatise on the topic.[2]

Coverage

The casebook addresses in a detailed fashion the international tax consequences, from a United States perspective, of transactions carried out by individuals and corporations. The text focuses on three situations: (1) the United States taxation of domestic individuals and corporations with respect to income arising from sources without the United States (i.e., foreign source income), (2) the United States taxation of their foreign counterparts on both their United States and foreign source income, and (3) the United States taxation of United States persons utilizing foreign persons to conduct their foreign activities.

Generally speaking, domestic individuals (i.e., citizens and residents) and domestic corporations are subject to United States taxation on all income, whatever its source. Thus, the United States tax rates are applied regardless of whether the income is derived in one of the 50 states or in a foreign country. However, any taxes which the domestic individual or corporation pays to a foreign jurisdiction may qualify for either a deduction or a credit against its United States tax liability, and certain foreign source earnings may be exempt from United States taxation.

In contrast to the tax treatment of domestic individuals and corporations, a foreign individual or corporation is not, by virtue of any *in personam* nexus, subject to tax by the United States. Foreign individuals and corporations resident in tax treaty jurisdictions are subject to United States taxation only if they derive income from within the United States (i.e., United States source income) or if they derive income which is "attributable to" a United States per-

---

[2] *See, e.g.,* Postlewaite, INTERNATIONAL TAXATION: CORPORATE AND INDIVIDUAL vols. 1-5 (Carolina Academic Press 3d. ed. 1998).

manent establishment. Passive income is typically subject to a rate of 15 percent or less with no allowance of deductions, and business income is subject to the graduated rates reduced by attendant deductions. Nontreaty residents receive somewhat similar yet broadened treatment since a 30 percent rate is imposed on passive income, and the attributable to a permanent establishment standard is broadened to an effectively connected to a trade or business standard.

Finally, the more limited taxing net attributable to foreign persons creates incentives for domestic persons to utilize a foreign enterprise (i.e., a corporation) to convert their investment or business activities into investments of a "foreign person." Congress, however, has developed various safeguard regimes limiting, but not precluding, such efforts.

Chapter 1
Residency

§ 1.01 Overview of Taxing Structure for Individuals
Cook v. Tait, 265 U.S. 47 (1924)

§ 1.02 Overview of Taxing Structure for Domestic and Foreign Corporations

§ 1.03 The Residency Scheme—In General

§ 1.04 Citizenship

§ 1.05 Residency

§ 1.06 The Green Card Test

§ 1.07 The Substantial Presence Test

§ 1.08 The 30-Day De Minimis Rule

§ 1.09 The Tax-Home Exception
Weible v. United States, 244 F.2d 158 (9th Cir. 1957)

§ 1.10 Exempt and Other Special Categories of Alien Individuals

§ 1.11 Residency Commencement and Termination
Problem 1

§ 1.01 Overview of Taxing Structure for Individuals

In the United States scheme of taxation, individuals are grouped into two basic categories: (1) United States citizens and resident aliens and (2) nonresident aliens. Those in the first category are taxed by the United States on their worldwide income. Nonresident alien individuals resident in a treaty jurisdiction are taxed only upon certain income which is derived in the United States or is attributable to a permanent establishment in the United States. Capital gains income of such nonresident aliens is typically exempt from United States taxation. If the foreign person constitutes a resident of a country that has not entered an income tax treaty with the United States, the taxing net may be further expanded and/or the tax rates increased. In light of these differences, it is clear that for individuals the determination of United States residency status is a matter of great importance.

Cook v. Tait
Supreme Court of the United States
265 U.S. 47 (1924)

Mr. Justice MCKENNA delivered the opinion of the Court. . . .

Plaintiff is a native citizen of the United States, and was such when he took up his residence and became domiciled in . . . Mexico. A demand was made upon him by defendant in error, designated defendant, to make a return of his income for the purpose of taxation under the revenue laws of the United States. Plaintiff complied with the demand, but under protest; the income having been derived from property situated in . . . Mexico. A tax was assessed against him in the sum of $1,193.38, the first installment of which he paid, and for it, as we have said this action was brought.

The question in the case . . . is, as expressed by plaintiff, whether Congress has power to impose a tax upon income received by a native citizen of the United States who, at the time the income was received, was permanently resident and domiciled in . . . Mexico, the income being from real and personal property located in Mexico.

Plaintiff assigns against the power, not only his rights under the Constitution of the United States, but under international law, and in support of the assignments cites many cases. It will be observed that the foundation of the assignments is the fact that the citizen receiving the income and the property of which it is the product are outside of the territorial limits of the United States. These two facts, the contention is, exclude the existence of the power to tax. Or to put the contention another way, to the existence of the power and its exercise, the person receiving the income and the property from which he receives it must both be within the territorial limits of the United States to be within the taxing power of the United States. The contention is not justified, and that it is not justified is the necessary deduction of recent cases. . . .

We may make further exposition of the national power as the case depends upon it. It was illustrated at once in *United States v. Bennett* by a contrast with the power of a state. It was pointed out that there were limitations upon the latter that were not on the national power. The taxing power of a state, it was decided, encountered at its borders the taxing power of other states and was limited by them. There was no such limitation, it was pointed out, upon the national power, and that the limitation upon the states affords, it was said, no ground for constructing a barrier around the

United States, "shutting that government off from the exertion of powers which inherently belong to it by virtue of its sovereignty."

The contention was rejected that a citizen's property without the limits of the United States derives no benefit from the United States. The contention, it was said, came from the confusion of thought in "mistaking the scope and extent of the sovereign power of the United States as a nation and its relations to its citizens and their relation to it." And that power in its scope and extent, it was decided, is based on the presumption that government by its very nature benefits the citizen and his property wherever found, and that opposition to it holds on to citizenship while it "belittles and destroys its advantages and blessings by denying the possession by government of an essential power required to make citizenship completely beneficial." In other words, the principle was declared that the government, by its very nature, benefits the citizen and his property wherever found, and therefore has the power to make the benefit complete. Or, to express it another way, the basis of the power to tax was not and cannot be made dependent upon the situs of the property in all cases, it being in or out of the United States, nor was not and cannot be made dependent upon the domicile of the citizen, that being in or out of the United States, but upon his relation as citizen to the United States and the relation of the latter to him as citizen. The consequence of the relations is that the native citizen who is taxed may have domicile, and the property from which his income is derived may have situs, in a foreign country and the tax be legal—the government having power to impose the tax.

Judgment affirmed.

§ 1.02 Overview of Taxing Structure for Domestic and Foreign Corporations

A similar dichotomy arises under the United States taxing system with respect to corporations. Two types of corporations exist—domestic and foreign. A domestic corporation is one organized or created under the laws of the United States or any of its states. A foreign corporation is defined as one which is not domestic.

Proper classification of the corporate entity is critical, since it determines the method of taxation under the United States tax laws. The Code broadly stipulates that every corporation is liable to the tax imposed under it. However, for international tax purposes, the application of § 11 to foreign corporations is limited by the taxing thresholds of § 882. As discussed above, qualification for tax treaty benefits may further reduce the tax liability to the United States.

It is immaterial whether a domestic corporation, subject to the tax imposed by § 11, derives income from sources within or without the United States. As a general rule, a domestic corporation is subject to United States taxation on all of its income, whether such income arises from foreign or United States business or investment activity. However, various policy considerations have led Congress in the past to modify this general taxing scheme with respect to certain specially defined entities. These domestic corporations have been afforded, as incentives to their organization, either special credits or a reduced rate of taxation.

A domestic corporation is taxed on all income even though some or all of its income may be derived through a foreign division or branch. A division or branch of a corporation is considered a part of that entity notwithstanding the fact that it may be staffed separately and directed by local management. A foreign branch is to be distinguished from a foreign subsidiary, which even though wholly owned, is a separate juridical entity and is treated as such for tax purposes. If a subsidiary is formed in a foreign jurisdiction, it is a foreign corporation and thus is not subject to the broad worldwide income taxing standard applicable to a domestic corporation.

§ 1.03 The Residency Scheme—In General

In the corporate context, the residency issue is easily resolved since the classification turns exclusively on the objective fact of where the enterprise was formed—a fact which can be readily ascertained with a minimum of effort. However, whether the United States possesses taxing jurisdiction over a foreign individual is not so easily determined. Prior to the enactment of § 7701(b) in 1984, this determination was essentially a question of fact focusing on whether the individual under scrutiny had a closer connection to the United States or the jurisdiction from which he came. Under this open-ended standard, it was impossible to chart a precise boundary between resident and nonresident alien individuals. The Ninth Circuit best described the residency issue as "[having] an evasive way about it, with as many colors as Joseph's coat."

Under § 7701(b), the prior facts-and-circumstances determination of residency status has been largely replaced by a more objective and mechanical test. While certain contexts mandate a reversion to the historical facts-and-circumstances standard, most of the issues regarding residency are now more simply resolved with a greater degree of certainty.

§ 1.04 Citizenship

United States citizens are taxed on their worldwide income from whatever source derived. The determination of United States citizenship is straightforward. The Regulations provide that every person born or naturalized in the United States and subject to its jurisdiction is a citizen. United States citizens who are also citizens of another jurisdiction are likewise encompassed in the worldwide income taxing net. An individual who has filed a declaration of intention to become a citizen, but who has not been admitted to citizenship through naturalization, is deemed an alien and not a citizen.

§ 1.05 Residency

The extent of a foreign citizen's liability for United States tax is predicated upon the critical inquiry of whether that individual is a resident alien individual or a nonresident alien individual of the United States. A resident alien individual generally is treated as a citizen for United States tax purposes. He or she is taxed on worldwide income. In contrast, nonresident alien individual status shrinks the United States taxing net to encompass only specified types of income.

The Code has adopted an objective determination of whether an alien individual is a United States resident. Such status in certain cases may be overriden by tax treaties. There are two basic tests by which residency is determined based on the individual's legal status and his physical presence in the United States. Under § 7701(b), an alien individual will be considered to be a United States resident with respect to any calendar year if and only if: (1) the individual is a lawful permanent resident of the United States at any time during the calendar year (the "green card test"); or (2) the individual is present in the United States for a particular time period (the "substantial presence test"). In all other cases, the individual is classified as a nonresident alien for tax purposes.

These tests represent the exclusive methods for determining whether an alien individual is considered a United States resident. If an individual is not described in these tests, he or she will not be considered a United States resident regardless of the degree or extent of contacts the person has with the United States.

§ 1.06 The Green Card Test

The first objective measure of United States residency focuses on the alien's legal status within the jurisdiction. An alien is treated as a United States resident if that individual is a lawful permanent resident of the United States at *any time* during the year at issue. Under this so-called "green card" test, an individual is a lawful permanent resident of the United States if he or she holds a green card at any time during the year and his or her status as a green card holder has neither been revoked nor determined administratively or judicially to have been abandoned. An alien individual who holds a green card may abandon resident alien status (subject to the physical presence test) by surrendering his green card to the Immigration and Naturalization Service or a consular officer.

For purposes of determining the alien individual's period of residence, residency terminates on the last day of the year on which the individual is lawfully admitted for permanent residence provided the individual has a closer connection to a foreign country for the remainder of the year and is not a United States resident at any time during the next year.

§ 1.07 The Substantial Presence Test

The second residency test, the substantial presence test, focuses on the alien individual's physical presence in the United States. Under the substantial presence test, an alien individual is treated as a resident alien if he or she is present in the United States (1) on at least 31 days of the current year and (2) at least 183 aggregate days during the current and two preceding taxable years.

An alien individual's presence in the United States for purposes of this test is determined using a composite, weighted measure of the alien's days of physical presence over a three-year period. The number of days an individual is present in the United States for a given year is computed as the aggregate of: (1) the number of days on which he or she was present in the United States during the current year; (2) the number of days on which he or she was present during the first preceding year; and (3) the number of days on which he or she was present during the second preceding year. For this purpose, fractional days of presence are counted as whole days. If this sum equals or exceeds 183 days, the individual meets the substantial presence test (absent the 30-day or tax-home exceptions discussed below) and thus is treated as a United States resident. However, actual presence of 183 days or more for the year in question is incontrovertible evidence of residence.

The mechanics of the substantial presence test may be illustrated by the following example. If A, a Greek national, has been present in the United States 210 days during Year 3, 9 days during Year 2, and 18 days during Year 1, he is a resident under the substantial presence test on the basis of his stay in Year 3 alone. For the year under consideration, if the foreign individual has *actual* presence of 183 days or more, he will be classified as a resident regardless of his presence in the United States in the preceding two years. However, if A's presence in the United States in Year 3 was only 180 days, he would nonetheless meet the requisite days of presence for resident status since his weighted average for the three-year measurement period exceeds 183 days (i.e., 180 x 1 = 180 (Year 3), plus, 9 x 1/3 = 3 (Year 2), plus, 18 x 1/6 = 3 (Year 1), yielding a total of 186 days).

An individual is treated as being present in the United States on any day if the individual is physically present in the United States at any time during such day. There are, however, various categories of individuals for which certain days are not counted as days of presence. Exceptions are provided for certain exempt individuals and certain individuals whose presence is transitory or temporary. Exempt individuals include, *inter alia*, certain teachers and trainees and certain students. In addition, individuals intending, but unable, to leave the United States because of a medical condition or problem arising while the individual was present in the United States are not considered to be present in the United States during that time. Regular commuters to United States employment who reside in Canada or Mexico or individuals in transit between two foreign points who are physically present in the United States for less than 24 hours are not deemed to be present in the United States during such transitory periods.

§ 1.08 The 30-Day De Minimis Rule

Notwithstanding any prior significant presence by an alien individual, if an alien individual is in the United States for 30 days or less in the calendar year, a de minimis exception to the substantial presence test applies. Under this exception, if an alien individual is physically present within the United States for 30 days or less during the current year, that individual will not be considered a United States resident even if the 183-day formula would otherwise be met.

§ 1.09 The Tax-Home Exception

Section 7701 negates resident status otherwise determined under the substantial presence test where the facts and circumstances and the individual's physical presence during the current year indicate that the individual has more significant ties to another jurisdiction. Under the tax-home exception, an alien individual is treated as a nonresident even if he meets the substantial presence test for any current year if the individual (1) is present within the United States on fewer than 183 days during the current year; (2) establishes that, for the current year, his "tax home" is in a foreign country; and (3) has a closer connection to such foreign country than to the United States. A tax home is determined by reference to the concept employed by § 162(a)(2) (applicable to the deductibility of travelling expenses incurred while away from home). Under these standards, a tax home is located at an individual's regular or principal place of business. If the individual lacks a regular or principal place of business, his tax home is his principal place of abode.

To avail himself or herself of the tax-home exception, the individual must establish the existence of a foreign tax home and a closer connection to the jurisdiction in which that tax home is located. In determining whether an individual has established a closer connection to a foreign country than to the United States, the individual must unequivocally demonstrate a significant lifestyle nexus to that country. Relevant facts and circumstances include, but are not limited to:

1. The location of the individual's permanent home;
2. The location of the individual's family;
3. The location of personal belongings, such as automobiles, furniture, clothing, and jewelry, owned by the individual and his or her family;
4. The location of social, political, cultural, or religious organizations with which the individual has a current relationship;
5. The location where the individual conducts routine banking activity (i.e., the location of personal bank accounts);
6. The location where the individual conducts business activities (other than those constituting his tax home);
7. The location of the jurisdiction in which the individual holds a driver's license;
8. The location of the jurisdiction in which the individual votes;

9. The country of residence designated by the individual on forms and documents; and
10. The types of official forms and documents filed by the individual.

The tax-home exception is not available for any year in which an individual has applied for a green card, has taken other affirmative steps to become a permanent resident, or has an application for adjustment of status pending.

Weible v. United States
United States Court of Appeals, Ninth Circuit
244 F.2d 158 (1957)

ROSS, DISTRICT JUDGE.

This is an action for refund of income taxes paid by appellant Glenn Weible . . . and his wife Patricia. During this period Weible was employed abroad. . . .

Weible, the taxpayer, had been employed by Max Factor and Company for some years prior to World War II, from 1938 to 1941. During the war he was employed by Lockheed, and in 1945 again entered Max Factor's employment, this time for the specific purpose of planning and constructing of manufacturing plants for the company in foreign countries, and the training of personnel to operate the same. The contract of employment was oral and by it Weible agreed to undertake the duties connected with these foreign assignments and to remain permanently outside the United States in the performance of these duties except for short periods of training and consultation. The periods of foreign employment which followed were as follows: Mexico, from January until May, 1946; Australia, from June, 1946, to October, 1948; Canada, from October, 1948, until July, 1949; England, from July, 1949 to December, 1950; South America, March, 1951, until date.

Without going into the evidence it is sufficient to state that in each country Weible became "integrated," at least to the extent of establishing social and business contacts with the local inhabitants. Since his job was the construction of manufacturing plants and the training of operating personnel his contacts in each country, as one may well imagine and as the record indicates, were many and varied, and much of his success appears to have been based on his ability to be and become a part of the social and commercial society of the particular countries in which he resided. . . .

Appellants present the question before the court in this fashion: "The only question presented is whether appellants were bona fide residents of a foreign country or countries within the meaning of Section [911] and thus entitled to the income exemption provided by that section. . . ."

Findings of fact, conclusions of law and judgment were entered on April 6, 1955. The court concluded that appellant Glenn Weible was not a bona fide resident of . . . Australia and Canada and England . . . and that therefore the earnings of Glenn Weible from Max Factor were taxable during this period. . . .

Appellants' specifications of error . . . are as follows:

(1) The court erred in failing to find that pursuant to his agreement with his employer and during the years 1947, 1948, and 1949 Weible agreed to and intended to remain continuously and indefinitely in a foreign country or countries in the performance of his duties except for short periods of training and consultation.

(2) The court erred in failing to find that the purpose of Weible in going to Australia, Canada and England was of such a nature that an extended stay in those countries may have been necessary for its accomplishment. . . .

Domicile and Residence

It does seem appellants' charge, to the effect that appellee is attempting to fuse two rather difficult words, "domicile" and "residence," has some merit. To permit that would be to create a hybrid and but compound the present confusion. But if we are to resolve the questions now before us it is necessary that we come to grips once and for all with the meaning of these expressions. . . . Since countless pages have been devoted to the distinctions between the two words our treatment will be short. . . .

"Residence" means living in a particular locality, but "domicile" means living in the locality with intent to make it a fixed and permanent home. "Residence" simply requires bodily presence as an inhabitant in a given place, while "domicile" requires bodily presence in that place, and also an intention to make it one's domicile.

Domicile is the most steadfast of the words, and is pretty well anchored in legal literature so far as meaning is concerned. Residence, on the other hand, has an evasive way about it, with as many colors as Joseph's coat. It reflects the context in which it is found, whereas "domicile" controls the context. Residence is physical, whereas domicile is generally a compound of physical presence plus an intention to make a certain definite place one's permanent abode, though, to be sure, domicile often hangs on the slender thread of intent alone, as for instance where one is a wanderer over the earth. Residence is not an immutable condition of domicile. . . .

The word "resident" is a term of many and varied meanings. It was, therefore, appropriate for the Commissioner of Internal Revenue, with the approval of the Secretary of the Treasury, to adopt interpretative regulations. As used in the statute and as interpreted by the regulation "residence" means broadly, presence as an inhabitant in a given place, not as a transient, but either indefinite as to time or for a purpose that is of such a nature that an extended stay be necessary for its accomplishment, although the person intends at all times to return to his domicile when the purpose has been consummated or abandoned. . . .

In view of the foregoing discussion we are of the Opinion that Weible was not only a "resident" of Australia, Canada and England during the years 1947, 1948 and 1949, but on the facts of his case was a "bona fide" resident. . . .

White v. Hoefferbert was similar to the Weible case. Taxpayer sought a refund from the Commissioner under Section [911] on the ground that his income was personal salary from sources without the United States while he was a bona fide resident of foreign countries. He was denied the refund and instituted suit in the District Court to recover the alleged overpayment. After hearing the evidence the court said that as a mixed question of law and fact the taxpayer's position was correct and that he was entitled to the refund claimed.

> "The principal and indeed the only issue in the case is whether on the facts the taxpayer was a bona fide resident of foreign countries during the entire taxable years involved, within the meaning of the Revenue Code, § [911]. The physical facts are not really in dispute."

Here the court said that the taxpayer's original engagement as a foreign service officer was for an indefinite period of time and it was only reasonable to believe that his intention was to remain in the foreign service of that company as a career or at least for many years. It was pointed out that on each visit of the taxpayer to the United States his intention was to return to Spain. In our case Weible on each visit intended to return to the foreign country in which he was then residing, or to such other foreign country as Max Factor might send him. The comments made by the court in the *White* case so aptly apply to the Weible situation that we quote further:

> "On hearing the taxpayer's extended testimony I found him a highly creditable and very well informed witness, and have no difficulty in finding his expression of intentions with regard to his foreign residence were in entire good faith. There is not the slightest suggestion in the case of any attempt by him to evade taxes. His foreign residence was solely due to the important business interests of the I.T. & T. in European countries. His case seems fairly typical of many citizens of the United States who accept foreign service for American enterprises with large interests abroad."

This case is factually similar to the Weible case in another respect, as is apparent from the following:

> "The only item of evidence introduced by the defendant in any way tending to contradict the taxpayer was his statement in filling out a printed form of 'Application for Registration' before the United States Vice Consul at Stockholm in which, after stating other factual matters * * * there was a short sentence reading 'I intend to return to the United States within six months to

reside permanently.' Divorced from its context this statement would, of course, be entitled to ponderable weight as bearing upon the bona fides of the taxpayer with respect to the duration of his employment for the I.T. & T. and his intended residence in Sweden. However, the statement was entirely satisfactorily explained by the taxpayer. * * * The evidence taken as a whole is entirely satisfactory and convincing that the particular statement under the circumstances did not contradict the main and really undisputed facts of the case. . . ."

Appellee on numerous occasions in its brief referred to Weible as a "sojourner" in the countries in which he resided. Surely, on the basis of any definition, that was an unfair descriptive adjective to be applied to Weible. Then, again, it appears that there has been some unwarranted use of the words "residence" and "domicile," which, if not deliberate, was at least careless.

The appellee would also have us believe that one must practically renounce his American citizenship to acquire a Section [911] residence in a foreign country. We are reminded of threading the camel through the needle.

The income tax law has spread its tentacles into everyone's life, and into every phase of life. Presently it is the most important factor in the economic welfare of our citizens. At its best there is much to be wondered at, both in the reading and the administrative application. Humble citizen to multi-millioned corporation has the right to assert and take every benefit available. This without stigma attached. It appears, to this writer, at least, that in relation to these exemption statutes the attitude of the bureaus responsible for their administration have too long been "try and get it." Such was not the intent of Congress.

The judgment is reversed and the case remanded with directions to enter judgment for the plaintiffs, appellants here.

§ 1.10 Exempt and Other Special Categories of Alien Individuals

Under the objective definition of resident alien contained in § 7701(b), certain alien individuals and their activities are accorded special exemptions from resident status. Certain days of presence of these "exempt" or special aliens are not counted towards the individual's United States residency. Special rules apply to specified categories of exempt aliens, those alien individuals unable to leave the United States for medical reasons, and certain individuals commuting to or travelling through the United States. Basically, days spent in the United States by such individuals will not be counted for purposes of determining presence under the substantial presence test.

The exempt category of alien individuals includes, *inter alia*, teachers or trainees and students. The Code and Regulations provide detailed definitions of the individuals in these exempt categories. For teachers and students, visa requirements are imposed and substantial compliance with such provisions is mandated. Special timing limitations are imposed on the teacher and student exemptions where such individuals are recurrently present in the United States. Lengthy stays eventually lose the protection of the exemption. Such limitations prevent a timeless pursuit of experience and knowledge while enjoying a tax-holiday courtesy of the United States government.

For individuals suffering a medical condition or problem, presence does not arise for any day on which an individual objectively intended to leave the United States but was unable to leave the United States because of a medical condition or problem arising while the individual was present therein. The Regulations expressly provide that the condition causing the failure to leave must not be a known pre-existing problem or condition. Presumably, a foreign individual with a known heart condition could not avail himself of the exception if he had a heart attack while visiting the United States. The medical exemption applies only to qualified medical stays extending beyond the individual's intended date of departure.

As illustrated by the Regulations, if a foreign individual intending to depart the United States on a flight scheduled for March 31 is injured and hospitalized by a serious accident in the United States on March 25, only post-March 31 days are excluded for purposes of the substantial presence test. The exemption contains definite limitations. For instance, a stay for purposes of treating a condition arising during a *prior* United States stay does not qualify. In addition, the individual cannot exclude days of presence that are considered to extend beyond a reasonable period in which to depart. Once the individual has recovered, the exemption ceases for any days of presence after the expiration of a reasonable period for making arrangements to leave.

Days in transit between foreign points are also, quite practically, excluded as days of presence for the substantial presence test. Such a traveller most likely cannot utilize his brief stay in the United States for any purpose sufficiently significant to extend residency nexus. The exemption is designed to protect individuals travelling between airports to change planes or those experiencing brief United States layovers. The exemption is conditioned on physical presence of less than 24 hours and the absence of any nontravel activities. Thus, should the individual attend a business meeting while in transit, the exemption will not apply.

§ 1.11 Residency Commencement and Termination

A resident individual's period of residency in the United States is measured differently depending on whether the individual obtained resident status via satisfying the green card test and/or the substantial presence test. If an individual satisfies the green card test but does not otherwise meet the substantial presence test, the individual's "residency starting date" is the first day of physical presence during the calendar year as a lawful permanent resident. If an alien individual satisfies the green card test for the current year but is not physically present in the United States during the current year, the individual's residency starting date is the first day of the following year.

If the substantial presence test is satisfied, residency generally commences on the first day the individual is present in the United States. However, a de minimis rule may apply in which nominal presence is disregarded. If during a period of actual presence (for example, a house-hunting trip) an individual can evidence that he had a closer connection to a foreign country than to the United States, up to ten days of presence can be disregarded for purposes of determining the residency start date. For example, if a Greek national flew to Philadelphia for a four-day unsuccessful search for housing in January, returned again in March for five days in which he procured housing commencing June 1, his residency period begins upon his arrival on June 1 notwithstanding his actual presence in the United States in January and March.

Similar rules apply for determining the alien individual's residency termination date. Residency terminates under the green card test on the last day of the calendar year on which the individual is deemed to be lawfully admitted for permanent residence provided he or she has a closer connection to a foreign country for the remainder of the year and he or she is not a United States resident at any time during the next calendar year.

Under the substantial presence test, provided that after the last date of physical presence in the United States the individual has a closer connection to a foreign country for the balance of the calendar year and is not a United States resident in the next year, his or her last day of presence will close the period of residency. Again, the nominal presence rules may be utilized to disregard up to ten days of actual presence. It must be noted, however, that though these days are disregarded for purposes of determining residency commencement and termination dates, they are still considered for determining whether an individual meets the substantial presence test.

PROBLEM 1—RESIDENCY

Code: §§ 1(a), 2(d), 11(a), 11(d), 871(a)(1), 871(a)(2), 871(b), 881(a), 882(a), 7701(a)(4)-(5), 7701(b)(1)-(3), 7701(b)(5)-(7)

Regulations: §§ 301.7701(b)-1(b), (c), and (e); 301.7701(b)-2(a)-(d)(2); 301.7701(b)-3(a), (b)(1), (4), (6), and (7)(iii), (c), and (d); 301.77701(b)-4(a)-(c)(2) and (d) examples (1)-(4)

1. What income of a citizen, resident individual, or domestic corporation is taxed by the United States? What income of a nonresident individual or a foreign corporation is taxed by the United States?

2. A, a citizen of Italy, came to New York City hoping to make a fortune in the "Big Apple" before returning to his native Italy. During the year, his salary totaled $15,000 and he had interest income from Italy of $5,000. What are the tax consequences?

3. P has never been in the United States prior to his move to New York City on January 1. P moved to New York City after applying for, and receiving, all requisite approval and permission from the Immigration and Naturalization Service to remain in the United States for as long as he wished.

    a. Will P be considered a resident alien under § 7701(b)? Under what test(s) might P be construed to be a resident alien?

    b. Assume instead P moved to New York City under a temporary visa on January 1, where he lived until his application for permanent residence was approved on November 15. What result?

    c. What if P moved to New York City on October 15, and his application for permanent residence in the United States was granted on December 1. Would P be considered a resident alien for any portion of the tax year? Under what test(s)? What would be the first day of his residency under § 7701(b)(2)?

4. H, a citizen of Spain, was present in the United States for 90 days during Year 1, 120 days in Year 2, and 150 days in Year 3. H was not a lawful permanent resident of the United States during any of those years and was not present in the United States during any year before Year 1.

a. In what year(s), if any, would H be considered a resident alien? What if H was present in the United States for 120 days in Year 3?
b. If H were present in the United States for 360 days in Year 1, 360 days in Year 2, and 30 days in Year 3, would he satisfy the substantial presence test for Year 3?
c. Assume alternatively that H was present in the United States for 150 days in Year 1, and 150 days in Year 2. He spent the remainder of his time in Spain where his wife and children still live and where he operates a thriving business. In addition, H is registered to vote and is licensed to drive in Spain. H travels to the United States in order to sell the widgets that his business produces in Spain. Will H be considered a resident alien in the United States for federal income tax purposes?

5. J, a citizen of Germany, is a student at Miami University in Oxford, Ohio. J is permitted to remain in the United States because the INS issued him a student visa. He was present as a first year student in the United States for 270 days in Year 1, 270 days in Year 2, and 270 days in Year 3.

a. Is J considered a resident alien?
b. Assume that J's student visa expired on May 1, Year 3, yet J remained in the United States until December 31, Year 3 under a temporary visa. Does your answer change?
c. Assume that J's student visa expired on May 1, Year 3. As J was driving to the Cincinnati airport, he was distracted by the roar of the crowd emanating from Riverfront Stadium following a Reds' homerun and drove into an embankment. J recovered from the accident but only after being immobilized in a body cast until December 28, Year 3. If J flew home to Germany on December 31, Year 3, would he be treated as a resident alien under the substantial presence test?

Chapter 2
Source Rules

§ 2.01　Introduction
§ 2.02　Source Rules for Interest
§ 2.03　Exceptions to the Interest Source Rule
§ 2.04　Source Rules for Dividends—Generally
§ 2.05　Dividends from United States Corporations
§ 2.06　Dividends from Foreign Corporations
§ 2.07　Source Rules for Personal Services Compensation
　　　　Revenue Ruling 87-38, 1987-1 C.B. 176
§ 2.08　Source Rules for Rents and Royalties
　　　　Boulez v. Commissioner, 83 T.C. 584 (1984)
§ 2.09　Source Rules for Dispositions of United States Real Property Interests
§ 2.10　Source Rules for Sales of Personal Property
§ 2.11　Sales of Inventory Property
§ 2.12　Sales of Noninventory Property
§ 2.13　Section 862—Income from Sources Without the United States
§ 2.14　Source Rules for Other Income
　　　　Revenue Ruling 89-67, 1989-1 C.B. 233
　　　　Problem 2

§ 2.01 Introduction

The source rules are relevant to United States individuals and corporations. Undoubtedly, the most important domestic application of these rules is in applying the overall limitation on the foreign tax credit, discussed in Chapter 4. Under § 901, a credit is generally allowed for income taxes paid by a United States person to a foreign government. Under § 904, this credit is limited by a computation which focuses upon the ratio of foreign source taxable income to taxable income from all sources. As the percentage of foreign source taxable income increases, the greater the allowable credit becomes. Thus, it is in the domestic taxpayer's best interest to scrutinize the origin of his income.

A similar concern arises in qualifying for the exclusion by a United States individual under § 911. As qualification turns on foreign source earned income, again the source rules are critical.

As discussed at Chapters 9-11, the source rules are relevant to foreign persons as well. A foreign person resident in a treaty country is subject to United States tax only on income derived from United States sources, the rules for which are established by treaty or are expressly incorporated from the Code, or income attributable to a permanent establishment. Investment income is typically taxed at a rate of 15 percent or less and business profits are subject to the graduated rates. A non-treaty foreign person generally is subject to United States tax only on income derived from United States sources or income effectively connected to a domestic trade or business. The graduated rates of §§ 1, 11, 871(b), and 882(a) are applied to income effectively connected (which typically requires a United States source) to a domestic trade or business. A 30 percent flat rate is levied on the taxpayer's other United States source gross income which generally consists of investment income.

The basic rules for sourcing income are contained in §§ 861, 862, 863, and 865. Underpinning these rules is the general proposition that the source of income is the jurisdiction from which that income is derived. Such an inquiry poses both factual and jurisdictional issues.

The initial issue to be determined is whether there is an appropriate nexus between the income derived and a foreign jurisdiction or the United States sufficient to classify that income as possessing a foreign or a United States source. For example, in the case of income derived from the rendition of services, the fact that the recipient of the services resides in a foreign country and pays for those services with a check drawn on a foreign bank are two significant "jurisdictional contacts" with the foreign country. However, other significant focal points may be where the funds are received and deposited and where the services are rendered. While each of these contacts could be defended as a basis upon which sourcing is logically premised, Congress has concluded that the place where the services are rendered is the most relevant contact for source classification of such compensation. The governing rule selected by Congress for the sourcing of various receipts may be grounded on the notion that the prescribed treatment is the most relevant and appropriate basis upon which to source income or simply may be grounded upon the administrative ease of applying that rule.

The source rules essentially classify income in one of three ways: as income from a United States source; income without a United States source; or income from partly within and partly without the United States. The rules operate based upon specific categories of income, such as interest, dividends, or income from the manufacture and sale of property. Categories of income not expressly addressed by a particular sourcing rule are basically sourced administratively or judicially, oftentimes with reference to the statutory rule which is most congruous with the transaction or income type under consideration.

Sections 861 and 862 enumerate eight categories of income—e.g., interest, dividends, personal services, rentals and royalties, profits from the disposition of a United States real property interest, profits from the sale of inventory property, etc. Section 865, a companion statute, sources income from the sale of personal property not governed by § 861(a)(6). With respect to these categories, §§ 861 and 862 generally adopt a *singular* focus and enumerate those circumstances under which such income will constitute exclusively United States source income or exclusively foreign source income.

Under § 863, discussed in Chapter 11, other categories of income are enumerated which have a significant relationship with jurisdictions other than the United States, e.g., manufacture of inventory abroad and sale within the United States and vice versa. In order to properly reflect the "contributions" of the respective jurisdictions to the derivation of such income, allocation rules are provided which result in a portion of the income possessing a United States source and the remainder having a foreign source.

Since the focus of the source rules is on income, losses are not sourced under § 861 but instead are classified for tax purposes under the allocation and apportionment rules of Regulation § 1.861-8. Regulations for the sourcing of losses arising under § 865 regarding the sale of personal property have been recently proposed at § 1.865-2.

Effective tax planning may require scrutiny of the source rules of several countries. Not all jurisdictions have the same criteria for source purposes. For instance, while the United States focuses on the jurisdiction where services are rendered, another jurisdiction may employ a different standard, such as the residence of the payor. Thus, in an international setting, it is possible for a single transaction spanning two taxing jurisdictions to possess *two* countries of source. Both the foreign jurisdiction and the United States may conclude that the income arises *exclusively* within their respective borders.

§ 2.02 Source Rules for Interest

Generally, the source of interest income is controlled by the residence or the place of incorporation of the obligor. Under § 861(a)(1), two types of interest are deemed to possess a United States source: interest from the United States or the District of Columbia (governmental interest) and interest from the interest-bearing obligations of United States residents and domestic corporations.

Interest arising from the debts of private obligors is sourced in the United States if the true obligor is a United States resident or a domestic corporation. Determining the domesticity of a corporation is particularly straightforward since, under § 7701(a)(4), the only issue is whether the entity was created or organized under the laws of any state or the United States. However, as regards other obligors, the term "resident" has proven to be an elusive one. The Regulations provide that the term includes an individual who, at the time of payment of the interest, is a resident of the United States and a domestic or foreign partnership which at any time during its taxable year is engaged in trade or business in the United States. These terms are fraught with ambiguity, resulting in difficulties in determining when an individual is truly resident in the United States or when an enterprise is engaged in a United States trade or business.

Related difficulties arise because of the statute's relatively simplistic assumption that there is only one obligor for any given debt transaction. Consider, for example, the result when X, a United States resident, and Y, a nonresident alien, jointly execute an "interest-bearing obligation." Should the source of the interest depend upon who ultimately pays the obligation? Should each co-obligor's ability to pay the note be examined in determining income source? Or, to simplify, should any interest payment be considered as 50 percent United States source and 50 percent foreign source, regardless of who actually satisfies the obligation? Neither the statute nor the Regulations pertaining to interest source offer any guidance. Analogous difficulties arise when Y, a United States resident, acts as a guarantor of the debt of X, a nonresident alien individual.

The definition of interest subject to sourcing under § 861(a)(1) is quite broadly defined. Although the statute refers only to "interest on bonds, notes, or other" interest-bearing obligations, § 861(a)(1) includes interest imputed under §§ 483 and 1273 original issue discount. Payments which are disguised forms of interest will likewise be classified according to the interest source rules.

§ 2.03 Exceptions to the Interest Source Rule

The residence of the obligor generally dictates the source of interest income. There are, however, a number of exceptions to this basic rule. These exceptions are premised on both grounds of policy and practicality.

Interest payments made by a United States resident or corporation that is essentially "domestic" in name only are not deemed to arise from a United States source. Interest paid by United States persons conducting an objectively active foreign business is treated as foreign source income. This exception provides for foreign sourcing if over a three-year period at least 80 percent of the gross income of the domestic corporation or the resident alien individual is derived from an active foreign business. In such a case, *all* of the interest received on the debts of that individual or corporation will be foreign sourced. Income is active foreign business income if it is derived by the individual or corporation from non-United States sources and is attributable to the active conduct of a business abroad.

Under another exception, interest on deposits with *foreign* branches of a United States corporation or partnership, if that branch is engaged in the banking business, will be considered foreign sourced. A companion rule exists for interest on deposits with foreign branches of a United States corporation or partnership which is a savings and loan or similar institution.

§ 2.04 Source Rules for Dividends—Generally

Under § 861(a)(2), the dividend source rules, like those for interest, focus upon certain characteristics of the payor. For corporate payors, both rules generally focus upon the situs of incorporation of the payor. Thus, the dividend source rules make the initial distinction for source purposes between domestic and foreign corporations. However, as discussed below, a further, more refined attempt is made to track the earnings and profits derived by the corporation and to account for the origin of those earnings via the source rules.

The Regulations state that the term "dividend" encompasses distributions defined in § 316, hinting that the concept of dividends for these purposes is linked to variations in corporate earnings and profits. Thus, distributions out of earnings and profits described in § 301(c)(1) are dividends subject to the sourcing rules of § 861(a)(2).

§ 2.05 Dividends from United States Corporations

The § 861(a)(2) sourcing rules focus on two principal areas: dividends from a domestic corporation and dividends from a foreign corporation. Dividends received from domestic corporations are United States source income with a minor exception for certain distributions of Domestic International Sales Corporations.

§ 2.06 Dividends from Foreign Corporations

Dividends from foreign corporations with a de minimis United States business nexus are generally spared United States source classification. Under § 861(a)(2)(B), if, over a three-year period, less than 25 percent of the gross income of a foreign corporation is effectively connected with a United States trade or business, any dividend received from that corporation will be deemed foreign source income. However, even if 25 percent or more of the payor's income over that period is effectively connected (or treated as such), a portion of the dividend received by the stockholder equal to the corporate ratio of effectively connected gross income to all gross income will be deemed United States source income.

For example, if Y corporation, formed and organized in Greece, in Year 4 pays a $10,000 dividend to Z, a United States shareholder, and its percentage of income effectively connected to a United States trade or business for Year 1–Year 3 was 22 percent, the entire dividend would be foreign source. If the applicable percentage was 40 percent, the dividend would be bifurcated for source purposes: $4,000 would be domestic source and $6,000 would be foreign source.

§ 2.07 Source Rules for Personal Services Compensation

The source rules for services follow the locale where those services were performed. Under § 861(a)(3), compensation for labor or personal services performed in the United States has a domestic source. This rule holds true irrespective of the residence of the payor, the place in which the contract for services was made, or the place or time of payment. Thus, the Swedish model who poses at various United States national parks in return for a fee of $15,000 will have $15,000 of domestically sourced income.

A de minimis exception to the place-of-performance rule is contained in § 861(a)(3)(A)-(C). This exception is intended "to permit residents of other countries to make brief visits to the United States for business purposes, such as the buying and selling of goods, without being subject, before leaving the country, to a demand for payment of tax on their compensation during the period of their stay here." This exception provides that compensation for services performed in the United States will be considered foreign source income if: (1) the labor or services are performed by a nonresident alien individual temporarily present in the United States for no more than 90 days during the year; (2) the aggregate compensation of that individual is $3,000 or less; and (3) the services are performed as an employee of or under a contract with (a) a nonresident alien, foreign partnership, or foreign corporation not engaged in a trade or business within the United States or (b) a United States citizen or resident individual, a United States partnership, or a United States corporation, if such services are performed for its foreign office or place of business.

Other problems surrounding the source of compensation include distinguishing compensation from other types of income and allocating compensation between foreign sources and United States sources. The first difficulty arises when a taxpayer performs services which eventually culminate in a patent, trade process, or other property interest. If a right to use that property is thereafter granted to a foreign entity, difficult characterization issues arise in deciding whether the resulting payments are royalties (subject to a separate source rule) or compensation.

A second and more common problem concerns the allocation of compensation when labor is performed by an employee both within and without the United States. The Regulations specify that apportionment may be made on whatever basis "most correctly reflects the proper source of income" but go on to state that in "many cases apportionment on the time basis will be acceptable." Two examples are presented which emphasize, seemingly to the exclusion of other methods, apportionment based upon a ratio of work days spent in the United States to total work days for which the compensation is paid. Thus, when apportionment is made by an individual on a time basis, the Service should face great difficulty in disturbing that allocation by using a method considered more reasonable.

Revenue Ruling 87-38
1987-1 C.B. 176

ISSUE

Advice has been requested concerning the method of allocating income between sources within the United States and sources without the United States under the circumstances described below.

FACTS

The taxpayer, a resident and citizen of Canada, is employed by a professional hockey club (club), a United States corporation. Prior to the regular season the taxpayer reported to and participated in a 30-day training period at a camp of the club located in Canada. The taxpayer entered into a new standard player's contract (contract) while participating in the training camp activities. The taxpayer received a per diem allowance during the period while at the training camp in addition to a per diem allowance and other amounts for playing in the exhibition games during that period. The contract also provided per diem allowances for each playoff series in which the player's team participated.

The salary agreed to by the taxpayer under the terms of the standard player's contract, which exceeded $15,000 per year, could be paid in semi-monthly installments beginning October 1 and ending with the final league game or playoff game. Since the regular playing season is shorter than the 1-year period covered by the contract, the taxpayer had the option to elect and did elect to receive the salary over a 12-month period. Thus, the taxpayer received salary payments during the time period when not actually playing hockey for the club. During this time period, taxpayer engaged in physical activities (such as weight lifting and running) to maintain good physical conditioning. Taxpayer was required by the contract to report to the training camp in good physical condition. During the regular season, the taxpayer played in hockey games both in Canada and in the United States.

Section 1 of the standard player's contract provides, in effect, that the term of the contract is for one year starting October 1 of the pertinent year and that the payment of the salary under the contract shall be in consecutive semi-monthly installments following the commencement of the regular league schedule of games. However, if the player has not been an employee of the club for the whole period of the club's games during the regular season and any playoffs for which the club qualifies, the player receives a part of the salary determined by the ratio of the number of days of actual employment during the regular season and playoff games for which the club qualifies to the number of days of the pre-season training camp, regular season, and playoff games for which the club qualifies.

Section 2 of the contract requires the player to report to the club's training camp and to participate in all exhibition, regular season, and playoff games.

Section 3 of the contract provides, in part, that the player agrees to report and to practice at such time and place as the club may designate and to participate in such exhibition games as may be arranged by the club within 30 days prior to the first league game. If the player fails to report and participate in the exhibition games, a fine not exceeding $500 may be imposed by the club and deducted from the compensation stipulated in the contract.

Under section 15 of the contract, if the player is suspended, the player agrees that there shall be deducted from the player's salary an amount equal to the exact portion of the salary as the number of days of suspension bears to the total number of days of the pre-season training camp, the regular season, and playoff games for which the club qualifies. . . .

HOLDING

Since the services of the taxpayer during the pre-season training camp, the regular season, and the playoff games were performed partly within and partly without the United States, pursuant to the terms of section 1.861-4(b) of the regulations, an amount is to be included in the gross income of the taxpayer for federal income tax purposes that bears the same relation to the total compensation under the contract for the current taxable year as the actual number of days of performance of the labor or service within the United States during the pre-season training camp, regular season, and playoff game period for the current taxable year bears to the total number of days in the season beginning with the first day of the pre-season training camp, and ending with the last day of the regular season or the last day on which the team plays in a playoff game.

In the case of a player signing-on after the regular playing season commences, an amount is to be included in the gross income of the taxpayer that bears the same relation to the total compensation under the contract for the current taxable year as the actual number of days of performance of the labor or service within the United States during the regular season and any playoff games for which the club qualifies bears to the total number of days in the period from the date of the beginning of the player's employment with the team to the last day of the regular season or the last day on which the team plays in a playoff game.

In the case of a suspended player, an amount is to be included in the gross income of the taxpayer that bears the same relation to the total compensation received by the player under the contract for the current taxable year as the actual number of days of performance of the labor or service within the United States, not including the period of suspension, during the pre-season training camp, the regular season, and any playoff games for which the club qualifies bears to the total number of days in the pre-season training camp, regular season, and any playoff games for which the club qualifies, not including the period of suspension.

These allocations apply to a taxpayer's entire salary received by the taxpayer from his club. Furthermore, days spent in the United States between a regular season and playoff games are considered as days in which services are rendered in the United States as are days spent in the United States between playoff games. These conclusions apply to all open years.

As noted above, the taxpayer receives a per diem allowance during the period at the training camp in Canada and certain amounts for playing in exhibition games during that period. The per diem payments for attending the training camp are from a source at the location of the training camp. The separate amounts specifically paid for participation in certain exhibition games and any amounts paid for playing in playoff games and the per diem payments made in connection therewith are from a source at the location of those games. These allocation formulas provide general rules, although specific cases may require modifications to the formulas. . . .

§ 2.08 Source Rules for Rents and Royalties

Rents and royalties are generally sourced to the jurisdiction of the situs of the property giving rise to the income. Rents and royalties derived from the use of property located in the United States are domestic source income. This source rule is a sweeping provision drafted to encompass every type of literary and industrial right, including royalties for the United States use of intangible assets such as patents, copyrights, secret processes and formulas, goodwill, trademarks, tradebrands, franchises, and other like property. The situs of the use of the property in question is the only significant factor in determining the source of rental or royalty income.

The principal classification problem lies in distinguishing royalties from other kinds of income. Differentiating royalty income from sales income can be especially difficult, particularly when the payment structure of a given transaction is contingent upon receipts which the licensee or purchaser derives from the use or disposition of the property. The difference between a license and a sale is frequently explained by the notion that only in the latter case has the vendor transferred all of his or her rights in the bundle of rights he or she possesses. However, significant uncertainty arises in many situations as to what rights truly comprise that bundle.

If a nonresident alien writer, for example, assigns to a domestic corporation in perpetuity the United States and Canadian serial rights to his novel, yet retains movie, stage, and book rights, the question arises as to whether the transfer is a sale or a mere license of just one of the rights stemming from the novel. Given the difficulties in classifying a transaction as a license or a sale, Congress recently legislated a resolution as to the sourcing of income from intangible assets. Regardless of whether the transaction in substance is a sale, if intangible assets are sold on a contingent payment basis, § 865(d)(1)(B) dictates that the royalty source rules of § 861(a)(4) be employed. Thus, if income from a sale of an intangible asset in a taxable year is contingent (based on productivity, disposition, or use), the source rules of § 861(a)(4) override those of § 865. Accordingly, income derived from the transfer will generally be sourced to the jurisdiction in which the property is used. However, the general classification issue continues for all transactions not addressed by the statute, namely those transactions involving dispositions of tangible property, regardless of contingencies, and those transactions involving dispositions of intangible property in which payment is independent of any contingencies based on use or productivity.

Once payments are classified as rents or royalties, the familiar problem of allocating income between countries arises. The general jurisdiction-of-use rule would dictate an allocation between United States and foreign sources on some reasonable basis, presumably on a relative time, mileage, income derived, or some similar approach.

Boulez v. Commissioner
United States Tax Court
83 T.C. 584 (1984)

KORNER, JUDGE:
Respondent determined a deficiency in petitioner's individual income tax for the calendar year 1975 in the amount of $20,685.61. After concessions, the issue which we are called upon to decide is whether certain payments received by petitioner in the year 1975 constitute sale "royalties," ... and are therefore exempt from tax by the United States, or whether said payments constitute compensation for personal services ... and are therefore taxable by the United States. ...

OPINION

Petitioner contends that the payments to him in 1975 by CBS, Inc. were not taxable by the United States, because they were "royalties" .... Respondent ... contends that the payments in question were taxable to petitioner by the United States because they represented compensation for personal services performed in the United States by petitioner. ...

[W]e must decide whether the payments received by petitioner in 1975 from CBS, Inc. constituted royalties or income from personal services. ... This issue, in turn, involves two facets:

(1) Did petitioner intend and support to license or convey to CBS Records, and did the latter agree to pay for, a property interest in the recordings he was engaged to make, which would give rise to royalties?

(2) If so, did petitioner have a property interest in the recordings which he was capable of licensing or selling?

The first of the above questions is purely factual, depends upon the intention of the parties, and is to be determined by an examination of the record as a whole, including the terms of the contract entered into between petitioner and CBS Records, together with any other relevant and material evidence.

The second question—whether petitioner had a property interest which he could license or sell—is a question of law. . . .

We will examine each of these questions in turn.

1. THE FACTUAL QUESTION

By the contract entered into between petitioner and CBS Records in 1969, as amended, did the parties agree that petitioner was licensing or conveying to CBS Records a property interest in the recordings which he was retained to make, and in return for which he was to receive "royalties?" . . .

The contract between the parties is by no means clear. On the one hand, the contract consistently refers to the compensation which petitioner is to be entitled to receive as "royalties," and such payments are tied directly to the proceeds which CBS Records was to receive from sales of recordings which petitioner was to make. Both these factors suggest that the parties had a royalty arrangement, rather than a compensation arrangement, in mind in entering into the contract. We bear in mind, however, that the labels which the parties affix to a transaction are not necessarily determinative of their true nature, and the fact that a party's remuneration under the contract is based on a percentage of future sales of the product created does not prove that a licensing or sale of property was intended, rather than compensation for services.

On the other hand, the contract between petitioner and CBS Records is replete with language indicating that what was intended here was a contract for personal services. Thus, paragraph 1 . . . clearly states that CBS Records was engaging petitioner "to render your services exclusively for us as a producer and/or performer. . . . It is understood and agreed that such engagement by us shall include your services as a producer and/or performer . . . ." Paragraph 3. of the contract then requires petitioner to "perform" in the making of a certain number of recordings in each year. Most importantly, in the context of the present question, paragraph 4. of the contract . . . makes it clear that CBS considered petitioner's services to be the essence of the contract: petitioner agreed not to perform for others with respect to similar recordings during the term of the contract, and for a period of five years thereafter, and he was required to "acknowledge that your services are unique and extraordinary and that we shall be entitled to equitable relief to enforce the provision of this paragraph 4."

Under paragraph 5. of the contract . . . it was agreed that the recordings, once made, should be entirely the property of CBS Records, "free from any claims whatsoever by you or any person deriving any rights or interests from you." Significantly, nowhere in the contract is there any language of conveyance of any alleged property right in the recordings by petitioner to CBS Records, nor any language indicating a licensing of any such purported right, other than the designation of petitioner's remuneration as being "royalties." The word "copyright" itself is never mentioned. Finally, under paragraph 13. of the contract, CBS Records was entitled to suspend or terminate its payments to petitioner "if, by reason of illness, injury, accident or refusal to work, you fail to perform for us in accordance with the provisions of this agreement. . . ."

Considered as a whole, therefore, and acknowledging that the contract is not perfectly clear on this point, we conclude that the weight of the evidence is that the parties intended a contract for personal services, rather than one involving the sale or licensing of any property rights which petitioner might have in the recordings which were to be made in the future.

2. THE LEGAL QUESTION

Before a person can derive income from royalties, it is fundamental that he must have an ownership interest in the property whose licensing or sale gives rise to the income. . . . [T]his Court held that in order for a payment to constitute a "royalty," the payee must have an ownership interest in the property whose use generates the payment. . . .

It is clear, then, that the existence of a property right in the payee is fundamental for the purpose of determining whether royalty income exists. . . .

Did the petitioner have any property rights in the recordings which he made for CBS Records, which he could either license or sell and which would give rise to royalty income here? We think not. . . .

In spite of [a] change in the law in 1971, however, petitioner's contractual relationship with CBS Records went on as before. Neither the amendment to that contract of 1971, nor the further amendment in 1974, made any reference to the change of the copyright laws, nor modified the basic contract in any respect which would be pertinent to the instant question. We conclude, therefore, that the parties saw no need to modify their contract because they understood that even after the Sound Recording Amendment of 1971, petitioner still had no licensable or transferable property rights in the recordings which he made for CBS Records, and we think this was correct.

The Copyright Act of 1909, even after its amendment by the Sound Recording Amendment of 1971, describes the person having a copyrightable interest in property as the "author or proprietor," 17 U.S.C. sec. 9, and further provides that "the word 'author' shall include an employer in the case of works made for hire." 17 U.S.C. sec. 26. The above is a statutory enactment of the long-recognized rule that where a person is employed for the specific purpose of creating a work, including a copyrightable item, the fruits of his labor, carried out in accordance with the employment, are the property of his employer. The rule creates a rebuttable presumption to this effect, which can be overcome by express contractual provisions between the employee and the employer, reserving to the former the copyrightable interest.

Here, the petitioner, a musical conductor of world-wide reputation, was employed to make recordings for CBS Records, and in doing so, was to exercise his peculiar and unique skills in accordance with his experience, talent, and best judgment. In these circumstances, we do not think that petitioner was an "employee" in the common law sense, but rather was an independent contractor, with the same relationship to CBS Records as a lawyer, an engineer, or an architect would have to his client, or a doctor to his patient. This, however, provides no grounds for distinction, since the "works for hire" rule applies to independent contractors just as it does to conventional employees.

In the instant case, the application of the "works for hire" rule means that petitioner had no copyrightable property interest in the recordings which he created for CBS Records, even after 1971. Petitioner was engaged for the specific purpose of making the recordings in question; his contract with CBS Records reserved no property rights in the recordings to him, and indeed made it specific that all such rights, whatever they were, were to reside in CBS Records. Under these circumstances, we do not think that petitioner has overcome the statutory presumption of the "works for hire" rule, nor that he has shown that he had any property interest in the recordings, either before 1971 or thereafter, which he could either license or sell to CBS Records so as to produce royalty income within the meaning of the treaty. This conclusion, in turn, reinforces our belief, which we have found as a fact, that the contract between petitioner and CBS Records was one for the performance of personal services. . . .

§ 2.09 Source Rules for Dispositions of United States Real Property Interests

Income from the disposition of real property (or a real property interest) located in the United States is gross income from domestic sources. If the property is located outside the United States, the income is foreign source. The critical factor is thus the situs of the property. The threshold issue in this determination is whether the property involved is real or personal property. If it is personalty, then the situs rule does not apply unless the property is "associated personal property" as defined in § 897. Such property generally includes personal property structurally or operationally associated with the use of real property.

§ 2.10 Source Rules for Sales of Personal Property

Historically, the rules for sourcing gain from the sale of personal property were governed by the title passage rule of § 861(a)(6). However in 1986 Congress fundamentally altered these source rules with regard to the disposition of noninventory personalty. Congress enacted § 865 which sets forth the source rules for most personal property transactions other than the sale of purchased inventory, for which the title passage rule of § 861(a)(6) was generally retained. Special rules are provided in § 863(b), discussed in Chapter 11, for cross-border transactions involving personal property which has been produced or manufactured and sold as inventory property.

§ 2.11 Sales of Inventory Property

The inventory source rules generally focus on the jurisdiction in which title passes. Under § 861(a)(6), income derived from the purchase of inventory property *outside* the United States and its sale *within* the United States is United States source income. Section 862(a)(6) supplies its converse: if inventory property is purchased *within* the United States and sold *outside* it, the income so derived is foreign source. Thus, the purchase of inventory in France by a Greek national and its sale in the United States with title passing to the buyer domestically will generate United States source income. A similar transaction with a purchase in the United States and title passing in France yields foreign source income.

Curiously, neither the Code nor the Regulations specifically addresses the source issue when inventory property is *both* purchased and sold domestically or when inventory property is *both* purchased and sold in a foreign country. It is clear, however, that the situs of sale controls in those cases as well. Thus, in the above hypotheticals, a purchase in France with title passing on the sale in France produces foreign source income, while a purchase in the United States with title passing on the sale in the United States generates United States source income.

A sale takes place "at the time when, and the place where, the rights, title, and interest of the seller in the property are transferred to the buyer." This passage of title issue is not peculiar to tax law. Rather, it is a question of local commercial law.

A major distinction should be noted between purchase-and-sale income and production-and-sale income. When dealing with purchase-and-sale income, no income is allocated to the purchase—only the sale is deemed responsible for generating the income. Thus, all income derived from the sale has its source where the sale took place. In production-and-sale situations, discussed in Chapter 11, some of the income is seen as a result of production activity and thus income does not stem from the sale alone. Consequently, the source of the income is bifurcated according to specified rules.

§ 2.12 Sales of Noninventory Property

In 1986, a new rule was mandated in § 865 for the sourcing of noninventory personal property, because Congress had grown weary of the potential for manipulation inherent in the title passage rule. This rule generally focuses on the *residence* of the selling taxpayer rather than the situs where title passes.

In general, under § 865, gain derived by a United States resident (i.e., an individual having a tax home in the United States or any corporation which is a United States person) from the sale of personal property is sourced in the United States. Conversely, gain derived by a nonresident is foreign sourced. Thus, for dispositions governed by § 865, instead of applying the factual analysis under prior law for determining the jurisdiction in which title passed, the new standard requires a determination of the taxpayer's residence or jurisdiction of formation or organization. Once determined, the gain is sourced accordingly. This standard as applied to entities is relatively simple and objective. For individuals, it may itself require a significant and subjective facts and circumstances analysis.

As regards individuals, it should be noted that the standards of § 7701(b), discussed in Chapter 1, are not controlling for determining residency. Instead, the critical factor is the location of the taxpayer's "tax home." The concept of tax home is an elusive one, often requiring a detailed consideration of many relevant facts and circumstances and implicating the innumerable tax cases arising under § 162(a)(2) addressing whether a taxpayer is away from home in the pursuit of business. The tax home concept applied on its own may give rise to seemingly incongruous results for sourcing purposes. A United States citizen or resident with a foreign tax home may be a nonresident for purposes of § 865, while an individual classified as a nonresident under § 7701(b) with a United States tax home will be classified as a resident under § 865.

As regards a United States citizen or resident alien, the tax home showing will not suffice for nonresidency status unless a tax of ten percent or more has been imposed upon the transaction by a foreign jurisdiction. For example, a United States citizen with a tax home in Tokyo who sells noninventory personal property to a Japanese resident will have foreign source income only if the gain is subject to a foreign tax of ten percent or more. Otherwise, United States source gain will arise regardless of the location of the tax home. Any corporation which is a United States person (i.e., organized in the United States) is a resident for purposes of § 865. Corporations not so classified are accorded nonresident status.

Once a person's or entity's status is properly determined, the source of income derived by that person from the sale of personal property follows his residence. Most individuals classified generally as nonresidents under § 7701(b) will have their tax home abroad under § 865, virtually ensuring that the gain from the sale of noninventory personal property will be classified as foreign source income. For example, a Greek citizen and resident with his tax home in Athens who sells noninventory personal property to a United States purchaser will have foreign source gain on the sale. A United States citizen or resident with his tax home in Chicago who sells personal property to a German resident will have United States source gain on the sale of property.

The general sourcing rule of § 865 focusing on residence, however, is subject to a considerable number of exceptions. As previously discussed, notwithstanding the residence rule, gain from the sale of inventory (with a notable exception discussed below) remains sourced with reference to the traditional title-passage rule. Inventory for purposes of § 865 is defined under the principles of § 1221.

Gain from the sale of depreciable personal property that is attributable to depreciation deductions (i.e., gain attributable to recapture under § 1245 or § 1250) is allocated between sources in the United States and sources outside the United States. The proportion of the gain sourced in the United States is determined by reference to a ratio consisting of the United States depreciation adjustments taken with respect to the property over the total depreciation adjustments. The remainder of the gain is sourced outside the United States. Thus, the taxpayer's residence in such cases is essentially irrelevant. Instead, the focus of the statute rests on the relative economic benefit. Any excess gain that is not attributable to depreciation deductions is sourced under the title passage rule of § 861(a)(6) for inventory property rather than the general residence rule of §865.

A special exception to the bifurcated approach of § 865 applies to property used predominantly within or without the United States.

In cases of such use, *all* of the depreciation deductions attributable to that property follow such use. Any excess gain on the sale of such property is sourced under the title passage rule.

Gain from the disposition of an intangible asset (other than goodwill) is sourced under the general residence rule only to the extent the payments in consideration of the sale are *not* contingent on the productivity, use, or disposition of the intangible asset. Contingent sales of intangible assets are sourced under the royalty source rules of § 861(a)(4). Thus, a foreign citizen with a foreign tax home who owns a patent and who is negotiating a sale with a United States purchaser must balance economic and tax issues. If the patent will be used in the United States, the potentially greater gain to be derived from a contingent sale must be balanced against the increased tax bill such a disposition will bring. The contingent sale/royalty rule would generate United States source since it focuses on the jurisdiction where the use is occurring, while a non-contingent sale would focus on the residence rules and afford the taxpayer gain with a foreign source.

However, gain from the sale of an intangible asset which has been amortized for tax purposes is sourced under the depreciable personal property tax rules of § 865(c) to the extent of such amortization. This rule applies regardless of whether the sale is contingent upon productivity or use. Therefore, in the above hypothetical, if the patent had previously been depreciated, gain to the extent of prior depreciation would first be tested by the depreciable personal property rules. Any remaining gain would be sourced either by the residence rules if the consideration is not contingent or by the royalty source rules of § 861(a)(4) if the consideration involves contingent payments. The inventory rules for sourcing excess gains under § 865(c)(2) are inapplicable to intangible assets.

Goodwill, although classified as an intangible asset, is subject to a separate source rule. Gain from the sale of goodwill is sourced in the country in which such goodwill was generated. In cases involving a multi-jurisdictional business, an allocation of the gain among various jurisdictions may be required. However, as goodwill in some cases is amortizable, the depreciable personal property rules of § 865(c) should govern to the extent of any amortization.

Special rules are provided for sales of personal property through offices or other fixed places of business. Different requirements are imposed under the source rule of § 865(e) for residents and nonresidents. See discussion at Chapter 11.

§ 2.13 Section 862—Income from Sources Without the United States

The previous discussion addressed §§ 861 and 865 which describe specific categories of income and determine when such items are United States source income. Section 862 merely confirms the converse. If, after the application of §§ 861 and 865, the item does not have a United States source, then, typically by definition, the income item has a foreign source.

Thus, gross income from sources without the United States includes interest and dividends other than those specified in § 861 and the accompanying Regulations. Foreign source income also includes compensation for labor or personal services performed outside the United States.

Rents and royalties from property located outside the United States are foreign source income. This includes payments for the use of patents, copyrights, secret processes and formulas, goodwill, trademarks, tradebrands, franchises, and other like property outside the United States.

Foreign source income is also produced by gains derived from the sale of real property located outside the United States. Other foreign source income enumerated under § 862 is profit derived from the purchase of inventory property *within* the United States and its sale or exchange *without* the United States. Section 865 also provides source rules for the sale of personal property which may result in a foreign source characterization.

§ 2.14 Source Rules for Other Income

Sections 861, 862, 863, and 865 do not establish a comprehensive scheme for sourcing all types of income. Some payments fall outside the parameters of these statutes, and one must look to general source principles to determine their source.

Once it was thought that the controlling factor of source for these payments was the residence of the payor. This view was encouraged by the Services's position in Revenue Ruling 69-108 in which it was held, apparently to the exclusion of all other factors, that the residence of the obligor decided the source of alimony. The Service thereafter veered away from that position and has instead decided: "In the absence of an overriding Code provision, the main factor in determining the source of income of payments received is whether the location of the property to which the payment related or the situs of the activities that resulted in its being made was in the United States or abroad." Thus, two source rules exist—one *in rem*, the other *in personam*. Difficulty may arise, however, in deciding which source rule applies in a given situation.

An excellent example of the contortions often required to determine the source of certain income items arose in *Bank of America v. United States,* 377 F.2d 575 (Ct. Cl. 1967). Therein, the court sourced acceptance, confirmation, and negotiation commissions derived by a bank by analogy of each to established source rules. Acceptance and confirmation commissions most resembled interest and were sourced according to those rules. Negotiation commissions mirrored income derived for services and thus were United States sourced.

Revenue Ruling 89-67
1989-1 C.B. 233

ISSUE

What is the source of an amount paid as a fellowship or a scholarship?

LAW AND ANALYSIS

Section 863(a) of the Internal Revenue Code of 1986 provides authority for the Commissioner to allocate or apportion items of gross income not specified in sections 861 and 862 to sources within and without the United States. No statutory rule is provided under section 861 or 862 for income received to support or subsidize a recipient's research or study activities.

Rev. Rul. 66-292, 1966-2 C.B. 280, held that the source of an amount received as a scholarship or fellowship is determined by where the research or study activities take place. A companion ruling, Rev. Rul. 66-291, 1966-2 C.B. 279, held that the source of an award for a puzzle contest is determined by where the activities required to solve the puzzle are performed. The rules contained in these revenue rulings are analogous to the rule contained in sections 861(a)(3) and 862(a)(3) of the Code that sources compensation from personal services where the services are performed. There is no indication in either cited revenue ruling, however, that the recipients performed any services for the payor, and Rev. Rul. 66-292 explicitly states to the contrary. The amount received to support or subsidize research and study and the amount received in respect of puzzle solving activities described in the two revenue rulings is not compensation for personal services because no services are performed. Absent a significant economic nexus with the place where the study and research and puzzle solving activities are performed, it is more appropriate to source these payments where the principal economic nexus exists, namely, at the residence of the payor. Thus, for example, scholarship or fellowship payments for research or study, and amounts paid for puzzle-solving activities, made by the United

States or a political subdivision thereof, a noncorporate U.S. resident, or a domestic corporation will be from U.S. sources. Similar payments by a foreign government or a foreign corporation will be foreign source payments. Payments made by an entity designated as a public international organization under the Internal Organizations Immunities Act will be foreign source payments. . . .

HOLDING

The source of a payment made as a scholarship, fellowship, or an award for puzzle solving contest activities is the residence of the payor. . . .

PROBLEM 2—SOURCE RULES

Code: §§ 861(a) and (c), 862(a), 865(a)-(d), (g), and (i), 897(c)

Regulations: §§ 1.861-4, 1.861-7, 1.863-1(d)(1)-(3)

T, an individual, was a citizen and bona fide resident of the United States. T is single and is on the cash method, calendar-year method of accounting. During the year, T owned the following assets:

1. 100 shares of the common stock of X Corporation—a domestic corporation;
2. 100 shares of the common stock of Y Corporation—a foreign corporation, 40 percent of its earnings over the past three years are effectively connected to a United States trade or business;
3. Rental real estate located in Modesto, California;
4. A loan to H, a citizen of the United States currently residing in Bolivia, in the amount of $7,000;
5. Deposit in a Chicago, Illinois bank, $20,000;
6. The rights to a patent created by T;
7. Vacant land held for investment located in Oregon; and
8. 50 shares of preferred stock of Z Corporation—a domestic corporation.

During the year, T received the following amounts:

a. Cash payment on the X Corporation stock, $20,000;
b. Cash payment on the Y Corporation stock, $13,000;
c. Rents from the rental property, $10,000;
d. Interest on the loan to H, $1,000;
e. Interest on deposit at Chicago, Illinois bank, $2,000;
f. Gain on sale of ten shares of Z Corporation stock, $5,000; and
g. Payment pursuant to sale to W Corporation of rights to use a patent in Switzerland for five percent of net profits from product produced through use of the process, $8,000.

1. What is the source of each item?
2. What is the source of the following items if:
   a. T was a plant manager for a French subsidiary of a United States corporation and received an annual salary of $70,000?

b. T received a $15,000 fellowship from M.I.T. to study the economic development of Poland?
c. T won $100,000 from the Illinois Little Lotto weekly drawing?
d. T sells inventory for a $3,000 profit from his United States wine distributorship to a Brazilian customer?
e. T sells 20 acres of vacant land in Vermont for a $35,000 gain?
f. T sells 50 shares of stock in Vermont Realty Inc., his wholly owned corporation, the sole asset of which is the property described in e., for a $40,000 gain?

Chapter 3
Section 911 Exclusion

§ 3.01 Taxation of Americans Abroad—Introduction
§ 3.02 Eligibility for the § 911 Exclusion
§ 3.03 The Tax Home Standard
§ 3.04 Bona Fide Residence Test
  Jones v. Commissioner, 927 F.2d 849 (5th Cir. 1991)
§ 3.05 Physical Presence Test
  Gelhar v. Commissioner, T.C. Memo 1992-162
§ 3.06 The Foreign Source Earned Income Limitation: § 911(b) Generally
  Revenue Ruling 80-254, 1980-2 C.B. 222
§ 3.07 Deferred Payments
§ 3.08 Amounts Received from a Sole Proprietorship or Partnership
§ 3.09 Limitation on the Amount of the Exclusion
§ 3.10 Employer-Provided Housing Exclusion
§ 3.11 Self-Provided Housing
§ 3.12 Computing the Foreign Earned Income Exclusion
  Problem 3

§ 3.01 Taxation of Americans Abroad—Introduction

In contrast to its method of taxing nonresident individuals and foreign corporations, the United States adopts a jealous posture as regards its residents, citizens, and domestic corporations. As a general rule, these persons must report, and subject to United States taxation, all of their income regardless of whether it is derived domestically or from abroad. Such a formula not only extends the reach of the government's taxing arm, but also raises the likelihood that the income will be taxed in more than one jurisdiction. In recognition of such possibilities, the United States permits its domestics to utilize the foreign tax credit to ameliorate the burdens of multiple taxation in the international arena.

The justification for such worldwide taxation is strongest when applied to a United States citizen and resident firmly settled within the United States borders and deriving income from foreign pursuits. Such members of society regularly draw on the governmental benefits available to its citizenry. However, with respect to those members who have journeyed abroad in order to search for employment, to relocate pursuant to their employer's instructions, to retire, or to merely travel, an argument exists that such individuals do not similarly burden the United States government. While dramatic settings can arise to make the position untenable, in many cases another government possesses the primary connection to such taxpayer with the United States relationship to that party secondary at best. In light of this more remote tie to the taxpayer and his foreign earnings, the United States has partially or fully exempted such earnings from United States tax.

In § 911, Congress provides an exclusion of foreign earnings as well as the exclusion of housing allowances. In 1997, Congress authorized a $2,000 per year increase in the ceiling permitting a maximum exclusion of $80,000 per year beginning in 2002. Beginning in 2007, the exclusion will be indexed annually for inflation. For purposes of this chapter, the $80,000 amount will be utilized. The rationale behind giving tax advantages to Americans overseas has never been unanimously agreed upon. Perhaps the most influential reasons for granting such tax advantages are that they are required to spur United States trade overseas; to provide equitable treatment for Americans facing escalating costs abroad; and to combat a perceived balance of payments problems.

§ 3.02 Eligibility for the § 911 Exclusion

If a domestic individual can show that his "tax home" is in a foreign country, there are two ways to reach the promised land (i.e., qualified individual status under § 911). First, a United States citizen may establish that he has been a bona fide resident of a foreign country or countries for an uninterrupted period which includes an entire taxable year. Alternatively, a citizen *or* resident of the United States is a qualified individual if he or she, during any period of 12 consecutive months, is present in a foreign country or countries during at least 330 full days in such period.

Qualification under either test means an individual may claim the § 911 exclusion for certain foreign earned income and the attendant housing costs amount "for such taxable year or for any taxable year which contains part of such period." The exclusion is elective. Notwithstanding the riches that appear on the surface of § 911, it is not a foregone conclusion that all who are eligible will stake claim to such benefits. For example, under § 911(d)(6), a taxpayer claiming the exclusion is not entitled to any attendant exclusions, deductions, and credits.

§ 3.03 The Tax Home Standard

The threshold criterion for the § 911 exclusion requires the taxpayer's tax home to be in a foreign country. Without a foreign tax home, the taxpayer cannot qualify for the exclusion regardless of whether he meets the presence or bona fide residency standards. Layered upon this requirement is the dictate that an individual cannot have a foreign tax home if he has an abode in the United States.

The tax home concept derives from the § 162(a)(2) "away from home" requirement applied to business and travel expenses and is laden with significant interpretive precedent in the domestic context. The Regulations attempt to flesh out the concept by providing:

> An individual's tax home is considered to be located at his regular or principal (if more than one regular) place of business or, if the individual has no regular or principal place of business because of the nature of the business, then at his regular place of abode in a real and substantial sense. An individual shall not, however, be considered to have a tax home in a foreign country for any period for which the individual's abode is in the United States. Temporary presence of the individual in the United States does not necessarily mean that the individual's abode is in the United States during that time. Maintenance of a dwelling in the United States by an individual, whether or not that dwelling is used in the United States by the individual's spouse and dependents, does not necessarily mean that the individual's abode is in the United States.

Treas. Reg § 1.911-2(b).

The requirement is probably of minimal significance for meeting the bona fide residence requirement but may be telling as regards the presence test. Given the Congressional abbreviation of the presence testing period (the current standard of 330 days in 12 months was contracted from the prior test of 510 days in 18 months), the fear may be that one without significant foreign immersion may otherwise qualify for the exclusion. The tax home doctrine acts as an additional safeguard against such potential abuse. The typical setting in which the tax home doctrine has been successfully invoked by the Service is where the employee hopscotches his living patterns, e.g., 28 days abroad, oftentimes on an oil rig, followed by a 28-day period in the United States or the employee attempts to mask his disguised vacation.

However, the issue is further complicated by the most recent Congressional pronouncement under § 162. In 1992, Congress, in an effort to minimize claims for the deduction of travel expenses, amended § 162(a) to provide that the taxpayer "shall not be treated as being temporarily away from home during any period of employment if such period exceeds one year." While the enactment tightened the standards for deductions under § 162, it may well have broadened the standards for exclusion under § 911 since the Regulations provide that the term "tax home" for purposes of § 911 has "the same meaning which it has for purposes of section 162(a)(2)."

§ 3.04 Bona Fide Residence Test

One means by which a taxpayer evidences his or her eligibility for the § 911 exclusion is to establish a genuine nexus to or presence in a foreign country. Whether a citizen is a bona fide resident of a foreign country is a question of fact that primarily concentrates on the qualitative indicia of having truly established a lifestyle in that country. The Regulations under § 871, which describe general principles relating to residency status, are specifically incorporated by § 911. One of the purposes behind § 911 and its lineage has been to expand overseas trade. To effectuate this intent, a liberal reading of the bona fide residence requirement probably should be made.

Claimants have the burden of establishing their foreign residency, and the claimed period must span an *entire* taxable year. Barring death, a taxpayer must possess such residence for the entirety of his taxable year. Thus, a calendar year taxpayer arriving in New Zealand on January 12, Year 1 and establishing residency would fail the residency test if he terminated his residence any time prior to December 31, Year 2. In the case of an early termination, not all is lost as the taxpayer may be able to meet the physical presence test instead.

Generally, whether an individual is a resident for purposes of § 911 depends upon his intention as to the purpose of his trip and the nature and length of his stay abroad. The Service determines whether an individual qualifies largely on the basis of relevant facts and circumstances. The following factors appear relevant.

It is possible for a taxpayer to qualify under § 911(d)(1)(A) while residing in more than one country during the tax year. For example, if an individual resides in France from January 1 to November 30, then transfers to England, that transfer will not prevent foreign residency status. This conclusion holds even if, before taking up a new post in England, the taxpayer takes the opportunity to vacation during December in the United States and does not arrive in England until January 2 of the following year. It is imperative that the claimant establish that he acquired English residency status.

The Regulations define a United States resident to be, among other things, someone who enters the United States for a purpose which may require an extended stay and who thus "makes his home temporarily in the United States." Thus, by analogy, failure to purchase or rent a house or room abroad will weigh heavily against the taxpayer, unless he or she can show, considering the demands of his employment, that it would be unreasonable to expect him to do so.

Failure to bring a spouse to the place of foreign employment may count against the taxpayer.

An individual is not a bona fide resident of a foreign country if the person makes a statement to the authorities of that foreign country claiming to be a nonresident of that country and is not taxed by that country by reason of nonresidency. Thus, an individual who makes such a statement generally is denied § 911 benefits regardless of any other facts which might support a residency claim.

Formerly, the Service took the position that if individuals were able to establish themselves as tax-exempt before foreign tax authorities, that was the equivalent of a statement of foreign nonresidency. The Service retreated from its previous stand and now concedes that an exemption from tax provided in a treaty or other international agreement will not in itself prevent a citizen from being a bona fide resident of a foreign country.

Of course, physical presence is of itself determinative of eligibility for § 911 benefits. Presence is also, however, a factor in determining eligibility under the bona fide residency standard. Excessive absence from the stated jurisdiction of residence undercuts assertions of residency.

However, temporary visits to the United States or elsewhere on vacation or business trips should not deprive the citizen of his status as a bona fide resident of a foreign country. The crucial question is, of course, when an absence becomes *unreasonable,* so as to sever foreign residency status. A representative of a domestic employer who is assigned indefinitely abroad and recalled to the United States for a one-month or less consultation with his employer should not forfeit foreign residency status.

The above rules apply only when bona fide residence has been established. Presumably, a representative of a United States employer who is assigned overseas indefinitely may establish residence immediately upon arrival.

Generally, a citizen who lives in a foreign country with no definite intention as to the length of stay will be considered a resident of that country under United States law. Thus, an employer who contemplates sending citizens abroad would be well advised for § 911 purposes not to have any definitive terms in the contract of employment regarding the length of foreign stay by employees, nor even the rights of domestic recall for relatively insignificant employee offenses. Once this quality of indefiniteness is achieved, however, it does not appear that a generalized boilerplate clause, providing for domestic recall with specified notice to the employee, endangers foreign residency status.

Where other factors exist which adequately support a taxpayer's claim of bona fide residency, the fact that the taxpayer's stay abroad is limited by visa to a certain time period has been scantily regarded by the courts. Also, in some countries, it may be nearly impossible to obtain a visa enabling an individual to stay in the particular country for an indefinite period; obviously, where this is the case, a limited visa will be of little significance in determining residency.

Selling a United States home is undoubtedly strong evidence of the taxpayer's intent to reside abroad. Conversely, failure to sell a home should logically weigh against the taxpayer. However, by analogy to the domestic residency Regulations, a mere floating intention of a citizen residing abroad to return to the United States should not deprive him of foreign residency status. The taxpayer's renting of his or her United States home may be evidence of an intent to reside abroad for a sufficiently lengthy period of time.

Jones v. Commissioner
United States Court of Appeals, Fifth Circuit
927 F.2d 849 (1991)

GOLDBERG, CIRCUIT JUDGE:
In a notice dated December 8, 1987, the Commissioner of Internal Revenue (the "Commissioner") determined deficiencies in George H. and Betty A. Jones' (collectively hereinafter referred to as "Taxpayers") income tax for the taxable years ending December 31, 1981, 1982 and 1983, in the amounts of $7,355, $37,513, and $37,031 respectively. The case was subsequently tried before the tax court. Finding that Jones failed to prove he was a bona fide resident of Japan during the applicable period, the tax court determined deficiencies in Taxpayers' income tax. . . .

I. Facts and Proceedings Below

When George H. Jones ("Jones") retired from the air force in 1970, he entered into an employment agreement with International Air Service Company, Ltd. ("IASCO"), a California corporation in the business of furnishing flight crew personnel to aircraft operators. Pursuant to a contract between IASCO and Japanese Air Lines Co., Ltd. ("JAL"), Jones was assigned exclusively to JAL, flying out of Tokyo, Japan. While in Japan on this initial assignment, Taxpayers and their four children resided in a rented house in Japan.

Jones served with JAL, based in Tokyo, from 1971 through March 1972. On March 31, 1972, JAL furloughed Jones. Jones moved his family and belongings back to San Antonio, Texas, so he could attempt to obtain interim employment. On January 1, 1973, JAL recalled Jones to active duty and reassigned him to JAL's Tokyo base. Although he then moved back to Tokyo, his wife remained in San Antonio so that their son could graduate from high school, after which time Mrs. Jones and their youngest daughter anticipated joining Jones in Tokyo. During both his first and second assignment in Tokyo, Jones' flights consisted of routes within Japan and between Japan and Asia.

In March 1974 JAL reassigned Jones to Anchorage, Alaska, its only base located in the United States. Therefore, after Taxpayers' son graduated from high school in San Antonio, Mrs. Jones and Taxpayers' youngest daughter also moved to Anchorage. Taxpayers' youngest daughter only lived in Anchorage until she left for college. After moving to Anchorage, Mrs. Jones began a career for the first time. She eventually went to work for a newly-formed bank and worked directly for the chairman of the bank.

On March 3, 1980, and continuing through the years in issue, JAL transferred Jones back to Tokyo. Although Mrs. Jones had the opportunity to move to Tokyo as well, she decided to remain in Anchorage and pursue her own career until Jones' expected retirement in 1988. She continued to occupy the townhome that Taxpayers' jointly owned in Anchorage. Taxpayers filed joint United States income tax returns for the years in question, 1981, 1982, and 1983.

When he moved back to Tokyo, Jones moved into the Hotel Nikko Narita (the "Hotel"), where he stayed until his retirement in 1988. Jones apparently elected to stay at the Hotel instead of renting an apartment or a house for reasons of convenience, economy, and the society of other JAL crewmembers who also lived in the Hotel. He checked into and out of the Hotel in accordance with his schedule, and left his personal belongings in storage at the Hotel when he was away.

Although Taxpayers tried to see each other as frequently as possible, Jones was only able to fly on JAL with discount tickets for approved vacation periods. Unlike many domestic air carriers, JAL did not allow its flight crew members the privilege of flying free anytime a seat was available. This same policy applied to Mrs. Jones.

Although Jones did not own an automobile in Japan during the years in issue, he had renewed his Japanese driver's license so that he could occasionally borrow a car or rent a car when his family came to visit him. Jones also maintained his Alaska driver's license and two cars in the United States were co-titled in his name. Although he did not maintain a bank account in Japan and held no Japanese-based credit cards, he did maintain joint bank accounts with his wife in Alaska and San Antonio, and held U.S.-based credit cards. During the years in question, Jones was registered to vote in Alaska and voted absentee in United States elections.

Jones held a commercial multi-entry visa, renewable every four years, which allowed him to stay in Japan a maximum of three years per entry. The only limitation was a requirement that he leave Japan at least once every three years. Since his profession dictated frequent trips outside Japan, this was not a problem for Jones.

Jones paid both Japanese and United States income taxes for the years at issue. Jones' Japanese income tax returns were prepared at his expense by a Japanese accountant in Japan. After moving to Japan, Jones received a dividend check, representing a 1981 payment under the Alaska Permanent Fund Distribution Program. Because entitlement was based on Alaskan residence, Jones returned the check, explaining that he was no longer an Alaska resident.

During the years in issue, JAL assigned Jones to flights which were either intercontinental between Japan and the United States, or intracontinental segments of such international flights within Japan and the United States. Jones had no control over which flights he was scheduled to fly. During the relevant period, Jones spent less than 165 nights a year in Japan. Since Anchorage was JAL's only U.S. base, and one of the normal stopover cities on Japan/U.S. routes, Jones' job required that he be in Anchorage frequently. When overnight in Anchorage, Jones stayed in the townhouse co-owned by Taxpayers.

During the years in issue, Jones did not have extensive contact with Japanese culture. He did visit a local Japanese doctor for medical attention and he participated in certain recreational activities, including jogging and playing golf. Jones socialized with co-workers also living at the Hotel and occasionally drove into Tokyo for dinner and entertainment.... Taxpayers claimed exclusions of $76,050 and $81,272, respectively, under Section 911 of the Code....

II. Discussion....

The only issue this court must address is whether Jones was a "qualified individual" within the meaning of section ... 911 of the Code. To be entitled to ... the exclusion available under Code Section 911 of foreign earned income, a taxpayer had to have a tax home in a foreign country and demonstrate (1) that he had either been a "bona fide resident" of a foreign country for an uninterrupted period including an entire taxable year (the "bona fide residency test"), or (2) that he had been physically present in a foreign country for a certain period of time (the "physical presence test"). Jones concedes that he does not meet the "physical presence test." Therefore, Jones must show that his tax home was in Japan and that he was a bona fide resident of Japan during the applicable period....

This court must determine residence in light of congressional intent, which was to encourage foreign trade by encouraging foreign employment for citizens of the United States, and to place them in an equal position with citizens of other countries going abroad who are not taxed by their own countries.

For purposes of section ... 911, the test of a taxpayer's bona fide residence in a foreign country is the test of alien residence established in Code Section 871. Treasury Regulation Section 1.871-2(b) provides in pertinent part that:

> An alien actually present in the United States who is not a mere transient or sojourner is a resident of the United States for purposes of the income tax.... One who comes to the United States for a definite purpose which in its nature may be promptly accomplished is a transient; but, if his purpose is of such a nature that an extended stay may be necessary for its accomplishment, and to that end the alien makes his home temporarily in the United States, he becomes a resident, though it may be his intention at all times to return to his domicile abroad when the purpose for which he came has been consummated or abandoned. Residence is therefore much less than domicile which requires an intent to make a fixed and permanent home.

When determining whether a taxpayer was a bona fide resident of a foreign country, courts consider a number of objective factors, first enunciated in *Sochurek v. Commissioner*, 300 F.2d 34 (7th Cir. 1962). These factors include:

(1) intention of the taxpayer;
(2) establishment of his home temporarily in the foreign country for an indefinite period;

(3) participation in the activities of his chosen community on social and cultural levels, identification with the daily lives of the people and, in general, assimilation into the foreign environment;
(4) physical presence in the foreign country consistent with his employment;
(5) nature and duration of his employment; whether his assignment abroad could be promptly accomplished within a definite or specified time;
(6) assumption of economic burdens and payment of taxes to the foreign country;
(7) status of resident contrasted to that of transient or sojourner;
(8) treatment accorded his income tax status by his employer;
(9) marital status and residence of his family;
(10) nature and duration of his employment; whether his assignment abroad could be promptly accomplished within a definite or specified time;
(11) good faith in making his trip abroad; whether for purpose of tax evasion.

While all these factors may not be present in every situation, those appropriate should be properly considered and weighed. A taxpayer must offer "strong proof" of bona fide residence in a foreign country to qualify for the foreign earned income exclusion under section 911.

In upholding the Commissioner's assessment, the tax court seemed to place particular emphasis on the fact Jones chose to live in the Hotel, rather than renting an apartment or a home in Japan, and the fact that Jones' wife chose to live in Anchorage, rather than give up her job and move to Japan with her husband. The tax court also noted that Jones had a number of ties to the United States, while he remained relatively unassimilated into the Japanese community. The tax court's analysis, however, overlooks the other . . . factors.

First, the tax court failed to consider Jones' intent. Jones obviously intended to become a resident of Japan and therefore he accordingly returned to the State of Alaska a dividend check which was based on Alaskan residence. A taxpayer's intent plays perhaps the most important part in determining the establishment and maintenance of a foreign residence.

Jones established his home in Japan, presumably for the remainder of his career. Jones' job as a pilot was ongoing and both JAL and Jones intended Jones to live and work in Japan until his retirement. Therefore, Jones' purpose for being in Japan was of such a nature that an extended stay was necessary. Due to his flight schedule, JAL required his physical presence in Japan and such presence was consistent with his employment.

In addition, Jones argues that he should not be penalized because the economic realities of Japan lead him to choose to live in the Hotel, instead of renting an apartment or buying a home. The Commissioner and the tax court seemed bothered by the apparent temporary nature of a hotel, but it is not necessary for a taxpayer to establish a fixed, permanent place of abode in order to be a "resident" of a foreign country.

Furthermore, Jones was apparently only away from his home in Japan when his business required it, or when he was on vacation. The fact that Jones was able to stay at his home in Anchorage during flights was merely fortuitous and should not be held against Jones. If JAL had not previously based Jones in Anchorage, Taxpayers would not have owned property there. In addition, if JAL had scheduled Jones to fly only Asian trips, as he had done when he was previously assigned to Japan, Jones would not have had occasion to layover in Anchorage. Nevertheless, business and vacation trips to the United States should not affect Jones' residency.

Jones paid resident Japanese income taxes. Jones' Japanese income tax returns were prepared at his expense by a Japanese accountant. Both JAL and IASCO viewed Jones as a resident of Japan for Japanese income tax purposes. In fact, JAL required IASCO to withhold Japanese income taxes from Jones' payroll checks. The last . . . factor also arguably supports Jones' claim to bona fide residency because the Commissioner has never suggested that Jones took the job in Japan for the purposes of tax evasion.

Both in his briefs and during oral argument, the Commissioner seemed to rely heavily on the fact that Jones' wife did not move to Japan during his last assignment to Tokyo. The Commissioner seems to argue that Taxpayers' should be punished because Mrs. Jones chose to stay in Anchorage and pursue a career, rather than move to Japan with her husband. When JAL reassigned Jones to Japan in 1980, Taxpayers' children were all away at school or married. For the first time in a number of years, Mrs. Jones was free to devote herself to a career. She would most likely not have been able to find comparable employment if she had joined her husband in Japan.

We are besieged with cases and statistics and erudite writing about the necessity for the equalization of rights and opportunities for men and women in our society. It would be strange indeed if the Congress of the United States which has legislated frequently and ardently for the equality of the sexes, should in the field of taxation find that a woman who desires to establish herself in the field of business, and her husband who obviously encouraged her, should be penalized because she is pursuing something which the Congress thinks is in the interest of our nation and its economy. Penalizing Taxpayers for Mrs. Jones' decision in no way furthers the clearly enunciated legislative purpose behind section . . . 911 of encouraging foreign employment of United States' citizens.

Although Jones' admittedly did not learn to speak Japanese and was relatively unassimilated into the Japanese culture, the majority of . . . factors support Jones' contention that he was a bona fide resident of Japan during the relevant period. Jones was not a mere transient or sojourner in Japan. Even though he intended to eventually return to his domicile in the United States after he retired from JAL, his purpose for being in Japan required him to remain there for at least eight years. Although Jones may have felt a little like a sojourner in a foreign land, as Moses did after he left Egypt and fled to Midian, under the applicable modern day tax statutes we are required to classify him as a bona fide resident of Japan, and not a mere transient or sojourner.

Section 911 . . . speaks to the modern age. . . . Today, husbands and wives, men and women, have the right to separate careers. With respect to Jones' tax residence, he was neither a domiciliary nor a transient. He was a resident of Japan. The Code clearly could have used the word domicile or transient; neither of these are strange to our congressional enactments and legislation. Instead, the Code speaks in terms of residence. Since we find that Jones was a bona fide resident of Japan during the relevant time period, we reverse the tax court.

Tax Home

Because the tax court determined that Jones was not a bona fide resident of Japan, it did not reach the question of whether Jones' tax home was in Japan. As we stated earlier, however, in order to qualify for the tax benefits available pursuant to section . . . 911, the taxpayer must prove both that he was a bona fide resident of a foreign country and that his tax home was in a foreign country. . . .

Treasury Regulation Section 1.911-2(b) sets forth the general rule that a taxpayer's tax home is at his principal place of business or employment. However, section 911, and the regulations promulgated pursuant to [it], provide the overriding exception that if an individual's abode is in the United States, then he is legally incapable of establishing that his tax home is in a foreign country.

Recently the tax court has had an opportunity to discuss the abode limitation, and this court has affirmed at least two of these opinions. In these cases, this court has adopted the following definition of abode:

> "Abode" has been variously defined as one's home, habitation, residence, domicile, or place of dwelling. While an exact definition of 'abode' depends upon the context in which the word is used, it clearly does not mean one's principal place of business. Thus, "abode" has a domestic rather than a vocational meaning, and stands in contrast to "tax home." . . .

The facts in this case can easily be distinguished from oil rig and compound worker cases. . . . In those cases, when the taxpayers were on duty on oil rigs or in the oil field compounds, they slept in employer-provided housing, ate employer-provided meals and returned home to the United States after each work period on employer-provided flights. In addition, the taxpayer's family was not allowed to join him abroad. These taxpayers were not incurring any costs associated with living abroad; rather, they were essentially commuting on a regular basis from their homes in the United States.

In contrast, Jones had to pay for his vacation travel to the United States. Jones also paid for his meals and his housing while abroad. Jones also incurred the additional cost of paying Japanese income taxes. In addition, Mrs. Jones had the opportunity to move to Japan if she had so desired, but she elected to keep her job in Anchorage for her own personal reasons. Therefore, Jones' abode was in Japan and not in the United States, and his tax home was also in Japan during the relevant period.

III. Conclusion

We are compelled to conclude that the tax court erred as a matter of law. Taxpayers have established that Jones was a bona-fide foreign resident of Japan and had his tax home in Japan during the years in question. Therefore, the tax court decision is reversed and remanded with direction to the tax court to expunge the deficiency assessed and enter judgment for the Taxpayers.

§ 3.05 Physical Presence Test

Another (and probably safer) way to qualify for § 911 is through the physical presence test. The physical presence test is not concerned with the qualitative nature of foreign residency that a United States citizen or resident establishes, the person's intentions with respect to returning to the United States, or the nature and purpose of the stay abroad. Instead, the test is a mathematical one, focusing only on the length of time a taxpayer stays in a foreign country or countries.

A citizen or resident meets the physical presence test if, during a period of 12 consecutive months, he is physically present in a foreign country (or countries) for 330 full days (approximately 11 months). The 12-month period may begin with any day. However, this period must end on the day before the corresponding day in the twelfth succeeding month. The period may begin before or after the taxpayer's arrival in the foreign jurisdiction and, similarly, may end before or after departure from that jurisdiction. The 330-day requirement need not be a consecutive period of presence.

A qualifying day is a period of 24 continuous hours beginning at midnight and ending the following midnight. Special rules, however, are provided for passing over international waters. If a taxpayer leaves the United States to travel directly to a foreign country or returns directly to the United States from a foreign country, the time spent over international waters does not count toward the 330-day total. If, however, the taxpayer is already present in a foreign country and merely travels from one foreign country to another, time spent over international waters *will* count if the trip takes less than 24 hours.

The required presence need not be for business purposes. Thus, vacation time in a foreign country counts towards presence as well as any time spent for any other purpose. These principles can best be illustrated by a number of examples:

1. X, a citizen, leaves the United States for England by air on June 10. She arrives in England at 9:00 a.m. on June 11. Her first qualifying day is June 12.

2. Assume that in 1. above, X passes over the coast of England at 11:00 p.m. on June 10 and arrives in England on June 11 at 12:30 a.m. Her first qualifying day is June 11. (The term "foreign country" includes the air space above a country).

3. X, who is present in London for purposes of § 911, leaves London by air at 11:00 p.m. on August 15 and arrives in Stockholm at 5:00 a.m. on August 16. Since her trip took less than 24 hours, she loses no qualifying days.

4. X, who is present in London for purposes of § 911, leaves Southampton, England, by ship at 10:00 p.m. on July 6 and arrives in Nice at 6:00 a.m. on July 8. Since the trip took more than 24 hours, X loses, as qualifying days, July 6, 7, and 8. If X remains in Nice, her next qualifying day will be on July 9.

The physical presence test is, by virtue of its mechanical nature, undoubtedly more certain than the factual labyrinth involved in establishing and determining bona fide residency. Moreover, under the presence test, the whereabouts of the taxpayer at particular times can be easily verified by customs stamps on the passport. Thus, it seems likely that the bona fide residence test is significant only when the taxpayer has spent a substantial amount of time in the United States during the course of a foreign assignment. For this reason, the rules concerning permissible return visits to the United States discussed under the bona fide residence standard assume much importance.

Presence must be established during a consecutive 12-month period. Too often, it is assumed that the 12-month period commences on the first full day of foreign presence. In other words, it is often assumed that a taxpayer who arrives in London on February 1 begins both his foreign presence *and* the 12-month testing period on February 2. However, the Regulations expressly provide that the period may begin before or after arrival abroad and, similarly, may end before or after departure from the foreign jurisdiction. Thus, in the above example, the taxpayer could employ the period of January 13 of the year of arrival to January 12 of the following year.

Gelhar v. Commissioner
T.C. Memo 1992-162

DINAN, SPECIAL TRIAL JUDGE:
Respondent determined a deficiency of $7,536 in petitioners' Federal income tax for the taxable year 1987. . . .

After concessions by respondent, the only issue for decision is whether petitioners were qualified individuals within the meaning of section 911(d)(1), eligible to exclude foreign earned income from their gross income for 1987. . . .

Petitioner Lynn W. Gelhar (hereinafter petitioner) is a Professor of Civil Engineering at the Massachusetts Institute of Technology (MIT). Petitioner's employment as a professor at MIT began in July 1982. On February 26, 1986, petitioner received informal approval for a requested sabbatical leave for the period July 1, 1986, through June 30, 1987. On August 7, 1986, petitioner received formal approval for the sabbatical.

Petitioners' primary residence has been in Concord, Massachusetts, since November 1982. From June 1, 1986, until June 1, 1987, petitioners leased their furnished residence in Concord, Massachusetts, to an unrelated party. During the term of the lease, petitioners did not maintain any other place of abode in the United States. Because they could not show that they had a legal residence as of January 1, 1987, petitioners' names were removed from the Register of Voters list for the Town of Concord.

On June 1, 1986, petitioners left the United States. They visited Belgium, Sweden, and Switzerland between June 2, 1986, and September 3, 1986. On September 3, 1986, they left Switzerland and returned to the United States. They were in the United States from September 3, 1986, until September 6, 1986, when they left for Switzerland and France. They visited Switzerland and France between September 7, 1986, and December 2, 1986, when they returned to the United States. They were in the United States from December 2, 1986, until December 5, 1986, when they left for France, Greece, Singapore, Australia, and New Zealand. Petitioners visited France, Greece, Singapore, Australia, and New Zealand between December 6, 1986, and May 24, 1987. They returned to the United States at Honolulu, Hawaii, on May 25, 1987. Petitioners were present in foreign countries for 345 days from June 2, 1986, through May 24, 1987. They returned to Concord, Massachusetts, on June 1, 1987.

From January 1, 1987, until May 24, 1987, petitioner resided in Australia and New Zealand while working for the University of Western Australia and an agency of the Australian Government and carrying out other professional work. While on the sabbatical leave, petitioner maintained continuing responsibilities with MIT. These responsibilities included advising MIT graduate students and administering ongoing research projects at MIT.

Sabbatical leave, by definition, is "leave with full or half pay granted (as every seventh year) to one holding an administrative or professional position (as college professor) for rest, travel, or research." Webster's Third New International Dictionary (1971). Petitioner's sabbatical leave salary for the period July 1, 1986, to June 30, 1987, was $33,100. While it was anticipated by MIT that an individual on sabbatical leave would return to normal academic duties at MIT after the sabbatical, no formal contractual obligation to do so existed. Both before and after his sabbatical, petitioner actively sought employment at other academic institutions. Following the termination of his sabbatical, petitioner resumed his duties at MIT during the summer of 1987.

Petitioners submitted a Form 2555, Foreign Earned Income, with their 1987 return on which they claimed a foreign earned income exclusion of $23,007. Respondent determined in her notice of deficiency that petitioners were not entitled to the foreign earned income exclusion claimed.

Respondent argues that petitioners do not qualify for the foreign earned income exclusion because they maintained a tax home in Concord, Massachusetts, during petitioner's sabbatical leave. Petitioners contend that they maintained a foreign tax home during petitioner's sabbatical leave and that their absence from Concord, Massachusetts, was of an indefinite or indeterminate nature. We agree with respondent. . . .

Pursuant to section 911(a), a qualified individual may elect to exclude from gross income certain foreign earned income. In order to qualify for the exclusion, a two-prong test must be satisfied. First, the taxpayer must have a "tax home" in a foreign country during the tax year in question. Second, the taxpayer must satisfy the bona fide residence test or the physical presence test. Respondent has conceded that petitioners satisfy the physical presence test.

For purposes of section 911, a tax home means an individual's home for purposes of section 162(a)(2) (relating to travel expenses while away from home). However, section 911(d)(3) also provides an overriding restriction on the tax home concept of section 162(a)(2) in that "An individual shall not be treated as having a tax home in a foreign country for any period for which his abode is within the United States."

A taxpayer's home within the meaning of section 162(a)(2), is generally the area or vicinity of the taxpayer's principal place of employment rather than the location of his family residence. An exception to this rule exists where the taxpayer's employment in a particular location is temporary, as opposed to indefinite, or indeterminate.

Employment is considered temporary when it is expected that it will last for only a short period of time. Employment is indefinite when the prospect is that the work will continue for an indeterminate and substantially long period of time. Employment which is originally temporary may become indefinite due to changed circumstances, or simply from the passage of time. The question of whether employment is of a temporary or indefinite nature is essentially a factual one. No single element is determinative and there are no rules of thumb, durational or otherwise.

In this case, petitioner was employed by MIT and lived in Concord, Massachusetts, until petitioners left the United States on June 1, 1986, to take advantage of petitioner's sabbatical leave for the period July 1, 1986, to June 30, 1987.

During his sabbatical leave, petitioner was still employed by MIT. Petitioners rented their home in Concord, Massachusetts, fully furnished for a period of only 1 year which coincided with the period of petitioner's sabbatical leave. Petitioner returned to his employment at MIT and his home in Concord at the conclusion of his sabbatical. His 5 months of employment in Australia and New Zealand, which commenced in January 1987, was clearly not intended to extend beyond May 1987, and was temporary.

Because we find that petitioner's employment during 1987 in Australia and New Zealand was temporary, it follows that petitioners did not establish a tax home in Australia and/or New Zealand during that time.

Since we have found that petitioner's employment in Australia and New Zealand was temporary and that petitioner did not establish a tax home in either of those locations in 1987, we need not decide whether petitioners maintained an abode in the United States during the period of petitioner's sabbatical leave.

Decision will be entered under Rule 155.

§ 3.06 The Foreign Source Earned Income Limitation: § 911(b) Generally

One of the two income items qualifying for exclusion from gross income under § 911 is the amount of the foreign earned income of the taxpayer. The phrase initially raises a source issue as well as a definitional concern over the term "earned income." Generally, earned income is cash or property given in return for the sweat of the taxpayer's brow: wages, salaries, professional fees, and other amounts received as compensation for personal services actually rendered. Earned income is derived from foreign sources if attributable to the individual's services performed in a foreign country or countries during either the individual's bona fide residency period or period of presence in a foreign country. Without properly sourced foreign earned income, no benefits are available under § 911 regardless of the taxpayer's compliance with the presence or residency standards. Thus, income earned for services performed in the United States is not eligible for the exclusion.

Traditionally, the Service has interpreted earned income to parallel the § 861(a)(3) concept of compensation—that is, something to be distinguished from royalties, sales income, and other particular source rule categories. This attitude led to some hair-splitting distinctions in deciding which source rule applied and whether an item of income represented earned income.

However, for purposes of the § 911 exclusion, the courts have interpreted earned income more broadly than § 861(a)(3) income. In *Tobey v. Commissioner,* 60 T.C. 227 (1973), for instance, the Tax Court drew a distinction between earned income and other income by characterizing the former as the result of a taxpayer's effort and the latter as that which is a return of capital. In the court's view, the fact that a "product" which results from the taxpayer's labor is later "sold" is irrelevant; gain derived from the sale of such self-created property is properly characterized as earned income. Thus, under the facts of the case, the court held that gain from the sale of paintings created by a domestic artist was earned income. The Service subsequently indicated its willingness to fall into line with the court's relatively expansive definition.

Revenue Ruling 80-254
1980-2 C.B. 222

Rev. Rul. 71-315, 1971-2 C.B. 271, holds that royalties paid to a writer by a publisher for the transfer of property rights of the writer in the writer's products are not earned income within the meaning of section 911(b) of the Internal Revenue Code. Rev. Rul. 71-315 also provides that amounts received by a writer under a personal service contract to write weekly articles for a newspaper and to write a book are earned income within the meaning of section 911(b).

In *Tobey v. Commissioner,* 60 T.C. 227 (1973), *acq.* 1979-1 C.B. 1, the United States Tax Court held that income from the sale of paintings created by the taxpayer is earned income under section 911 of the Code.

HOLDING

Because of the acquiescence in *Tobey*, the royalties paid to the writer in Rev. Rul. 71-315, by the publisher for the transfer of property rights of the writer in the writer's products are now considered to be earned income within the meaning of section 911(b) of the Code.

Rev. Rul. 71-315 correctly holds that amounts received by the writer under a contract to write weekly articles for a newspaper and to write a book are earned income under section 911(b). . . .

§ 3.07 Deferred Payments

Income earned for services performed abroad must be attributed to the taxable year in which the employee performed those services. For purposes of computing the foreign earned income limitation, foreign earned income deferred until the next taxable year after the year in which the services generating the income were performed is *not* taken into account in the year of receipt. Rather, the deferred earned income is deemed earned in the year of performance and thus absorbs the limitation for the taxable year of performance.

For example, assume B, a United States citizen, is a qualified individual performing services in Hungary during Year 1 and Year 2. B earns a salary of $60,000 for Year 1 and $90,000 in Year 2. B is employed for the full year during both Year 1 and Year 2, but he receives a payment of $150,000 in Year 2 for two years of salary. In Year 2, B is entitled to exclude $140,000 received in that year under § 911. The exclusion is comprised of B's Year 1 exclusion of $60,000 ($80,000 limited to the $60,000 of foreign earned income attributable to that year) and B's Year 2 exclusion capped at $80,000. The unutilized $20,000 of exclusion for Year 1 *cannot* be carried over to absorb B's $10,000 of Year 2 foreign earned income that exceeds his $80,000 § 911 limitation for that year.

If income is deferred in excess of one taxable year beyond the year in which the services were performed, the income no longer constitutes foreign earned income. Individuals engaged in certain long-term employment contracts involving deferred payments may forfeit the § 911 exclusion. For example, if in the above hypothetical B had instead received his Year 1 salary of $60,000 in Year 3 and his Year 2 salary of $90,000 in Year 4, he would not be entitled to the § 911 exclusion for the foreign income earned in either Year 1 or Year 2.

§ 3.08 Amounts Received from a Sole Proprietorship or Partnership

Generally, business income is regarded as a return on capital and thus is not regarded as earned income. However, if the taxpayer performs services for the business, amounts received as compensation may be considered earned income if those amounts reasonably reflect the value of the taxpayer's services. In the case of a noncorporate business in which both personal services and capital are material income-producing factors, a reasonable allowance as compensation for the individual's services is treated as earned income, but such allowance is capped at 30 percent of the taxpayer's share of the net profits of that business.

§ 3.09 Limitation on the Amount of the Exclusion

A financial limitation is placed on the amount of the foreign earned income exclusion. The exclusion is limited to the amount of foreign earned income, computed on a daily basis, at an annual rate of $80,000. There is no carryover of "excess" earned income. The limitation tracks the earned income attributable to each taxable year. For instance, assume A is employed in Greece for two years (Year 1- Year 2) and earns a salary of $70,000 per year. However, the payment of $20,000 of his Year 1 salary is deferred until Year 2. The § 911 exclusion operates to impose a limit of $80,000 of earnings *per taxable year*. Thus, for Year 1, a $70,000 exclusion is available for the $50,000 received in Year 1 plus the $20,000 that was received in Year 2, but which was attributable to Year 1. In Year 2, the $70,000 salary attributable to and received therein is likewise excluded.

§ 3.10 Employer-Provided Housing Exclusion

Section 911 provides that, at the election of a qualified individual, that individual may exclude from gross income his foreign earned income and his housing cost amount. An individual's housing cost amount is an amount equal to the excess of the individual's reasonable housing expenses for the taxable year over a base level of housing costs (an amount equal to 16 percent of the salary of a step 1, grade GS-14 federal employee). Housing expenses include all reasonable expenses paid by or on behalf of an individual for housing for the taxpayer, his spouse, and dependents in a foreign country, including expenses such as rent or fair rental value, utilities, or insurance. Housing expenses do not include interest, taxes, or co-op expenses which are deductible under § 163, § 164, or § 216(a). The housing exclusion applies *in addition to* the $80,000 earned income exclusion and is determined prior to the § 911(a)(1) foreign earned income exclusion. Housing expenses do not include the cost of purchasing a house, capital improvements, and other capital expenditures; the cost of purchased furniture, accessories, or domestic labor; amortized payments of principal with respect to an evidence of indebtedness secured by a mortgage on the taxpayer's housing; and certain other items.

The base housing amount is equal to the product of 16 percent of the annual salary of a step 1, grade GS-14 federal government employee multiplied by the ratio of the number of qualifying days to the number of days in the taxable year. For this purpose, a qualifying day is defined as a day within the period during which an individual meets the tax home requirement and either the bona fide residence or the physical presence test. In many cases, the qualifying period will constitute the entire taxable year. However, for the years of arrival and departure, the taxpayer often will not meet the presence or residency requirements for the entire year. In such cases, a more precise determination is required.

For example, assume that an individual leaves New York at 7:00 p.m. on October 4, Year 1; arrives in the United Kingdom at 6:00 a.m. on October 5; establishes residency; and remains in the United Kingdom for the next three years making his tax home there. His number of qualifying days during Year 1 under the residency standard will be 87 days (October 6 through December 31). However, if the taxpayer qualifies under the presence test, his qualifying days may exceed the days of actual presence. The Regulations specifically provide that the 12-month period for the presence test may include days when the taxpayer is either not present in a foreign country or does not maintain a foreign tax home. Thus, if in the above example the individual's foreign presence is continuous from the date of his arrival, his 12-month qualifying period may predate his arrival up to a maximum of 35 days (365 days–330 days). The statutory test requires his presence in a foreign country for 330 days during *any* 12-month period. In this case, the period, at the individual's election, could commence on September 1. If so, the number of qualifying days would increase too.

The § 911(a)(2) housing cost amount exclusion is available only to the extent of the lesser of the housing cost amount attributable to an individual's employer provided amounts or his or her foreign source earned income for the taxable year and is determined prior to the § 911(a)(1) foreign earned income exclusion. Employer provided amounts include any foreign source earned income paid or incurred on behalf of an individual by the employer including salary, reimbursements for housing expenses, educational expenses, or other specified amounts. The term is sufficiently broad that any employee, even if not compensated specifically for housing purposes, may still qualify to the extent of his or her own expenditures on his behalf. The implicit assumption is that indirect employer-provided amounts, e.g., an increased salary, should receive the same treatment as payments to an identically situated taxpayer whose salary does not reflect the amount of the employer-provided housing allowance. The only earnings which will not be employer-provided are those arising from an individual's self-employment.

§ 3.11 Self-Provided Housing

For self-employed taxpayers, different rules apply. Where a self-employed qualifying taxpayer pays for housing, such amounts are treated as a deduction, not an exclusion, allowable in computing adjusted gross income. The deduction is limited to the excess of (1) the foreign earned income of the individual for the year over (2) the amount of such income excluded by the foreign earned income exclusion and the housing cost amount. Thus, if all of an individual's foreign earned income is excluded by the foreign earned income exclusion, that individual is not entitled to a deduction for self-provided housing costs.

§ 3.12 Computing the Foreign Earned Income Exclusion

Once the exclusion for the housing cost amount has been determined, the taxpayer may then proceed to determine his foreign earned income exclusion. The amount of foreign earned income that can be excluded is the lesser of the excess of the individual's foreign earned income over the excluded housing cost amount or the annual exclusion rate prorated to reflect the individual's qualifying days. The § 911(a)(1) foreign earned income exclusion is computed after the § 911(a)(2) housing cost exclusion.

In order to compute the § 911(a)(1) foreign earned income exclusion, the following procedure must be followed:

The first step involves a determination of how many qualifying days an individual is able to establish during his or her taxable year, i.e., a day within the period during which an individual meets the tax home requirement and either the bona fide residence or the physical presence test. In many cases, the qualifying period will constitute the entire taxable year. However, for the years of arrival and departure, the taxpayer often will not meet the presence or residency requirements for the entire year. In such cases, a more precise determination is required.

For example, assume that an individual leaves New York at 7:00 p.m. on October 4, Year 1; arrives in the United Kingdom at 6:00 a.m. on October 5; establishes residency; and remains in the United Kingdom for the next three years making his tax home there. His number of qualifying days during Year 1 under the residency standard will be 87 days (October 6 through December 31). However, as discussed above, if the taxpayer qualifies under the presence test, his qualifying days may exceed the days of actual presence. Thus, if in the example the individual's foreign presence is continuous from the date of his arrival, his 12-month qualifying period may predate his arrival up to a maximum of 35 days (365 days–330 days). The statutory test requires his presence in a foreign country for 330 days during *any* 12-month period. The period, at the individual's election, could commence on September 1. If so, the number of qualifying days for Year 1 would increase to 112. As noted below, the proper selection of the 12-month period can increase the amount of the § 911(a) limitation, which in most cases, proves advantageous to the taxpayer.

The amount of the § 911(a)(1) exclusion which will be available in any year is determined by the following formula:

$$\frac{\text{Number of qualifying days in the taxable year}}{\text{Number of days in the taxable year}} \times \$80,000$$

Thus, in the example above, the available § 911(a)(1) exclusion would be $19,068 ($80,000 x (87 days/365 days)) for a residency claim and $24,548 ($80,000 x (112 days/365 days)) for presence qualification.

Determining the amount of foreign earned income received during the year requires the integration of three notions: the concept of when income is received by an individual; the definition of earned income; and the source of the earned income. The concepts of earned income and its source have been previously considered. The taxpayer's accounting method governs the determination. Thus, a taxpayer who renders foreign services worth $60,000 in Year 1 but does not receive such funds until Year 2 has received, and will report, foreign earned income in Year 2 if he is a cash method taxpayer. If instead he were an accrual method taxpayer, he would report the income in Year 1.

Foreign earned income generally is considered to be earned in the taxable year in which the individual performed the services giving rise to the income, regardless of the year of receipt. Thus, an amount received in a taxable year for services rendered in the prior year is attributable to the earlier year. The attribution of bonuses and substantially nonvested property is made with reference to all of the facts and circumstances. For example, if an individual receives a bonus which is attributable to services performed (or to be performed) in more than one taxable year, the amount of the bonus is allocated among the years on the basis of the services performed (or to be performed).

After determining the amount of foreign earned income attributable to the current year, the § 911 exclusion is available to the extent of the lesser of that portion of the foreign earned income in excess of the housing cost amount excluded under § 911(a)(2) or the exclusion limitation. However, for purposes of this example, it is assumed that the § 911(a)(2) exclusion is not available, e.g., the employer provides housing within the meaning of § 119. Thus, in the above example, where the limitation was computed to be $19,068 or $24,548, the taxpayer's § 911 exclusion would equal that amount if his foreign earned income (e.g., $40,000) were greater than the determined figure. If his foreign earned income were less (e.g., $10,000), then his § 911(a)(1) exclusion would be limited to the amount of foreign earned income.

If foreign earned income received by a taxpayer is attributable to years other than the year of receipt, a final calculation must be made in order to determine whether the exclusion is available for the year to which the amount is attributable. The § 911 availability in the year of receipt is irrelevant for these amounts. For example, if in the example above (assuming residence qualification) the individual received $16,000 of foreign earned income (salary) during Year 1 and received a further $3,500 performance bonus on January 4, Year 2 attributable to services performed during November, Year 1, under the Regulations only $3,068 (the remaining § 911(a) exclusion for Year 1 ($19,068 − $16,000)) of the $3,500 bonus may be excluded under the § 911(a)(1) foreign earned income exclusion for Year 2.

The remaining $432 may not be excluded under § 911(a)(1) even if, for the remainder of Year 2, the individual received only $60,000 foreign earned income ($20,000 less than the maximum of $80,000 § 911(a)(1) exclusion available for Year 2).

PROBLEM 3—SECTION 911 EXCLUSION

Code: §§ 1(a)-(d), 11(a), 164(a)(3) and (b)(3), 275(a)(4), 901(a) and (b)(1), 904(a), 911(a)-(d)(7)

Regulations: §§ 1.911-2(a)-(d), 1.911-3(a)-(d), 1.911-4(a)-(b)(4) and (d), 1.911-6(a)

1. A, who lives in Chicago, Illinois, derives $22,000 in salary from his employer. Furthermore, A deposits funds in a Swiss bank account, which yield $4,000 in interest, deposited to his account on December 31. What is A's taxable income for United States taxing purposes? What result if A pays $3,200 in tax to Switzerland on the interest income? What if A paid Switzerland $500 in tax?

2. C, a United States citizen, is transferred to Sydney, Australia to work for her employer's subsidiary for a four-year period. She arrives on December 31, Year 1 and commences employment on January 1, Year 2. Her annual salary is $100,000 and her foreign housing expenses are $2,000 per month. Assume that the salary of a GS-14 step 1 is $50,000.

    a. What is her tax liability to the United States under the residency test of § 911?
    b. What if her salary is $75,000 per year?
    c. What if her employment period was two years?
    d. What if she arrived in Australia on January 11, Year 2 and departed on December 27, Year 3?
    e. What if she arrived on December 31, Year 1 and departed January 2, Year 3?
    f. What result if C pays income tax of $12,000 to Australia on her salary? What if, under the Australian tax law, she is not liable for any tax? What if she is not liable under the United States-Australia tax treaty because thereunder she is a resident of the United States? What if she declares herself to be a nonresident of Australia and therefore under the Australian tax law is not liable for tax?

3. D, a United States citizen employed by an Illinois corporation, is transferred on July 1, Year 1, to work with its subsidiary located in France. Upon transfer, D is informed that he can expect to work at the branch for approximately 18 months, with

a return to the United States scheduled for December 31, Year 2. A's yearly salary is $100,000 and foreign housing expenses are $2,000 per month. Assume that the salary of a GS-14 step 1 is $50,000.

a. What tax results in Year 1 under the presence test of § 911?
b. What result if D invests a portion of her salary in a French bank, earning interest of $5,000 per year?
c. What if D requests that $30,000 of her Year 1 and Year 2 salary be payable in Year 3 and Year 4 respectively?

Chapter 4
Foreign Tax Credit

§ 4.01 Introduction
§ 4.02 Credit Versus Deduction
§ 4.03 Persons Eligible to Take the Credit
§ 4.04 Creditable Taxes—General Principles
§ 4.05 Requirements for Credit
Nissho Iwai American Corp. v. Commissioner, 89 T.C. 765 (1987)
Revenue Ruling 90-107, 1990-2 C.B. 178
§ 4.06 Taxes on Business Income
§ 4.07 Taxes on Dividends, Interest, Other Passive Income, and Compensation
§ 4.08 Taxes "In Lieu Of" Income Taxes: § 903
§ 4.09 The § 904 Limitation upon the Amount of Taxes Which May Be Credited—In General
§ 4.10 The Separate Computations of the Overall § 904 Limitation
§ 4.11 Carryback and Carryover of Excess Taxes Paid: § 904(c)
§ 4.12 Corporations Eligible to Utilize the Foreign Tax Credit—Domestic Stockholders in Foreign Corporations: § 902
First Chicago Corp. v. Commissioner, 96 T.C. 421 (1991)
§ 4.13 Calculating the Taxes Deemed Paid by Domestic Corporations
§ 4.14 The § 78 Gross-Up
§ 4.15 Two Variations on the § 904 Limitation: Capital Gains and Losses
§ 4.16 Recapture of Foreign Losses: § 904(f)
Problem 4

§ 4.01 Introduction

For the most part, individuals and corporations are subject to potential taxation in two places: the jurisdiction from which they derive their income (the country of income source) and the jurisdiction in which they are organized or resident (the country of residence). Thus, a United States individual or corporation earning $500 in Germany may be taxed both by Germany (assuming a 40 percent rate yielding a $200 tax) and the United States (assuming a 35 percent rate yielding a $175 tax). Without relief from one or both of the jurisdictions, the tax bill on $500 of income would thus be $375, imposing upon the taxpayer an effective tax rate of 75 percent.

This near confiscatory rate of tax would have a particularly deleterious effect on international operations. To prevent this double taxation, the United States employs the use of a foreign tax credit, by which the United States extends a dollar-for-dollar credit for foreign income taxes paid. In the credit context, the country of residence defers to the country of income source. Thus, in the above example, a foreign tax credit for the German tax payments would eliminate United States tax and yield an overall tax rate of 40 percent. The amount of the credit is linked to the amount of foreign source income derived by the taxpayer.

§ 4.02 Credit Versus Deduction

Under § 901(b)(1), a credit against tax may be taken by a United States citizen and a domestic corporation for foreign "income, war profits, and excess profits taxes." Alternatively, a deduction for such taxes is available under § 164(a)(3). A taxpayer must select *either* the credit or the deduction. As a rule, both cannot be enjoyed. However, the taxpayer may alternate annually between the credit and the deduction depending upon which is more favorable.

In most cases, the § 901 credit is more advantageous than the deduction because a credit reduces tax on a dollar-for-dollar basis, while a deduction merely reduces the amount of income upon which the tax will be levied. The credit may also be favored because § 265(a)(1) denies a deduction for expenses (including foreign taxes) allocable to income exempt from United States tax, while the § 901 credit may be taken even though the foreign tax in question is attributable to such income.

However, the deduction may be preferable to the credit. Most notably, the § 901 credit is curtailed by the source rule limitation of

§ 904. This limitation does not apply to § 164(a)(3) deductions. Additionally, the deduction is infinitely superior to the credit when a tax is not creditable because it fails to meet the statutory and regulatory requirements for creditability.

§ 4.03 Persons Eligible to Take the Credit

The § 901 "direct" foreign tax credit is primarily available to United States residents, citizens, and corporations. A § 902 "indirect" foreign tax credit arises only in the corporate context. It is available to domestic corporations owning at least ten percent of the voting stock of a foreign corporation which pays or accrues foreign taxes upon earnings it distributes as a dividend to the domestic corporate parent.

§ 4.04 Creditable Taxes—General Principles

The Regulations construct a two-pronged test to determine whether a foreign levy is a creditable tax. The first portion of the Regulations address whether a foreign levy qualifies as an income tax for § 901 purposes by determining whether the levy is a tax and whether its predominant character is that of a tax in the "United States sense." The latter portion of the Regulations address rules for determining both the amount of tax creditable and the identity of the payor of the tax. The definitional issue of which payments constitute a tax and which do not permeates the discussion of the foreign tax credit.

With the exception of § 902, a credit is extended only to the taxpayer incurring a foreign tax liability. A taxpayer incurs a tax liability if the remedies for nonpayment run against him. Thus, the imposition of legal liability is the determinative factor with regard to creditability as opposed to who actually pays the tax. The fact that a withholding agent remits the tax does not deprive the party actually burdened by the tax from qualifying as the taxpayer for credit purposes. Provided the agent had the right to withhold such funds, the amount of the proceeds withheld constitutes both income to, and a tax payment by, the taxpayer. In essence, the transaction is viewed as though the taxpayer had received the full amount of the proceeds and then personally paid the foreign tax.

The Regulations also focus on determining the *amount* of foreign tax paid. The scope of the computation is narrow, precluding the availability of the credit for refundable amounts, subsidies, multiple levies, and noncompulsory payments. The Regulations limit the creditability of foreign taxes to those taxes which would result from a "reasonable" application of foreign tax law. Anything in excess of that standard constitutes a noncompulsory amount for which the credit is not available. Thus, to maximize the potential for creditability, the taxpayer should apply foreign tax law (including applicable tax treaties) so as to reduce foreign income and taxes. However, a taxpayer is not expected to alter its business form, conduct, or mode of operations in order to demonstrate that an amount is "compulsory."

§ 4.05 Requirements for Credit

To credit a payment to a foreign country, a taxpayer must show that the payment is an *income* tax. This determination is made independently for each separate foreign levy. In order to constitute a creditable income tax, the levy must be a tax and its predominant character must be that of an "income tax in the United States sense." In order to constitute a tax, the payment must be a *compulsory* payment to a foreign government which is intended as such. Fines, penalties, interest, royalties, and charges for specific economic benefits thus do not represent a tax for purposes of the credit. Since the preferential treatment of a credit is superior typically to that of a deduction, the payment must be more than a payment for which a deduction, such as a royalty payment, would be available and would adequately compensate for the expenditure.

The tax must be designed, similar to most United States taxes, to reach *net* gain. The Regulations elaborate that the net gain requirement is dependent upon compliance with a realization test and a net income test. Additionally, the tax may not be a "soak-up" tax, i.e., one for which liability is dependent upon the availability of the credit against the taxpayer's tax obligation to another country.

This definitional issue has garnered much controversy. The Service and the courts have elaborated on what foreign taxes may be credited. This elaboration appears to evince a significant tightening of standards.

Nissho Iwai American Corp. v. Commissioner
United States Tax Court
89 T.C. 765 (1987)

JACOBS, JUDGE:

OPINION

At the outset, it should be noted that this case involves the unusual situation in which a taxpayer seeks to recognize income. The reason for this is because attached to the recognition of income is the potential availability of a foreign tax credit; and taxwise, the foreign tax credit is worth more than the detrimental recognition of the income. . . .

Petitioner claimed a credit for the entire amount of Brazilian withholding tax. In his notice of deficiency, respondent disallowed 85 percent of the claimed credit. . . .

A foreign tax is creditable only if the taxpayer is legally liable under foreign law for the tax. However, legal liability for a tax and the obligation to pay the tax are not necessarily the same. For example, under a withholding system, legal liability for the tax and the obligation to pay the tax are different. The Federal wage withholding system illustrates this difference—the employer is the person obligated to withhold the tax and to pay the withheld tax to the government; the employee is the person legally liable for the tax.

Under Brazilian law, interest paid to foreign lenders (i.e., lenders residing or domiciled abroad) is subject to an income tax at the rate of 25 percent. The Brazilian borrower is required to withhold that percentage from each payment of interest; as a practical matter, the interest payment cannot be made unless and until the Brazilian withholding tax is paid. Respondent argues that the Brazilian withholding tax is a tax upon the payment, rather than receipt, of interest. We disagree.

United States tax law is the standard for deciding whether a foreign levy is a creditable income tax. After reviewing translations of the applicable Brazilian law, it is our opinion that the tax is on the receipt of the interest. The tax is imposed on the foreign lender; the Brazilian borrower is simply the person required to pay the tax on behalf of the foreign lender. Accordingly, we believe that the Brazilian withholding tax per se is potentially creditable to the lender. We now turn to the amount of the Brazilian withholding tax which is creditable. . . .

Respondent contends that if petitioner is legally liable for the Brazilian tax, that portion of the tax which was returned . . . by way of the subsidy is not creditable. . . .

[A]mounts of tax paid or accrued to a foreign country do not include amounts used directly or indirectly as a subsidy to either the taxpayer or a person who is engaged in a business transaction with the taxpayer where the subsidy is determined directly or indirectly by reference to the amount of income tax, or the base used to compute the income tax, imposed by the country on the taxpayer. Here, the amount of the subsidy received [by the payor] is clearly based on the amount of the withholding tax. . . .

The purpose of the foreign tax credit is to reduce international double taxation. Here, no double taxation occurred; in fact, because petitioner's loan . . . was a net loan, petitioner was not 'out of pocket' for any of the Brazilian taxes. As far as petitioner is concerned, its receiving credit for the Brazilian taxes in any amount essentially constitutes a windfall. The question to be resolved is how much of a windfall petitioner is to receive. . . .

Here, [the payor] absorbed the entire amount of the Brazilian withholding tax on behalf of petitioner. Simultaneous with the payment of the tax, [the payor] received a subsidy from the Brazilian government based on the amount of tax paid. Petitioner argues that an amount collected as a tax does not 'lose its status as such by virtue of the fact that the taxing authority (foreign or domestic) allocates that amount to a specific program.' While in general we agree with petitioner's argument, in the situation involved herein, payment of the tax and receipt of the subsidy are in lockstep. Common sense dictates that payment of the tax and receipt of the subsidy be viewed together in determining the amount of foreign taxes creditable for purposes of section 901. If we accept payment of the Brazilian tax as one transaction and receipt of the subsidy as another, we would ignore the true unity of the transaction and elevate form over substance; this we shall not do.

To reflect the foregoing and concessions by the parties,

Decision will be entered under Rule 155.

Revenue Ruling 90-107
1990-2 C.B. 178

ISSUE

What are the foreign tax credit consequences of the receipt of a Brazilian investment certificate obtained in connection with the payment of a creditable Brazilian income tax?

FACTS

P, a domestic corporation, owns all of the stock of FS, a Brazilian corporation.

In order to increase development, Brazil offers a special income tax incentive to companies investing in certain government approved projects. Under the incentive program, companies may designate annually a portion of their Brazilian income tax to one of several investment funds, which coordinate development programs in Brazil. Once the designation and full payment of the tax are made, the investment fund issues to the company an investment certificate in an amount equal to the tax designation. The recipient of an investment certificate has three options: it may 1) retain the investment certificate and thereby become a shareholder in the investment fund; 2) convert the investment certificate, through a government regulated exchange, into a direct ownership interest in certain other companies participating in the investment fund; or 3) sell the investment certificate on one of the country's public stock exchanges.

FS's Brazilian income tax liability for year 1 was 100 X cruzados. In January of year 2, FS timely paid its Brazilian income tax, and, as a participant in a Brazilian development program, FS designated 25x cruzados to an investment fund. Later in year 2, FS received a 25x investment certificate. . . .

LAW AND ANALYSIS

. . . .

[T]he Regulations state that "[a]n amount is not tax paid to a foreign country to the extent it is reasonably certain that the amount will be refunded, credited, rebated, abated, or forgiven." [The] regulation illustrates that to the extent that the rebate is in the form of property, the amount of tax paid for section 901 purposes is the difference between the initial amount of tax paid and the fair market value of the property received.

When FS made its 100x cruzado payment to the Brazilian authorities in January of year 2, it was reasonably certain that a portion of this amount would be refunded to FS in the form of property, an investment certificate. Accordingly, . . . the amount of Brazilian income tax paid by FS for year 1 is 100x cruzados less the fair market value of the investment certificate ascertained at the time of payment of the tax. . . .

HOLDING

The amount of creditable foreign tax is the initial amount of tax paid, reduced by the fair market value of the investment certificate ascertained at the time of payment of the tax.

§ 4.06 Taxes on Business Income

Foreign taxes imposed on income from business operations are a prime concern of the Rulings and Regulations. Basically, the Service denies creditability to foreign taxes which could conceivably be levied even though the taxpayer has suffered a net loss in that country. If, upon review of the language or administration of a foreign tax statute, the Service concludes that the tax might be levied upon a net loss, it may contend that the tax is not a creditable income tax in the United States sense.

A creditable § 901 tax must be an income tax within the United States meaning of the term. To pass this test, various requirements must be met.

The Regulations provide that the realization requirement is met if the event which is taxable would result at its occurrence or thereafter in the realization of income under the standards of the Code. A tax which is triggered by a purchase, a tax computed on the basis of rental value, and a tax triggered by the manufacture of a product rather than its sale generally would violate this requirement since none of these events gives rise to a realization event as expressed by § 1001 of the Code.

Some general exceptions to the realization requirement are afforded under the § 901 Regulations. First, a tax may be credited if it represents only a slight, as opposed to substantial, deviation from the United States realization concept. Basically, this exception should apply to taxes levied on a wide variety of income types, some types being realized in the domestic sense and others not. If the unrealized types (e.g., rental income from a personal residence or receipt of stock dividends) are insignificant in light of the realized items included in the tax base, the tax may be credited. In such a case, the tax is evaluated as a whole. Once blessed, it is applicable to all who fall within its net, including any taxpayers whose predominant or exclusive reason for being subject to the tax is the receipt of the exceptional unrealized items. Additionally, imposition of a post-realization tax is acceptable if the United States tax system employs a similar tax.

A second exception is provided for taxes levied on nonrealization events which occur before events which would result in domestic realization. Provided that a second tax is not levied upon the actual realization, the surrogate earlier event satisfies the standard. An example is given in the Regulations wherein a tax is levied upon a deemed distribution by a corporation to its shareholders. It is provided that the base upon which the tax is imposed is the shareholder's pro rata share of the corporation's taxable income less the pro rata share of corporate tax. The example provides that a credit may be taken for the deemed distribution. The exception is conditioned on the fact that the foreign jurisdiction does not impose a second tax on the actual distribution of funds. If such were the case, the second, and not the first, tax would qualify for the credit.

In order to satisfy the net income test, the tax must permit either recovery of actual significant costs, including capital expenditures, or a surrogate allowance that closely approximates these amounts. The Service emphasizes that expenses incurred in producing gross trade or business income are not inherently so slight as to ensure that they will almost never exceed the amount of that gross income and thus not produce a loss. Because of this, a foreign tax on business income that does not permit the deduction of generally significant expenses incurred in producing that income is not "almost certain" to fall on net income. Thus, the tax is not creditable.

The critical issues in this area are (1) which expenses are significant; and (2) when (if ever) will the nondeductibility of significant expenses be tolerated. The Regulations provide that the foreign tax law must permit the recovery of the more significant costs incurred in producing the product. If actual expenses are not permitted but an alternative procedure which reasonably approximates such costs is employed, then the net gain requirement is met. Furthermore, the fact that such costs may be recovered more slowly under foreign law than would be the case under United States law will not invalidate the tax.

§ 4.07 Taxes on Dividends, Interest, Other Passive Income, and Compensation

The creditability of taxes on investment income items and employee compensation in theory is determined by the same requirements discussed above for business taxes. However, the Regulations acknowledge some distinctions between these receipts and others and also lessen some of the specific requirements. Withholding taxes on dividends, interest, royalties, and other types of passive income are likely to be creditable taxes, even if taxation of these items is on a gross basis.

§ 4.08 Taxes "In Lieu Of" Income Taxes: § 903

The reluctance of the Service in the § 901 area has focused increased attention on § 903 as an alternative means of securing a credit for foreign taxes. Section 903 provides that, for purposes of the foreign tax credit, the term "income, war profits, and excess profits taxes" shall include taxes paid in lieu of a foreign income tax. The Senate Finance Committee, in passing § 903, indicated that the statute was intended to enjoy a broad construction:

> Thus if a foreign country in imposing income taxation authorized, for reasons growing out of the administrative difficulties of determining net income or taxable basis within that country, a United States domestic corporation doing business in such country to pay a tax in lieu of such income tax but measured, for example, by gross income,

gross sales or a number of units produced within the country, such tax has not heretofore been recognized as a basis for a credit. Your committee has deemed it desirable to extend the scope of this section.

Under the Regulations, to qualify as a § 903 "in lieu of" tax, the tax must meet the general definition of a tax. This definition focuses upon compulsory levies and the nature of the tax as a substitute for, and not in addition to, an income tax or series of income taxes otherwise imposed. Thus, a tax on gross or fictitious income stands a better chance of being credited under § 903 than under § 901 given that the base of the tax need not bear any relationship to realized net income. The tax is considered creditable under § 903 only if the foreign country has a general income tax law in force; the taxpayer would, in the absence of a specific provision applicable to him, be subject to that general income tax; and the general income tax is not imposed on the taxpayer because he is subject to the substituted tax.

§ 4.09 The § 904 Limitation upon the Amount of Taxes Which May Be Credited—In General

Once the amount of foreign taxes creditable under §§ 901-903 has been ascertained, the taxpayer must then examine the § 904 limitations which are imposed upon the credit. That statute provides that the credit is limited to an amount determined under the following formula:

$$\text{Maximum foreign tax credit} = \frac{\text{Foreign source taxable income}}{\text{Worldwide taxable income}} \times \text{United States tax on worldwide income}$$

The object of the § 904 limitation is to protect the claim of the United States to tax the domestic source income of its own taxpayers. Thus, the § 904 limitation attempts to effectively limit the credit to the United States tax liability that would be imposed on the taxpayer's foreign source income. For example, assume that a domestic corporation subject to an effective tax rate of 30 percent derives $40 of income from a domestic source and $70 of income in a foreign country subject to an effective tax rate of 50 percent (yielding a foreign tax liability of $35). In the absence of a limitation, the creditable foreign tax ($35) would completely eliminate any domestic tax otherwise owing ($33—which is 30 percent of worldwide income of $110). If such were the case, the United States would have completely surrendered its claim to tax. Instead, the § 904 limitation caps the credit at $21 ($70/$110 x $33).

Under the § 904 limitation, the tax attributable to the higher foreign tax rate is viewed as a noncreditable cost of investing or conducting business in that country. In essence, the statutory approach does not permit any portion of the domestic tax payment attributable to United States source income to be offset by foreign taxes. From a policy standpoint, United States source income does not fall within the category of doubly taxed income.

Concerning the § 904 limitation, the following points should be stressed. A foreign tax may be considered creditable under § 901 even though it is levied upon income which is exempt from domestic taxation. The § 904 limitation, on the other hand, focuses upon *taxable* income and thus excludes, from both the numerator and the denominator, income which is exempt from United States tax. Because the limitation is based upon taxable income, it necessarily involves the allocation of deductions for foreign source income. The subject of allocating and apportioning expenses is complex. Generally, expenses are allocated to the class of income to which they bear a factual relationship.

As a general rule, the source of income rules are controlling for purposes of the foreign tax credit. Thus, the taxpayer's transactions are to be tested against the rules of §§ 861-863 and 865. Once sourced, the income is integrated accordingly into the § 904 limitation as United States or foreign source income. However, in some cases, Congress for various policy reasons has altered the source of income or loss rules solely for foreign tax credit purposes. Thus, even if a particular transaction otherwise generates foreign source income or loss, Congress may have legislated a different standard to apply for sourcing purposes for determining the allowable foreign tax credit.

§ 4.10 The Separate Computations of the Overall § 904 Limitation

Various policy considerations have led Congress to specify that the § 904 calculation must be applied separately to special classes of income, often referred to as income "baskets." Broadly speaking, the purpose of the separate basket-limitation is to ensure that a taxpayer's foreign tax credit is limited to the United States tax imposed on foreign source income by severely restricting a taxpayer's ability to average low-tax foreign source income with high-tax income in an effort to utilize "excess" foreign tax credits.

Assume, for example, that C, a domestic corporation, derives foreign business income taxed at a 40 percent rate. C's total taxable income for the year is $100,000 of which $25,000 is attributable to the foreign activity. The remaining $75,000 is attributable to United States projects. C pays $10,000 in foreign tax. C's tentative tax computed under § 11 without regard to the foreign tax credit is $23,250. C's residual income limitation would be: $23,250 x $25,000/$100,000 = $5,813. Thus, C may only claim a foreign tax credit of only $5,813, even though it paid $10,000 in foreign taxes.

If, in addition to the above facts, $5,000 of C's $100,000 taxable income consists of interest income from another foreign country which is exempt from tax in that country either by statute or tax treaty, C's residual income limitation would be increased to $6,975 ($23,250 x $30,000/$100,000). This results in $1,162 more of the foreign taxes being creditable through the generation of the non-taxed foreign source interest income.

To preclude such a manipulation of the foreign tax credit limitation, Congress has mandated the use of nine separate baskets. The baskets include, *inter alia*, a passive income basket, a high withholding tax interest basket, and an all other income basket. Such categorization precludes the effective usage of various types of enumerated (and arguably malleable) income types to increase the numerator of the § 904 limitation for credit purposes.

Additional statutory safeguards exist with respect to the use of domestic losses to offset foreign taxable income. To ensure that the taxpayer does not allocate the losses to the category which would be most favorable to the taxpayer, the statute mandates that the loss be allocated proportionately among the various income baskets.

When the § 904 limitation was first enacted, one of the most popular ways of generating low-tax foreign source income to reduce the shrinking effect of the limitation was to derive passive income in a low-tax or non-tax foreign jurisdiction. This effort increased the foreign source income numerator of the § 904 limitation ratio without the corresponding payment of significant foreign taxes. To prevent this tactic, § 904(d) as originally enacted provided that the limitation must be separately applied against passive income. Passive income generally is defined as income which is classified as interest, dividends, royalties, rents, etc. Expressed as an equation, the § 904(d) passive income limitation is:

$$\text{Maximum passive income basket foreign tax credit} = \frac{\text{Foreign source § 904(d) passive income}}{\text{Worldwide taxable income}} \times \text{United States tax on worldwide income}$$

By way of example, assume that a United States individual derives $100,000 of foreign taxable income with a foreign tax liability of $40,000 and $100,000 of domestic taxable income, yielding a worldwide taxable income of $200,000 subject to an assumed domestic tax rate of 30 percent. In addition, the taxpayer derived $20,000 of foreign dividend income subject to a treaty rate of five percent (additional foreign tax of $1,000). Thus, the total domestic tax liability would equal $66,000 ($220,000 worldwide taxable income x 30 percent). In such a case, the separate basket limitations would be applicable. The passive income basket would be the ratio of $20,000 foreign taxable dividend income to $220,000 worldwide taxable income which equals 9.1 percent. The ratio is applied to the domestic tax liability of $66,000, but the credit cannot exceed the actual taxes paid on such income of $1,000. The overall limitation would be applicable to the remainder of the activity and would give rise to a 45.5 percent ratio ($100,000 foreign taxable income/$220,000 worldwide taxable income) applied against the domestic tax liability of $66,000, yielding a credit of $30,030. The foreign tax of $40,000 would exceed the $30,030 limit and result in a $9,970 foreign tax credit carryover.

A second basket is established for high withholding tax interest. While such income would generally be included in the passive income basket discussed above, the legislative concern was the offsetting of high-taxed interest with low-taxed, or exempt, interest. To prevent this, Congress constructed another basket. High-taxed interest is any interest subject to a withholding tax of at least five percent which is not imposed on a net basis.

Expressed in equation form, the § 904(d) high withholding tax interest limitation is:

$$\text{Maximum high withholding tax interest income basket foreign tax credit} = \frac{\text{Net foreign source § 904(d) high tax interest income}}{\text{Worldwide taxable income}} \times \text{United States tax on worldwide income}$$

Income which does not fall within one of the eight precise categories of § 904 is subject to the residual, general § 904 limitation. Generally, to lessen the effect of the limitation, the tax planning objective is to create as much foreign source income as possible, without running afoul of the special rules.

§ 4.11 Carryback and Carryover of Excess Taxes Paid: § 904(c)

The amount of foreign taxes paid or accrued in a taxable year may exceed the foreign tax credit limitation determined under § 904(a). This scenario results in the taxpayer having excess unused foreign tax credits. On the other hand, the § 904(a) limitation in a given year may exceed the amount of foreign taxes paid, thus resulting in an excess limitation. Section 904(c) provides for a carryback and carryover of taxes from taxable years in which the taxpayer incurs excess foreign taxes to years in which the taxpayer has an excess limitation.

The amount of unused foreign taxes in a given year is determined by subtracting the maximum credit allowed under § 904(a) from the taxes paid to all foreign countries. The unused foreign tax can be carried back two taxable years and forward five taxable years. The Code establishes the order of years to which the unused foreign tax is to be carried, i.e., the second preceding year, the first preceding year, then the first, second, third, fourth, and fifth succeeding taxable years. To the extent that the unused foreign tax is not absorbed by the final carryover years, it is irretrievably lost.

Tax payments carried back or over to an excess limitation year are deemed to be taxes paid in the excess limitation year. The maximum amount of unused foreign tax which can be treated as paid or accrued in the taxable year to which the taxes are carried is the full amount of the unused foreign taxes to the extent a sufficient excess limitation exists in that year to absorb it. In other words, the amount of unused foreign tax treated as paid or accrued in an excess limitation year is the lesser of the amount of unused foreign tax sought to be carried to the excess limitation year or the excess limitation for the year to which the taxes are carried. The excess limitation in any taxable year is the amount by which the limitation applicable to that year exceeds the sum of taxes actually paid for that year, taxes deemed paid for that year, and unused foreign taxes from other years carried to that year with the earliest year considered first.

The same basic principles discussed above apply to carrybacks and carryovers of income subject to the separate baskets of § 904(d). However, unused foreign tax and the excess limitation must be computed separately for each type of income.

§ 4.12 Corporations Eligible to Utilize the Foreign Tax Credit—Domestic Stockholders in Foreign Corporations: § 902

The foreign tax credit is generally allowed only to the taxpayer who paid, or on whose behalf were paid, foreign taxes to a foreign government. However, a domestic corporation meeting prescribed requirements of stock ownership in a foreign corporation is permitted to claim the credit for foreign taxes paid by that foreign subsidiary attributable to earnings distributed to that domestic shareholder. In essence, the distribution "piggybacks" to the distributee the amount of foreign taxes incurred in earning such amounts.

The § 902 *deemed paid* provisions have undergone substantial modifications since their creation. Current law permits a domestic corporation which receives a dividend from a foreign corporation in any taxable year to take a credit for taxes deemed paid if it owns at least ten percent of the voting stock of the foreign corporation. For purposes of § 902, the payor foreign corporation is designated a *first-tier corporation*.

The deemed paid provisions extend down to sixth-tier subsidiaries. For example, a first-tier corporation to which dividends are paid by a foreign corporation in which the first corporation owns at least ten percent of the voting stock (a *second-tier* corporation) is deemed to have paid a portion of the taxes actually paid or accrued by the second-tier corporation. An additional ownership limitation is imposed for lower-tier subsidiaries. In order to claim the credit for lower-tier corporations, the domestic corporate parent must have at least five percent indirect ownership in those foreign corporations. In a two-tier arrangement, for example, the percentage of stock owned by the domestic corporation in the first-tier corporation multiplied by the percentage of stock held by the first-tier corporation in the second-tier corporation must equal at least five percent.

Assume that domestic corporation A owns 30 percent of foreign corporation B (first-tier corporation). Corporation B owns 40 percent of foreign corporation C (second-tier corporation). Corporation C owns 50 percent of foreign corporation D (third-tier corporation). Is A entitled to a § 902 deemed paid credit for taxes paid by B, C, and/or D?

In this case, both the ten percent direct ownership and the five percent indirect ownership requirements are met.

Ten Percent Direct Ownership:
A owns more than ten percent of B (30 percent)

> B owns more than ten percent of C (40 percent)
> C owns more than ten percent of D (50 percent)

AND

> Five Percent Indirect Ownership:
> A owns greater than five percent of C (second-tier) through B (first-tier) (30% x 40% = 12%)
> A owns greater than five percent of D (third-tier) through C (second-tier) and B (first-tier) (12% x 50% = 6%)

Thus, domestic corporation A can claim the foreign tax credit for taxes paid and deemed paid by all three of the tier corporations.

First Chicago Corp. v. Commissioner
United States Tax Court
96 T.C. 421 (1991)

GERBER, JUDGE:

OPINION

The controversy here concerns a question of first impression involving the interpretation of the 10-percent requirement of section 902. . . . We must specifically decide whether [the] provisions would permit petitioner to avail itself of the deemed foreign tax credit.

GENERAL BACKGROUND

Section 901 provides for the allowance to a domestic corporation of a credit on certain foreign taxes paid or accrued during a taxable year to any foreign country or possession of the United States. Section 901 also provides, in the case of a corporate taxpayer, an allowance of a credit for taxes "deemed to have been paid under sections 902 and 960." . . .

Accordingly, section 902, in addition to the foreign tax credit for foreign tax actually paid or accrued by a domestic taxpayer under section 901, imputes a credit, in certain circumstances, to domestic corporations for a proportionate (in relation to the domestic corporation's shareholdings) amount of tax paid by a dividend-paying foreign corporation.

SECTION 902(a)—THE STATUTE AND LEGISLATIVE HISTORY

In the face of the statutory language "a domestic corporation which owns at least 10 percent of the voting stock of a foreign corporation," petitioner first argues that "[t]he language . . . and the rationale for section 902(a) together fully support treating the consolidated group as one entity for purposes of determining whether the 10% voting stock requirement of section 902(a) has been met." If we should hold otherwise, petitioner's alternative position is that, factually, [its] affiliates held the shares as agents or nominees on behalf of [it]. Respondent counters that neither the language nor the intent of section 902(a) . . . would permit aggregating the shares of affiliated corporate taxpayers in order to meet the qualifications of section 902(a). Respondent also argues that the facts indicate that . . . subsidiaries and affiliates were not agents or nominees . . . . Respondent also asserts that section 902(a) requires 10-percent voting power rather than 10 percent of the voting stock and that [petitioner] and its affiliates did not have 10 percent of the voting power.

Petitioner argues that the legislative history supports aggregation under section 902(a). First, we consider whether the legislative history regarding section 902(a) should be consulted, and if consulted, whether it supports petitioner's argument that section 902(a) should be read to include an affiliated group.

Normally, there is:

> "no more persuasive evidence of the purpose of a statute than the words by which the legislature undertook to give expression to its wishes. Often these words are sufficient in and of themselves to determine the purpose of the legislation. In such cases we have followed their plain meaning. . . ."

When, however, the meaning leads to absurd results or the results are "plainly at variance with the policy of the legislation as a whole," courts have followed the purpose, rather than the literal words of the statute.

It is clear that the general congressional intent underlying sections 901 and 902 was to avoid double (foreign and domestic) taxation of foreign income and dividends by allowing a credit for certain taxes paid or deemed paid with respect to dividends received. Moreover, in the legislative history . . . that principle was reaffirmed, but the requirement that a domestic corporation own a majority of the voting stock of the foreign corporation was reduced to the current "ten percent or more" standard.

Petitioner, however, asks us to focus upon what it considers to be part of the legislative history concerning the Revenue Act of 1918, ch. 18, 40 Stat. 1057. During floor debate of a 1918 Revenue Act predecessor of the current foreign tax credit sections, one senator proposed the aggregation of related domestic taxpayers in order to meet the majority voting requirement (which was required at that time). The proposal did not, however, find its way into enacted legislation, and, to date, has not appeared as part of the statutory language. To the extent one would consider this to be material in the legislative history, it should not be denominated as a reflection of congressional intent because it reflects the view or proposal of only one senator and, more importantly, was not incorporated in the resulting legislation. Accordingly, we find no express or implied congressional intent to include consolidated shareholdings or aggregation of shareholdings in order to meet the 10-percent or more threshold for application of section 902. . . .

PETITIONER'S AGENT OR NOMINEE POSITION

Having decided that petitioner and its affiliated group are not entitled to aggregate, we next consider petitioner's alternative theory that its affiliates held shares . . . as agents and nominees. Petitioner offered this alternative argument, which essentially posits that each subsidiary held the . . . shares as an agent or nominee . . . . Under those circumstances, petitioner contends that it held 10 percent in one shareholder. On this point, the parties' arguments converge upon a recent Supreme Court case which addressed the question of whether the tax attributes of the property held by an agent can be attributed to the principal. . . .

The four indicia of agency status are as follows: (1) Whether the corporation operates in the name and for the account of the principal; (2) whether the corporation binds the principal by its actions; (3) whether the corporation transmits money received to the principal; and (4) whether receipt of income is attributable to the services of employees of the principal and to assets belonging to the principal.

Although a subsidiary corporation satisfying these indicia may be considered a true agent of its parent in a general sense, two other requirements are also imposed. The first requirement mandates that the subsidiary's agency relationship with its parent cannot be derived exclusively from the fact that it is owned by its parent-principal. This factor addresses the separate-entity doctrine. . . . It demands proof positive that the agency relationship exists separate and apart from the subsidiary's ownership by its principal and that it is not in substance a tax-avoiding manipulation of an otherwise independent legal entity. These concerns are satisfied where unequivocal evidence of the genuineness of the agency relationship exists.

Assuming unequivocal evidence of a genuine agency relationship is present, it must lastly be established that the subsidiary's business purpose was the carrying on of the normal duties of an agent. Reference to general agency principles will determine whether this second requirement is satisfied. . . .

To fit within this framework, petitioner first argues that its sole purpose for spreading the ownership of . . . shares amongst several affiliates, rather than having one shareholder, was to obtain a voting benefit under Article 16 of the Articles of Association . . . prohibiting any shareholder, regardless of the number of shares held, more than six votes. Petitioner advances the obvious and convincing business purpose that they wished to protect a sizable investment . . . by exercising their shareholders' rights to cause the election of officers and board members in order to participate in management. Respondent agrees that this was a valid business purpose of petitioner, but points out that certain of the affiliates also obtained business benefits from ownership . . . shares. The "Edge Act subsidiaries," for example, were required to maintain capital of at least $2 million and the . . . shares were counted in the satisfaction of that requirement. Nevertheless, we find that the principal business proposal of placing ownership . . . shares in subsidiaries was to maintain and possibly enhance control over the investment.... Having found ... that the property was held in a manner which reflects that it could have been the subject of an agency (or nominee) relationship, we proceed to see if an agency relationship existed....

The parties' initial controversy over the "six ... factors" concerns the requirement of whether the corporation's relations with its principal are not dependent upon the fact that it is owned by the principal. Although petitioner acknowledges that the [*Commissioner v.*] *Bollinger*[, 485 U.S. 340 (1988),] court set out the six ... factors, it argues that the Supreme Court ruled for the taxpayer without deciding whether the fifth one had been met and without holding the taxpayer to a strict or literal compliance with some or all of the remaining "factors." Respondent argues that the Supreme Court did not eliminate or ignore the fifth factor or decide that a wholly owned subsidiary could be an agent for its owner.

After noting that the relationship between a corporation-agent and its owner-principal is always based on ownership and the owner can cause the relationship to be altered or terminated at any time, the Supreme Court stated that this requirement (the fifth factor) was an attempt to protect the separate-entity doctrine.... In that connection, the Court expressed the view that it agreed "that it is reasonable for the Commissioner to demand unequivocal evidence of genuineness [of the agency relationship] in the corporation-shareholder context...." The essence of this analysis is that petitioner must show the genuineness of the agency relationship, separate and apart from its general authority to control the corporate subsidiaries.

The facts in our record do contain numerous circumstantial bits of evidence which could be interpreted to imply the existence of an agency relationship [with] and its affiliates. But there is no direct and/or explicit evidence that an agency relationship existed.... As pointed out by the Supreme Court, the element of control is always present between a corporation and its owner. That control is similar to the type of control found in an agency relationship. Accordingly, petitioner must decisively show that a "genuine agency" was intended.... Petitioner has failed to show such a relationship existed [with] and its affiliates during the years under consideration....

As pointed out above, there are several factors and facts in this record which indicate that the affiliated corporations involved were acting in concert and on behalf of affiliated members. It is most significant that this type of action is usual in consolidated groups with common ownership.... [T]he inherent commonality in such relationships requires the showing of a genuine agency relationship.... We find in this case that petitioner has not shown an agency relationship (an agency in fact) existed in this case....

To reflect the foregoing,

Decision will be entered under Rule 155.

§ 4.13 Calculating the Taxes Deemed Paid by Domestic Corporations

In general, a domestic parent corporation cannot claim a credit for foreign taxes paid by its foreign subsidiary unless the subsidiary makes a dividend distribution to the parent. This dividend is viewed under the Code as a manifestation of accumulated profits. It is the payment of the dividend which triggers the deemed paid provisions. The amount of the credit allowable is directly proportional to the size of the dividend as a percentage of available post-1986 undistributed earnings. The actual computation numerically expressed is:

$$\text{Section 902 credit} = \text{Post-1986 foreign taxes paid or deemed paid by first-tier corporation} \times \frac{\text{Dividends paid by first tier corporation to domestic corporation}}{\text{Post-1986 undistributed earnings of first-tier corporation} - \text{Foreign taxes paid or accrued}}$$

(Section 902 credit = amount of tax paid by first tier which is deemed paid by a domestic corporation)

The taxes which a first-tier corporation is deemed to have paid through a lower-tier corporation are calculated by applying the same formula.

By way of example, assume domestic corporation X owns 100 percent of foreign corporation Y. Assume that Y distributes its first dividend of $300 at a time in which total net undistributed earnings equaled $1,000. If its foreign tax payments during its period of existence had totaled $500, the deemed paid credit would total $150 ($300/$1,000 x $500).

It should be noted that a dividend distribution from a foreign subsidiary to its parent corporation may produce *both* direct and indirect credits for the year of distribution. If a foreign jurisdiction taxes shareholders upon the receipt of a dividend from the foreign corporation, in addition to the § 902 determinations discussed above, a § 901 credit may be available to the distributee corporation as well.

The practical significance of the § 902 formula lies in the fact that a domestic corporation, by choosing to enter a foreign market through a subsidiary instead of a branch, will not have entirely forfeited its claim to a foreign tax credit. Furthermore, the formula might be seen as an attempt to ensure that the transfer of income from a subsidiary to a parent will occur through the conventional mechanism of the dividend payment, rather than the more circuitous routes of providing loans, goods, or services at a less than arm's-length price.

§ 4.14 The § 78 Gross-Up

When a domestic corporation elects to take the foreign tax credit for taxes paid by a foreign corporation, the amount of taxes deemed paid must be treated and reported as dividend income. That is, the amount of the actual dividends received are "grossed up" to include an additional amount equal to the tax deemed paid on those dividends. Thus, in the example in § 4.13, X would have additional deemed dividend income of $150 in addition to its $150 § 902 credit.

The § 78 gross-up prevents "over crediting" of foreign taxes. This statutory approach is an attempt to neutralize the benefits of utilizing a foreign subsidiary rather than a branch for foreign operations. When a foreign branch is utilized, the direct foreign tax credit is available, yet all of the income from foreign sources is subject to United States tax. The use of a wholly-owned subsidiary instead results in the availability of the foreign tax credit with domestic taxation of the dividend income only. The remainder of the foreign earnings are not subject to domestic taxation. The gross-up concept eliminated this disparity as to distributed earnings of the subsidiary. However, unequal treatment remains in cases of retained earnings.

§ 4.15 Two Variations on the § 904 Limitation: Capital Gains and Losses

When a United States person has foreign source capital gains or losses, special rules apply to the computation of the § 904 foreign tax credit limitation.

If an individual or a corporation has a foreign net capital gain but, because of domestic capital losses, has an overall capital loss, without a safeguard provision the § 904 limitation would be enhanced at no cost to the taxpayer in terms of his domestic tax liability. In that case, the foreign gain would increase the numerator of the § 904 limitation while the overall loss would have no effect on the denominator. For example, if a domestic corporation had a $500 foreign capital gain and a $600 domestic capital loss, the numerator of the § 904 limitation (forcign taxable income) would increase by $500 but the denominator (worldwide taxable income) would be unaffected since capital losses are permitted only to the extent of capital gain. Thus, the § 904(b) limitation could be increased by the derivation of capital gain.

To prevent this inflation, § 904(b) provides that the numerator of the § 904 fraction includes gain from the sale or exchange of capital assets only to the extent of foreign source capital gain net income. This limitation is expressed as the lesser of capital gain net income from sources without the United States or capital gain net income. Capital gain net income, in turn, is "the excess of the gains from sales or exchanges of capital assets over the losses from such sales or exchanges." The definitions require the taxpayer to source capital gains and losses. This treatment precludes a person having an overall capital loss from including foreign capital gain in the § 904 numerator. Thus, the taxpayer with a $500 foreign capital gain and a $600 domestic capital loss would include none of the gain in the numerator because the lesser amount under the statute is net capital gain, in this setting an amount equal to zero ($500 gain does not exceed $600 loss). If instead the domestic capital loss totaled $300, only $200 would enter the numerator.

The source of capital gains from the sale of personal property is generally the residence of the seller with some noteworthy exceptions, while the source for capital gain from the sale of real property is the location of the property.

Additional rules are provided to preclude the favorable use of foreign capital gains, should they be lightly taxed by the United States, from affording additional benefits in the tax credit arena. The operative condition for the application of § 904(b)(2)(B) is the existence of a capital gain rate differential (i.e., where the highest tax rate for ordinary income exceeds that for capital gain). This differential can arise for individuals, since the highest rate for ordinary income is 39.6 percent and the highest rate for capital gain is 20 percent. However, to date, notwithstanding the efforts of various administrations, no such differential exists for corporations since the highest rate for either type of income is 35 percent.

With regard to individuals, the statute mandates that if foreign capital gain exists for the year, the numerator of the limitation is reduced by the product of the rate differential times the foreign source net capital gain. A similar approach is required with regard to the denominator of the § 904 limitation. The rate differential is defined as a fraction, the numerator of which is the difference between the highest tax rate on ordinary income and the highest tax rate on capital gain and the denominator of which is the highest rate on ordinary income.

By way of example, assume that a domestic taxpayer has $4,000 of domestic taxable income and $1,000 of foreign capital gain income. Without § 904(b), the limitation ratio would be 20 percent ($1,000 foreign taxable income divided by $5,000 of worldwide taxable income). However, because capital gain is more lightly taxed than ordinary income, Congress concluded that the limitation ratio for § 904 should likewise reflect this tax-favored treatment. Thus, under § 904(b), the limitation would be reduced by an amount equal to the fraction of 19.6 (39.6 − 20)/39.6 times the capital gain. This would generate a $500 reduction (19.6/39.6 x $1,000) of both the numerator and the denominator of the §904 limitation which reduces the limitation ratio from 20 percent to 11 percent (($1,000 − $500)/($5,000 − $500) = $500/$4,500). Accordingly, the limitation under § 904 is reduced in order to reflect the fact that the capital gain income is lightly taxed by the United States.

§ 4.16 Recapture of Foreign Losses: § 904(f)

As evidenced by the discussion of the safeguard rules promulgated under § 904(b) respecting capital gains and losses and their impact on the § 904 limitation, similar concerns arise with regard to the generation and treatment of foreign losses. As losses in the year incurred will limit a taxpayer's worldwide income, they have a beneficial effect on the credit limitation as the denominator is reduced accordingly. However, subsequent profits from the same foreign activity would otherwise have a full effect on both the numerator and the denominator of the limitation. When these effects were viewed together, Congress concluded that such treatment was excessively favorable to the taxpayer. As a consequence, foreign losses are affected by three separate rules of § 904(f): (1) the confinement of losses to their separate baskets under § 904(d); (2) the resourcing of certain losses; and (3) the resourcing, and at times recognition, of income from certain property dispositions.

The foreign tax credit limitation is applied to various baskets under § 904(d). Absent an allocation mechanism, if the taxpayer generated a loss for the year with regard to some or all of its operations, uncertainty would arise as to what income was to be offset with what loss. Section 904(f)(3) provides that allocation mechanism.

The intention of § 904(f) is to prioritize loss usage and hold it against foreign income even if the loss does not arise in the same basket. Section 904(f) thereby reduces the numerator, and the resulting benefits, of the foreign tax credit limitation for particular baskets. Furthermore, rules are provided for allocating subsequent income to those categories which previously absorbed the foreign loss. In essence, a recapture rule is provided to ensure that a one-shot foreign loss does not minimize the impact of the § 904(d) limitation baskets. Additionally, this rule is to be distinguished from the treatment of an overall foreign loss (discussed further below) since the taxpayer has overall foreign income (i.e., foreign income exceeds foreign loss).

If a domestic taxpayer sustains an overall loss from foreign activities during the year, that loss offsets the taxpayer's domestic income in the loss year. If the taxpayer in subsequent years earns an overseas profit, § 904(f) requires that foreign source income in an amount equal to that previously deducted loss be recharacterized as having been derived from a domestic source. The source of the income is thus changed to preclude a double benefit in the foreign tax credit context.

In general, § 904(f)(3) provides that any taxpayer who sustains an overall foreign loss must recapture that loss in later taxable years. Recapture is accomplished by recasting a portion of subsequently derived foreign income as domestic source income. The amount of metamorphosed income is limited to the lesser of the amount of the previously unrecaptured loss or 50 percent of foreign taxable income for that year. A larger percentage may be recaptured if the taxpayer so elects. This election should be advantageous when the taxpayer has a domestic loss which reduces his tax liability in a later year. Through acceleration of the recapture, it is possible to exhaust the overall foreign loss account before the advent of more profitable years.

Section 904(f)(3) provides for recapture of a loss incurred upon the disposition of property which was predominantly used in a trade or business conducted outside of the United States prior to the time the loss has been recaptured under the rules discussed above. A disposition includes "a sale, exchange, distribution, or gift of property whether or not gain or loss is recognized on the transfer." Property which is not in fact nor expected to be a material factor in the realization of income by the taxpayer is excluded from the disposition recapture rules.

In the event of such a disposition, the taxpayer is deemed to receive and *recognize* taxable income regardless of whether another Code section would usually accord nonrecognition treatment to the transaction. The amount recognized upon the disposal is the lesser of the difference in the fair market value and adjusted basis of the property (i.e., the inherent gain on the property) or the remaining unrecaptured balance in the overall foreign loss account. Thus, recapture of income from dispositions of foreign trade or business property is accelerated to 100 percent, and the full amount of the gain (to the extent of nonrecaptured foreign losses) is subject to reclassification as domestic source income.

PROBLEM 4—FOREIGN TAX CREDIT

Code: §§ 164(a)(3), 164(b)(3), 275(a)(4), 78, 901(a), 901(b), 902(a), 902(b), 903, 904(a), 904(d)(1)(B), 904(d)(1)(I), and 904(f)

Regulations: §§ 1.901-1(c), 1.901-2(a), and 1.901-2(b)

1. T, a United States citizen, is opening a coffee shop in Venezuela.

   a. During the year, T incurs the following tax liabilities which he pays promptly:
      i. Real property tax;
      ii. Value added tax;
      iii. Venezuelan Federal income tax on his business income;
      iv. Venezuelan state income tax; and
      v. Venezuelan withholding tax (25 percent rate) on dividends.

      Which of these taxes are creditable under § 901 or § 903?

   b. With respect to creditable taxes, may T credit some and deduct others?

2. Z is a domestic corporation. Its principal business activity consists of the manufacture and sale of industrial machinery, and its main plant and offices are located in Delaware. Z also has a branch plant located in France where Z manufactures and sells its products in Europe. During the year, Z realized $100,000 of taxable income from its United States plant activities, and $75,000 of taxable income, exclusive of the French taxes, from its foreign branch activities. Assume that Z's United States tax liability (pre-credit) is $50,000. The foreign branch paid $40,000 in corporate income taxes to France.

   a. What is Z's tax liability for the year?
   b. What if the taxes paid to France are $20,000?

3. Throughout the year, domestic corporation A owns all of the one class of stock of B, a French corporation which was formed January 1. B engages in France in the manufacture of machinery which is sold in France and also other countries. B has gains, profits, and income of $100,000, and pays foreign income taxes imposed on those gains, profits, and income of $40,000. On December 31, B pays a dividend of $30,000 to A. What is A's income and net United States tax liability with respect to the dividend assuming that the tax rate is 15 percent?

4. For the year, A owns all of the one class of stock of foreign corporation B, which in turn owns all of the one class of stock of foreign corporation C. C corporation has gains, profits, and income of $300,000 and pays foreign income taxes on those gains, profits, and income of $90,000. On December 31, C pays a $100,000 dividend to B. B has $300,000 of gains, profits, and income made up of $200,000 from its own business operations and the $100,000 dividend received from C. B pays $50,000 of foreign income tax on those gains, profits, and income. On December 31, B pays a dividend of $125,000 to A. What is A's income and net United States tax liability with respect to the dividend assuming that the tax rate is 25 percent?

5. What result in 2. if Z realizes taxable income from its United States plant of $50,000; taxable income from its Brazilian plant of $30,000 (paying $15,000 in taxes); taxable income from its Canadian plant of $40,000 (paying $25,000 in taxes); and a taxable loss of $20,000 from its Mexican plant (paying no taxes). Assume that Z's domestic tax liability (pre-credit) is $20,000.

6. Assume in 5. that the Canadian gain was long-term capital in nature and no taxes were paid to Canada.

   a. What result if the gain arose through the sale of personalty? What result if realty?
   b. What if Z were a United States citizen?
   c. What result if Z realizes a $40,000 long-term United States capital loss and the United States tax liability (pre-credit) is $15,000?

7. Z Corporation, a domestic corporation, commenced foreign operations in Year 1 by establishing a Brazilian branch which produced a loss of $40,000, while its domestic operations generated a $40,000 gain. In Year 2, its Brazilian operations resulted in taxable income of $100,000 with an attendant tax payment of $40,000, while its domestic operations generated taxable income of $75,000. What is Z's tax liability for Year 2 if its pre-credit tax liability was $80,000?

Chapter 5
Tax Treaties—
An Overview

§ 5.01 Overview
§ 5.02 Negotiation of Treaties
§ 5.03 Ratification of Treaties
§ 5.04 Interpretive and Supplementary Materials
§ 5.05 Relationship of Tax Treaties to United States Federal Law
§ 5.06 Tax Treaties and Double Taxation
§ 5.07 Persons Eligible for Treaty Benefits
§ 5.08 Saving Clauses
§ 5.09 Anti-Treaty Shopping Clauses
§ 5.10 Nondiscrimination Clauses
Revenue Ruling 91-58, 1991-2 C.B. 340
§ 5.11 Competent Authority Procedures
United States-Canada Income Tax Treaty
United States-Canada Protocol to the Income Tax Treaty—1995
Technical Explanation of United States Model Income Tax Treaty
United States Model Income Tax Treaty
Problem 5

§ 5.01 Overview

As of August 1, 1998, over 50 income tax treaties have been entered between the United States and foreign countries. Income tax treaties, in theory, serve two important purposes. From a tax vantage point, treaties purport to mitigate potential double taxation. They provide consistent rules specifically governing the taxation of income items such as business profits, income from real property, dividends, interest, royalties, and other items. Treaties also set forth specialized rules applicable to certain classes of persons, such as students, teachers, athletes, artists, and apprentices. These governing provisions generally determine which treaty country retains the right to tax such items or persons. From a foreign policy perspective, tax treaties are designed to stimulate trade and investment between the two signatory countries and add a degree of certainty to cross-border transactions.

The critical importance of tax treaties cannot be overemphasized in tax planning and decision making. Treaties possess authority that overrides the tax treatment otherwise provided by the Internal Revenue Code. Moreover, Treasury recently announced that it will devote nearly 40 percent of its efforts to negotiating and renegotiating tax treaties. Accordingly, one must be familiar with and consult relevant tax treaties when analyzing cross-border transactions. Given the increasing globalization of markets and the rapid pace at which treaties are being negotiated and renegotiated, a firm grasp of basic treaty themes and concepts is a necessary analytical tool in the tax adviser's repertoire.

§ 5.02 Negotiation of Treaties

The formulation and ratification of tax treaties reflects a concerted multi-step effort among several divisions of the federal government and a host of interested parties. Treaties are the culmination of extensive, complex, and often protracted negotiations between representatives of the United States and the foreign country's counterparts. Primary responsibility for the negotiation of tax treaties and their related protocols rests with the staffs of the Treasury Department's Office of International Tax Counsel and the Office of Tax Analysis (International). Personnel of the Internal Revenue Service and the State Department also play a pivotal advisory role in the negotiation process.

The blueprint for the United States position in treaty negotiations is drawn from the Model Income Tax Treaty formulated by the Treasury Department. The latest version of this document was issued September 20, 1996 and is reproduced at the end of this chapter.

§ 5.03 Ratification of Treaties

As treaty provisions emerge from negotiations, the agreed-upon text is initialed, signifying the signatories' acquiescence to certain provisions. Once the State Department translates and approves the treaty text, the treaty is signed by the appropriate officials of the United States (i.e., the Secretary of State or the United States Ambassador) and the foreign country. The signed treaty is then forwarded to the President with a letter of submittal, describing generally the key provisions of the treaty and requesting the President to forward the treaty to the Senate for ratification. The President forwards the treaty with a letter of transmittal requesting Senate approval.

Once the treaty is submitted to the Senate, it is referred to the Senate Foreign Relations Committee. The Committee reviews the explanations of the treaty prepared by the Treasury Department and the Joint Committee on Taxation, as well as the comments and statements of interested parties. The Committee may hold hearings on the proposed treaty. After its review, the Committee submits the treaty to the Senate floor for ratification, either on its negotiated terms or as amended by the Committee. The full Senate then deliberates on the proposed treaty and ultimately must consent to ratification by a vote of two-thirds of the members present.

After Senate ratification, the President confirms the treaty by signing a ratification instrument. The treaty only comes into force when both treaty countries ratify the treaty and exchange ratification instruments. The date that ratification instruments are exchanged generally marks the date upon which the treaty is considered to be "in force." A treaty which is in force is not, however, always "in effect." Treaties may contain prospective or retroactive effective dates.

§ 5.04 Interpretive and Supplementary Materials

Fortunately, the often terse text of treaties is frequently supplemented by more detailed explanations and examples prepared by congressional committees or administrative agencies. These materials provide a road map to the formation and application of particular provisions and often encapsulate the negotiation process. The following materials are the principal interpretive and supplemental sources arising in conjunction with tax treaties:

1. *Protocols*—Existing and proposed tax treaties may be amended by a supplemental treaty called a protocol. A protocol, like a treaty, must be duly enacted via proper ratification procedures.

2. *Treasury Department Technical Explanations*—The Technical Explanation serves as the official guide to the tax treaty, functioning

comparably to the legislative history behind a statute. Technical Explanations explain, interpret, and often apply the particular provisions of the treaty. They also highlight the policy, compromises, and agreements driving particular treaty provisions.

§ 5.05 Relationship of Tax Treaties to United States Federal Law

Article VI, paragraph 2 of the United States Constitution states that treaties, along with the Constitution itself and all laws in pursuance thereof, "shall be the supreme law of the land." Thus, treaties and the Internal Revenue Code are generally accorded equal weight.

To deal with potential inconsistencies and conflicts between the two authorities, courts have adopted a "last-in-time" rule of construction which provides that the later-enacted provision controls. Given the fact that virtually all of the 50 income tax treaties of the United States were entered or renegotiated after the adoption of the Internal Revenue Code of 1954, generally treaty provisions will control. However, under the last-in-time approach, if a treaty and a later-enacted Code provision conflict, the Code provision will prevail unless the subsequent enactment does not plainly indicate an intent to supersede the treaty.

The Code provides no bright-line rules for determining how treaty clauses interact with Code sections. In fact, the Code gingerly approaches the potential conflict. The general principle that treaty obligations must be considered in tandem with Code provisions is broadly reiterated in § 7852(d)(1), which accords treaties and Code provisions equivalence, stating that neither source of law shall have preferential status. In conjunction, § 894(a)(1) imposes the relatively vague directive that Code provisions are to be applied to taxpayers with "due regard" to any applicable United States treaty obligation. While counterintuitive to a tax lawyer who, by definition, consults the Code first, in the world of international taxation inbound investment must be evaluated in light of a non-legislative, non-statutory document, i.e., any controlling income tax treaty. Answers derived therefrom must be double checked against the Code to ensure that an overriding provision has not been subsequently enacted by Congress.

§ 5.06 Tax Treaties and Double Taxation

A foreign individual or entity investing in the United States or a United States individual or entity investing in a foreign country runs a severe risk that more than one country will claim the right to tax all or part of that investment. For example, if a United Kingdom corporation deposits cash in an interest-bearing account with a United States bank, two countries may claim a right to tax any interest received: the United Kingdom, as the country of corporate domicile and the United States, as the country from which the income is derived. The danger arises not only that income will be taxed twice but also, if the combined tax rate is high enough, at a near-confiscatory rate. These potential clashes theoretically have prompted the United States to enter into numerous tax treaties in an attempt to both contour a uniform and pre-emptive scheme of taxation and to minimize the potential for double taxation.

Treaties attempt to ameliorate double taxation in two ways. First, treaties delineate specific types of income (i.e., business profits, dividends, interest, etc.) and provide precise rules for the taxation of these items. The country of income source generally gives way under the treaty regime to the recipient's country of domicile. Treaties generally provide that under certain conditions the recipient of a particular item of income will be taxed at a lesser tax rate or will be exempt from taxation in the country from which that income is derived.

The second way by which treaties minimize the potential for double taxation is through the establishment of "competent authority" procedures. Competent authority procedures afford taxpayers the opportunity to present disputes regarding treaty provisions to the officials of their home country for resolution.

§ 5.07 Persons Eligible for Treaty Benefits

Signatory countries jealously guard the benefits of tax treaties by expressly limiting the categories of persons eligible for such benefits. In most cases, only a corporation or other person that is a "resident" of one of the foreign signatory countries may claim the benefits of an income tax treaty. For example, Article 7(1) of the United States-Canada treaty states that "the business profits of a resident of a Contracting State shall be taxable only in that State unless the resident carries on business in the other Contracting State through a permanent establishment situated therein." Similarly, Article 10 of that treaty provides that dividends paid by "a company which is a resident of a Contracting State to a resident of the other Contracting State" are eligible for preferential withholding tax rates.

Treaties generally define those individuals and entities that qualify as residents. They typically consider an individual a resident of a treaty country if that individual is within the taxing jurisdiction of that country as a resident. For corporations, residency generally arises in either its country of incorporation or the country of its management seat.

It is possible that a person may be a resident of both signatory countries. In such a case, most treaties contain a "tiebreaker rule" to definitively place a dual resident firmly in one country for purposes of applying the treaty. The United States-Canada treaty tiebreaker rule is typical of such provisions. If an entity is a resident under the domestic law of both the United States and Canada, that entity is for purposes of the treaty deemed to be a resident only of the country under whose laws it is created. Similarly, if, by virtue of the above definition, an individual is a resident of both countries, then his or her status for purposes of the treaty is determined under the following priority scheme:

1. He or she is deemed to be a resident of the country in which he or she has a permanent home available. If a permanent home is available in both countries or in neither country, he or she is deemed to be a resident of the country to which his or her personal and economic relations (i.e., "vital interests") are closer.
2. If the center of vital interests cannot be determined, he or she is deemed to be a resident of the country in which a habitual abode exists.
3. If a habitual abode exists in both countries or in neither country, he or she is deemed to be a resident of the country of citizenship.
4. If he or she is a citizen of both countries or of neither country, the competent authorities of the countries resolve the residency quandary by mutual agreement.

§ 5.08 Saving Clauses

The basic premise of tax treaties requires the United States to extend benefits to foreign residents of a tax treaty country in exchange for that country's reciprocal grant of benefits to United States persons. This reciprocal agreement does not, however, force the United States to forfeit its right to subject its citizens (including, without limitation, those permanently living abroad) to domestic tax on their worldwide income. Even those persons residing or doing business in a tax treaty country remain in the domestic taxing fold. Thus, United States citizens are generally not permitted to avoid taxation by cloaking themselves in foreign residency and claiming United States treaty benefits extended to foreign residents. This taxing grasp manifests itself in tax treaties through "saving clauses," which subject United States citizens living abroad to continued domestic taxation.

§ 5.09 Anti-Treaty Shopping Clauses

The "anti-treaty shopping" provisions of most tax treaties present another hurdle to be cleared by a claimant of the treaty benefit. Such provisions operate to restrict treaty benefits to those individuals and entities legitimately connected to the treaty country. Treaty shopping limitations prevent citizens of other countries that do not have United States tax treaties from exploiting those benefits by selectively conducting their affairs in favorable treaty countries.

The treaty shopping targeted by such provisions typically involves the establishment of a corporation or other entity entitled to tax treaty benefits by "third-country investors" not directly entitled to the tax treaty benefits being claimed by the corporation or entity. For example, under the Code, dividends paid by a United States corporation to a foreign corporation which is not a resident of a treaty signatory are subject to a 30 percent withholding tax. Under Article 10(2)(a) of the United States-Netherlands tax treaty, however, dividends paid by a 25 percent owned United States subsidiary to its Dutch parent are generally eligible for a five percent withholding tax rate. Absent an anti-treaty shopping clause, to secure that favorable rate of tax, a resident of a third country (for example, Brazil) that does not have a tax treaty with the United States could merely interpose a Dutch corporation between himself and his controlled United States corporation. Thus, the Brazilian third-country investor could successfully shop for advantageous treaty benefits by simply establishing a Dutch corporation.

Treaty shopping is frowned upon by the United States for both policy and pragmatic reasons. As a matter of broad tax treaty policy, the United States intends that particular treaty benefits be available only to individual residents and entities established within of the signatory country. Moreover, on a strategic level, tax treaty negotiators contend that, if treaty shopping continues unabated, the incentive for countries to step forward and meaningfully negotiate a treaty with the United States is eroded. In the prior example, for instance, if Brazilian residents could merely avail themselves of United States-Netherlands tax treaty benefits by utilizing Dutch corporations, the United States and its citizens are effectively deprived of any reciprocally favorable tax treatment in Brazil.

Given the unintended benefits accruing to third-country beneficiaries via treaty shopping, it is now established United States treaty policy to include anti-treaty shopping clauses in new or revised tax treaties. For example, a person (other than an individual) which is a resident of a treaty jurisdiction is not entitled to relief from taxation in the other jurisdiction unless more than 50 percent of that the beneficial interest in such person is owned, directly or indirectly, by one or more individual residents of that jurisdiction and the entity's income is not used in substantial part, directly or indirectly, to meet liabilities to persons who are residents of a third jurisdiction. These restrictions prevent the use of entities as mere conduits or leveraged shells through which income is funneled to third-country investors after enjoying a brief tax holiday in a treaty country.

§ 5.10 Nondiscrimination Clauses

Aside from reducing international double taxation, tax treaties also attempt to ensure that the residents of each signatory country are not discriminated against in a tax sense by the tax authorities of the other country. This protection is afforded in most tax treaties by operation of a "nondiscrimination clause." In a typical clause, the United States promises on a reciprocal basis not to tax a foreign person residing in a treaty country at a higher rate than a United States person in the same circumstances nor to deprive that person of any deduction or credit available to United States citizens in the same circumstances.

The relatively imprecise verbiage contained in typical nondiscrimination clauses begs the question of when a foreign person is "in the same circumstances" as a United States person and thus is entitled to parallel tax treatment. The Service has shed some light on the proper construction of this phrase, albeit negatively, by defining what circumstances are *not* "the same circumstances." For instance, it appears that a nonresident person seldom can rely on a nondiscrimination clause, because that nonresident, subject to limited taxation by the United States, seldom is in the same circumstances as a United States citizen or resident who is subject to worldwide taxation.

Revenue Ruling 91-58
1991-2 C.B. 340

ISSUE

May nationals of the United Kingdom who are residents of the United States within the meaning of section 7701(b) of the Code qualify for the exclusions and deduction provided by section 911 by establishing that they have been bona fide residents of a foreign country or countries for an uninterrupted period that includes an entire taxable year.

FACTS

X is a domestic corporation that provides specialized services in the United States and foreign countries. X employees nationals (citizens) of the United Kingdom whose tax homes are in the United Kingdom or other foreign countries. Although these nationals are employed by X in the United Kingdom and other foreign countries, they are residents of the United States, within the meaning of section 7701(b).

LAW AND ANALYSIS

Section 911 of the Code provides that a "qualified individual" may elect to exclude or deduct certain amounts from gross income. A citizen of the United States is a qualified individual if either of the following tests is met: (1) the individual's tax home is in a foreign country and the individual establishes to the satisfaction of the Secretary that he or she has been a bona fide resident of a foreign country or countries for an uninterrupted period which includes an entire taxable year (the "bona fide residence test"); or (2) the individual's tax home is in a foreign country and, during any period of 12 consecutive months, he or she is present in a foreign country or countries during at least 330 full days in such period (the "physical presence test"). The determination of whether a United States citizen is a bona fide resident of a foreign country is made by applying the principles of section 871 and the regulations thereunder. By its terms, section 911(d)(1)(B) provides that an alien resident of the United States is a qualified individual only if he or she satisfies the requirements of the physical presence test. . . .

The principles set forth in Rev. Rul. 72-330 are applicable to the instant situation. Therefore, absent a specific treaty provision or a provision of the regulations under the treaty to the contrary, the non-discrimination article in a United States income tax treaty will be applied without regard to the saving clause in the treaty.

Paragraph (1) of Article 24 (Non-discrimination) of the United States-United Kingdom Income Tax Convention (the Treaty) provides that individuals who are nationals of a Contracting State and who are residents of the other Contracting State shall not be subjected in that other State to any taxation or any requirement connected therewith which is other or more burdensome than the taxation and connected requirements to which nationals of that other State in the same circumstances are or may be subjected. Paragraph (3) (Personal Scope) of the Treaty contains the saving clause and provides that a Contracting State may tax its residents and its nationals as if the Treaty had not come into effect. However, paragraph (4) of Article I of the Treaty provides, in part, that the saving clause shall not affect the application of Article 24 (Non-discrimination).

Because citizens of the United States may be treated as qualified individuals for purposes of section 911(d) of the Code under either the bona fide residence test or the physical presence test, requiring nationals of the United Kingdom to satisfy the physical presence test subjects them to a requirement connected with section 911 which is more burdensome than the taxation and connected requirements to which citizens of the United States in the same circumstances are subjected. Accordingly, nationals of the United Kingdom must be treated as qualified individuals for purposes of section 911 if they satisfy the requirements of the bona fide residence test.

HOLDING

Nationals of the United Kingdom who are residents of the United States within the meaning of section 7701(b) of the Code may qualify for the exclusion and deduction provided by section 911 by establishing to the satisfaction of the Secretary that they have been bona fide residents of a foreign country or countries under the residency rules of section 1.871-2(b) of the regulations for a period that includes an entire taxable year. . . .

§ 5.11 Competent Authority Procedures

Double taxation can arise in several ways which may not be specifically addressed in the articles of a treaty. To safeguard against the effects of such omissions as well as to ensure the intended application of the treaty, most tax treaties contain a "competent authority" provision.

Competent authority provisions set forth procedures by which a taxpayer that is subject to double taxation or other inconsistent treatment by a signatory country and who lacks specific relief via the treaty can petition for relief. To invoke these procedures, the taxpayer presents his or her case to the designated competent authority. If the taxpayer's prayer for relief is meritorious, the authority may present the matter to its foreign counterpart with a view toward finding an equitable solution.

United States-Canada Income Tax Treaty

(Signed September 26, 1980; In Force August 16, 1984; Effective August 16, 1984; and Amended by Protocols Signed June 14, 1983 and March 28, 1984)

The United States of America and Canada, desiring to conclude a Convention for the avoidance of double taxation and the prevention of fiscal evasion with respect to taxes on income and on capital, have agreed as follows:

Article I
PERSONAL SCOPE

This Convention is generally applicable to persons who are residents of one or both of the Contracting States. . . .

. . . .

Article III
GENERAL DEFINITIONS

1. For the purposes of this Convention, unless the context otherwise requires: . . .

    (e) The term "person" includes an individual . . . a company and any other body of persons . . .
    (g) The term "competent authority" means:
        (i) In the case of Canada, the Minister of National Revenue or his authorized representative; and
        (ii) In the case of the United States, the Secretary of the Treasury or his delegate. . . .

2. As regards the application of the Convention by a Contracting State any term not defined therein shall, unless the context otherwise requires and subject to the provisions of Article XXVI (Mutual Agreement Procedure), have the meaning which it has under the law of that State concerning the taxes to which the Convention applies.

Article IV
RESIDENCE

1. For the purposes of this Convention, the term "resident of a Contracting State" means any person who, under the laws of that State, is liable to tax therein by reason of his domicile, residence, place of management, place of incorporation or any other criterion of a similar nature. . . .

2. Where by reason of the provisions of paragraph 1 an individual is a resident of both Contracting States, then his status shall be determined as follows:

    (a) He shall be deemed to be a resident of the Contracting State in which he has a permanent home available to him;

if he has a permanent home available to him in both States or in neither State, he shall be deemed to be a resident of the Contracting State with which his personal and economic relations are closer (centre of vital interests);
(b) If the Contracting State in which he has his centre of vital interests cannot be determined, he shall be deemed to be a resident of the Contracting State in which he has an habitual abode;
(c) If he has an habitual abode in both States or in neither State, he shall be deemed to be a resident of the Contracting State of which he is a citizen; and
(d) If he is a citizen of both States or of neither of them, the competent authorities of the Contracting States shall settle the question by mutual agreement.

3. Where by reason of the provisions of paragraph 1 a company is a resident of both Contracting States, then if it was created under the laws in force in a Contracting State, it shall be deemed to be a resident of that State. . . .

Article V
PERMANENT ESTABLISHMENT

1. For the purposes of this Convention, the term "permanent establishment" means a fixed place of business through which the business of a resident of a Contracting State is wholly or partly carried on.

2. The term "permanent establishment" shall include especially:

(a) A place of management;
(b) A branch;
(c) An office;
(d) A factory;
(e) A workshop; and
(f) A mine, an oil or gas well, a quarry or any other place of extraction of natural resources.

3. A building site or construction or installation project constitutes a permanent establishment if, but only if, it lasts more than 12 months. . . .

. . . .

5. A person acting in a Contracting State on behalf of a resident of the other Contracting State—other than an agent of an independent status to whom paragraph 7 applies—shall be deemed to be a permanent establishment in the first-mentioned State if such person has, and habitually exercises in that State, an authority to conclude contracts in the name of the resident.

6. Notwithstanding the provisions of paragraphs 1, 2 and 5, the term "permanent establishment" shall be deemed not to include a fixed place of business used solely for, or a person referred to in paragraph 5 engaged solely in, one or more of the following activities:

2. Subject to the provisions of paragraph 3, where a resident of a Contracting State carries on business in the other Contracting State through a permanent establishment situated therein, there shall in each Contracting State be attributed to that permanent establishment the business profits which it might be expected to make if it were a distinct and separate person engaged in the same or similar activities under the same or similar conditions and dealing wholly independently with the resident and with any other person related to the resident. . . .

3. In determining the business profits of a permanent establishment, there shall be allowed as deductions expenses which are incurred for the purposes of the permanent establishment, including executive and general administrative expenses so incurred, whether in the State in which the permanent establishment is situated or elsewhere. Nothing in this paragraph shall require a Contracting State to allow the deduction of any expenditure which, by reason of its nature, is not generally allowed as a deduction under the taxation laws of that State.

4. No business profits shall be attributed to a permanent establishment of a resident of a Contracting State by reason of the use thereof for either the mere purchase of goods or merchandise or the mere provision of executive, managerial or administrative facilities or services for such resident. . . .

. . . .

6. Where business profits include items of income which are dealt with separately in other Articles of this Convention, then the provisions of those Articles shall not be affected by the provisions of this Article.

7. For the purposes of the Convention, the business profits attributable to a permanent establishment shall include only those profits derived from the assets or activities of the permanent establishment. . . .

. . . .

Article X
DIVIDENDS

1. Dividends paid by a company which is a resident of a Contracting State to a resident of the other Contracting State may be taxed in that other State.

2. However, such dividends may also be taxed in the Contracting State of which the company paying the dividends is a resident and according to the laws of that State; but if a resident of the other Contracting State is the beneficial owner of such dividends, the tax so charged shall not exceed:

(a) 10 per cent of the gross amount of the dividends if the beneficial owner is a company which owns at least 10 per cent of the voting stock of the company paying the dividends;

(b) 15 per cent of the gross amount of the dividends in all other cases.

(a) The use of facilities for the purpose of storage, display or delivery of goods or merchandise belonging to the resident;
(b) The maintenance of a stock of goods or merchandise belonging to the resident for the purpose of storage, display or delivery;
(c) The maintenance of a stock of goods or merchandise belonging to the resident for the purpose of processing by another person;
(d) The purchase of goods or merchandise, or the collection of information, for the resident; and
(e) Advertising, the supply of information, scientific research or similar activities which have a preparatory or auxiliary character, for the resident.

7. A resident of a Contracting State shall not be deemed to have a permanent establishment in the other Contracting State merely because such resident carries on business in that other State through a broker, general commission agent or any other agent of an independent status, provided that such persons are acting in the ordinary course of their business.

8. The fact that a company which is a resident of a Contracting State controls or is controlled by a company which is a resident of the other Contracting State, or which carries on business in that other State (whether through a permanent establishment or otherwise), shall not constitute either company a permanent establishment of the other. . . .

Article VI
INCOME FROM REAL PROPERTY

1. Income derived by a resident of a Contracting State from real property . . . situated in the other Contracting State may be taxed in that other State.

2. For the purposes of this Convention, the term "real property" shall have the meaning which it has under the taxation laws of the Contracting State in which the property in question is situated and shall include any option or similar right in respect thereof. . . .

3. The provisions of paragraph 1 shall apply to income derived from the direct use, letting or use in any other form of real property and to income from the alienation of such property.

Article VII
BUSINESS PROFITS

1. The business profits of a resident of a Contracting State shall be taxable only in that State unless the resident carries on business in the other Contracting State through a permanent establishment situated therein. If the resident carries on, or has carried on, business as aforesaid, the business profits of the resident may be taxed in the other State but only so much of them as is attributable to that permanent establishment.

This paragraph shall not affect the taxation of the company in respect of the profits out of which the dividends are paid.

3. The term "dividends" as used in this Article means income from shares or other rights, not being debt-claims, participating in profits, as well as income subjected to the same taxation treatment as income from shares by the taxation laws of the State of which the company making the distribution is a resident.

4. The provisions of paragraph 2 shall not apply if the beneficial owner of the dividends, being a resident of a Contracting State, carries on business in the other Contracting State of which the company paying the dividends is a resident, through a permanent establishment situated therein, or performs in that other State independent personal services from a fixed base situated therein, and the holding in respect of which the dividends are paid is effectively connected with such permanent establishment or fixed base. . . .

Article XI
INTEREST

1. Interest arising in a Contracting State and paid to a resident of the other Contracting State may be taxed in that other State.

2. However, such interest may also be taxed in the Contracting State in which it arises, and according to the laws of that State; but if a resident of the other Contracting State is the beneficial owner of such interest, the tax so charged shall not exceed 15 per cent of the gross amount of the interest. . . .

. . . .

4. The term "interest" as used in this Article means income from debt-claims of every kind, whether or not secured by mortgage, and whether or not carrying a right to participate in the debtor's profits, and in particular, income from government securities and income from bonds or debentures, including premiums and prizes attaching to such securities, bonds or debentures, as well as income assimilated to income from money lent by the taxation laws of the Contracting State in which the income arises. However, the term "interest" does not include income dealt with in Article X (Dividends).

5. The provisions of paragraphs 2 and 3 shall not apply if the beneficial owner of the interest, being a resident of a Contracting State, carries on business in the other Contracting State in which the interest arises, through a permanent establishment situated therein, or performs in that other State independent personal services from a fixed base situated therein, and the debt-claim in respect of which the interest is paid is effectively connected with such permanent establishment or fixed base. . . .

6. For the purposes of this Article, interest shall be deemed to arise in a Contracting State when the payer is that State itself, or a political subdivision, local authority or resident of that State. Where, however, the person paying the interest, whether he is a resident of a Contracting State or

not, has in a State other than that of which he is a resident a permanent establishment or a fixed base in connection with which the indebtedness on which the interest is paid was incurred, and such interest is borne by such permanent establishment or fixed base, then such interest shall be deemed to arise in the State in which the permanent establishment or fixed base is situated and not in the State of which the payer is a resident. . . .

Article XII
ROYALTIES

1. Royalties arising in a Contracting State and paid to a resident of the other Contracting State may be taxed in that other State.

2. However, such royalties may also be taxed in the Contracting State in which they arise, and according to the laws of that State; but if a resident of the other Contracting State is the beneficial owner of such royalties, the tax so charged shall not exceed 10 per cent of the gross amount of the royalties.

3. Notwithstanding the provisions of paragraph 2, copyright royalties and other like payments in respect of the production or reproduction of any literary, dramatic, musical or artistic work (but not including royalties in respect of motion picture films and works on film or videotape for use in connection with television) arising in a Contracting State and beneficially owned by a resident of the other Contracting State shall be taxable only in that other State.

4. The term "royalties" as used in this Article means payments of any kind received as a consideration for the use of, or the right to use, any copyright of literary, artistic or scientific work (including motion picture films and works on film or videotape for use in connection with television), any patent, trade mark, design or model, plan, secret formula or process, or for the use of, or the right to use, tangible personal property or for information concerning industrial, commercial or scientific experience, and, notwithstanding the provisions of Article XIII (Gains), includes gains from the alienation of any intangible property or rights described in this paragraph to the extent that such gains are contingent on the productivity, use or subsequent disposition of such property or rights.

5. The provisions of paragraphs 2 and 3 shall not apply if the beneficial owner of the royalties, being a resident of a Contracting State, carries on business in the other Contracting State in which the royalties arise, through a permanent establishment situated therein, or performs in that other State independent personal services from a fixed base situated therein, and the right or property in respect of which the royalties are paid is effectively connected with such permanent establishment or fixed base. . . .

6. For the purposes of this Article, royalties shall be deemed to arise in a Contracting State when the payer is that State itself, or a political subdivision, local authority or resident of that State. However:

  (a) Except as provided in subparagraph (b), where the person paying the royalties, whether he is a resident of a Contracting State or not, has in a State other than that of which he is a resident a permanent establishment or a fixed base in connection with which the obligation to pay the royalties was incurred, and such royalties are borne by such permanent establishment or fixed base, then such royalties shall be deemed to arise in the State in which the permanent establishment or fixed base is situated and not in the State of which the payer is a resident; and

(b) Where the royalties are for the use of intangible property or tangible personal property in a Contracting State, then such royalties shall be deemed to arise in that State and not in the State of which the payer is a resident. . . .

Article XIII
GAINS

1. Gains derived by a resident of a Contracting State from the alienation of real property situated in the other Contracting State may be taxed in that other State.

2. Gains from the alienation of personal property forming part of the business property of a permanent establishment which a resident of a Contracting State has . . . in the other Contracting State or of personal property pertaining to a fixed base which is . . . available . . . to a resident of a Contracting State in the other Contracting State for the purpose of performing independent personal services, including such gains from the alienation of such a permanent establishment or of such a fixed base, may be taxed in that other State.

3. Gains derived by a resident of a Contracting State from the alienation of:

(a) Shares forming part of a substantial interest in the capital stock of a company which is not a resident of that State the value of which shares is derived principally from real property situated in the other Contracting State . . . may be taxed in that other State, provided that the laws in force in the first-mentioned State at the time of such alienation would, in comparable circumstances, subject to taxation gains derived by a resident of that other State. . . .

4. Gains from the alienation of any property other than that referred to in paragraphs 1, 2 and 3 shall be taxable only in the Contracting State of which the alienator is a resident. . . .

Article XIV
INDEPENDENT PERSONAL SERVICES

Income derived by an individual who is a resident of a Contracting State in respect of independent personal services may be taxed in that State. Such income may also be taxed in the other Contracting State if the individual has or had a fixed base regularly available to him in that other State but only to the extent that the income is attributable to the fixed base.

Article XV
DEPENDENT PERSONAL SERVICES

1. . . . [S]alaries, wages and other similar remuneration derived by a resident of a Contracting State in respect of an employment shall be taxable only in that State unless the employment is exercised in the other Contracting State. If the employment is so exercised, such remuneration as is derived therefrom may be taxed in that other State.

2. Notwithstanding the provisions of paragraph 1, remuneration derived by a resident of a Contracting State in respect of an employment exercised in a calendar year in the other Contracting State shall be taxable only in the first-mentioned State if:

   (a) Such remuneration does not exceed ten thousand dollars ($10,000) in the currency of that other State; or
   (b) The recipient is present in the other Contracting State for a period or periods not exceeding in the aggregate 183 days in that year and the remuneration is not borne by an employer who is a resident of that other State or by a permanent establishment or a fixed base which the employer has in that other State. . . .

. . . .

Article XXII
OTHER INCOME

1. Items of income of a resident of a Contracting State, wherever arising, not dealt with in the foregoing Articles of this Convention shall be taxable only in that State, except that if such income arises in the other Contracting State it may also be taxed in that other State. . . .

. . . .

Article XXV
NON-DISCRIMINATION

1. Citizens of a Contracting State, who are residents of the other Contracting State, shall not be subjected in that other State to any taxation or any requirement connected therewith which is other or more burdensome than the taxation and connected requirements to which citizens of that other State in the same circumstances are or may be subjected.

2. Citizens of a Contracting State, who are not residents of the other Contracting State, shall not be subjected in that other State to any taxation or any requirement connected therewith which is other or more burdensome than the taxation and connected requirements to which citizens of any third State in the same circumstances (including State of residence) are or may be subjected. . . .

Article XXVI
MUTUAL AGREEMENT PROCEDURE

1. Where a person considers that the actions of one or both of the Contracting States result or will result for him in taxation not in accordance with the provisions of this Convention, he may, irrespective of the remedies provided by the domestic law of those States, present his case in writing to the competent authority of the Contracting State of which he is a resident or, if he is a resident of neither Contracting State, of which he is a national.

2. The competent authority of the Contracting State to which the case has been presented shall endeavor, if the objection appears to it to be justified and if it is not itself able to arrive at a satisfactory solution, to resolve the case by mutual agreement with the competent authority of the other Contracting State, with a view to the avoidance of taxation which is not in accordance with the Convention. . . .

3. The competent authorities of the Contracting States shall endeavor to resolve by mutual agreement any difficulties or doubts arising as to the interpretation or application of the Convention. . . .

. . . .

Article XXIX
MISCELLANEOUS RULES

1. The provisions of this Convention shall not restrict in any manner any exclusion, exemption, deduction, credit or other allowance now or hereafter accorded by the laws of a Contracting State in the determination of the tax imposed by that State.

2. Except as provided in paragraph 3, nothing in the Convention shall be construed as preventing a Contracting State from taxing its residents (as determined under Article IV (Residence)) and, in the case of the United States, its citizens . . . as if there were no convention between the United States and Canada with respect to taxes on income and on capital. . . .

United States-Canada Protocol to the Income Tax Treaty—1995

(Signed March 17, 1995; In Force September 9, 1995; Generally Effective January 1, 1996)

The United States of America and Canada, desiring to conclude a Protocol to amend the Convention with Respect to Taxes on Income and on Capital signed at Washington on September 26, 1980, as amended by the Protocols signed on June 14, 1983 and March 28, 1984 (hereinafter referred to as "the Convention"), have agreed as follows: . . .

. . . .

Article 3

1. Paragraph I of Article IV (Residence) of the Convention shall be deleted and replaced by the following:

"1. For the purposes of this Convention, the term "resident" of a Contracting State means any person that, under the laws of that State, is liable to tax therein by reason of that person's domicile, residence, citizenship, place of management, place of incorporation or any other criterion of a similar nature.... For the purposes of this paragraph, an individual who is not a resident of Canada under this paragraph and who is a United States citizen or an alien admitted to the United States for permanent residence (a "green card" holder) is a resident of the United States only if the individual has a substantial presence, permanent home or habitual abode in the United States, and that individual's personal and economic relations are closer to the United States than to any third State." . . .

2. A new sentence shall be added at the end of paragraph 3 of Article IV (Residence) of the Convention as follows:

"Notwithstanding the preceding sentence, a company that was created in a Contracting State, that is a resident of both Contracting States and that is continued at any time in the other Contracting State in accordance with the corporate law in that other State shall be deemed while it is so continued to be a resident of that other State." . . .

. . . .

Article 5

1. The references in paragraphs 2(a) and 6 of Article X (Dividends) of the Convention to a rate of tax of "10 per cent" shall be deleted and replaced by references to a rate of tax of "5 per cent" . . . .

. . . .

Article 6

1. The reference in paragraph 2 of Article XI (Interest) of the Convention to "15 per cent" shall be deleted and replaced by a reference to "10 per cent". . . .

. . . .

Article 7

1. Paragraph 3 of Article XII (Royalties) of the Convention shall be deleted and replaced by the following:

"3. Notwithstanding the provisions of paragraph 2,
(a) Copyright royalties and other like payments in respect of the production or reproduction of any literary, dramatic, musical or artistic work (other than payments in respect of motion pictures and works on film, videotape or other means of reproduction for use in connection with television);

(b) Payments for the use of, or the right to use, computer software;
(c) Payments for the use of, or the right to use, any patent or any information concerning industrial, commercial or scientific experience (but not including any such information provided in connection with a rental or franchise agreement); and
(d) Payments with respect to broadcasting as may be agreed for the purposes of this paragraph in an exchange of notes between the Contracting States; arising in a Contracting State and beneficially owned by a resident of the other Contracting State shall be taxable only in that other State."

2. Paragraph 6 of Article XII (Royalties) of the Convention shall be deleted and replaced by the following:

"6. For the purposes of this Article,
(a) Royalties shall be deemed to arise in a Contracting State when the payer is a resident of that State. Where, however, the person paying the royalties, whether he is a resident of a Contracting State or not, has in a State a permanent establishment or a fixed base in connection with which the obligation to pay the royalties was incurred, and such royalties are borne by such permanent establishment or fixed base, then such royalties shall be deemed to arise in the State in which the permanent establishment or fixed base is situated and not in any other State of which the payer is a resident; and
(b) Where subparagraph (a) does not operate to treat royalties as arising in either Contracting State and the royalties are for the use of, or the right to use, intangible property or tangible personal property in a Contracting State, then such royalties shall be deemed to arise in that State." . . .

. . . .

Article 18

A new Article XXIX A (Limitation on Benefits) shall be added to the Convention as follows:

"Article XXIX A
Limitation on Benefits

1. For the purposes of the application of this Convention by the United States,
(a) A qualifying person shall be entitled to all of the benefits of this Convention, and

(b) Except as provided in paragraphs 3, 4 and 6, a person that is not a qualifying person shall not be entitled to any benefits of the Convention.

2. For the purposes of this Article, a qualifying person is a resident of Canada that is:

(a) A natural person; ...
(c) A company ... in whose principal class of shares or units there is substantial and regular trading on a recognized stock exchange;
(d) A company more than 50 per cent of the vote and value of the shares (other than debt substitute shares) of which is owned, directly or indirectly, by five or fewer persons each of which is a company ... referred to in subparagraph (c), provided that each company ... in the chain of ownership is a qualifying person or a resident or citizen of the United States;
(e)(i) A company 50 per cent or more of the vote and value of the shares (other than debt substitute shares) of which is not owned, directly or indirectly, by persons other than qualifying persons or residents or citizens of the United States . . . where the amount of the expenses deductible from gross income that are paid or payable by the company ... for its preceding fiscal period (or, in the case of its first fiscal period, that period) to persons that are not qualifying persons or residents or citizens of the United States is less than 50 per cent of its gross income for that period; ...

3. Where a person that is a resident of Canada and is not a qualifying person of Canada, or a person related thereto, is engaged in the active conduct of a trade or business in Canada ... the benefits of the Convention shall apply to that resident person with respect to income derived from the United States in connection with or incidental to that trade or business, including any such income derived directly or indirectly by that resident person through one or more other persons that are residents of the United States. Income shall be deemed to be derived from the United States in connection with the active conduct of a trade or business in Canada only if that trade or business is substantial in relation to the activity carried on in the United States giving rise to the income in respect of which benefits provided under the Convention by the United States are claimed. . . .

. . . .

6. Where a person that is a resident of Canada is not entitled under the preceding provisions of this Article to the benefits provided under the Convention by the United States, the competent authority of the United States shall, upon that person's request, determine on the basis of all factors including the history, structure, ownership and operations of that person whether

(a) Its creation and existence did not have as a principal purpose the obtaining of benefits under the Convention that would not otherwise be available; or
(b) It would not be appropriate, having regard to the purpose of this Article, to deny the benefits of the Convention to that person.

The person shall be granted the benefits of the Convention by the United States where the competent authority determines that subparagraph (a) or (b) applies.

7. It is understood that the fact that the preceding provisions of this Article apply only for the purposes of the application of the Convention by the United States shall not be construed as restricting in any manner the right of a Contracting State to deny benefits under the Convention where it can reasonably be concluded that to do otherwise would result in an abuse of the provisions of the Convention." . . .

Technical Explanation of United States Model Income Tax Treaty

(September 20, 1996)

PURPOSE OF MODEL CONVENTION . . .

The Model is drawn from a number of sources. Instrumental in its development was the U.S. Treasury Department's draft Model Income Tax Convention, published on June 16, 1981 ("the 1981 Model") and withdrawn as an official U.S. Model on July 17, 1992, the Model Double Taxation Convention on Income and Capital, and its Commentaries, published by the OECD, as updated in 1995 ("the OECD Model"), existing U.S. income tax treaties, recent U.S. negotiating experience, current U.S. tax laws and policies and comments received from tax practitioners and other interested parties.

For over thirty years the United States has actively participated in the development of the OECD Model, and the United States continues its support of that process. Accordingly, the publication of a U.S. Model does not represent a lack of support for the work of the OECD in developing and refining its Model treaty. To the contrary, the strong identity between the provisions of the OECD and U.S. Models reflects the fact that the United States drew heavily on the work of the OECD in the development of the U.S. Model. . . .

Like the OECD Model, the Model is intended to be an ambulatory document that may be updated from time to time to reflect further consideration of various provisions in light of experience, subsequent treaty negotiations, economic, judicial, legislative or regulatory developments in the United States, and changes in the nature or significance of transactions between U.S. and foreign persons. . . . The Model will be more useful if it is understood which developments have given rise to alterations in the Model, rather than leaving such judgements to be inferred from actual treaties concluded after the release of the Model. The manner and timing of such updates will be subsequently determined. . . .

For this reason and others, the Model is not intended to represent an ideal United States income tax treaty. Rather, a principal function of the Model is to facilitate negotiations by helping the negotiators identify differences between income tax policies in the two countries. In this regard, the Model can be especially valuable with respect to the many countries that are conversant with the OECD Model. Such countries can compare the Model with the OECD Model and very quickly identify issues for discussion during tax treaty negotiations. By helping to identify legal and policy differences between the two treaty partners, the Model will facilitate the negotiations by enabling the negotiators to move more quickly to the most important issues that must be resolved. Reconciling these differences will lead to an agreed text that will differ from the Model in numerous respects. Another purpose of the Model . . . is to provide a basic explanation of U.S. treaty policy for all interested parties, regardless of whether they are prospective treaty partners.

Since the Model is intended to facilitate negotiations and not to provide a text that the United States would propose that the treaty partner accept without variation, it should not be assumed that a departure from the Model text in an actual treaty represents an undesirable departure from U.S. treaty policy. The United States would not negotiate a treaty with a country without thoroughly analyzing the tax laws and administrative practices of the other country. For these reasons, it is unlikely that the United States ever will sign an income tax convention that is identical to the Model.

Therefore, variations from the Model text in a particular case may represent a modification that the United States views as necessary to address a particular aspect of the treaty partner's tax law, or even represent a substantive concession by the treaty partner in favor of the United States. Time is another relevant consideration, as treaty policies evolve in other countries just as they do in the United States. Furthermore, language differences (even with English-speaking countries) sometimes necessitate changes in Model language. Consequently, it would not be appropriate to base an evaluation of an actual treaty simply on the number of differences between the treaty and the Model. Rather, such an evaluation must be based on a firm understanding of the treaty partner's tax laws and policies, how that law interacts with the treaty and the provisions of U.S. tax law, precedents in the partner's other treaties, the relative economic positions of the two treaty partners, the considerations that gave rise to the negotiations, and the numerous other considerations that give rise to any agreement between two sovereign nations.

United States Model Income Tax Treaty
(September 20, 1996)

The United States of America and . . ., desiring to conclude a Convention for the avoidance of double taxation and the prevention of fiscal evasion with respect to taxes on income, have agreed as follows:

Article 1
GENERAL SCOPE

1. This Convention shall apply only to persons who are residents of one or both of the Contracting States, except as otherwise provided in the Convention.

2. The Convention shall not restrict in any manner any benefit now or hereafter accorded:

    a)   by the laws of either Contracting State; or
    b)   by any other agreement between the Contracting States. . . .

. . . .

4. Notwithstanding any provision of the Convention . . . a Contracting State may tax its residents (as determined under Article 4 (Residence)), and by reason of citizenship may tax its citizens, as if the Convention had not come into effect. . . .

. . . .

Article 3
GENERAL DEFINITIONS

1. For the purposes of this Convention, unless the context otherwise requires:

    a)   the term "person" includes an individual . . . a company, and any other body of persons;
    b)   the term "company" means any body corporate or any entity that is treated as a body corporate for tax purposes according to the laws of the state in which it is organized;
    c)   the terms "enterprise of a Contracting State" and "enterprise of the other Contracting State" mean respectively an enterprise carried on by a resident of a Contracting State, and an enterprise carried on by a resident of the other Contracting State;

. . . .

e) the term "competent authority" means:

    (i)   in the United States: the Secretary of the Treasury or his delegate; and
    (ii)   in _____: _____;

. . . .

h) the term "national" of a Contracting State, means:

  (i) any individual possessing the nationality or citizenship of that State; and
  (ii) any legal person . . . deriving its status as such from the laws in force in that State. . . .

2. As regards the application of the Convention at any time by a Contracting State any term not defined therein shall, unless the context otherwise requires, or the competent authorities agree to a common meaning pursuant to the provisions of Article 25 (Mutual Agreement Procedure), have the meaning which it has at that time under the law of that State for the purposes of the taxes to which the Convention applies, any meaning under the applicable tax laws of that State prevailing over a meaning given to the term under other laws of that State.

Article 4
RESIDENCE

1. Except as provided in this paragraph, for the purposes of this Convention, the term "resident of a Contracting State" means any person who, under the laws of that State, is liable to tax therein by reason of his domicile, residence, citizenship, place of management, place of incorporation, or any other criterion of a similar nature.

  a) The term "resident of a Contracting State" does not include any person who is liable to tax in that State in respect only of income from sources in that State or of profits attributable to a permanent establishment in that State. . . .

2. Where by reason of the provisions of paragraph 1, an individual is a resident of both Contracting States, then his status shall be determined as follows:

  a) he shall be deemed to be a resident of the State in which he has a permanent home available to him; if he has a permanent home available to him in both States, he shall be deemed to be a resident of the State with which his personal and economic relations are closer (center of vital interests);
  b) if the State in which he has his center of vital interests cannot be determined, or if he does not have a permanent home available to him in either State, he shall be deemed to be a resident of the State in which he has an habitual abode;
  c) if he has an habitual abode in both States or in neither of them, he shall be deemed to be a resident of the State of which he is a national;
  d) if he is a national of both States or of neither of them, the competent authorities of the Contracting States shall endeavor to settle the question by mutual agreement.

3. Where by reason of the provisions of paragraph 1 a company is a resident of both Contracting States, then if it is created under the laws of one of the Contracting States or a political subdivision thereof, it shall be deemed to be a resident of that State. . . .

Article 5
PERMANENT ESTABLISHMENT

1. For the purposes of this Convention, the term "permanent establishment" means a fixed place of business through which the business of an enterprise is wholly or partly carried on.

2. The term "permanent establishment" includes especially:

   a) a place of management;
   b) a branch;
   c) an office;
   d) a factory;
   e) a workshop; and
   f) a mine, an oil or gas well, a quarry, or any other place of extraction of natural resources. . . .

. . . .

4. Notwithstanding the preceding provisions of this Article, the term "permanent establishment" shall be deemed not to include:

   a) the use of facilities solely for the purpose of storage, display or delivery of goods or merchandise belonging to the enterprise;
   b) the maintenance of a stock of goods or merchandise belonging to the enterprise solely for the purpose of storage, display or delivery;
   c) the maintenance of a stock of goods or merchandise belonging to the enterprise solely for the purpose of processing by another enterprise;
   d) the maintenance of a fixed place of business solely for the purpose of purchasing goods or merchandise, or of collecting information, for the enterprise;
   e) the maintenance of a fixed place of business solely for the purpose of carrying on, for the enterprise, any other activity of a preparatory or auxiliary character;
   f) the maintenance of a fixed place of business solely for any combination of the activities mentioned in subparagraphs a) through e).

5. Notwithstanding the provisions of paragraphs 1 and 2, where a person—other than an agent of an independent status to whom paragraph 6 applies—is acting on behalf of an enterprise and has and habitually exercises in a Contracting State an authority to conclude contracts that are binding on the enterprise, that enterprise shall be deemed to have a permanent establishment in that State in respect of any activities that the

person undertakes for the enterprise, unless the activities of such person are limited to those mentioned in paragraph 4 that, if exercised through a fixed place of business, would not make this fixed place of business a permanent establishment under the provisions of that paragraph.

6. An enterprise shall not be deemed to have a permanent establishment in a Contracting State merely because it carries on business in that State through a broker, general commission agent, or any other agent of an independent status, provided that such persons are acting in the ordinary course of their business as independent agents.

7. The fact that a company that is a resident of a Contracting State controls or is controlled by a company that is a resident of the other Contracting State, or that carries on business in that other State (whether through a permanent establishment or otherwise), shall not constitute either company a permanent establishment of the other.

Article 6
INCOME FROM REAL PROPERTY
(IMMOVABLE PROPERTY)

1. Income derived by a resident of a Contracting State from real property (immovable property), . . . situated in the other Contracting State may be taxed in that other State.

2. The term "real property (immovable property)" shall have the meaning which it has under the law of the Contracting State in which the property in question is situated.

3. The provisions of paragraph 1 shall apply to income derived from the direct use, letting, or use in any other form of real property.

4. The provisions of paragraphs 1 and 3 shall also apply to the income from real property of an enterprise and to income from real property used for the performance of independent personal services.

5. A resident of a Contracting State who is liable to tax in the other Contracting State on income from real property situated in the other Contracting State may elect for any taxable year to compute the tax on such income on a net basis as if such income were business profits attributable to a permanent establishment in such other State. Any such election shall be binding for the taxable year of the election and all subsequent taxable years unless the competent authority of the Contracting State in which the property is situated agrees to terminate the election.

Article 7
BUSINESS PROFITS

1. The business profits of an enterprise of a Contracting State shall be taxable only in that State unless the enterprise carries on business in the other Contracting State through a permanent establishment situated therein. If the enterprise carries on business as aforesaid, the business profits of the enterprise may be taxed in the other State but only so much of them as are attributable to that permanent establishment.

2. Subject to the provisions of paragraph 3, where an enterprise of a Contracting State carries on business in the other Contracting State through a permanent establishment situated therein, there shall in each Contracting State be attributed to that permanent establishment the business profits that it might be expected to make if it were a distinct and independent enterprise engaged in the same or similar activities under the same or similar conditions. For this purpose, the business profits to be attributed to the permanent establishment shall include only the profits derived from the assets or activities of the permanent establishment.

3. In determining the business profits of a permanent establishment, there shall be allowed as deductions expenses that are incurred for the purposes of the permanent establishment, including a reasonable allocation of executive and general administrative expenses, research and development expenses, interest, and other expenses incurred for the purposes of the enterprise as a whole (or the part thereof which includes the permanent establishment), whether incurred in the State in which the permanent establishment is situated or elsewhere.

4. No business profits shall be attributed to a permanent establishment by reason of the mere purchase by that permanent establishment of goods or merchandise for the enterprise. . . .

. . . .

6. Where business profits include items of income that are dealt with separately in other Articles of the Convention, then the provisions of those Articles shall not be affected by the provisions of this Article.

7. For the purposes of the Convention, the term "business profits" means income from any trade or business, including income derived by an enterprise from the performance of personal services, and from the rental of tangible personal property. . . .

. . . .

Article 10
DIVIDENDS

1. Dividends paid by a resident of a Contracting State to a resident of the other Contracting State may be taxed in that other State.

2. However, such dividends may also be taxed in the Contracting State of which the payor is a resident and according to the laws of that State, but if the dividends are beneficially owned by a resident of the other Contracting State, except as otherwise provided, the tax so charged shall not exceed:

- a) 5 percent of the gross amount of the dividends if the beneficial owner is a company that owns directly at least 10 percent of the voting stock of the company paying the dividends;
- b) 15 percent of the gross amount of the dividends in all other cases.

This paragraph shall not affect the taxation of the company in respect of the profits out of which the dividends are paid. . . .

. . . .

5. For purposes of the Convention, the term "dividends" means income from shares or other rights, not being debt-claims, participating in profits, as well as income that is subjected to the same taxation treatment as income from shares under the laws of the State of which the payor is a resident.

6. The provisions of paragraphs 1 and 2 shall not apply if the beneficial owner of the dividends, being a resident of a Contracting State, carries on business in the other Contracting State, of which the payor is a resident, through a permanent establishment situated therein, or performs in that other State independent personal services from a fixed base situated therein, and the dividends are attributable to such permanent establishment or fixed base. . . .

Article 11
INTEREST

1. Interest arising in a Contracting State and beneficially owned by a resident of the other Contracting State may be taxed only in that other State.

2. The term "interest" as used in this Convention means income from debt-claims of every kind, whether or not secured by mortgage, and whether or not carrying a right to participate in the debtor's profits, and in particular, income from government securities and income from bonds or debentures, including premiums or prizes attaching to such securities, bonds or debentures, and all other income that is subjected to the same taxation treatment as income from money lent by the taxation law of the Contracting State in which the income arises. . . .

3. The provisions of paragraph 1 shall not apply if the beneficial owner of the interest, being a resident of a Contracting State, carries on business in the other Contracting State, in which the interest arises, through a permanent establishment situated therein, or performs in that other State independent personal services from a fixed base situated therein, and the interest is attributable to such permanent establishment or fixed base. . . .

Article 12
ROYALTIES

1. Royalties arising in a Contracting State and beneficially owned by a resident of the other Contracting State may be taxed only in that other State.

2. The term "royalties" as used in this Convention means:

(a) any consideration for the use of, or the right to use, any copyright of literary, artistic, scientific or other work (including computer software, cinematographic films, audio or video tapes or disks, and other means of image or sound reproduction), any patent, trademark, design or model, plan, secret formula or process, or other like right or property, or for information concerning industrial, commercial, or scientific experience; and

(b) gain derived from the alienation of any property described in subparagraph (a), provided that such gain is contingent on the productivity, use, or disposition of the property.

3. The provisions of paragraph 1 shall not apply if the beneficial owner of the royalties, being a resident of a Contracting State, carries on business in the other Contracting State through a permanent establishment situated therein, or performs in that other State independent personal services from a fixed base situated therein, and the royalties are attributable to such permanent establishment or fixed base. . . .

Article 13
GAINS

1. Gains derived by a resident of a Contracting State that are attributable to the alienation of real property situated in the other Contracting State may be taxed in that other State.

2. For the purposes of this Convention the term "real property situated in the other Contracting State" shall include:

a) real property referred to in Article 6 (Income from Real Property (Immovable Property));
b) a United States real property interest; and
c) an equivalent interest in real property situated in ___.

3. Gains from the alienation of personal property that are attributable to a permanent establishment that an enterprise of a Contracting State has in the other Contracting State, or that are attributable to a fixed base that is available to a resident of a Contracting State in the other Contracting State for the purpose of performing independent personal services, and gains from the alienation of such a permanent establishment (alone or with the whole enterprise) or of such a fixed base, may be taxed in that other State. . . .

. . . .

5. Gains from the alienation of any property other than property referred to in paragraphs 1 through 4 shall be taxable only in the Contracting State of which the alienator is a resident.

Article 14
INDEPENDENT PERSONAL SERVICES

1. Income derived by an individual who is a resident of a Contracting State in respect of the performance of personal services of an independent character shall be taxable only in that State, unless the individual has a

fixed base regularly available to him in the other Contracting State for the purpose of performing his activities. If he has such a fixed base, the income attributable to the fixed base that is derived in respect of services performed in that other State also may be taxed by that other State. . . .

. . . .

Article 15
DEPENDENT PERSONAL SERVICES

1. . . . [S]alaries, wages, and other remuneration derived by a resident of a Contracting State in respect of an employment shall be taxable only in that State unless the employment is exercised in the other Contracting State. If the employment is so exercised, such remuneration as is derived therefrom may be taxed in that other State.

2. Notwithstanding the provisions of paragraph 1, remuneration derived by a resident of a Contracting State in respect of an employment exercised in the other Contracting State shall be taxable only in the first-mentioned State if:

- a) the recipient is present in the other State for a period or periods not exceeding in the aggregate 183 days in any twelve month period commencing or ending in the taxable year concerned;
- b) the remuneration is paid by, or on behalf of, an employer who is not a resident of the other State; and
- c) the remuneration is not borne by a permanent establishment or a fixed base which the employer has in the other State. . . .

. . . .

Article 21
OTHER INCOME

1. Items of income beneficially owned by a resident of a Contracting State, wherever arising, not dealt with in the foregoing Articles of this Convention shall be taxable only in that State. . . .

. . . .

Article 22
LIMITATION ON BENEFITS

1. A resident of a Contracting State shall be entitled to benefits otherwise accorded to residents of a Contracting State by this Convention only to the extent provided in this Article.

2. A resident of a Contracting State shall be entitled to all the benefits of this Convention if the resident is:

- a) an individual; . . .
- c) a company, if
  - i) all the shares in the class or classes of shares representing more than 50 percent of the voting power and

value of the company are regularly traded on a recognized stock exchange, or

ii) at least 50 percent of each class of shares in the company is owned directly or indirectly by companies entitled to benefits under clause i), provided that in the case of indirect ownership, each intermediate owner is a person entitled to benefits of the Convention under this paragraph; . . .

f) a person other than an individual, if:
   i) On at least half the days of the taxable year persons described in subparagraphs a), b), c), d) or e) own, directly or indirectly (through a chain of ownership in which each person is entitled to benefits of the Convention under this paragraph), at least 50 percent of each class of shares or other beneficial interests in the person, and
   ii) less than 50 percent of the person's gross income for the taxable year is paid or accrued, directly or indirectly, to persons who are not residents of either Contracting State (unless the payment is attributable to a permanent establishment situated in either State), in the form of payments that are deductible for income tax purposes in the person's State of residence.

3. a) A resident of a Contracting State not otherwise entitled to benefits shall be entitled to the benefits of this Convention with respect to an item of income derived from the other State, if:
   i) the resident is engaged in the active conduct of a trade or business in the first-mentioned State,
   ii) the income is connected with or incidental to the trade or business, and
   iii) the trade or business is substantial in relation to the activity in the other State generating the income.

b) For purposes of this paragraph, the business of making or managing investments will not be considered an active trade or business unless the activity is banking, insurance or securities activity conducted by a bank, insurance company or registered securities dealer.

c) Whether a trade or business is substantial for purposes of this paragraph will be determined based on all the facts and circumstances. In any case, however, a trade or business will be deemed substantial if, for the preceding taxable year, or for the average of the three preceding taxable years, the asset value, the gross income, and the payroll expense that are related to the trade or business in the first-mentioned State equal at least 7.5 percent of the resident's (and any related parties') proportionate share of the asset value, gross income and payroll expense, respectively, that are related to the activity that generated the income in the other State, and the average of the three ratios exceeds 10 percent.

d) Income is derived in connection with a trade or business if the activity in the other State generating the income is a line of business that forms a part of or is complementary to the trade or business. Income is incidental to a trade or business if it facilitates the conduct of the trade or business in the other State.

4. A resident of a Contracting State not otherwise entitled to benefits may be granted benefits of the Convention if the competent authority of the State from which benefits are claimed so determines. . . .

. . . .

Article 24
NON-DISCRIMINATION

1. Nationals of a Contracting State shall not be subjected in the other Contracting State to any taxation or any requirement connected therewith that is more burdensome than the taxation and connected requirements to which nationals of that other State in the same circumstances, particularly with respect to taxation on worldwide income, are or may be subjected. This provision shall also apply to persons who are not residents of one or both of the Contracting States.

2. The taxation on a permanent establishment or fixed base that a resident or enterprise of a Contracting State has in the other Contracting State shall not be less favorably levied in that other State than the taxation levied on enterprises or residents of that other State carrying on the same activities. The provisions of this paragraph shall not be construed as obliging a Contracting State to grant to residents of the other Contracting State any personal allowances, reliefs, and reductions for taxation purposes on account of civil status or family responsibilities that it grants to its own residents. . . .

PROBLEM 5—TAX TREATIES—AN OVERVIEW

Code: §§ 894, 7852(d), 871(a)(1)-(2), 871(b), 881(a), 882(a)-(c)

Reading Materials: Canadian Tax Treaty, Canadian Protocol, Model Income Tax Treaty

1. What is the purpose of income tax treaties? Having studied the concept of the foreign tax credit in Chapter 4, is the articulated rationale of "eliminating double taxation" accurate?

2. What is the rate of tax on business income derived from the United States by a resident of a country which has not entered an income tax treaty with the United States? *See* §§ 871(b) and 882. What is the rate of tax on business income derived by the Canadian resident from within the United States? *See* Article VII.

3. What is the rate of tax on investment income derived from the United States by a resident of a country which has not entered an income tax treaty with the United States? *See* §§ 871(a) and 881.

    a. What is the rate of tax on investment dividend income derived from the United States by a Canadian resident? *See* Article X(2), Protocol Article 5.
    b. What is the treatment of interest income? *See* Article XI, Protocol Article 6.
    c. What is the treatment of royalty income? *See* Article XII, Protocol Article 7(1).
    d. What is the treatment of rental income from real property? *See* Article VI.
    e. What is the treatment of rental income from personal property? *See* Article XV.
    f. What is the treatment of gain from the disposition of real property? *See* Articles VI and XIII(1).
    g. What is the treatment of gains from the disposition of personal property? *See* Article XIII(4).

4. What result if the taxpayer, a United States citizen, retires in Canada and derives $30,000 of dividend income from United States sources? *See* Article XXIX(2).

5. What result in 3g. if the United States Congress enacts a provision taxing such gains?

6. Which non-United States persons can utilize the United States-Canadian tax treaty and qualify for benefits? *See* Article IV, Protocol Articles 3 and 18.

7. What is the concern over treaty shopping? Why does the United States oppose such posturing?

8. Can a Canadian resident who is a United States nonresident alien file a joint return with respect to any income subject to tax by the United States? *See* § 6013(a) and Article XXV.

9. How are terms utilized in a treaty defined? *See* Article III(2).

10. What tax consequences arise for any income not specifically addressed by treaty? *See* Article XXII.

11. Under what circumstances is income considered derived from a treaty country? *See* Articles III(2) and XI(6).

12. How, if at all, does the Model Treaty differ from the Canadian treaty? What is the future role of the Model Treaty?

Chapter 6
Tax Treaties and Passive Income

§ 6.01 Introduction
§ 6.02 Dividends
§ 6.03 Interest
§ 6.04 Royalties
§ 6.05 Gains from the Disposition of Property
§ 6.06 Income from Real Property
§ 6.07 Residual Income Clauses
Technical Explanation of United States-Canada Income Tax Treaty
Technical Explanation of the Protocol to the United States-Canada Income Tax Treaty—1995
Problem 6

§ 6.01 Introduction

In this Chapter, the tax treaty principles governing specific types of passive income are analyzed. While tax treaties address both outbound and inbound transactions (i.e., United States residents deriving income from a foreign jurisdiction and foreign residents deriving income from within the United States), the discussion in this Chapter focuses primarily on inbound transactions. However, the provisions apply equally to outbound activity.

As a general rule, the Code taxes passive income of nonresident, nontreaty persons at a 30 percent rate of tax. Tax treaties almost without exception impose a rate which is one-half or less than the statutory rate.

§ 6.02 Dividends

Absent a tax treaty, if a foreign person receives a United States source dividend which is not effectively connected to the conduct of a domestic trade or business, that dividend is subject to a 30 percent withholding tax. United States tax treaties generally reduce that statutory tax rate significantly. For instance, under many treaties, this 30 percent tax is reduced to 15 percent provided it is not attributable to a permanent establishment or a fixed base and is further reduced to five percent if the dividend recipient owns at least ten percent of the voting stock of the payor. Tax treaties often reflect this two-tier rate structure with variations on the required level of ownership for securing the nominal tax rate.

The determination of whether a payee corporation is entitled to a lower tax rate on dividends under a particular treaty has been the subject of several Rulings. For instance, in Revenue Ruling 75-118, a Netherlands holding company received a dividend from its wholly owned domestic subsidiary. The Service ruled that the Netherlands corporation was entitled to the nominal five percent treaty rate where the holding company held the stock of three domestic corporations and numerous foreign corporations; acquired the shares of the payor corporation as a partial liquidation distribution in anticipation of a change in Canadian law; and had complete dominion and control over the funds it received without obligation to transfer the funds to its parent.

The potential for a nominal withholding tax rate based solely on corporate ownership is ripe for abuse and controversy. The Service quite properly is reluctant to extend the lower related-party treaty rate if a parent-subsidiary relationship has been established primarily for the purpose of securing the favorable tax rate. This appears to hold true even where the required level of parental ownership of the subsidiary's stock clearly exists and even in the absence of a prohibitive treaty provision to that effect.

§ 6.03 Interest

Interest received by a resident of a treaty country is generally entitled to preferential treaty benefits. Treaties generally provide that interest received from a United States payor and beneficially owned and derived by a treaty country resident is not subject to withholding or other tax so long as the interest is not attributable to a permanent establishment. Some tax treaties, however, do not completely exempt domestic source interest income from United States taxation. Rather, such interest is subject to a reduced tax rate.

For treaty purposes, "interest" is generally quite broadly construed. It includes not only traditional interest payments for the use or forbearance of money but may also include unstated interest, such as original issue discount and imputed interest. Absent language to the contrary, interest does not, however, include call premiums, swap payments, or guarantee fees. Such amounts do not represent compensation for the use of money.

§ 6.04 Royalties

Royalties derived from the United States are generally exempt from tax or subject to a reduced rate of tax under most tax treaties. For instance, treaties often provide that royalties derived and beneficially owned by a resident of a contracting state are taxable only in that state. Under such treaties, royalties derived by a foreign licensor from United States sources are exempt from taxation. Accordingly, if those royalties are not attributable to a permanent establishment, they are also exempt from withholding tax. Some tax treaties, however, do not extend a complete exemption in the source country for royalty income. Rather, royalties are subject to a reduced rate of tax.

The term "royalties" generally encompasses payments received for the use of, or the right to use, any copyright of literary, artistic, or scientific work (often excluding cinematographic, radio, or television films), any patent, trademark, secret formula, process, or other like right or property, or information concerning industrial, commercial, or scientific experience. Many treaties also include as royalties gains derived from the alienation of any such right or property which are contingent on the productivity, use, or disposition thereof.

§ 6.05 Gains from the Disposition of Property

Under most treaties, gains derived from the transfer of property are generally taxable only in the country of the transferor's residence. However, in many treaties, the United States retains jurisdiction to tax those gains derived from the transfer of United States real property, personal property attributable to a United States permanent establishment or fixed base, or intangible assets where the amount of gain is contingent on the productivity, use, or disposition of the intangible asset. Such property interests possess a sufficient nexus to the United States to warrant this reservation of a right to tax the gain received upon their disposition.

§ 6.06 Income from Real Property

Most treaties do not provide for a reduction of the statutory rate for income derived from real property. The income is typically subject to tax in the situs jurisdiction regardless of whether the income is derived annually, e.g., rental income, or whether the income is derived from a disposition of the property, e.g., gain from the sale of the property.

§ 6.07 Residual Income Clauses

Some treaties contain a residual exemption for income items not specifically addressed by other provisions of the treaty. Residual provisions generally grant taxing authority over unaddressed income to the recipient's home country. For instance, many such clauses provide that items of income that are not dealt with in other articles are taxable only in the recipient's country of residence unless the income arises in the other contracting state. The term "arise" in these provisions typically is interpreted as requiring the application of the source rules of the country of source.

Technical Explanation of United States-Canada Income Tax Treaty
(Signed on September 26, 1980)

INTRODUCTION

In this technical explanation of the Convention between the United States and Canada signed on September 26, 1980 ("the Convention"), references are made to the Convention and Protocol between Canada and the United States with respect to Income Taxes signed on March 4, 1942, as amended by the Convention signed on June 12, 1950, the Convention signed on August 8, 1956 and the Supplementary Convention signed on October 25, 1966 (the "1942 Convention"). These references are intended to put various provisions of the Convention into context. . . .

The technical explanation is an official guide to the Convention. It reflects policies behind particular Convention provisions, as well as understandings reached with respect to the interpretation and application of the Convention.

Article I
PERSONAL SCOPE

Article I provides that the Convention is generally applicable to persons who are residents of either Canada or the United States or both Canada and the United States. The word "generally" is used because certain provisions of the Convention apply to persons who are residents of neither Canada nor the United States. . . .

. . . .

Article III
GENERAL DEFINITIONS

Article III provides definitions and general rules of interpretation for the Convention. Paragraph 1(a) states that the term "Canada," when used in a geographical sense, means the territory of Canada, including any area beyond the territorial seas of Canada which, under international law and the laws of Canada, is an area within which Canada may exercise rights with respect to the seabed and subsoil and their natural resources. This definition differs only in form from the definition of Canada in the 1942 Convention; paragraph 1(a) omits the reference in the 1942 Convention to "the Provinces, the Territories and Sable Island" as unnecessary. . . .

Paragraph 1(e) provides that the term "person" includes an individual, an estate, a trust, a company, and any other body of persons. Although both the United States and Canada do not regard partnerships as taxable entities, the definition in the paragraph is broad enough to include partnerships where necessary. . . .

The term "competent authority" is defined in paragraph 1(g) to mean, in the case of Canada, the Minister of National Revenue or his authorized representative and, in the case of the United States, the Secretary of the Treasury or his delegate. The Secretary of the Treasury has delegated the general authority to act as competent authority to the Commissioner of the Internal Revenue Service, who has redelegated such authority to the Assistant Commissioner (Compliance) with the concurrence, in certain cases, of the Assistant Commissioner (Technical). The Assistant Commissioner (Compliance) has redelegated authority to the Director of International Operations to administer programs for routine and specific exchanges of information and mutual assistance in collection and to the Director, Examination Division, to administer programs for simultaneous and industrial exchanges of information. . . .

Paragraph 2 provides that, in the case of a term not defined in the Convention, the domestic tax law of the Contracting State applying to the Convention shall control, unless the context in which the term is used requires a definition independent of domestic tax law or the competent authorities reach agreement on a meaning pursuant to Article XXVI (Mutual Agreement Procedure). The term "context" refers to the purpose and background of the provision in which the term appears.

Pursuant to the provisions of Article XXVI, the competent authorities of the Contracting States may resolve any difficulties or doubts as to the interpretation or application of the Convention. An agreement by the competent authorities with respect to the meaning of a term used in the Convention would supersede conflicting meanings in the domestic laws of the Contracting States.

Article IV
RESIDENCE

Article IV provides a detailed definition of the term "resident of a Contracting State." The definition begins with a person's liability to tax as a resident under the respective taxation laws of the Contracting States. A person who, under those laws, is a resident of one Contracting State and not the other need look no further. However, the Convention definition is also designed to assign residence to one State or the other for purposes of the Convention in circumstances where each of the Contracting States believes a person to be its resident. The Convention definition is, of course, exclusively for purposes of the Convention.

Paragraph 1 provides that the term "resident of a Contracting State" means any person who, under the laws of that State, is liable to tax therein by reason of his domicile, residence, place of management, place of incorporation, or any other criterion of a similar nature. The phrase "any other criterion of a similar nature" includes, for U.S. purposes, an election under the Code to be treated as a U.S. resident. . . .

Paragraphs 2, 3, and 4 provide rules to determine a single residence for purposes of the Convention for persons resident in both Contracting States under the rules set forth in paragraph 1. Paragraph 2 deals with individuals. A "dual resident" individual is initially deemed to be a resident of the Contracting State in which he has a permanent home available to him. If the individual has a permanent home available to him in both States or in neither, he is deemed to be a resident of the Contracting State with which his personal and economic relations are closer. If the personal and economic relations of an individual are not closer to one Contracting State than to the other, the individual is deemed to be a resident of the Contracting State in which he has an habitual abode. If he has such an abode in both States or in neither State, he is deemed to be a resident of the Contracting State of which he is a citizen. If the individual is a citizen of both States or of neither, the competent authorities are to settle the status of the individual by mutual agreement.

Paragraph 3 provides that if, under the provisions of paragraph 1, a company is a resident of both Canada and the United States, then it shall be deemed to be a resident of the State under whose laws (including laws of political subdivisions) it was created. Paragraph 3 does not refer to the State in which a company is organized, thus making clear that the tiebreaker rule for a company is controlled by the State of the company's original creation. Various jurisdictions may allow local incorporation of an entity that is already organized and incorporated under the laws of another country. Paragraph 3 provides certainty in both the United States and Canada with respect to the treatment of such an entity for purposes of the Convention. . . .

. . . .

Article VI
INCOME FROM REAL PROPERTY

Paragraph 1 provides that income derived by a resident of a Contracting State from real property situated in the other Contracting State may be taxed by that other State. Income from real property includes, for purposes of Article VI, income from agriculture or forestry. Also, while "income derived . . . from real property" includes income from rights such as an overriding royalty or a net profits interest in a natural resource, it does not include income in the form of rights to explore for or exploit natural resources which a party receives as compensation for services (e.g., exploration services); the latter income is subject to the provisions of Article VII (Business Profits), XIV (Independent Personal Services), or XV (Dependent Personal Services), as the case may be. As provided by paragraph 3, paragraph 1 applies to income derived from the direct use, letting or use in any other form of real property and to income from the alienation of such property.

Generally speaking, the term "real property" has the meaning which it has under the taxation laws of the Contracting State in which the property in question is situated, in accordance with paragraph 2. In any case, the term includes any option or similar right in respect of real property, the usufruct of real property, and rights to explore for or to exploit mineral deposits, sources, and other natural resources. The reference to "rights to explore for or to exploit mineral deposits, sources and other natural resources" includes rights generating either variable or fixed payments. The term "real property" does not include ships and aircraft.

Unlike Article XIII A of the 1942 Convention, Article VI does not contain an election to allow a resident of a Contracting State to compute tax on income from real property situated in the other State on a net basis. Both the Internal Revenue Code and the Income Tax Act of Canada generally allow for net basis taxation with respect to real estate rental income, although Canada does not permit such an election for natural resource royalties. Also, unlike the 1942 Convention which in Article XI imposes a 15 percent limitation on the source basis taxation of rental or royalty income from real property, Article VI of the Convention allows a Contracting State to impose tax on such income under its internal law. . . .

. . . .

Article X
DIVIDENDS

Paragraph 1 allows a Contracting State to impose tax on its residents with respect to dividends paid by a company which is a resident of the other Contracting State.

Paragraph 2 limits the amount of tax that may be imposed on such dividends by the Contracting State in which the company paying the dividends is resident if the beneficial owner of the dividends is a resident of the other Contracting State. The limitation is 10 percent of the gross amount of the dividends if the beneficial owner is a company that owns 10 percent or more of the voting stock of the company paying the dividends; and 15 percent of the gross amount of the dividends in all other cases. Paragraph 2 does not impose any restrictions with respect to taxation of the profits out of which the dividends are paid.

Paragraph 3 defines the term "dividends," as the term is used in this Article. Each Contracting State is permitted to apply its domestic law rules for differentiating dividends from interest and other disbursements.

Paragraph 4 provides that the limitations of paragraph 2 do not apply if the beneficial owner of the dividends carries on business in the State in which the company paying the dividends is a resident through a permanent establishment or fixed base situated there, and the stockholding in respect of which the dividends are paid is effectively connected with such permanent establishment or fixed base. In such a case, the dividends are taxable pursuant to the provisions of Article VII (Business Profits) or Article XIV (Independent Personal Services), as the case may be. Thus, dividends paid in respect of holdings forming part of the assets of a permanent establishment or fixed base or which are otherwise effectively connected with such permanent establishment or fixed base (i.e., dividends attributable to the permanent establishment or fixed base) will be taxed on a net basis using the rates and rules of taxation generally applicable to residents of the State in which the permanent establishment or fixed base is situated. . . .

Article XI
INTEREST

Paragraph 1 allows interest arising in Canada or the United States and paid to a resident of the other State to be taxed in the latter State. Paragraph 2 provides that such interest may also be taxed in the Contracting State where it arises, but if a resident of the other Contracting State is the beneficial owner, the tax imposed by the State of source is limited to 15 percent of the gross amount of the interest.

Paragraph 3 provides a number of exceptions to the right of the source State to impose a 15 percent tax under paragraph 2. The following types of interest beneficially owned by a resident of a Contracting State are exempt from tax in the State of source: a) interest beneficially owned by a Contracting State, a political subdivision, or a local authority thereof, or an instrumentality of such State, subdivision, or authority, which interest is not subject to tax by such state; b) interest beneficially owned by a resident of a Contracting State and paid with respect to debt obligations issued at arm's length which are guaranteed or insured by such State or a political subdivision thereof, or by an instrumentality of such State or subdivision (not by a local authority or an instrumentality thereof), but only if the guarantor or insurer is not subject to tax by that State; c) interest paid by a Contracting State, a political subdivision, or a local authority thereof, or by an instrumentality of such State, subdivision, or authority, but only if the payor is not subject to tax by such State; and d) interest beneficially owned by a seller of equipment, merchandise, or services, but only if the interest is paid in connection with a sale on credit of equipment, merchandise, or services and the sale was made at arm's length. Whether such a transaction is made at arm's length will be determined in the United States under the facts and circumstances. The relationship between the parties is a factor, but not the only factor, taken into account in making this determination. . . .

Paragraph 4 defines the term "interest," as used in Article XI, to include, among other things, debt claims of every kind as well as income assimilated to income from money lent by the taxation laws of the Contracting State in which the income arises. In no event, however, is income dealt with in Article X (Dividends) to be considered interest.

Paragraph 5 provides that neither the 15 percent limitation on tax in the Contracting State of source provided in paragraph 2 nor the various exemptions from tax in such State provided in paragraph 3 apply if the beneficial owner of the interest is a resident of the other Contracting State carrying on business in the State of source through a permanent establishment or fixed base, and the debt claim in respect of which the interest is paid is effectively connected with such permanent establishment or fixed base (i.e., the interest is attributable to the permanent establishment or fixed base). In this case, interest income is to be taxed in the Contracting State of source as business profits—that is, on a net basis.

Paragraph 6 establishes the source of interest for purposes of Article XI. Interest is considered to arise in a Contracting State if the payer is that State, or a political subdivision, local authority, or resident of that State. However, in cases where the person paying the interest, whether a resident of a Contracting State or of a third State, has in a State other than that of which he is a resident a permanent establishment or fixed base in connection with which the indebtedness on which the interest was paid was incurred, and such interest is borne by the permanent establishment or fixed base, then such interest is deemed to arise in the State in which the permanent establishment or fixed base is situated and not in the State of the payer's residence. Thus, pursuant to paragraphs 6 and 2, and Article XXII (Other Income), Canadian tax will not be imposed on interest paid to a U.S. resident by a company resident in Canada if the indebtedness is incurred in connection with, and the interest is borne by, a permanent establishment of the company situated in a third State. "Borne by" means allowable as a deduction in computing taxable income. . . .

Article XII
ROYALTIES

... Paragraph 1 of Article XII of the Convention provides that a Contracting State may tax its residents with respect to royalties arising in the other Contracting State. Paragraph 2 provides that such royalties may also be taxed in the Contracting State in which they arise, but that if a resident of the other Contracting State is the beneficial owner of the royalties the tax in the Contracting State of source is limited to 10 percent of the gross amount of the royalties.

Paragraph 3 provides that, notwithstanding paragraph 2, copyright royalties and other like payments in respect of the production or reproduction of any literary, dramatic, musical, or artistic work, including royalties from such works on videotape cassettes for private (home) use, if beneficially owned by a resident of the other Contracting State, may not be taxed by the Contracting State of source. This exemption at source does not apply to royalties in respect of motion picture films and works on film or videotape for use in connection with television broadcasting. Such royalties are subject to tax at a maximum rate of 10 percent in the Contracting State in which they arise, as provided in paragraph 2 (unless the provisions of paragraph 5, described below, apply).

Paragraph 4 defines the term "royalties" for purposes of Article XII. "Royalties" means payments of any kind received as consideration for the use of the right to use any copyright of literary, artistic, or scientific work, including motion picture films and works on film or videotape for private (home) use or for use in connection with television broadcasting, any patent, trademark, design or model, plan, secret formula or process, or any payment for the use of or the right to use tangible personal property or for information concerning industrial, commercial, or scientific experience. The term "royalties" also includes gains from the alienation of any intangible property or rights described in paragraph 4 to the extent that such gains are contingent on the productivity, use, or subsequent disposition of such intangible property or rights. Thus, a guaranteed minimum payment derived from the alienation of (but not the use of) any right or property described in paragraph 4 is not a "royalty." Any amounts deemed contingent on use by reason of Code section 871(e) are, however, royalties under paragraph 2 of Article III (General Definitions), subject to Article XXVI (Mutual Agreement Procedure). The term "royalties" does not encompass management fees, which are covered by the provisions of Article VII (Business Profits) of XIV (Independent Personal Services), or payments under a bona fide cost-sharing arrangement. Technical service fees may be royalties in case where the fees are periodic and dependent upon productivity or a similar measure.

Paragraph 5 provides that the 10 percent limitation on tax in the Contracting State of source provided by paragraph 2, and the exemption in the Contracting State of source for certain copyright royalties provided by paragraph 3, do not apply if the beneficial owner of the royalties carries on business in the State of source through a permanent establishment or fixed base and the right or property in respect of which the royalties are paid is effectively connected with such permanent establishment or fixed base (i.e., the royalties are attributable to the permanent establishment or fixed base). In that event, the royalty income would be taxable under the provisions of Article VII (Business Profits) or XIV (Independent Personal Services), as the case may be.

Paragraph 6 establishes rules to determine the source of royalties for purposes of Article XII. The first rule is that royalties arise in a Contracting State when the payer is that State, or a political subdivision, local authority, or resident of that State. Notwithstanding that rule, royalties arise not in the State of the payer's residence but in any State, whether or not a Contracting State, in which is situated a permanent establishment or fixed base in connection with which the obligation to pay royalties was incurred, if such royalties are borne by such permanent establishment or fixed base. Thus, royalties paid to a resident of the United States by a company resident in Canada for the use of property in a third State will not be subject to tax in Canada if the obligation to pay the royalties is incurred in connection with, and the royalties are borne by, a permanent establishment of the company in a third State. "Borne by" means allowable as a deduction in computing taxable income.

A third rule, which overrides both the residence rule and the permanent establishment rule just described, provides that royalties for the use of intangible property or tangible personal property arise in the Contracting State in which such property is used. Thus, consistent with the provisions of Code section 861(a)(4), if a resident of a third State pays royalties to a resident of Canada for the right to use intangible property in the United States, such royalties are considered to arise in the United States and are subject to taxation by the United States consistent with the Convention. Similarly, if a resident of Canada pays royalties to a resident of a third State, such royalties are considered to arise in the United States and are subject to U.S. taxation if they are for the right to use intangible property in the United States. The term "intangible property" encompasses all the items described in paragraph 4, other than tangible personal property. . . .

Article XIII
GAINS

Paragraph 1 provides that Canada and the United States may each tax gains from the alienation of real property situated within that State which are derived by a resident of the other Contracting State. The term "real property" is defined for this purpose in paragraph 2 of Article VI (Income From Real Property). The term "alienation" used in paragraph 1 and other paragraphs of Article XIII means sales, exchanges and other dispositions or deemed dispositions (e.g., change of use, gifts, death) that are taxable events under the taxation laws of the Contracting State applying the provisions of the Article.

Paragraph 2 of Article XIII provides that the Contracting State in which a resident of the other Contracting State "has or had" a permanent establishment or fixed base may tax gains from the alienation of personal property constituting business property if such gains are attributable to such permanent establishment or fixed base. Unlike paragraph 1 of Article VII (Business Profits), paragraph 2 limits the right of the source State to tax such gains to a twelve-month period following the termination of the permanent establishment or fixed base.

Paragraph 3 authorizes the Contracting State of source to tax gains derived from the alienation of certain stock and other interests, if such interests ultimately reflect value derived from real property situated in that State. The right to tax in the State of source applies when there is an alienation of either shares forming part of a substantial interest in the capital stock of a company which is not a resident of the taxpayer's State of residence, or an interest in a partnership, trust, or estate, but only if the value of such shares or interest, as the case may be, is derived principally from real property in the Contracting State of source. The term "principally" means more than 50 percent. The right accorded to the State of source depends, however, on the domestic law in force in the Contracting State of residence. Thus, if at the time of alienation the latter State does not, by reason of its domestic law, impose tax upon gains derived from the alienation of a class of shares or interests (such as shares in companies which are not residents of that State), then the State of source may not impose tax in reciprocal circumstances.

Subparagraph (c) of paragraph 3 provides that the term "real property" as used in the paragraph, does not include property—other than mines, oil or gas wells, rental property, or property used for agriculture or forestry—in which a business is carried on. The term does include the shares of a company which derive their value principally from real property (wherever located) and an interest in a partnership, trust, or estate the direct disposition of which would be subject to tax under the paragraph. Thus, taxation in the Contracting State of source is preserved through several tiers of entities if the value of the shares or interest alienated is ultimately dependent principally upon real property in that State.

A "substantial interest" exists only if, on or after the effective date of the Convention provided in Article XXX (Entry Into Force), the resident and any persons related to him own 10 percent or more of the shares of any class of the capital stock of a company. It is the intention that once a "substantial interest" exists, all stock that is part of such "substantial interest" is covered by paragraph 3, even if the percentage of ownership declines to less than 10 percent. The term "related persons" is not defined by the rules of Article IX (Related Persons); rather, the term is defined pursuant to paragraph 2 of Article III (General Definitions).

Paragraph 4 reserves to the Contracting State of residence the sole right to tax gains from the alienation of any property other than property referred to in paragraphs 1, 2, and 3. . . .

. . . .

Article XXII
OTHER INCOME

Paragraph 1 provides that a Contracting State of which a person is a resident has the sole right to tax items of income, wherever arising, if such income is not dealt with in the prior Articles of the Convention. If such income arises in the other Contracting State, however, it may also be taxed in that State. The determination of where income arises for this purpose is made under the domestic laws of the respective Contracting States unless the Convention specifies where the income arises (e.g., paragraph 6 of Article XI (Interest)) for purposes of determining the right to tax, in which case the provisions of the Convention control. . . .

. . . .

Article XXV
NON-DISCRIMINATION

Paragraphs 1 and 2 of Article XXV protect individual citizens of a Contracting State from discrimination by the other Contracting State in taxation matters. Paragraph 1 provides that a citizen of a Contracting State who is a resident of the other Contracting State may not be subjected in that other State to any taxation or requirement connected with taxation which is other or more burdensome than the taxation and connected requirements imposed on similarly situated citizens of the other State.

Paragraph 2 assures protection in a case where a citizen of a Contracting State is not a resident of the other Contracting State. Such a citizen may not be subjected in the other State to any taxation or requirement connected to taxation which is other or more burdensome than the taxation and connected requirements to which similarly situated citizens of any third State are subjected. The reference to citizens of a third State "in the same circumstances" includes consideration of the State of residence. Thus, pursuant to paragraph 2, the Canadian taxation with respect to a citizen of the United States resident in, for example, the United Kingdom may not be more burdensome than the taxation of a U.K. citizen resident in the United Kingdom. Any benefits available to the U.K. citizen by virtue of an income tax convention between the United Kingdom and Canada would be available to the U.S. citizen resident in the United Kingdom if he is otherwise in the same circumstances as the U.K. citizen. . . .

Article XXVI
MUTUAL AGREEMENT PROCEDURE

Paragraph 1 provides that where a person considers that the actions of one or both of the Contracting States will result in taxation not in accordance with the Convention, he may present his case in writing to the competent authority of the Contracting State of which he is a resident or, if he is a resident of neither Contracting State, of which he is a national. Thus, a resident of Canada must present to the Minister of National Revenue (or his authorized representative) any claim that such resident is being subjected to taxation contrary to the Convention. A person who requests assistance from the competent authority may also avail himself of any remedies available under domestic laws.

Paragraph 2 provides that the competent authority of the Contracting State to which the case is presented shall endeavor to resolve the case by mutual agreement with the competent authority of the other Contracting State, unless he believes that the objection is not justified or he is able to arrive at a satisfactory unilateral solution. Any agreement reached between the competent authorities of Canada and the United States shall be implemented notwithstanding any time or other procedural limitations in the domestic laws of the Contracting States, except where the special mutual agreement provisions of Article IX (Related Persons) apply, provided that the competent authority of the Contracting State asked to waive its domestic time or procedural limitations has received written notification that such a case exists within six years from the end of the taxable year in the first-mentioned State to which the case relates. The notification may be given by the competent authority to take action, or a person related to the taxpayer. Unlike Article IX, Article XXVI does not require the competent authority of a Contracting State to grant unilateral relief to avoid double taxation in a case where timely notification is not given to the competent authority of the other Contracting State. Such unilateral relief may, however, be granted by the competent authority in its discretion pursuant to the provisions of Article XXVI and in order to achieve the purposes of the Convention. In a case where the provisions of Article IX apply, the provisions of paragraphs 3, 4, and 5 of that Article are controlling with respect to adjustments and corresponding adjustments of income, loss, or tax and the effect of the Convention upon time or procedural limitations of domestic law. Thus, if relief is not available under Article IX because of fraud, the provisions of paragraph 2 of Article XXVI do not independently authorize such relief.

Paragraph 3 provides that the competent authorities of the Contracting States shall endeavor to resolve by mutual agreement any difficulties or doubts arising as to the interpretation or application of the Convention. In particular, the competent authorities may agree to the same attribution of profits to a resident of a Contracting State and its permanent establishment in the other Contracting State; the same allocation of income, deductions, credits, or allowances between persons; the same determination of the source of income; the same characterization of particular items of income; a common meaning of any term used in the Convention; rules, guidelines, or procedures for the elimination of double taxation with respect to income distributed by an estate or trust, or with respect to a partnership; or to increase any dollar amounts referred to in the Convention to reflect monetary or economic developments. The competent authorities may also consult and reach agreements on rules, guidelines, or procedures for the elimination of double taxation in cases not provided for in the Convention.

The list of subjects of potential mutual agreement in paragraph 3 is not exhaustive; it merely illustrates the principles set forth in the paragraph. As in the case of other U.S. tax conventions, agreement can be arrived at in the context of determining the tax liability of a specific person or in establishing rules, guidelines, and procedures that will apply generally under the Convention to resolve issues for classes or taxpayers. It is contemplated that paragraph 3 could be utilized by the competent authorities, for example, to resolve conflicts between the domestic laws of Canada and the United States with respect to the allocation and apportionment of deductions.

Paragraph 4 provides that each Contracting State will endeavor to collect on behalf of the other State such amounts as may be necessary to ensure that relief granted by the Convention from taxation imposed by the other State does not enure to the benefit of persons not entitled to such relief. Paragraph 4 does not oblige either Contracting State to carry out administrative measures of a different nature from those that would be used by Canada or the United States in the collection of its own tax or which would be contrary to its public policy.

Paragraph 5 confirms that the competent authorities of Canada and the United States may communicate with each other directly for the purpose of reaching agreement in the sense of paragraphs 1 through 4. . . .

Technical Explanation of the Protocol to the United States-Canada Income Tax Treaty—1995

(Signed on September 26, 1980, as Amended by the Protocols Signed on June 14, 1983, and March 28, 1984)

The Protocol, signed at Washington on March 17, 1995 (the "Protocol"), amends the Convention Between the United States of America and Canada with Respect to Taxes on Income and on Capital, signed at Washington on September 26, 1980, as amended by the Protocols signed on June 14, 1983 and March 28, 1984 (collectively referred to as the "Convention"). This technical explanation is an official guide to the Protocol. It explains policies behind particular provisions, as well as understandings reached during the negotiations with respect to the interpretation and application of the Protocol. The technical explanation is not intended to provide a complete comparison between the Protocol and the Articles of the Convention that it amends. To the extent that the Convention has not been amended by the Protocol, the Technical Explanation of the Convention remains the official explanation. References to "he" or "his" should be read to mean "he" or "she" or "his" or "her.". . .

. . . .

Article 3

Article 3 of the Protocol amends Article IV (Residence) of the Convention. It clarifies the meaning of the term "resident" in certain cases and adds a special rule, found in a number of recent U.S. treaties, for determining the residence of U.S. citizens and "green-card" holders.

The first sentence of paragraph 1 of Article IV sets forth the general criteria for determining residence under the Convention. It is amended by the Protocol to state explicitly that a person will be considered a resident of a Contracting State for purposes of the Convention if he is liable to tax in that Contracting State by reason of citizenship. Although the sentence applies to both Contracting States, only the United States taxes its non-resident citizens in the same manner as its residents. Aliens admitted to the United States for permanent residence ("green card" holders) continue to qualify as U.S. residents under the first sentence of paragraph 1, because they are taxed by the United States as residents, regardless of where they physically reside.

U.S. citizens and green card holders who reside outside the United States, however, may have relatively little personal or economic nexus with the United States. The Protocol adds a second sentence to paragraph 1 that acknowledges this fact by limiting the circumstances under which such persons are to be treated, for purposes of the Convention, as U.S. residents. Under that sentence, a U.S. citizen or green card holder will be treated as a resident of the United States for purposes of the Convention, and, thereby, be entitled to treaty benefits, only if (1) the individual has a substantial presence, permanent home, or habitual abode in the United States, and (2) the individual's personal and economic relations with the United States are closer than those with any third country. If, however, such an individual is a resident of both the United States and Canada under the first sentence of the paragraph, his residence for purposes of the Convention is determined instead under the "tie-breaker" rules of paragraph 2 of the Article.

The fact that a U.S. citizen who does not have close ties to the United States may not be treated as a U.S. resident under Article IV of the Convention does not alter the application of the saving clause of paragraph 2 of Article XXIX (Miscellaneous Rules) to that citizen. However, like any other individual that is a resident alien under U.S. law, a green card holder is treated as a resident of the United States for purposes of the saving clause only if he qualifies as such under Article IV.

New paragraph 1(a) confirms that the term "resident" of a Contracting State includes the Government of that State or a political subdivision or local authority of that State, as well as any agency or instrumentality of one of these governmental entities. This is implicit in the current Convention and in other U.S. and Canadian treaties, even where not specified. . . .

Article 3 of the Protocol adds a sentence to paragraph 3 of Article IV of the current Convention to address the residence of certain dual resident corporations. Certain jurisdictions allow local incorporation of an entity that is already organized and incorporated under the laws of another country. Under Canadian law, such an entity is referred to as having been "continued" into the other country. Although the Protocol uses the Canadian term, the provision operates reciprocally. The new sentence states that such a corporation will be considered a resident of the State into which it is continued. Paragraph 5 of Article 21 of the Protocol governs the effective date of this provision. . . .

. . . .

Article 5

Article 5 of the Protocol amends Article X (Dividends) of the Convention. Paragraph 1 of Article 5 amends paragraph 2(a) of Article X to reduce from 10 percent to 5 percent the maximum rate of tax that may be imposed by a Contracting State on the gross amount of dividends beneficially owned by a company resident in the other Contracting State that owns at least 10 percent of the voting stock of the company paying the dividends. . . .

Article 6

Article 6 of the Protocol amends Article XI (Interest) of the Convention. Paragraph 1 of the Article reduces the general maximum withholding rate on interest under paragraph 2 of Article XI from 15 percent to 10 percent. . . .

Article 7

Article 7 of the Protocol modifies Article XII (Royalties) of the Convention by expanding the classes of royalties exempt from withholding of tax at source. Paragraph 3, as amended by the Protocol, identifies four classes of royalty payments arising in one Contracting State and beneficially owned by a resident of the other that are exempt at source: (1) subparagraph (a) preserves the exemption in paragraph 3 of the present Convention for copyright royalties in respect of literary and other works, other than certain such payments in respect of motion pictures, videotapes, and similar payments; (2) subparagraph (b) specifies that computer software royalties are also exempt; (3) subparagraph (c) adds royalties paid for the use of, or the right to use, patents and information concerning industrial, commercial, and scientific experience, other than payments in connection with rental or franchise agreements; and (4) subparagraph (d) allows the Contracting States to reach an agreement, through an exchange of diplomatic notes, with respect to the application of paragraph 3 of Article XII to payments in respect of certain live broadcasting transmissions.

The specific reference to software in subparagraph (b) is not intended to suggest that the United States views the term "copyright" as excluding software in other U.S. treaties (including the current treaty with Canada).

The negotiators agreed that royalties paid for the use of, or the right to use, designs or models, plans, secret formulas, or processes are included under subparagraph 3(c) to the extent that they represent payments for the use of, or the right to use, information concerning industrial, commercial, or scientific experience. In addition, they agreed that royalties paid for the use of, or the right to use, "know how," as defined in paragraph 11 of the Commentary on Article 12 of the OECD Model Income Tax Treaty, constitute payments for the use of, or the right to use, information concerning industrial, commercial, or scientific experience. The negotiators further agreed that a royalty paid under a "mixed contract," "package fee," or similar arrangement will be treated as exempt at source by virtue of paragraph 3 to the extent of any portion that is paid for the use of, or the right to use, property or information with respect to which paragraph 3 grants an exemption.

The exemption granted under subparagraph 3(c) does not, however, extend to payments made for information concerning industrial, commercial, or scientific experience that is provided in connection with a rental or franchise agreement. For this purpose, the negotiators agreed that a franchise is to be distinguished from other arrangements resulting in the transfer of intangible property. They agreed that a license to use intangibles (whether or not including a trademark) in a territory, in and of itself, would not constitute a franchise agreement for purposes of subparagraph 3(c) in the absence of other rights and obligations in the license agreement or in any other agreement that would indicate that the arrangement in its totality constituted a franchise agreement. For example, a resident of one Contracting State may acquire a right to use a secret formula to manufacture a particular product (e.g., a perfume), together with the right to use a trademark for that product and to market it at a non-retail level, in the other Contracting State. such an arrangement would not constitute a franchise in the absence of any other rights or obligations under that arrangement or any other agreement that would indicate that the arrangement in its totality constituted a franchise agreement. Therefore, the royalty payment under that arrangement would be exempt from withholding tax in the other Contracting State to the extent made for the use of, or the right to use, the secret formula or other information concerning industrial, commercial, or scientific experience; however, it would be subject to withholding tax at a rate of 10 percent, to the extent made for the use of, or the right to use, the trademark.

The provisions of paragraph 3 do not fully reflect the U.S. treaty policy of exempting all types of royalty payments from taxation at source, but Canada was not prepared to grant a complete exemption for all types of royalties in the Protocol. Although the Protocol makes several important changes to the royalty provisions of the present Convention in the direction of bringing Article XII into conformity with U.S. policy, the United States remains concerned about the imposition of withholding tax on some classes of royalties and about the associated administrative burdens. In this connection, the Contracting States have affirmed their intention to collaborate to resolve in good faith any administrative issues that may arise in applying the provisions of subparagraph 3(c). The United States intends to continue to pursue a zero rate of withholding for all royalties in future negotiations with Canada, including discussions under Article 20 of the Protocol, as well as in negotiations with other countries.

As noted above, new subparagraph 3(d) enables the Contracting States to provide an exemption for royalties paid with respect to broadcasting through an exchange of notes. This provision was included because Canada was not prepared at the time of the negotiations to commit to an exemption for broadcasting royalties. Subparagraph 3(d) was included to enable the Senate to give its advice and consent in advance to such an exemption, in the hope that such an exemption could be obtained without awaiting the negotiation of another full protocol. Any agreement reached under the exchange of notes authorized by subparagraph 3(d) would lower the withholding rate from 10 percent to zero and, thus, bring the Convention into greater conformity with established U.S. treaty policy.

Paragraph 2 of Article 7 of the Protocol amends the rules in paragraph 6 of Article XII of the Convention for determining the source of royalty payments. Under the present Convention, royalties generally are deemed to arise in a Contracting State if paid by a resident of that State. However, if the obligation to pay the royalties was incurred in connection with a permanent establishment or a fixed base in one of the Contracting States that bears the expense, the royalties are deemed to arise in that State.

The Protocol continues to apply these basic rules but changes the scope of an exception provided under the present Convention. Under the present Convention, a royalty paid for the use of, or the right to use, property in a Contracting State is deemed to arise in that State. Under the Protocol, this "place of use," exception applies only if the Convention does not otherwise deem the royalties to arise in one of the Contracting States. Thus, the "place of use" exception will apply only if royalties are neither paid by a resident of one of the Contracting States nor borne by a permanent establishment or fixed base in either State. For example, if a Canadian resident were to grant franchise rights to a resident of Chile for use in the United States, the royalty paid by the Chilean resident to the Canadian resident for those rights would be U.S. source income under this Article, subject to U.S. withholding at the 10 percent rate provided in paragraph 2. . . .

Royalties generally are considered borne by a permanent establishment or fixed base if they are deductible in computing the taxable income of that permanent establishment or fixed base. . . .

. . . .

Article 14

. . . Article 14 also adds a new paragraph 6 to Article XXVI (Mutual Agreement Procedure). Paragraph 6 provides for a voluntary arbitration procedure, to be implemented only upon the exchange of diplomatic notes between the United States and Canada. Similar provisions are found in the recent U.S. treaties with the Federal Republic of Germany, the Nether-

example, a Canadian company that is not publicly traded but that is owned, one-third each, by three companies, two of which are Canadian resident corporations whose principal classes of shares are substantially and regularly traded on a recognized stock exchange, will qualify under subparagraph (d). . . .

Ownership/base erosion test.

Subparagraph (e) of paragraph 2 provides a two-part test under which certain other entities may be qualifying persons, based on ownership and "base erosion." Under the first of these tests, benefits will be granted to a Canadian resident company if 50 percent or more of the vote and value of its shares (other than debt substitute shares), or to a Canadian resident trust if 50 percent or more of its beneficial interest, is not owned, directly or indirectly, by persons other than qualifying persons or U.S. residents or citizens. The wording of these tests is intended to make clear that, for example, if a Canadian company is more than 50 percent owned by a U.S. resident corporation that is, itself, wholly owned by a third-country resident other than a U.S. citizen, the Canadian company would not pass the ownership test. This is because more than 50 percent of its shares is owned indirectly by a person (the third-country resident) that is not a qualifying person or a citizen or resident of the United States. . . .

The second test of subparagraph (e) is the so-called "base erosion" test. A Canadian company or trust that passes the ownership test must also pass this test to be a qualifying person. This test requires that the amount of expenses that are paid or payable by the Canadian entity in question to persons that are not qualifying persons or U.S. citizens or residents, and that are deductible from gross income, be less than 50 percent of the gross income of the company or trust. This test is applied for the fiscal period immediately preceding the period for which the qualifying person test is being applied. If it is the first fiscal period of the person, the test is applied for the current period.

The ownership/base erosion test recognizes that the benefits of the Convention can be enjoyed indirectly not only by equity holders of an entity, but also by that entity's obligees, such as lenders, licensors, service providers, insurers and reinsurers, and others. For example, a third-country resident could license technology to a Canadian-owned Canadian corporation to be sub-licensed to a U.S. resident. The U.S. source royalty income of the Canadian corporation would be exempt from U.S. withholding tax under Article XII (Royalties) of the Convention (as amended by the Protocol). While the Canadian corporation would be subject to Canadian corporation income tax, its taxable income could be reduced to near zero as a result of the deductible royalties paid to the third-country resident. If, under a Convention between Canada and the third country, those royalties were either exempt from Canadian tax or subject to tax at a low rate, the U.S. treaty benefit with respect to the U.S. source royalty income would have flowed to the third-country resident at little or no tax cost, with no reciprocal benefit to the United States from the third country. The ownership/base erosion test therefore requires both that qualifying persons or U.S. residents or citizens substantially own the entity and that the entity's deductible payments be made in substantial part to such persons. . . .

Active trade or business test.

Paragraph 3 provides an eligibility test for benefits for residents of Canada that are not qualifying persons under paragraph 2. This is the so-called "active trade or business" test. Unlike the tests of paragraph 2, the active trade or business test looks not solely at the characteristics of the person deriving the income, but also at the nature of the activity engaged in by that person and the connection between the income and that activity. Under the active trade or business test, a resident of Canada deriving an item of income from the United States is entitled to benefits with respect to that income if that person (or a person related to that person under the principles of Internal Revenue Code section 482) is engaged in an active trade or business in Canada and the income in question is derived in connection with, or is incidental to, that trade or business.

Income that is derived in connection with, or is incidental to, the business of making or managing investments will not qualify for benefits under this provision, unless those investment activities are carried on with customers in the ordinary course of the business of a bank, insurance company, registered securities dealer, or deposit-taking financial institution.

Income is considered derived "in connection" with an active trade or business in the United States if, for example, the income-generating activity in the United States is "upstream," "downstream," or parallel to that conducted in Canada. Thus, if the U.S. activity consisted of selling the output of a Canadian manufacturer or providing inputs to the manufacturing process, or of manufacturing or selling in the United States the same sorts of products that were being sold by the Canadian trade or business in Canada, the income generated by that activity would be treated as earned in connection with the Canadian trade or business. Income is considered "incidental" to the Canadian trade or business if, for example, it arises from the short-term investment of working capital of the Canadian resident in U.S. securities.

An item of income will be considered to be earned in connection with or to be incidental to an active trade or business in Canada if the income is derived by the resident of Canada claiming the benefits directly or indirectly through one or more other persons that are residents of the United States. Thus, for example, a Canadian resident could claim benefits with respect to an item of income earned by a U.S. operating subsidiary but derived by the Canadian resident indirectly through a wholly-owned U.S. holding company interposed between it and the operating subsidiary. This language would also permit a Canadian resident to derive income from the United States through one or more U.S. residents that it does not wholly own. For example, a Canadian partnership in which three unrelated Canadian companies each hold a one-third interest could form a wholly-owned U.S. holding company with a U.S. operating subsidiary. The "directly or indirectly" language would allow otherwise available treaty benefits to be claimed with respect to income derived by the three Canadian partners through the U.S. holding company, even if the partners were not considered to be related to the U.S. holding company under the principles of Internal Revenue Code section 482.

Income that is derived in connection with, or is incidental to, an active trade or business in Canada, must pass an additional test to qualify for U.S. treaty benefits. The trade or business in Canada must be substantial in relation to the activity in the United States that gave rise to the income in respect of which treaty benefits are being claimed. To be considered substantial, it is not necessary that the Canadian trade or business be as large as the U.S. income-generating activity. The Canadian trade or business cannot, however, in terms of income, assets, or other similar measures, represent only a very small percentage of the size of the U.S. activity.

The substantiality requirement is intended to prevent treaty-shopping. For example, a third-country resident may want to acquire a U.S. company that manufactures television sets for worldwide markets; however, since its country of residence has no tax treaty with the United States, any dividends generated by the investment would be subject to a U.S. withholding tax of 30 percent. Absent a substantiality test, the investor could establish a Canadian corporation that would operate a small outlet in Canada to sell a few of the television sets manufactured by the U.S. company and earn a very small amount of income. That Canadian corporation could then acquire the U.S. manufacturer with capital provided by the third- country resident and produce a very large number of sets for sale in several countries, generating a much larger amount of income. It might attempt to argue that the U.S. source income is generated from business activities in the United States related to the television sales activity of the Canadian parent and that the dividend income should be subject to U.S. tax at the 5 percent rate provided by Article X of the Convention, as amended by the Protocol. However, the substantiality test would not be met in this example, so the dividends would remain subject to withholding in the United States at a rate of 30 percent.

In general, it is expected that if a person qualifies for benefits under one of the tests of paragraph 2, no inquiry will be made into qualification for benefits under paragraph 3. Upon satisfaction of any of the tests of paragraph 2, any income derived by the beneficial owner from the other Contracting State is entitled to treaty benefits. Under paragraph 3, however, the test is applied separately to each item of income.

Derivative benefits test.

Paragraph 4 of Article XXIX A contains a so-called "derivative benefits" rule not generally found in U.S. treaties. This rule was included in the Protocol because of the special economic relationship between the United

States and Canada and the close coordination between the tax administrations of the two countries.

Under the derivative benefits rule, a Canadian resident company may receive the benefits of Articles X (Dividends), XI (Interest), and XII (Royalties), even if the company is not a qualifying person and does not satisfy the active trade or business test of paragraph 3. To qualify under this paragraph, the Canadian company must satisfy both (i) the base erosion test under subparagraph (e) of paragraph 2, and (ii) an ownership test.

The derivative benefits ownership test requires that shares (other than debt substitute shares) representing more than 90 percent of the vote and value of the Canadian company be owned directly or indirectly by either (i) qualifying persons or U.S. citizens or residents, or (ii) other persons that satisfy each of three tests. The three tests that must be satisfied by these other persons are as follows:

First, the person must be a resident of a third State with which the United States has a comprehensive income tax convention and be entitled to all of the benefits under that convention. Thus, if the person fails to satisfy the limitation on benefits tests, if any, of that convention, no benefits would be granted under this paragraph. Qualification for benefits under an active trade or business test does not suffice for these purposes, because that test grants benefits only for certain items of income, not for all purposes of the convention.

Second, the person must be a person that would qualify for benefits with respect to the item of income for which benefits are sought under one or more of the tests of paragraph 2 or 3 of this Convention, if the person were a resident of Canada and, for purposes of paragraph 3, the business were carried on in Canada. For example, a person resident in a third country would be deemed to be a person that would qualify under the publicly-traded test of paragraph 2 of this Convention if the principal class of its shares were substantially and regularly traded on a stock exchange recognized either under the treaty between the United States and Canada or under the treaty between the United States and the third country. Similarly, a company resident in a third country would be deemed to satisfy the ownership/base erosion test of paragraph 2 under this hypothetical analysis if, for example, it were wholly owned by an individual resident in that third country and most of its deductible payments were made to individual residents of that country (i.e., it satisfied base erosion).

The third requirement is that the rate of U.S. withholding tax on the item of income in respect of which benefits are sought must be at least as low under the convention between the person's country of residence and the United States as under this Convention.

Competent authority discretion.

Paragraph 6 provides that when a resident of Canada derives income from the United States and is not entitled to the benefits of the Convention under other provisions of the Article, benefits may, nevertheless be granted at the discretion of the U.S. competent authority. In making a determination under this paragraph, the competent authority will take into account all relevant facts and circumstances relating to the person requesting the benefits. In particular, the competent authority will consider the history, structure, ownership (including ultimate beneficial ownership), and operations of the person. In addition, the competent authority is to consider (1) whether the creation and existence of the person did not have as a principal purpose obtaining treaty benefits that would not otherwise be available to the person, and (2) whether it would not be appropriate, in view of the purpose of the Article, to deny benefits. The paragraph specifies that if the U.S. competent authority determines that either of these two standards is satisfied, benefits shall be granted.

For purposes of implementing paragraph 6, a taxpayer will be expected to present his case to the competent authority for an advance determination based on the facts. The taxpayer will not be required to wait until it has been determined that benefits are denied under one of the other provisions of the Article. It also is expected that, if and when the competent authority determines that benefits are to be allowed, they will be allowed retroactively to the time of entry into force of the relevant treaty provision or the establishment of the structure in question, whichever is later (assuming that the taxpayer also qualifies under the relevant facts for the earlier period).

General anti-abuse provisions.

Paragraph 7 was added at Canada's request to confirm that the specific provisions of Article XXIX A and the fact that these provisions apply only for the purposes of the application of the Convention by the United States should not be construed so as to limit the right of each Contracting State to invoke applicable anti-abuse rules. Thus, for example, Canada remains free to apply such rules to counter abusive arrangements involving "treaty-shopping" through the United States, and the United States remains free to apply its substance-over-form and anti-conduit rules, for example, in relation to Canadian residents. This principle is recognized by the Organization for Economic Cooperation and Development in the Commentaries to its Model Tax Convention on Income and on Capital, and the United States and Canada agree that it is inherent in the Convention. The agreement to state this principle explicitly in the Protocol is not intended to suggest that the principle is not also inherent in other tax conventions, including the current Convention with Canada. . . .

PROBLEM 6—TAX TREATIES AND PASSIVE INCOME

Regulation: § 1.871-12

Reading Material: United States-Canada Income Tax Treaty where relevant

T, an individual, was a citizen and bona fide resident of Canada. T is single and is on the cash method, calendar-year method of accounting. T has never been present in the United States. During the year, T owned the following assets:

1. 100 shares of the common stock of X Corporation—a United States corporation;

2. 100 shares of the common stock of Y Corporation—a Brazilian corporation;

3. Rental real estate located in Modesto, California (T's activities in this connection do not constitute engaging in a trade or business);

4. A loan to H, a citizen of the United States currently residing in Bolivia, in the amount of $7,000;

5. Deposit in a Chicago, Illinois bank, $20,000;

6. The rights to a patent created by T;

7. Vacant land held for investment in Oregon; and

8. 50 shares of preferred stock of Z Corporation—a United States corporation.

During the year, T received the following amounts:

a. Cash payment on the X Corporation stock, $20,000;
b. Cash payment on the Y Corporation stock, $13,000, 40 percent of its earnings for the past three years were effectively connected with a United States trade or business;
c. Rents from the rental property, $10,000;
d. Interest on the loan to H, $1,000;
e. Interest on deposit at Chicago, Illinois bank, $2,000;
f. Gain on sale of 10 shares of Z Corporation stock, $5,000; and
g. Payment pursuant to sale to W of United States rights to patent for five percent of net profits from product produced through its use, $8,000.

T's expenses for the year included:

a. Depreciation and expenses with respect to the United States rental property, $3,000;
b. Loss on the sale of five shares of Z Corporation stock, $1,000; and
c. Medical expenses, $4,500.

1. What tax consequences arise for T under the United States-Canada tax treaty assuming that none of his holdings constitutes a permanent establishment?

   a. What result if T is present in the United States for 190 days during the year?
   b. What result if T is a Brazilian and forms a Canadian corporation to conduct the activities?
   c. What result if T is a United States citizen?
   d. What result if T has a United States permanent establishment and receives a dividend from an investment unrelated to the permanent establishment?

2. Suppose in 1. that T had a $13,000 gain on the sale of T's unimproved United States realty. What result?

Chapter 7

Tax Treaties and Business Income

§ 7.01 The Taxation of Business Profits—Generally
§ 7.02 Carrying on a United States Business
Revenue Ruling 58-63, 1958-1 C.B. 624
§ 7.03 Fixed Place of Business
Unger v. Commissioner, 936 F.2d 1316 (D.C. Cir. 1991)
§ 7.04 Duration of Permanent Establishment
§ 7.05 Use of Another's Fixed Place of Business
§ 7.06 Use of Agents
§ 7.07 Dependent Agents
Revenue Ruling 90-80, 1990-2 C.B. 170
§ 7.08 Agents Versus Purchasers
Revenue Ruling 76-322, 1976-2 C.B. 487
§ 7.09 Agents Versus Lessees
§ 7.10 Scope of Business Profits Article
Revenue Ruling 86-156, 1986-2 C.B. 297
§ 7.11 Business Profits Attributable to a Permanent Establishment
§ 7.12 Determination of Income Attributable to a Permanent Establishment
§ 7.13 Allocation and Apportionment of Expenses to a Permanent Establishment
§ 7.14 Dependent Personal Services—Employees
Revenue Ruling 86-145, 1986-2 C.B. 297
§ 7.15 Independent Personal Services—Independent Contractors
§ 7.16 Computation of United States Tax Liability Under a Tax Treaty
§ 7.17 Disclosure of Treaty-Based Return Positions
Technical Explanation of United States-Canada Income Tax Treaty
Problem 7

§ 7.01 The Taxation of Business Profits— Generally

This Chapter addresses the tax treaty principles governing the receipt of business income and income from the rendition of dependent and independent services. While tax treaties address both outbound transactions (i.e., United States residents deriving income from a foreign jurisdiction) and inbound transactions (i.e., foreign residents deriving income from within the United States), the discussion in this chapter focuses primarily on inbound transactions. However, the provisions apply equally to outbound activity.

The United States taxation of business profits under a tax treaty may differ from the treatment of those profits under the Code. If a foreign individual or foreign corporation is engaged in a trade or business within the United States, the income of that taxpayer which is effectively connected with the business is subject to tax on a net basis at the usual graduated rates applicable to citizens, resident individuals, and domestic corporations.

However, income tax treaties provide that business income is taxable in the United States only if an enterprise possesses a "permanent establishment" in the United States. In the absence of a permanent establishment, the income is not taxable even if a domestic trade or business exists. Moreover, if the taxpayer has a permanent establishment, tax treaties generally tax only those "business profits" that are "attributable to" the permanent establishment. While the concepts of trade or business and effectively connected are similar to the concepts of permanent establishment and attributable to, the treaty concepts require a greater nexus and/or immersion in the country of source than do the statutory standards.

From the standpoint of the tax treaty claimant, therefore, at least four threshold questions must be asked to determine the claimant's eligibility for a treaty exemption of its business profits. First, it must be determined whether that person is "carrying on a business in the United States." Second, is that business conducted through a "permanent establishment"? Third, what are "business profits"? Finally, what business profits are "attributable" to the permanent establishment?

§ 7.02 Carrying on a United States Business

The standard for determining whether a foreign person is carrying on a business in the United States for tax treaty purposes is likely the same standard employed in determining if a person is engaged in a domestic trade or business under § 864, discussed in Chapter 9. As a generalization, the standard is similar to that required for deductibility of expenses under § 162, i.e., regularity and continuity. If a foreign person does not conduct a trade or business under § 864, it will be exempt from domestic tax on its active business profits without reliance on any treaty exemption.

Revenue Ruling 58-63
1958-1 C.B. 624

Advice has been requested whether a nonresident alien individual, owning a racing stable in France and engaged in the operation of same for profit, who enters a horse in a race in the United States, is exempt from United States income tax on the winnings therefrom.

A citizen and resident of France owned and operated a horse racing stable, located in France, for profit. He was invited to enter an outstanding horse in a race to be held in the United States. He and the racing association agreed that the horse would not compete in any other races while in the United States. The racing association invited him to view the race and participate in the social events connected therewith. The invitation was accepted. The horse won the race and the owner was paid the winner's purse.

The operation of a racing stable for profit is a business enterprise. The entry of a horse in a race in this country constitutes being "engaged in trade or business within the United Sates," within the meaning of section 871(c) of the Internal Revenue Code of 1954. Accordingly, income derived therefore is subject to United States income tax unless exempted by some other provision of law.

Article 3 of the income tax convention between the United States and France provides, in part, that an enterprise of one of the contracting states is not subject to taxation by the other contracting state in respect of its industrial and commercial profits except in respect of such profits allocable to its permanent establishment in the later state. A "French enterprise" includes every form of undertaking carried on by an individual resident of France in France. "Industrial and commercial profits" include profits derived from the industrial activity of a French enterprise. The term "permanent establishment" includes branches, mines and oil wells, plantations, factories, workshops, stories, purchasing and selling and other offices, agencies, warehouses, and other fixed places of business.

Accordingly, it is held that a nonresident alien individual does not have a permanent establishment in the United States merely by entering a race horse in a single race in the United States and coming to the United States to view the race and to participate in the social events connected therewith. While the winner's purse received by the owner of a racing stable operated for profit constitutes industrial or commercial profits, this income is exempt from United States income tax under Article 3 of the income tax convention between the United States and France.

§ 7.03 Fixed Place of Business

The existence of a "permanent establishment" in a tax treaty country is often the critical nexus for that treaty country's taxation of business profits. Treaties generally equate a permanent establishment with a fixed place of business. A permanent establishment is often described as "a fixed place of business through which the business of an enterprise is wholly or partly carried on." A permanent establishment may include (1) a place of management; (2) a branch; (3) an office; (4) a factory; (5) a workshop; (6) a warehouse; and (7) a mine, oil or gas well, a quarry, or any other place of extraction of natural resources.

Treaties also provide some guidance as to what activities will *not* constitute a permanent establishment. Many common arrangements with respect to merchandise or goods do not constitute permanent establishment. For instance, the use of facilities or the maintenance of a stock of goods solely for the purpose of storage, display, or delivery is not a permanent establishment. Neither does the use of a facility for ancillary business purposes generally equate to a permanent establishment. No permanent establishment arises from the maintenance of a fixed place of business solely for the purpose of purchasing goods or merchandise, collecting information, or carrying on any other activity of a preparatory or auxiliary character. Similarly, no permanent establishment exists if goods are maintained solely for processing by another.

Some treaties permit inventory to be stored by a foreign person in a United States warehouse for quick delivery to domestic customers without that inventory stock (or the warehouse in which it is stored) constituting a permanent establishment. Similarly, the use by a foreign person of a United States showroom or a demonstration room to display or demonstrate the use of its products to domestic customers will not constitute a United States permanent establishment.

Perhaps for pragmatic reasons, the Service has broadly construed the scope of the "preparatory or auxiliary activities" that do not give rise to a permanent establishment. In Revenue Ruling 72-418, the Service applied the exception to the activities of a United States office of a German bank. In that Ruling, the bank maintained a United States office to: obtain information on various banking and financial matters including credit reports on American banks; assist the bank's domestic and German customers with information and letters of introduction to American banks and firms; maintain contacts with American banks and firms and provide the same with information on German financial conditions; occasionally communicate with the bank's domestic debtors and obtain information on repayment possibilities; and advertise for the bank throughout the United States.

Despite these relatively substantial domestic activities, the Service ruled that the bank was exempt from tax on its United States profits under Article 2(1)(c) of the former German treaty. That treaty excluded from permanent establishment status any "fixed place of business for the collection of information for the enterprise, or for the purpose of advertising, for the supply of information, for scientific research or for similar activities, if they have a preparatory or auxiliary character."

Apparently, the Service reasoned that the German bank's core activities consisted of loan activity to United States customers and negotiating essential terms and conditions. Since the United States office did not engage in such core activities but confined itself to general marketing and informational activities, it engaged only in "preparatory or auxiliary" activities. Thus, that office did not give rise to a United States permanent establishment.

The Service construed the term "permanent establishment" with respect to the United States-Canada treaty in Revenue Ruling 77-45. There, a Canadian corporation contracted to plan and design a manufacturing plant in the United States. Most design and other services were performed by the corporation in Canada. However, employees were sent to the United States site to inspect contractor work performance, to prepare reports, and to perform other duties. The Service ruled that a permanent establishment did *not* exist under the Canadian treaty in force. Insufficient United States nexus existed given that the United States-based employees were not authorized to make major decisions covering basic plant design. In addition, employees used a United States building provided by the domestic client without separately bargained for consideration and the project lasted less than one year.

A permanent establishment may indirectly arise by virtue of a foreign person's ownership interest in a pass-through entity. For instance, a permanent establishment may be imputed to a foreign partner in a limited or general partnership if the partnership itself has a United States permanent establishment. If that partnership earns business profits, the foreign partner's distributive share of such profits retains its partnership-level character upon pass-through. As that partner is vicariously deemed to have a United States permanent establishment, the partner's share of partnership business profits will not be insulated from taxation under a treaty in the hands of the distributee partner. In contrast, stock ownership of, or affiliation with, entities or persons with a United States permanent establishment does not in itself appear to be sufficient grounds to impute a permanent establishment to the owner or affiliate.

Unger v. Commissioner
United States Court of Appeals, District of Columbia Circuit
936 F.2d 1316 (1991)

BUCKLEY, CIRCUIT JUDGE:
We are asked to determine whether the United States-Canada Income Tax Convention of 1942 permits the United States to tax a Canadian resident's distributable share of capital gain realized by a Massachusetts partnership in which he is a limited partner. On the settled authority of *Donroy, Ltd. v. United States*, 301 F.2d 200 (9th Cir.1962), we hold that it does.

I. Background

In 1984, the Charles River Park "C" Company ("Company"), a Massachusetts limited partnership, sold real estate in Boston, Massachusetts. The sale produced a long-term capital gain that was distributed among the Company's seven general and twenty-two limited partners. Among those limited partners was Robert Unger, a resident of British Columbia, Canada. His share of the gain totalled $289,260.

Mr. Unger did not include this sum as taxable income on his 1984 United States Nonresident Alien Income Tax Return. Instead, he indicated that as he had no "permanent establishment" in the United States, this income was exempt from taxation by the United States under the Tax Convention. The Internal Revenue Service disagreed....

II. Discussion

Article I of the Tax Convention provides in relevant part:

An enterprise of one of the contracting States is not subject to taxation by the other contracting State in respect of its industrial and commercial profits except in respect of such profits allocable in accordance with the Articles of this Convention to its permanent establishment in the latter State.

As defined in the Convention's first Protocol, "the term 'enterprise' includes every form of undertaking, whether carried on by an individual, partnership, corporation or any other entity," Protocol § 3(b); "the term 'permanent establishment' includes branches, . . . offices, agencies and other fixed places of business of an enterprise," *id.* § 3(f).

The question, then, turns on the nature of a limited partnership. If Mr. Unger's interest as a limited partner in the Company gives him an interest in its offices, he has a permanent establishment in Boston that makes his share of the Company's profits taxable by the United States. If he has no permanent establishment here, this income is exempt.

Two views have long competed regarding the basic nature of a partnership. The "aggregate theory" considers a partnership to be no more than an aggregation of individual partners. Under this theory, each partner has an interest in the property of the partnership; thus, Mr. Unger would be deemed to have a permanent establishment in the United States. The "entity theory" characterizes a partnership as a separate entity; under this view, the offices would be attributable to the partnership but not the partners, and Mr. Unger would not be deemed to have a permanent establishment in this country. Courts remain ambivalent in their treatment of partnerships, dealing with them as aggregates for certain purposes and as entities for others. . . .

The Internal Revenue Code . . . treats partnerships as aggregates for some purposes and as separate entities for others. A partnership must calculate income as a discrete entity. The obligation to pay taxes, however, passes through the partnership to the individual partners. The conflict between the aggregate and the entity views, then, carries over to the realm of federal taxation.

Mr. Unger argues that whatever the merits of the aggregate theory where ordinary partnerships are concerned, it should not be applied to limited partnerships. He maintains that a limited partner should be likened to (and taxed the same way as) a corporate shareholder, as both risk only the capital they have chosen to put at stake. In contrast, a general partner has full personal liability for partnership debts. Moreover, like a shareholder, a limited partner may not participate in the active management of the enterprise; indeed, if he should, he will lose his protected status and become fully liable as a general partner. Mr. Unger also points out that the distinctions between general and limited partnerships can be dispositive. Courts have chosen, for example, to protect partnership assets from execution by judgment creditors of a limited partner, and to ignore the citizenship of limited partners, but not that of general partners, in determining diversity jurisdiction.

Mr. Unger makes a number of valid observations about the intricacies and inconsistencies that exist in the law of partnership as it has evolved in various jurisdictions, but he fails to provide any persuasive reason, based on either Massachusetts partnership law or the facts of this case, for us to disregard what has come to be viewed as settled law under the Tax Convention.

In 1962, in *Donroy*, the Ninth Circuit was called upon to deal with an almost identical case. It involved Canadian corporations that were limited partners of two California partnerships whose principal offices were located in San Francisco. The court examined the relevant California partnership law and concluded that the aggregate theory was to be applied in determining whether the Canadian partners had a permanent establishment in the United States. It concluded that "the office or permanent establishment of the partnership is in law, the office of each of the partners—whether general or limited." The court also noted that "the United States and Canada look, not to the partnership as such, but to the distributive income of the individual partners for income tax purposes." Thus the application of the aggregate theory in *Donroy* was consistent with the manner in which partnership income was actually taxed by both parties to the Convention. . . .

Although Mr. Unger attempts to draw factual distinctions between the two cases, we find no material differences between them. Mr. Unger chose limited partnership interest as a form of passive investment, and asserts that the Canadian corporations in *Donroy* became limited partners in California limited partnerships in order to expand their business. This assertion apparently rests on statements the district court mentioned as issues for future litigation, and on the Canadian partners' compliance with California's rule that a limited partnership will not be licensed as a liquor wholesaler unless each of the limited partners is qualified to transact business in California. The requirement applied regardless of whether the limited partners actually engaged in the conduct of business. These slim reeds cannot support a conclusion that these limited partners were so actively involved in the conduct of business as to make *Donroy* inapplicable here.

As the Tax Court noted, the factual distinctions between these cases are inconsequential. Whatever their reasons, both Mr. Unger and the Canadian limited partners in *Donroy* participated in the same form of business organization; and *Donroy* held that, as a matter of law, it was the ownership of a limited partnership interest that resulted in a permanent establishment in the United States. As Mr. Unger has failed to cite any legal authority or factual differences that would require a contrary conclusion, we find that *Donroy* is dispositive of this case; and we do so for reasons that go beyond the respect that one circuit will normally accord the decisions of another. . . .

III. Conclusion

We hold that as a result of his limited partnership interest in the Company, Mr. Unger had a permanent establishment in the United States within the meaning of the United States-Canada Income Tax Convention. As a consequence, his share of the partnership gains is taxable by the United States. The Tax Court's decision is therefore affirmed.

§ 7.04 Duration of Permanent Establishment

Even if a foreign person uses a United States office or other fixed place of business, a permanent establishment should not arise if the use of that office or fixed place of business is brief or transitory rather than permanent. What represents brief, as opposed to permanent, use will vary based on the facts and circumstances of each particular case. Permanent establishment status has been avoided, however, in cases where the use of a fixed place of business lasted for less than 12 months. In contrast, conducting *significant* business operations at a site for abbreviated time periods has been found to give rise to a permanent establishment.

§ 7.05 Use of Another's Fixed Place of Business

Business exigencies, particularly for multinational entities, often necessitate the use by foreign employees of the domestic offices or establishments of a United States affiliate. This practical necessity implicates the issue of the permitted extent of such use before the foreign entity runs afoul of the permanent establishment provisions. Clearly, the use of United States hotel rooms by the employees of a foreign person on a temporary and transient basis should not give rise to a domestic permanent establishment. By analogy, the temporary and transient use of a domestic subsidiary's office by employees of a foreign parent corporation should not constitute a permanent establishment.

However, the tables may expectedly turn if the employees of a foreign corporation make frequent and continuous use of another's domestic office or fixed place of business for substantial periods of time. In that case, the fact that the office is not owned by the foreign corporation is not likely to be sufficient detachment to negate the existence of a permanent establishment.

§ 7.06 Use of Agents

The use of a United States office or other fixed place of business by employees of a foreign person may give rise to a permanent establishment. A similar risk arises if the foreign person conducts business through an agent who effectively serves as its United States alterego. United States tax treaties generally provide that the office of a person (an "agent") who acts on behalf of a foreign taxpayer (a "principal") may be imputed to that taxpayer under certain circumstances.

Most treaties contains two pertinent and typical treaty limitations on imputing an agent's trade or business to the principal. First, a foreign person does not have a permanent establishment solely because it conducts business in the United States through a broker, general commission agent, or any other agent of an *independent* status, so long as that agent acts in the ordinary course of its business. Second, if a foreign person conducts United States business through a *dependent* agent, that agent's activities are imputed only to that principal for which the agent has and habitually exercises in the United States the authority to conclude contracts in the name of principal.

Some delineating distinctions between independent and dependent agents exist. An independent agent is a general commission agent, broker, or other agent of an independent status acting in the ordinary course of his business in that capacity. Such an agent is a paid agent who, in pursuance of his usual trade or business, sells goods or merchandise consigned or entrusted to him for that purpose by or for the owner of such goods or merchandise.

A dependent agent is one which truly stands in the stead of the principal, conducting business in its place. A dependent agent is one who has the authority to negotiate and conclude contracts in the name of the principal or who holds stock or merchandise of the principal and regularly fills orders from that stock on behalf of the principal. Incidental or occasional contractual or merchandising activity is insufficient to render an agent a dependent agent. The dependent agent's power to conclude contracts on behalf of the principal or its power to fill orders must be exercised with "some frequency over a continuous period of time." Occasional or incidental activity does not evidence regularity.

§ 7.07 Dependent Agents

Recent United States tax treaties provide for a fairly generous cushion of dependent agent activity that may take place before a principal is deemed to have a permanent establishment. The domestic activities of a dependent agent will trigger imputation of a permanent establishment to the foreign principal only if that agent has and habitually exercises in the United States authority to conclude contracts "in the name of the principal." Thus, the mere fact that an agent concludes certain contracts in the United States is not per se evidence of a permanent establishment. Rather, a permanent establishment arises only if the agent executes contracts setting forth the name of its foreign *principal* as the contracting party.

Assume, for example, that a foreign corporation manufactures goods and ships those goods to its wholly owned domestic subsidiary. Under the above standard, the subsidiary may warehouse the goods and arrange for their delivery to the United States customer without creating a permanent establishment for the parent corporation, so long as the subsidiary does not "conclude contracts" for the sale of the goods."

Revenue Ruling 90-80
1990-2 C.B. 170

ISSUE

Are the foreign persons in the two situations described below subject to United States tax on gain from barter transactions in the United States?

. . .

FACTS

. . . .

Situation 2

D, a citizen and resident of FC [a treaty country], wished to invest $20,000 in the United States. On January 1, 1989, D entered into a written agreement (the Agreement) with C, a citizen and resident of the United States. The Agreement gives C the authority to negotiate and conclude barter transactions in D's name. C will act only on behalf of D in these transactions, will be under D's management and control, and will have no other employment during 1989.

Acting under the Agreement, C maintained an office and performed bartering activities. After paying C for his services, D made a profit of $70,000 on the 1989 barter transactions.

LAW AND ANALYSIS

Under section 1001 of the Code, gain or loss will be recognized on each separate barter exchange. The amount of gain or loss will be the difference between the adjusted basis of the property exchanged and the fair market value of the property received. . . .

. . . .

Situation 2

C has and habitually exercises in the United States the authority to conclude barter contracts and transactions in D's name. C is not an independent agent because C has no other employment during 1989 and is under D's management and control. Therefore, under Article 5 of the Convention, D has a permanent establishment in the United States in 1989 by virtue of the activities C undertakes for D and the office maintained by C for the purpose of conducting D's barter transactions.

Since D is treated as having a permanent establishment in the United States, under Article 7(1) of the Convention, the 1989 business profits of D that are attributable to its United States permanent establishment are taxable in the United States. The $70,000 profit that D derived from the barter transactions is attributable to D's United States permanent establishment, and thus, those profits are subject to tax . . . . D must file a 1989 United States tax return.

Accordingly, P does not have a permanent establishment in the United States within the meaning of the Convention. Therefore, the income derived by P from transactions with S, it's subsidiary, in accordance with the terms of the agreement discussed herein, is not subject to Federal income tax.

§ 7.09 Agents Versus Lessees

For tax treaty purposes, lessees are also distinguished from agents. A bona fide lessee of property or equipment is *not* an agent of the lessor. Thus, if a domestic entity leases personal property from a foreign lessor eligible for treaty benefits, neither the existence of the lease nor the presence of leased personal property within the United States should give rise to a United States permanent establishment for the lessor. In contrast, the lease of domestic *real* property by a foreign person may give rise to a permanent establishment merely by virtue of the United States nexus of that property. Such presence alone may suffice as a basis for generating a permanent establishment unless the tenant assumed primary responsibility for maintenance and repair while the lessor provided minimal services was *not* a domestic trade or business.

§ 7.10 Scope of Business Profits Article

If a treaty claimant has no permanent establishment in the United States, that claimant's business profits or industrial or commercial profits may be exempt from taxation. The term "business profits" generally includes income derived from any trade or business. Therefore, any income derived from the conduct of an active business is characterized as business profits.

The business profits article is powerful in that it can convert to taxable status the character of items typically governed by other treaty articles that would exempt or reduce taxation on those items. For instance, royalties may normally be exempt from United States tax as a "royalty," but by being characterized as business profits attributable to a permanent establishment, those royalties become taxable in the United States. Some treaties hinge the priority of competing articles on whether the income is attributable to a permanent establishment.

If a foreign person maintains and derives income through a United States permanent establishment, such income typically will be subject to tax by operation of the treaty's business profits article on a net basis. This treatment holds true even if that income represents, for instance, interest income which is the subject of a separate treaty article. Thus, if income arises from an active business and is derived through a United States permanent establishment, the tax treatment afforded by the business profits article of a tax treaty generally overrides other treaty articles dealing with specific types of income.

Conversely, if a foreign person does *not* maintain a United States permanent establishment or derives United States source income unrelated to a permanent establishment, the treaty article (if any) dealing with that specific type of income generally controls. For example, if a foreign corporation maintains a permanent establishment and receives a United States source dividend from a portfolio investment unrelated to that permanent establishment, the dividend income will be subject to a reduced withholding tax under the dividend article of the relevant tax treaty.

Revenue Ruling 86-156
1986-2 C.B. 297

ISSUE

Whether photocopy machines are "other like property" within the meaning of Article IX of the United States-Netherlands Income Tax Convention (the Treaty) and, if not, whether payments for the lease thereof constitute industrial or commercial profits within the meaning of Article III of the Treaty.

FACTS

P, a corporation organized under the laws of the Netherlands, owns 100 percent of the stock of S, a corporation organized under the laws of the United States. P manufactures photocopy machines and leases them to S, and S makes periodic rental payments to P. P carries on a portion of its manufacturing operations in the Netherlands. P is not engaged in a trade or business within the United States through a permanent establishment. S subleases the photocopy machines to its United States customers.

LAW AND ANALYSIS

Article IX of the Treaty . . . specifically exempted United States source royalties paid to a Netherlands corporation for the use of industrial, commercial, or scientific equipment, provided that the Netherlands corporation was not engaged in a trade or business within the United States through a permanent establishment.

Article IX(2) . . . exempts United States source royalties, rentals, or amounts paid as consideration for the use of, or right to use, copyrights, artistic or scientific works, patents, designs, plans, secret processes or formulae, trademarks, motion picture films, films or tapes for radio or television broadcasting, or other like property or rights, or information concerning industrial, commercial or scientific knowledge, experience or skill, provided that the Netherlands corporation does not have a permanent establishment within the United States to which such amounts are attributable.

Article III(1) of the Treaty . . . exempts industrial or commercial profits derived by a Netherlands enterprise to the extent not attributable to a permanent establishment in the United States. Article II(1)(g) defines a Netherlands enterprise as an industrial or commercial enterprise or undertaking carried on in the Netherlands by the taxpayer. Article III(5) of the Treaty . . . provides that industrial or commercial profits means income derived from the active conduct of a trade or business, but does not include income described in Article IX(2). . . .

Where payments for the use of industrial, commercial or scientific equipment are to be exempted by the royalties article in a treaty, that article specifically states that such property is included within its scope. Therefore, the phrase "other like property or rights" contained in Article IX(2) of the Treaty . . . modifies only the items specifically enumerated in Article IX(2). The items of tangible property included in Article IX(2) are tapes, films, and artistic or scientific works. None of the items enumerated could possibly incorporate equipment. Consequently, the phrase "other like property or rights" cannot be interpreted to refer to industrial, commercial, or scientific equipment. Payments for the use of industrial, commercial or scientific equipment, therefore, are not covered by Article IX(2) and are exempt, if at all, under the business profits article (Article III) of the Treaty.

Article III(5) of the Treaty defines "industrial or commercial profits" as "income derived from the active conduct of a trade or business." Article III(1) provides that the exemption for industrial or commercial profits derived by a Netherlands enterprise is applicable only to income that is not attributable to a permanent establishment in the United States.

The phrases "industrial or commercial profits" and "income derived from the active conduct of a trade or business" do not require such profits or income of the Netherlands enterprise be derived by an active trade or business within the United States, but merely require that the income be derived from the active conduct of a trade or business conducted in whole or in part in the Netherlands by the Netherlands enterprise.

Article III of the Treaty, therefore, exempts United States source rentals or other payments for the use of industrial, commercial, or scientific equipment, provided that such amounts are attributable to a trade or business actively conducted in whole or in part in the Netherlands by the Netherlands enterprise and are not attributable to a permanent establishment in the United States.

HOLDING

Under the facts of this case, the rentals for photocopy machines derived by P from S constitute industrial or commercial profits derived by a Netherlands enterprise. Furthermore, the rentals are not attributable to a permanent establishment of P in the United States. Therefore, the rentals are exempt from United States tax under Article III of the Treaty.

§ 7.11 Business Profits Attributable to a Permanent Establishment

Under many tax treaties, if a foreign person maintains a United States permanent establishment, any business profits "attributable to" that permanent establishment are subject to tax on a net basis at the graduated rates generally applicable to domestic taxpayers. Business profits are attributable to a permanent establishment if the assets or activities of that establishment play a meaningful role in generating those profits. For example, if a foreign taxpayer is engaged in a domestic trade or business through a permanent establishment and that taxpayer makes an isolated sale of inventory in the United States from an unrelated business wholly independent of the assets or activities of the permanent establishment, the domestic source profit realized is not attributable to the foreign person's permanent establishment.

In the tax treaty context, Congress, eager to stimulate foreign investment in the United States, requires that income be attributable to the taxpayer's permanent establishment before subjecting that income to the graduated rates. This treatment ensures that investment/passive income retains such status and bears a treaty rate of zero-15 percent, while "true" business income would be subjected to the graduated rates of § 1 or § 11. This distinction also ensures that a foreign person conducting a domestic trade or business does not confront the disincentive of high tax rates with respect to the nonbusiness investment of his surplus funds.

Though the fundamental taxing framework applicable to a foreign person's business income parallels that applicable to domestic persons, the method of computing a foreign person's net income from a permanent establishment subject to tax is distinct and complex. Generally, the determination of such income follows a three-step sequence. First, the gross income derived by the foreign person attributable to a permanent establishment must be segregated from any other foreign or domestic source income which is not attributable to that permanent establishment. Next, the foreign person's expenses related to the permanent establishment must be segregated. Once determined, these expenses must be allocated between income attributable to the permanent establishment and other income.

§ 7.12 Determination of Income Attributable to a Permanent Establishment

The first step in taxing a foreign person deriving business profits from a permanent establishment involves separating the income attributable to that business from other income. Attributable to income encompasses two principal categories of income: (1) fixed or determinable income and capital gain or loss from sources within the United States; and (2) some foreign source income.

The determination of whether income is attributable to a permanent establishment is discussed in the text of the Technical Explanations of many recently signed treaties. Mechanisms are provided for segregating passive income from business income. They generally utilize two tests: one to be applied to taxpayers such as foreign sellers or manufacturers dealing with tangible goods in the United States (the "asset use" test) and the other to be applied to taxpayers such as those conducting service-intensive businesses or those dealing with the licensing of intangible assets (the "material factor" test).

Foreign persons engaged in business, e.g., the manufacture or sale of tangible goods, in the United States who concomitantly derive passive income items in the course of that business generally face the asset use test. This test seeks to distinguish income derived from holding investment assets from income generated by using assets in the day-to-day operation of the permanent establishment. The asset use test focuses on whether the income is derived from assets used, or held for use, in the conduct of a United States trade or business through a permanent establishment.

Three factors are considered in deciding whether an asset is used, or held for use, in a United States business: (1) whether the asset is held for the principal purpose of promoting the *present* conduct of a United States trade or business; (2) whether the asset is acquired and held in the ordinary course of the trade or business; and (3) whether the asset is otherwise held in some direct relationship to the trade or business. If the asset is deemed to be a business asset under one of these standards, all income flowing from its use is attributable to the permanent establishment.

A rebuttable presumption generally exists that the requisite relationship is present for purposes of the asset use test if the asset is acquired with funds generated by the trade or business, the income generated from the asset is reinvested in that trade or business, and United States personnel actively involved in that business exercise significant management and control over the investment of the asset. This presumption can be rebutted if the foreign person demonstrates that an asset is held to carry out some future business purpose and not to meet present business needs.

Stock or securities dealing or service-intensive businesses involving the licensing of intangible assets confront the material factor test for determining whether passive income is attributable to that permanent establishment. The controlling determination is whether the activities of the domestic trade or business are a material factor in realizing that passive income.

Unlike the asset use test, which focuses narrowly on the role of particular income-generating assets in business operations, the material factor test focuses on the more overarching measure of the degree of correlation with the business activities of the foreign person's United States permanent establishment. Such income is considered "attributable to" if the United States activities of that business are a material factor in the realization of such items of income, gain, or loss.

Generally, a United States permanent establishment will not be a material factor in generating income if the core activities incident to the transaction are conducted abroad. For instance, such would be the case in a patent licensing context where the license negotiation and consummation occurs abroad by foreign employees and the United States branch plays no role in otherwise arranging for the licenses.

Many treaties provide that the determination of attributable to income can incorporate domestic rules which attribute income, even foreign source, to the taxing jurisdiction. Generally, income, gain, or loss from sources *without* the United States is not attributable to a domestic permanent establishment. However, limited exceptions are provided if the income is one of three specified types of income having a significant genesis in domestic business activities and if it is attributable to the corporation's office or other fixed place of business within the United States. The categories of income, which are discussed in detail in Chapter 10, are:

1. Rents, royalties, or gains from intangible property,
2. Dividends, interest, or gains from the sale of stock or securities, and
3. Income from the sale of personal property inventory items.

Income will *not* be attributable to a United States office or fixed place of business unless that establishment was a material factor in the realization of that income, i.e., it provides "a significant contribution to the production of that income" and its activities are an "essential economic element in the production of income."

If foreign sellers of inventory and other tangible property can prove that the property was sold for use, consumption, or disposition outside of the United States *and* that a foreign office materially participated in a sale, it is irrelevant if a domestic office also played a significant role. To determine whether a foreign office participated materially in a sale, the activities of that office must be scrutinized to determine if it performed significant services necessary for the consummation of the sale. Soliciting and negotiating are clearly significant services. In such a case, none of the foreign source sales income will be subject to United States taxation. For example, the receipt of a sales order by a United States office or fixed place of business will result in that locale being deemed a material factor in the realization of that income "except where the sales order is received unsolicited and that office is not held out to potential customers as the place to which such sales orders should be sent."

The country of ultimate use will generally be considered the country of destination of that property. If at the time of the sale, the taxpayer knew or should have known that the property would not be used in that country of destination, the onus rests upon the taxpayer to determine the true country of ultimate use. Without such proof, the United States is presumed to be that country. However, a taxpayer who sells property to a person whose principal business consists of selling from inventory to retail customers at foreign retail outlets may, in the interest of efficiency, presume that the property will be used abroad.

An office or fixed place of business is generally a place, site, structure, or other fixed facility through which a foreign person engages in business. The term includes a wide variety of geographic locales—factories, stores and other sales outlets, workshops, mines, quarries, and other places of natural resource extraction. The facility need not be continuously used by the foreign person or his agent to be so classified. If the facility happens to be another related or unrelated person's office or place of business, sporadic use of that office should not cause that office or fixed place of business to be imputed to the taxpayer-user.

Special rules are provided with regard to the offices in the United States of various agents employed by the foreign person. Agents are classified as either independent or dependent agents. The office of a general commission agent, broker, or other *independent* agent will not be considered an office of the foreign principal when that agent acts solely within the ordinary course of his business in that capacity. However, if an agent acts exclusively, or almost exclusively, for a particular foreign principal or if both principal and agent are controlled by the same interests, independent agent status may be threatened.

Generally, the office of a *dependent* agent will also be disregarded unless the agent has the authority to negotiate and conclude contracts in the name of the foreign principal and regularly exercises that authority *or* has a stock of merchandise belonging to the foreign person from which orders are regularly filled. A special rule applies to dependent agents who are also employees. If employee-agents regularly carry on the business of their employer in the ordinary course of their duties in a United States fixed facility, that fixed facility will be imputed to their foreign employer-principal. This result ensues regardless of the scope of the employee's authority to contract or fill orders on behalf of the foreign principal.

§ 7.13 Allocation and Apportionment of Expenses to a Permanent Establishment

Given the business genesis underlying the attributable to concept, it is only proper that the foreign person be entitled to offset that income with the expenses incurred to earn such income. Generally, a two-tiered method accomplishes this task; the two distinct tiers being, first, "allocation" and then, if necessary, "apportionment." The allocation process is the threshold determination which focuses on whether an expense is directly related to a particular class of gross income. In effect, the task of allocating deductions involves matching those deductions with the gross income to which they most directly relate.

Once deductions are matched with a particular class of gross income, the composition of that particular class of gross income must be analyzed to determine whether it is comprised solely of United States source income, solely foreign source income, or some combination of both. As the term and procedure suggest, the apportionment of allocated deductions within a class of gross income is required only in the last scenario. When apportionment is required, the deduction already allocated to that mixed-source class of gross income under the first-tier allocation procedure is, in effect, further divided between the foreign source income and United States source income comprising that class of gross income.

For example, assume that domestic accounting firm performing services in both the United Kingdom and the United States. The firm's headquarters is in the United States, and it has a branch office abroad staffed by resident members. In the course of its operations, the firm will derive United States and foreign source income from the rendition of services and possibly interest income from both jurisdictions from short-term investment of excess cash reserves. Expenses include those for personnel, rent, utilities, and the like.

Expenses directly related to the rendition of services, namely salaries, rent, etc., are allocable to the class of gross income derived from services. Some expenses, such as supervisory or general and administrative expense, are not definitely related to any class of income and are thus most likely allocated to *all* classes of gross income. As the two presumed classes of gross income (i.e., income from services and interest income) are comprised of both foreign and United States source gross income, allocated expenses must further be apportioned between those two types of income.

The process of apportioning deductions occurs within a class of gross income and matches deductions with the foreign or United States source income to which they are related. For these purposes, once a deduction has been allocated to a class of gross income, the source of the gross income item(s) comprising that class must be determined. If the class consists exclusively of attributable to income or exclusively of non-attributable income, the taxpayer fortunately may end its analysis after the allocation process is completed. The deduction is allocated in its entirety.

If the class of gross income to which a deduction has been allocated is comprised of *both* attributable to and non-attributable to income, that deduction must be apportioned between those two groupings of income. The apportionment process is accomplished in a fact-based manner which reflects to a reasonably close extent the factual relationship between the deduction and the gross income grouping. Examples of bases and factors which may be considered in making this factual determination include comparisons of sales, gross receipts, cost of goods sold, profit contributions, expenses and intangible costs incurred in generating the activity, and gross income.

§ 7.14 Dependent Personal Services— Employees

Tax treaties may contain special rules governing the taxation of income derived by an individual from performing personal services. Often these rules distinguish between dependent and independent personal services.

"Dependent personal services" treaty articles generally encompass those services performed by employees. Under many treaties, compensation derived by a foreign individual eligible for treaty benefits is not subject to United States tax if the recipient is present in the United States for 183 days or less in the taxable year, the compensation is paid by or on behalf of a foreign employer, and such amount is not borne by the employer's United States permanent establishment or fixed base. Some treaties also cap the amount of compensation that the recipient can receive to remain eligible for treaty benefits.

By contrast, under § 864(b), a nonresident individual who performs services in the United States is treated (but for a limited exception) as engaged in the conduct of a domestic trade or business. Thus, compensation attributable to such services is generally taxed on a net basis at the tax rates applicable to domestic taxpayers under § 1.

Treaties may also restrict benefits to employees who work for particular employers. For instance, an individual who performs services on behalf of a *foreign* employer may be protected by tax treaty only if the employee provides services for a treaty country employer resident in that country. In contrast, such an exemption will not apply to an individual who comes to the United States and works for a *domestic* employer.

A bona fide employer-employee relationship must exist between the foreign treaty individual and the foreign employer to secure such treaty exemptions. For example, if a foreign individual establishes a foreign corporation to "employ" him shortly before a United States tour, the Service will likely assert that no true employer-employee relationship exists. If the corporate employer lacks substance (i.e., it merely serves as a shell for the efforts of the individual), the Service will most likely treat the foreign corporate employer as an agent of the "employee" when the employer receives United States source payments.

This recharacterization serves to deny the application of the dependent services exemption to the foreign individual. However, under some treaties, the foreign individual's United States source compensation may still be exempt under an independent services article.

In some situations, treaty benefits cannot be extended if the compensation sought to be excluded is deducted on a United States tax return filed by the foreign employer or by another person. Such a limitation prevents double dipping into tax benefits by both exempting the recipient's income from taxation and claiming a corresponding deduction from the payor's United States taxable income.

Some tax treaties limit the amount of income that may be received by a claimant for dependent services, such as a $10,000 limit on domestic services. If the limit is exceeded, *all* United States source compensation is taxable; the first $10,000 may not be excluded.

Revenue Ruling 86-145
1986-2 C.B. 297

ISSUE

Whether the term "tax year concerned" as used in Article 15(2)(a) of the United States-United Kingdom Income Tax Convention ("Convention") . . . refers to the tax year in which personal services are performed or to the tax year in which compensation for those services is received.

FACTS

A, a United Kingdom resident, was present in the United States for more than 183 days in 1985. A performed personal services during that period for an employer who was not a resident of the United States and who had no permanent establishment or fixed base in the United States. With respect to 1985, A was a resident of the United Kingdom and was not deemed a resident of the United States under Article 4 of the Convention. A was present in the United States for 30 days in 1986 and during that period was paid for the services performed when present in the United States in 1985. In each of those years, A's United States tax year was the calendar year.

LAW AND ANALYSIS

Article 15(1) of the Convention provides the general rule that remuneration in respect of employment is taxable in the Contracting State where the employment is performed.

Article 15(2) of the Convention provides that, notwithstanding Article 15(1), remuneration derived by a resident of a Contracting State in respect of an employment exercised in the other Contracting State shall be taxable only in the first-mentioned State if:

    (a)   the recipient is present in that other State for a period not exceeding in the aggregate 183 days *in the tax year concerned;* and

    (b)   the remuneration is paid by, or on behalf of, an employer who is not a resident of that other State; and

    (c)   the remuneration is not borne as such by a permanent establishment or a fixed base which the employer has in that other State. [Emphasis added.]

The Treasury Department Technical Explanation of the Convention states that Article 15 of the Convention is based on Article 15 (Dependent Persons Services) of the 1977 OECD Model Convention (Model Convention). Article 15(1) of the Model Convention has a rule and exception similar to Article 15(2)(a) of the Convention. The focus of this exception is "employment of short duration abroad. . . . The exemption is limited to the 183-day period." Thus, the use of the term "in the tax year concerned" as part of the limitation on that exemption refers to the tax year in which the employment services being compensated are performed, and not to the tax year in which the compensation for the services is received.

Since A was present in the United States for more than 183 days in 1985, the exemption from United States taxation under Article 15(2) of the Convention is unavailable to A with respect to the services A rendered during that year. The exemption is unavailable with respect to those services notwithstanding that A was paid for them in 1986 when A was present in the United States for less than 183 days.

HOLDING

For purposes of the 183-day limitation to the exemption under Article 15(2)(a) of the Convention, the term "tax year concerned" refers to the tax year in which the services being compensated are performed in a Contracting State by a resident of the other Contracting State and not to the tax year in which compensation for services is received.

§ 7.15 Independent Personal Services—Independent Contractors

Tax treaties may exempt from United States taxation income earned by a foreign individual from services provided independently, namely as an independent contractor. Independent personal services are those "performed by an individual for his own account." Income derived by a foreign individual for the performance of independent services will generally be subject to tax only if the services are performed in the United States and the income is attributable to a domestic fixed base regularly available to the individual for the purpose of performing those services. The exemption for independent services income may be limited by treaty in a manner similar to the limitations imposed on dependent personal services. For instance, some treaties impose a limitation on the number of days a provider of independent services may be present in the United States.

The independent services exemption has been applied *inter alia* to a boxer; a promoter; a performer who gives concerts; a stage director; a production designer; a cameraman; and an individual serving on a board of directors. Independent services should also include professional services such as those performed by doctors, lawyers, and architects.

The existence of a fixed base from which independent services are performed serves much the same role in creating a taxing nexus as a permanent establishment. The term "fixed base" is premised on a permanent center of activity. A fixed base will generally be a site other than the individual's residence. If, however, an individual uses part of a residence for business purposes, that residence may nonetheless constitute a fixed base.

It appears that the concept of a fixed base may subsume the concept of a permanent establishment. For example, if a concert artist retained an independent, unrelated United States corporation as his representative to promote and arrange domestic tours and was present in the United States for 36 days during his tour, this should not give rise to a fixed base in the United States. Since the domestic corporation was an independent agent working in the ordinary course of its business, the artist did not have a permanent establishment. Therefore, the artist should not have a fixed base in the United States.

Extending the durational parameters with respect to a permanent establishment, it should be possible for a foreign person to spend a relatively short time period in the United States without creating a fixed base. Longer periods of presence may be acceptable, especially where a person is mobile.

§ 7.16 Computation of United States Tax Liability Under a Tax Treaty

A foreign treaty country resident deriving United States source income faces several potential tax scenarios in computing the amount of its tax liability: all, none, or part of its income may be governed by a treaty. Foreign persons facing the first two scenarios are easily handled, since the tax results are tallied exclusively under either the treaty or the Code.

The more difficult cases are those hybrid cases in which some of the foreign person's income is governed by treaty while the rest is not or, while governed by treaty, the statutory provision imposes a lower rate, e.g., interest income taxed at ten percent under the treaty but qualifying for the portfolio interest exception under the Code which exempts the income from tax. The Regulations provide that, in such cases, the foreign person's income is bifurcated between "treaty income" and "nontreaty income." Thereafter, the tax liabilities on treaty and nontreaty income are separately determined. Once calculated, the results are combined to yield the taxpayer's tentative tax liability. However, if the tentative tax liability exceeds the tax liability that would have arisen had no tax treaty been in effect and the statutory rates had been applied, the lesser United States tax liability determined under the Code will control.

§ 7.17 Disclosure of Treaty-Based Return Positions

Section 6114 ensures that the Service is afforded an opportunity to evaluate the legitimacy of foreign persons' claims that United States income is insulated from taxation by a governing tax treaty. Under § 6114, any person who claims that a tax treaty overrides or modifies otherwise applicable Code provisions must disclose and support that claim. However, the Service may in its discretion waive this requirement.

The Regulations state that a foreign person must file a tax return if that person takes a "treaty-based return position." A nonexclusive list of examples of such positions is given in the Regulations. Some of these positions are:

1. That a nondiscrimination clause of a tax treaty precludes or modifies the Code;
2. That a treaty reduces the rate of withholding tax on United States source interest income, dividends, royalties, or other types of fixed or determinable annual or periodical income;
3. That income derived from a domestic trade or business is not subject to tax because it is not attributable to a permanent establishment or fixed base.
4. That expenses may be apportioned and allocated to income derived from a domestic trade or business in a manner inconsistent with the Code;
5. That a treaty alters the source of any item of income or deduction; and
6. That a treaty grants a credit for a foreign tax otherwise not creditable under the Code.

The Service may waive treaty-based disclosure. A waiver generally occurs where a tax return would not be required, absent § 6114, if the taxpayer claims that a tax treaty has reduced or eliminated the rate of withholding tax otherwise applicable to United

States source interest, dividends, royalties, or other types of fixed or determinable annual or periodical income. The Regulations also waive reporting for individuals if the payments or income items otherwise reportable do not, in the aggregate, exceed $10,000.

Technical Explanation of United States-Canada Income Tax Treaty

INTRODUCTION

In this technical explanation of the Convention between the United States and Canada signed on September 26, 1980 ("the Convention"), references are made to the Convention and Protocol between Canada and the United States with respect to Income Taxes signed on March 4, 1942, as amended by the Convention signed on June 12, 1950, the Convention signed on August 8, 1956 and the Supplementary Convention signed on October 25, 1966 (the "1942 Convention"). These references are intended to put various provisions of the Convention into context. . . .

The technical explanation is an official guide to the Convention. It reflects policies behind particular Convention provisions, as well as understandings reached with respect to the interpretation and application of the Convention. . . .

. . . .

Article V
PERMANENT ESTABLISHMENT

Paragraph 1 provides that for the purposes of the Convention the term "permanent establishment" means a fixed place of business through which the business of a resident of a Contracting State is wholly or partly carried on. Article V does not use the term "enterprise of a Contracting State," which appears in the 1942 Convention. Thus, paragraph 1 avoids introducing an additional term into the Convention. The omission of the term is not intended to have any implications for the interpretation of the 1942 Convention.

Paragraph 2 provides that the term "permanent establishment" includes especially a place of management, a branch, an office, a factory, a workshop, and a mine, oil or gas well, quarry, or any other place of extraction of natural resources. Paragraph 3 adds that a building site or construction or installation project constitutes a permanent establishment if and only if it lasts for more than 12 months. . . .

Paragraph 5 provides that a person acting in a Contracting State on behalf of a resident of the other Contracting State is deemed to be a permanent establishment of the resident if such person has and habitually exercises in the first-mentioned State the authority to conclude contracts in the name of the resident. This rule does not apply to an agent of independent status, covered by paragraph 7. Under the provisions of paragraph 5, a permanent establishment may exist even in the absence of a fixed place of business. If, however, the activities of a person described in paragraph 5 are limited to the ancillary activities described in paragraph 6, then a permanent establishment does not exist solely on account of the person's activities.

There are a number of minor differences between the provisions of paragraphs 1 through 5 and the analogous provisions of the 1942 Convention. One important deviation is elimination of the rule of the 1942 Convention which deems a permanent establishment to exist in any circumstance where a resident of one State uses substantial equipment in the other State for any period of time. The Convention thus generally raises the threshold for source basis taxation of activities that involve substantial equipment (and that do not otherwise constitute a permanent establishment). Another deviation of some significance is elimination of the rule of the 1942 Convention that considers a permanent establishment to exist where a resident of one State carries on business in the other State through an agent or employee who has a stock of merchandise from which he regularly fills orders that he receives. The convention provides that a person other than an agent of independent status who is engaged solely in the maintenance of a stock of goods or merchandise belonging to a resident of the other State for the purpose of storage, display or delivery does not constitute a permanent establishment.

Paragraph 6 provides that a fixed place of business used solely for, or an employee described in paragraph 5 engaged solely in, certain specified activities is not a permanent establishment, notwithstanding the provisions of paragraphs 1, 2, and 5. The specified activities are: a) the use of facilities for the purpose of storage, display, or delivery of goods or merchandise belonging to the resident whose business is being carried on; b) the maintenance of a stock of goods or merchandise belonging to the resident for the purpose of storage, display, or delivery; c) the maintenance of a stock of goods or merchandise belonging to the resident for the purpose of processing by another person; d) the purchase of goods or merchandise, or the collection of information, for the resident; and e) advertising, the supply of information, scientific research, or similar activities which have a preparatory or auxiliary character, for the resident. Combinations of the specified activities have the same status as any one of the activities. The reference in paragraph 6(e) to specific activities does not imply that any other particular activities—for example, the servicing of a patent or a know-how contract or the inspection of the implementation of engineering plans—do not fall within the scope of paragraph 6(e) provided that, based on the facts and circumstances, such activities have a preparatory of auxiliary character.

Paragraph 7 provides that a resident of a Contracting State is not deemed to have a permanent establishment in the other Contracting State merely because such resident carries on business in the other State through a broker, general commission agent, or any other agent of independent status, provided that such persons are acting in the ordinary course of their business.

Paragraph 8 states that the fact that a company which is a resident of one Contracting State controls or is controlled by a company which is either a resident of the other Contracting State, whether through a permanent establishment or otherwise, does not automatically render either company a permanent establishment of the other. . . .

. . . .

Article VII
BUSINESS PROFITS

Paragraph 1 provides that business profits of a resident of a Contracting State are taxable only in that State unless the resident carries on business in the other Contracting State through a permanent establishment situated in that other State. If the resident carries on, or has carried on, business through such a permanent establishment, the other State may tax such business profits but only so much of them as are attributable to the permanent establishment. The reference to a prior permanent establishment ("or has carried on") makes clear that a Contracting State in which a permanent establishment existed has the right to tax the business profits attributable to that permanent establishment, even if there is a delay in the receipt or accrual of such profits until after the permanent establishment has been terminated.

Any business profits received or accrued in taxable years in which the Convention has effect, in accordance with Article XXX (Entry Into Force), which are attributable to a permanent establishment that was previously terminated are subject to tax in the Contracting State in which such permanent establishment existed under the provisions of Article VII.

Paragraph 2 provides that where a resident of either Canada or the United States carries on business in the other Contracting State through a permanent establishment in that other State, both Canada and the United States shall attribute to that permanent establishment business profits which the permanent establishment might be expected to make if it were a distinct and separate person engaged in the same or similar activities under the same or similar conditions and dealing wholly independently with the resident and with any other person related to the resident. The term "related to the resident" is to be interpreted in accordance with paragraph 2 of Article IX (Related Persons). The reference to other related persons is intended to make clear that the test of paragraph 2 is not restricted to independence between a permanent establishment and a home office.

Paragraph 3 provides that, in determining business profits of a permanent establishment, there are to be allowed as deductions those expenses which are incurred for the purposes of the permanent establishment, including executive and administrative expenses, whether incurred in the State in which the permanent establishment is situated or in any other State. However, nothing in the paragraph requires Canada or the United States to allow a deduction for any expenditure which would not generally be allowed as a deduction under its taxation laws. The language of this provision differs from that of paragraph 1 of Article III of the 1942 Convention, which states that in the determination of net industrial and commercial profits of a permanent establishment there shall be allowed as deductions "all expenses, wherever incurred" as long as such expenses are reasonably allocable to the permanent establishment. Paragraph 3 of Article VII of the Convention is not intended to have any implications for interpretation of the 1942 Convention, but is intended to assure that under the Convention deductions are allowed by a Contracting State which are generally allowable by that State.

Paragraph 4 provides that no business profits are to be attributed to a permanent establishment of a resident of a Contracting State by reason of the use of the permanent establishment for merely purchasing goods or merchandise or merely providing executive, managerial, or administrative facilities or services for the resident. Thus, if a company resident in a Contracting State has a permanent establishment in the other State, and uses the permanent establishment for the mere performance of stewardship of other managerial services carried on for the benefit of the resident, this activity will not result in profits being attributed to the permanent establishment.

Paragraph 5 provides that business profits are to be attributed to a permanent establishment by the same method in every taxable period unless there is good and sufficient reason to change such method. In the United States, such a change may be a change in accounting method requiring the approval of the Internal Revenue Service.

Paragraph 6 explains the relationship between the provisions of Article VII and other provisions of the Convention. Where business profits include items of income which are dealt with separately in other Articles of the Convention, those other Articles are controlling.

Paragraph 7 provides a definition for the term "attributable to." Profits "attributable to" a permanent establishment are those derived from the assets or activities of the permanent establishment. Paragraph 7 does not preclude Canada or the United States from using appropriate domestic tax law rules of attribution. The "attributable to" definition does not, for example, preclude a taxpayer from using the rules of section 1.864-4(c)(5) of the Treasury Regulations to assure for U.S. tax purposes that interest arising in the United States is attributable to a permanent establishment in the United States. (Interest arising outside the United States is attributable to a permanent establishment in the United States based on the principles of Regulations sections 1.864-5 and 1.864-6 and Revenue Ruling 75-253, 1975-2 C.B. 203.) Income that would be taxable under the Code and that is "attributable to" a permanent establishment under paragraph 7 is taxable pursuant to Article VII, however, even if such income might under the Code be treated as fixed or determinable annual or periodical gains or income not effectively connected with the conduct of a trade or business within the United States. The "attributable to" definition means that the limited "force-of-attraction" rule of Code section 864(c)(3) does not apply for U.S. tax purposes under the Convention. . . .

. . . .

Article XIV
INDEPENDENT PERSONAL SERVICES

Article XIV concerns the taxation of income derived by an individual in respect of the performance of independent personal services. Such income may be taxed in the Contracting State of which such individual is a resident. It may also be taxed in the other Contracting State if the individual has or had a fixed base regularly available to him in the other State for the purpose of performing his activities, but only to the extent that the income is attributable to that fixed base. The use of the term "has or had" ensures that a Contracting State in which a fixed base existed has the right to tax income attributable to that fixed base even if there is a delay between the termination of the fixed base and the receipt of accrual of such income.
. . .

Unlike Article VII of the 1942 Convention, which provides a limited exemption from tax at source on income from independent personal services, Article XIV does not restrict the exemption to persons present in the State of source for fewer than 184 days. Furthermore, Article XIV does not allow the $5,000 exemption at source of the 1942 Convention, which was available even if services were performed through a fixed base. However, Article XIV provides complete exemption at source if a fixed base does not exist.

. . . .

Article XV
DEPENDENT PERSONAL SERVICES

Paragraph 1 provides that, in general, salaries, wages, and other similar remuneration derived by a resident of a Contracting State in respect of an employment are taxable only in that State unless the employment is exercised in the other Contracting State. If the employment is exercised in the other Contracting State, the entire remuneration derived therefrom may be taxed in that other State but only if, as provided by paragraph 2, the recipient is present in the other State for a period or periods exceeding 183 days in the calendar year, or the remuneration is borne by an employer who is a resident of that other State or by a permanent establishment or fixed base which the employer has in that other State. However, in all cases where the employee earns $10,000 or less in the currency of the State of source, such earnings are exempt from tax in that State. "Borne by" means allowable as a deduction in computing taxable income. Thus, if a Canadian resident individual employed at the Canadian permanent establishment of a U.S. company performs services in the United States, the income earned by the employee from such services is not exempt from U.S. tax under paragraph 1 if such income exceeds $10,000 (U.S.) because the U.S. company is entitled to a deduction for such wages in computing its taxable income. . . .

PROBLEM 7—TAX TREATIES AND BUSINESS INCOME

Reading Material: United States-Canada Income Tax Treaty where relevant

1. F Corporation was organized under the laws of Canada. Its principal business activity consists of the worldwide sale of goods purchased in Canada.

    a. What result if F Corporation receives unsolicited orders from United States residents?

    b. What result if F Corporation sends catalogues to various individuals in the United States and advertises on television which leads to the placement of orders by United States residents?

2. Assume that all of F Corporation's office facilities are located in Canada. Respecting its sales made in the United States, orders for F's goods are solicited by their traveling salespersons operating out of the home office on a commission basis. Purchase orders are sent to the Canadian office where they are accepted by F Corporation and filled from inventory warehoused in Canada. F corporation maintains no inventory, plant, office, or other facilities in the United States.

    a. What is F Corporation's United States tax obligation for the year?

    b. Suppose that F Corporation maintained a branch office located in leased office space in Chicago. The branch maintained a leased warehouse for storage of purchased inventory. The United States salesmen operated out of its Chicago office, but all orders had to be accepted in Canada. What is F Corporation's United States tax liability?

3. Would F have a permanent establishment if it were a shareholder in a corporation conducting a trade or business in the United States? What if F was a significant shareholder? A majority shareholder? The sole shareholder?

4. Would F have a permanent establishment if it invested in a general partnership or limited liability company rather than a corporation?

5. T is a Canadian architect representing a client that is constructing a building in San Francisco, and, as part of his ser-

vices, the architect was on site on six different days during the year. What tax consequences, if any?

6. T is an employee (i.e., a commission salesperson) of a Canadian corporation selling products in the United States. T spends 130 days in the United States during the year in pursuit of his employment. What tax consequences, if any, arise?

Chapter 8
Nontreaty Persons—Investment Income

§ 8.01 General Taxing Pattern Applicable to Foreign Persons
§ 8.02 Taxation of Nonresident Individuals
§ 8.03 Taxation of Foreign Corporations
§ 8.04 Income Described in §§ 871(a) and 881(a)—In General
§ 8.05 Withholding of 30 Percent Tax at Source
§ 8.06 The Portfolio Interest Exception
         Problem 8

§ 8.01 General Taxing Pattern Applicable to Foreign Persons

In contrast to United States citizens and residents who are taxed broadly on worldwide income, the considerably more focused domestic taxing net applicable to foreign persons is generally cast at those particular items of income possessing a genesis in the United States—namely, income derived from United States sources and income derived from domestic trade or business activities. These income items may be taxed on either a gross or net basis, depending on the nature of the income derived. The sections that follow explore the common themes underpinning the basic taxing regimes applicable to nonresident alien individuals and foreign corporations who generally are unable to utilize an income tax treaty as well as the unique rules governing each type of taxpayer.

§ 8.02 Taxation of Nonresident Individuals

A nontreaty, nonresident individual is generally subject to United States tax on three classes of income. Such individuals are taxed on domestic source income items described in § 871, including dividends, interest, rents, and certain other types of "fixed or determinable" income. They are also taxed on income from the sale or exchange of capital assets, but only if the individual is present in the United States for at least 183 days during the taxable year. These items of income are taxed on a gross basis at a 30 percent tax rate. Unlike effectively connected income, the nonbusiness nature of these income items precludes claiming deductions and credits against such income in computing the nonresident's tax liability. In most cases, the United States tax on such income is enforced by withholding tax at the source.

Finally, a nonresident individual is taxed on income that is "effectively connected" with a United States trade or business. Income effectively connected with a United States trade or business is taxed on a net basis, subject to the graduated tax rates of § 1. As this class of income derives from trade or business activities, properly allocated deductions and credits are reflected in the individual's computation of his or her domestic tax liability. Nonresident individuals are also entitled to claim deductions in computing their effectively connected taxable income for casualty and theft losses related to United States property, charitable contributions, and a single personal exemption under § 151.

Two special statutes permit or require certain income derived by nonresidents to be treated as arising from a United States trade or business, thus subjecting that income to taxation on a net basis at graduated rates. First, § 871(d) permits nonresidents to elect to treat income derived from United States real property as effectively connected income. Similarly, § 897(a) treats gains and losses derived from sales and other dispositions of United States real property interests as if that gain or loss were effectively connected income.

Nonresident individuals are theoretically subject to the 30 percent gross income tax under § 871(a) on net capital gains derived from domestic sources if such individuals are present in the United States for 183 days or more during the taxable year. Gains and losses are recognized for purposes of § 871 only to the extent that those gains or losses would be recognized if they were effectively connected with a domestic trade or business. In practice, however, nonresident individuals who satisfy the 183-day presence requirement generally will be treated as United States residents for tax purposes under § 7701(b). Accordingly, gain from the sale of personal property by such individuals will be taxed at the graduated rates of § 1 and not at the 30 percent rate imposed under § 871. The 30 percent tax applicable to capital gains under § 871 will typically be imposed on those nonresident individuals whose actual presence is excluded by statute for purposes of determining residency under the 183-day standard of § 7701(b), but whose presence is counted for purposes of the 183-day threshold of § 871(a)(2).

§ 8.03 Taxation of Foreign Corporations

Foreign corporations, like nonresident individuals and unlike domestic corporations, incur United States tax only on specific classes of income derived from United States sources or activities. Foreign corporations are subject to such tax on domestic source passive income items described in § 881, including dividends, interest, rents, and certain other types of fixed or determinable income, and income effectively connected with a United States trade or business.

The first class of domestic source income is taxed on a gross basis at a 30 percent rate without the benefit of offsetting deductions. In most cases, the United States tax on such income is enforced by withholding at the source. In contrast, effectively connected income derived from a United States trade or business is taxed on a net basis under the graduated rates of § 11. As effectively connected income derives from trade or business activities, properly allocated deductions and credits are reflected in the corporation's computation of its domestic tax liability.

A foreign corporation derives effectively connected income only when the corporation is engaged in a United States trade or business or is deemed to be so engaged. Two special statutes permit or require certain income derived by foreign corporations to be treated as arising from a United States trade or business, thus subjecting that income to taxation on a net basis at graduated rates. First, § 882(d) permits a foreign corporation to elect to treat income derived from United States real property as effectively connected income. Similarly, § 897(a) treats gains and losses derived from sales and other dispositions of United States real property interests as if that gain or loss were effectively connected income.

In addition to the regular corporate income tax, as discussed at Chapter 11, foreign corporations engaged in a domestic trade or business are also subject to a branch profits tax imposed under § 884 on income attributable to that trade or business. The branch profits tax is intended to place foreign-owned branches on par with domestic subsidiaries for tax purposes. The branch profits tax equals 30 percent (or a lower tax treaty rate, if applicable) of a foreign corporation's "dividend equivalent amount." The dividend equivalent amount generally represents the foreign corporation's current effectively connected earnings and profits from a United States trade or business as adjusted for net increases and decreases in "United States net equity" and as adjusted in certain other ways. The foreign corporation's dividend equivalent amount is reduced by the corporation's federal income tax. Thus, broadly speaking, the branch profits tax for the highest-bracketed corporation equals 19.5 percent (30% of (100% – 35%)) of a foreign corporation's adjusted effectively connected taxable income. This tax attempts to mirror the 30 percent withholding tax imposed on a United States corporation when it repatriates its earnings to its foreign owners.

§ 8.04 Income Described in §§ 871(a) and 881(a)—In General

The domestic source income described in §§ 871(a) and 881(a) which is not derived from a domestic trade or business is generally subject to United States tax at a rate of 30 percent of the gross amount received. Given that the United States must reach beyond its confines to tax such income, this tax is generally imposed by withholding at the source of the income.

The income items subject to the 30 percent gross income tax under §§ 871 and 881 encompass primarily income from passive, nonbusiness activities. The gross income tax reaches such traditional items of investment income as interest, dividends, and rents. It likewise reaches the vague category of other fixed or determinable income. Though curiously neither § 871(a) nor § 881(a) state that United States source royalties (as distinct from rents) are subject to the 30 percent tax, it is clear under the Regulations that those royalties are so taxed.

The 30 percent tax does not apply to dividends and interest derived from certain investments. Interest on deposits with a bank or savings institution are spared so long as that interest is not effectively connected with a domestic trade or business. Dividends received from a domestic corporation which derives at least 80 percent of its gross income from active foreign business income also escape the tax. The portion of the dividend excluded from tax equals the ratio of the payor corporation's foreign source gross income to its total gross income. These special exclusions operate to remove from the United States taxing net interest derived from ordinary banking activities and dividends derived from corporations that are domestic in name only.

Gains from the sale or exchange of intangible assets or of any interest therein, to the extent such gains are contingent on the productivity, use, or disposition of the property, are also subject to the 30 percent tax. Gains from the sale or exchange of other property, however, are *not* deemed fixed or determinable income.

The gross income tax presents certain definitional and sourcing issues. In each of the above-described categories, a definitional issue is confronted as to the category to which a particular income item belongs. Given the statutory parallelism of §§ 861, 871, and 881, authorities arising under the sourcing rules of § 861 may prove relevant by analogy. Furthermore, such amounts are subject to tax only if they possess a United States source.

Little can be said with assurance regarding the nebulous fixed or determinable income category. It is extremely difficult to conclude under present law that an item of income should be exempt from the 30 percent tax of § 871 or § 881 because it is not fixed or determinable income. Neither the courts nor the Service have opened any substantial crevices on which the fearless tax adviser can gain a foothold.

§ 8.05 Withholding of 30 Percent Tax at Source

The 30 percent tax imposed under §§ 871(a) and 881(a) on domestic source income not effectively connected with a United States trade or business is generally enforced by withholding at the source. This tax collection mechanism is required given that the United States taxing arm must by definition extend to foreign persons outside of its jurisdiction. Under §§ 1441 and 1442, any foreign *or* domestic person having control, receipt, custody, disposal, or payment of any item of United States source income described in § 871 or § 881 is responsible for withholding the 30 percent tax from such payment and for remitting that tax to the Service. To encourage compliance, persons required to withhold such tax are themselves liable for that tax.

§ 8.06 The Portfolio Interest Exception

In general, §§ 871(a) and 881(a) provide that United States source interest payable to a foreign investor which is not effectively connected with a domestic trade or business is subject to a 30 percent withholding tax. Despite this general rule, the United States has long tried to assist its individuals and corporations in obtaining cost-effective long-term debt financing from foreign investors. To attract such favorable financing arrangements, domestic persons must be able to pay interest to foreign lenders free of a withholding tax.

Congress accommodated this practical need for low-cost financing by enacting a special exception from the 30 percent withholding tax for "portfolio interest" paid to a foreign payee. The portfolio interest exception enables United States persons to pay interest to foreign lenders on particular debt obligations without being subjected to a withholding tax. Interest paid on debt obligations in registered form qualifies for the portfolio interest exception if the payor or other withholding agent receives a statement made under penalty of perjury that the beneficial owner of the obligation is *not* a United States person. However, interest from those obligations cannot be effectively connected with the payee's United States trade or business. Assuming that the requirements ensuring foreign ownership are properly in place, a foreign investor may, subject to certain limitations, invest in United States and corporate obligations without being subjected to United States tax on any non-effectively connected interest therefrom.

Such preferences provided by statute may also prove beneficial to residents of a treaty country. While treaty provisions impose a tax rate on passive income typically lower than the statutory rate of 30 percent, as evidenced by the portfolio interest exception certain income may qualify for a statutory rate lower than the treaty rate. Under most income tax treaties, one of the articles generally provides that nothing in the treaty will preclude or pre-empt an exemption, income, or credit otherwise available.

PROBLEM 8—NONTREATY PERSONS—INVESTMENT INCOME

Code: §§ 871(a), (b), (d), (h), (i), 873

T, an individual, was a citizen and bona fide resident of Saudi Arabia. T is single and is on the cash method, calendar-year method of accounting. T has never been present in the United States. During the year, T owned the following assets:

1. 100 shares of the common stock of X Corporation—a domestic corporation;
2. 100 shares of the common stock of Y Corporation—a foreign corporation;
3. Rental real estate located in Modesto, California (T's activities in this connection do not constitute engaging in trade or business);
4. A loan to H, a citizen of the United States currently residing in Bolivia, in the amount of $7,000;
5. Deposit in a Chicago, Illinois bank, $20,000;
6. The rights to a patent created by T;
7. Vacant land held for investment in Oregon; and
8. 50 shares of preferred stock of Z Corporation—a domestic corporation.

During the year, T received the following amounts:

a. Cash payment on the X Corporation stock, $20,000—domestic source;
b. Cash payment on the Y Corporation stock, $13,000—$5,200 domestic source, $7,800 foreign source;
c. Rents from the rental property, $10,000—domestic source;
d. Interest on the loan to H, $1,000—foreign source;
e. Interest on deposit at Chicago, Illinois bank, $2,000—domestic source;
f. Gain on sale of ten shares of Z Corporation stock, $5,000—foreign source; and
g. Payment pursuant to sale to W Corporation of United States rights to a patent for five percent of net profits from product produced through its use, $8,000—domestic source.

T's expenses for the year included:
- a. Depreciation and expenses with respect to the United States rental property, $3,000;
- b. Loss on the sale of five shares of Z Corporation stock in the United States, $1,000; and
- c. Medical expenses, $4,500.

What is T's taxable United States income for the year and his tax liability assuming that none of the activities constitutes a trade or business?

Chapter 9

Nontreaty Persons— Existence of a Trade or Business

§ 9.01 Trade or Business Status—Generally
Revenue Ruling 88-3, 1988-1 C.B. 268
Revenue Ruling 58-63, 1958-1 C.B. 624

§ 9.02 Performance of Services
Johansson v. United States, 336 F.2d 809 (5th Cir. 1964)

§ 9.03 De Minimis Exception for Nominal Services

§ 9.04 Real Property

§ 9.05 Election to Be Taxed on a Net Basis
Revenue Ruling 92-74, 1992-2 C.B. 156

§ 9.06 Dispositions of United States Real Property Interests

§ 9.07 Sales Activity

§ 9.08 Purchasing Activity

§ 9.09 Representative Office Activity

§ 9.10 Partnerships

§ 9.11 Use of Dependent and Independent Agents

§ 9.12 Licensees and Lessees
Problem 9

§ 9.01 Trade or Business Status—Generally

The determination of whether a foreign person is "engaged in trade or business within the United States" is generally a question of fact for which there are no hard and fast rules. In fact, the Code shuns any affirmative definition of the concept, opting instead to delineate in the negative a handful of discrete situations that do *not* give rise to a trade or business. By necessity courts have therefore been left to establish the parameters for this determination.

Some general guidance can be gleaned from the body of cases construing the trade or business standard. For instance, a United States trade or business is generally characterized by "progression, continuity, or sustained activity." Moreover, this activity must occur during some substantial portion of the taxable year. Thus, if employees of a foreign corporation come to the United States for two weeks to negotiate and conclude the sale of merchandise to a domestic purchaser, such activity probably should not, standing alone, represent the conduct of a United States trade or business even if the value of the merchandise sold is substantial.

On a broad scale, courts have focused primarily upon the degree and significance of the activity undertaken by the person under scrutiny in assessing whether that person is engaged in a trade or business. A domestic trade or business has generally been found where the level of United States sales or operational activity is fairly extensive. For instance, trade or business status has been assigned to sales activity conducted through agents and to significant marketing and export activities. Conversely, no trade or business arises when the foreign person has minimal sales or operational activity in the United States. For example, no trade or business arose when a foreign person had an insignificant physical presence in the United States such as maintaining a barebones office or using an office for merely ministerial or collection functions. Similarly, no trade or business should arise via isolated sales or export activity.

Moreover, a United States trade or business generally supposes that a foreign person's domestic activities are directly related or pivotal to the active pursuit of profit. It appears that, in order for a foreign person to be engaged in a domestic trade or business, its "core activities" (i.e., those activities which are essential to the derivation of profit) must be conducted in the United States. Thus, a foreign person who merely collects revenues, maintains books, or performs other ministerial functions in the United States should not be engaged in a *United States* trade or business. Similarly, a foreign person maintaining a domestic "representative office" to gather information about general market conditions and to pass such information to its foreign home office should not have a domestic trade or business so long as that representative office does not actively solicit or negotiate with United States customers. In contrast, a foreign person rendering services or soliciting sales domestically should quite properly be deemed to be engaged in a trade or business.

The distinction between a foreign person's conduct of a United States trade or business and something less may be similar, in some circumstances, to the distinction between activities giving rise to

§ 162 business expenses and activities giving rise to deductions under § 212 related to the production of income. Thus, in appropriate cases, these analogous authorities construing the distinction between expenses under §§ 162 and 212 may prove to be valuable interpretive tools for counsel representing foreign taxpayers with United States activities.

Revenue Ruling 88-3
1988-1 C.B. 268

Rev. Rul. 73-227, 1973-1 C.B. 338, examines the activities of X, the foreign financing subsidiary of a United States parent, and holds that the United States source interest income that X earns is effectively connected with a United States trade or business under section 864(c) of the Internal Revenue Code of 1954.

Section 864(b) of the Code and the regulations promulgated thereunder provide rules for determining whether a foreign taxpayer is engaged in a trade or business within the United States. (These rules may differ in some respects from those used in determining whether a taxpayer is engaged in a trade or business under other sections of the Code.) The determination whether X is engaged in a trade or business within the United States must therefore be made by applying these rules to the facts described in the ruling. Rev. Rul. 73-227, however, does not do so. The ruling simply concludes without discussion of the applicable statute and regulations that X is engaged in a trade or business within the United States. Because the ruling does not discuss and apply the proper legal standard, its conclusion may be unsound.

In addition, the determination whether a taxpayer is engaged in a trade or business within the United States is highly factual. Such a determination is not ordinarily made in an advance ruling. See sections 2.01 and 4.01(2) of Rev. Proc. 87-6, 1987-1 I.R.B. 45.

Accordingly, Rev. Rul. 73-227 is revoked. Determinations under section 864 of the Code must be made by applying the regulations promulgated thereunder to the facts and circumstances of each case.

Similarly, as discussed in Chapter 7, the treaty concept of a permanent establishment, while occasionally coextensive with the statutory concept, typically requires a greater degree of activity within the United States than required for finding of a trade or business under the Code.

Revenue Ruling 58-63
1958-1 C.B. 624

Advice has been requested whether a nonresident alien individual, owning a racing stable in France and engaged in the operation of same for profit, who enters a horse in a race in the United States, is exempt from United States income tax on the winnings therefrom.

A citizen and resident of France owned and operated a horse racing stable, located in France, for profit. He was invited to enter an outstanding horse in a race to be held in the United States. He and the racing association agreed that the horse would not compete in any other races while in the United States. The racing association invited him to view the race and participate in the social events connected therewith. The invitation was accepted. The horse won the race and the owner was paid the winner's purse.

The operation of a racing stable for profit is a business enterprise. The entry of a horse in a race in this country constitutes being "engaged in trade or business within the United States," within the meaning of section 871(c) of the Internal Revenue Code of 1954. Accordingly, income derived therefore is subject to United States income tax unless exempted by some other provision of law.

§ 9.02 Performance of Services

Aside from a special de minimis provision applicable to alien individuals, a foreign person who renders services in the United States at any time within a taxable year is automatically deemed to be engaged in a domestic trade or business. Such income is normally deemed effectively connected with a trade or business and thus is generally subject to tax at graduated tax rates. Under this all-encompassing standard, services which under the more stringent criteria would not yield a trade or business will do so in this context. Such treatment is dramatic when contrasted with the more lenient treatment of such income in the tax treaty context, as discussed in Chapter 7. The standard tax treaty provision for independent or dependent services permits more frequent and extensive activity, i.e., the 183 day rule and the fixed base rule, before such services are taxable by the United States.

While this basic rule is simply stated, convoluted issues arise in identifying the nature of income from services and the location where those services were performed as well as segregating income derived from services from other income. As an example of the difficult definitional issues faced in the services context, assume that a foreign corporation entered into a contract with a domestic corporation, which allowed it to use for a specified period of time know-how relating to the treatment of certain chemicals. In conjunction with the contract, the foreign corporation made certain of its employees available in the United States to instruct the domestic corporation's employees on the techniques related to the know-how. In such a case, an allocation must be made between the amounts paid for the know-how and the amounts paid for the services of the foreign employees. In a similar situation, the Service commented that, since the "personal services have only a nominal value apart from the license to use such 'know how,' all but a nominal sum should be allocated to the license."

Johansson v. United States
United States Court of Appeals, Fifth Circuit
336 F.2d 809 (1964)

RIVES, CIRCUIT JUDGE.

On three occasions, Ingemar Johansson, a citizen of Sweden, fought Floyd Patterson for the heavyweight boxing championship of the world. All three fights took place in the United States. Taxes in the amounts of $598,181.92 for the calender year 1960 and $411,620 for the period January 1, 1961, through March 13, 1961, were assessed against Johansson on the income he earned from the Patterson fights and related activities. The Government brought an action against Johansson to collect the taxes assessed....

The first question for this court is whether Johansson may be taxed by the United States on the income he earned from his activities here during the period in question. Section 871(c) of the Internal Revenue Code of 1954 provides that [a nonresident alien individual engaged in trade or business within the United States shall be taxable.... For purposes of ... this section, ... the terms engaged in trade or business within the United States includes the performance of personal services within the United States at any time within the taxable year]. Since the express exceptions contained in section 871 are inapposite here, we must view that section as authorizing the assessments involved in this case unless an applicable tax convention requires a contrary result. The Income Tax Convention with Sweden, does not bar the assessments. See article XI(a), (d). However, Johansson claims an exemption [under the Income Tax Convention with Switzerland]....

. . . .

Applying this standard to the facts of the present case, the district court concluded that Johansson was not a resident of Switzerland during the period in question. This conclusion is fully supported by the evidence....

§ 9.03 De Minimis Exception for Nominal Services

The per se United States trade or business status generally accorded services yields to a special exception for nominal and incidental services performed by a nonresident alien individual. Such an individual will *not* be considered to be engaged in a United States trade or business if:

1. He or she is physically present in the United States for 90 days or less during the taxable year;
2. The amount of compensation attributable to the United States services is $3,000 or less; and
3. The individual is employed by, or is under contract with, a foreign person who is not engaged in a United States trade or business or by a foreign office of a United States person.

If the alien individual satisfies these criteria, all of his or her domestic source services income is freed from the trade or business affiliation. However, if a nonresident alien's domestic source services income exceeds $3,000, *all* of the income from services performed in the United States is taxed, not just the excess over $3,000. It is immaterial for purposes of the exception whether the nonresident alien individual is performing such services as an employee or otherwise.

§ 9.04 Real Property

A foreign person's mere ownership of United States real property standing alone will not automatically trigger trade or business status for that person. If, however, the foreign person's real property activity extends beyond the mere receipt of rent or other income and the payment of incidental ownership expenses, that person will be considered to be engaged in a trade or business provided the activity is continuous and regular.

By way of example, assume that F, a foreign corporation, owns an office building in the United States which it leases to tenants on a "net lease" basis. The leases provide for a minimum monthly rental and for the lessee's payment of real estate taxes, operating expenses, ground rent, repairs, interest and principal on existing mortgages, and insurance. An employee of F visits the United States one week each year to conduct new lease negotiations, attend conferences, make phone calls, draft documents, and make other significant decisions with respect to the lease. On similar facts, the Service ruled that such a corporation will *not* be considered to be engaged in a trade or business as a result of such net lease activity. Thus, absent an election to be treated as a domestic trade or business under § 882(d), all of the actual and imputed rent received by F will be subject to tax under § 881 at a 30 percent rate on a gross basis.

As an additional example, assume that F, a foreign person, owns four commercial properties in the United States. F employs a United States-based agent to manage the properties by executing leases, collecting rents, keeping books of account, supervising repairs, and paying taxes and mortgage interest. During the year in issue, F sells one of its properties and executes an option to purchase another. On similar facts, a foreign person was found to be engaged in a trade or business.

§ 9.05 Election to Be Taxed on a Net Basis

Under current law, a foreign person who owns and manages United States real property will most likely *want* to be considered engaged in a trade or business. First, if a foreign person is engaged in a trade or business, he will be permitted to deduct expenses attributable to his real property for United States tax purposes. Conversely, if the foreign person is not engaged in a trade or business, he will not be able to deduct those expenses, even if his ownership of the property is clearly profit-motivated.

Second, a foreign person may incur an operating loss attributable to the ownership and maintenance of United States real property. If a foreign person is engaged in a trade or business during his years of real property ownership, he will be able to utilize such losses to offset profits derived from other United States trades or businesses and, if such real property ownership is his only United States business, carry forward those losses until the taxable year in which he sells the property. If a foreign person derives a gain from the sale of United States real property, that gain is automatically deemed to arise from the conduct of a United States trade or business and hence is exposed to tax. Thus, if the foreign person has incurred losses during its ownership tenure, a carryforward of those losses will favorably offset such taxable gain.

However, a foreign person who net leases United States real property, has activities that are otherwise insubstantial with respect to such property, or is not otherwise engaged in any domestic trade or business may have difficulty establishing that he is engaged in a United States trade or business as a result of his real property activity. Thus, that person may be unable to reduce other United States source trade or business income by losses and expenses attributable to that property.

In such a case, a foreign person should consider making a "net income election" under § 871(d) or § 882(d) with respect to income derived from its United States real property interests. A net income election permits a foreign person deriving income from United States real property held for the production of income to treat "all such income" as effectively connected with the conduct of a United States trade or business. The election must be made for all classes of a foreign person's income from real property. The election applies only to United States source income which would otherwise not be effectively connected income. However, the election generally does not activate the effectively connected rules of § 864(c), since the election does not cause the foreign person to be treated as engaged in a domestic trade or business for most other purposes.

Importantly, the election may be equally available to income tax treaty residents. As discussed at Chapter 6, treaties often reserve to the situs country the right to tax such income without regard to the treaty. Thus, for example, a Canadian investing in United States rental property could elect under § 871(d) or § 882(d) and be taxed at the graduated rates on a net basis.

Revenue Ruling 92-74
1992-2 C.B. 156

ISSUE

How does an election under section 882(d) of the Internal Revenue Code with respect to property that is a United States real property interest affect the computation of net operating losses and capital gains and losses on disposition of the property?

FACTS

A foreign corporation makes an election under section 882(d) with respect to United States real property. The amounts involved and the circumstances of ownership are such that allowance of any losses or credits is not limited by section 469. Transactions with respect to the property lead to the following results in the current taxable year (and no other facts are relevant):

Situation 1. Current allowable deductions attributable to the property exceed current income from the property; the taxpayer has income from other United States trades or businesses, as well as income from other property subject to a section 882(d) election.

Situation 2. Current allowable deductions attributable to the property exceed current income from the property; the property is disposed of in the current year at a loss; the taxpayer has income from other United States trades or businesses, as well as income from other property subject to a section 882(d) election; and the taxpayer has no other capital gains or losses.

Situation 3. Current allowable deductions attributable to the property exceed current income from the property; the property is disposed of in the current year at a gain; the taxpayer has income from other United States trades or businesses, as well as income from other property subject to a section 882(d) election; and the taxpayer has no other capital gains or losses.

Situation 4. Current income from the property exceeds current allowable deductions attributable to the property; the property is disposed of in the current year at a loss; the taxpayer has income from other United States trades or businesses, as well as income from other property subject to a section 882(d) election; and the taxpayer has no other capital gains or losses.

LAW AND ANALYSIS

Section 882(d) of the Code allows a foreign corporation to elect to have certain income from real property held for the production of income treated as if it were effectively connected with the conduct of a trade or business within the United States. The legislative history of section 882(d) of the Code provides that the provisions relating to the applicability of such an election, as well as the manner of making or revoking the election, are identical to the provisions of section 871(d). . . .

HOLDINGS

An election under section 882(d) of the Code requires taxpayers to account for current operating gains and losses, and gains and losses on disposition of the property subject to the election, as follows:

Situation 1. Current allowable deductions attributable to the property exceed current income from the property. In the case of an election under section 882(d), the excess of current allowable deductions attributable to the property over current income from the property may be used to offset income from other United States trades or businesses, as well as income from other property subject to a section 882(d) election. If such deductions exceed the current income described above, the excess will constitute a net operating loss under section 172(c) of the Code. The normal carryback and carryover rules in section 172(b) apply with respect to the net operating loss.

Situation 2. Current allowable deductions attributable to the property exceed current income from the property; the property is disposed of in the current year at a loss; and the taxpayer has no other capital gains or losses. In the case of an election under section 882(d) of the Code, a foreign corporation is not entitled to a deduction for the current year for capital losses in excess of capital gains (section 1211(a)). In computing a net operating loss, the net capital loss may not be used in the computation, because it is not an allowable deduction under Chapter 1 of subchapter B of the Code (section 172(c)). A foreign corporation may use the excess of current allowable deductions attributable to the property over current income from the property to offset income from other United States trades or businesses, as well as income from other property subject to a section 882(d) election. If such deductions exceed the current income described above, the excess will constitute a net operating loss under section 172(c) of the Code.

The normal carryback and carryover rules in section 1212(a) apply with respect to the capital loss.

Situation 3. Current allowable deductions attributable to the property exceed current income from the property; the property is disposed of in the current year at a gain; and the taxpayer has no other capital gains or losses. In the case of a capital gain on disposition of real property not attributable to a United States trade or business by a foreign corporation, the gain is treated as effectively connected with a United States trade or business under section 897(a)(1) of the Code. Therefore, the gain is included in gross income under section 882(a)(2). If current allowable deductions attributable to the property exceed the total of current income from the property and gain on disposition, such excess may be used to offset income from other United States trades or businesses, as well as income from other property subject to a section 871(d) or 882(d) election. If such deductions exceed the income described above, the excess will constitute a net operating loss under section 172(c). The normal carryback and carryover rules in section 172(b)(1) apply with respect to the net operating loss.

Situation 4. Current income from the property exceeds current allowable deductions attributable to the property; the property is disposed of in the current year at a loss; and the taxpayer has no other capital gains or losses. In the case of an election under section 882(d) of the Code, a foreign corporation is not entitled to a deduction for the current year for capital losses in excess of capital gains (section 1211(a)). In computing a net operating loss, the net capital loss may not be used in the computation, because it is not an allowable deduction under Chapter 1 of subchapter B of the Code (section 172(c)).

The normal carryback and carryover rules in section 1212(a) apply with respect to the capital loss.

§ 9.06 Dispositions of United States Real Property Interests

Under § 897, gain or loss derived by a foreign person from the sale or other disposition of a United States real property interest is deemed to be effectively connected with the conduct of a domestic trade or business. Thus, such gains are exposed to United States tax at graduated tax rates regardless of whether the foreign person is actually engaged in a United States trade or business under the § 864 trade or business standard.

For this purpose, the term "United States real property interest" generally means an interest in real property (including an interest in a mine, well, or other natural deposit) located in the United States or the Virgin Islands and any interest (other than an interest solely as a creditor) in any domestic corporation if at least 50 percent in value of the realty and business assets of that corporation consists of United States real property interests. Thus, gain from the sale of shares of a United States corporation that owns real property can be reached by § 897.

§ 9.07 Sales Activity

Surprisingly little authority exists to determine when activity involving the sale of inventory within the United States represents the conduct of a domestic trade or business. It is generally assumed that the maintenance by a foreign person of a stock of inventory in the United States, coupled with the sales efforts of a United States-based *dependent* agent (such as an employee or an unrelated person acting on an exclusive or near exclusive basis for such person), will mean that such person is engaged in a domestic trade or business. Although less clear, it is probably likewise true that a foreign person will be so engaged if it conducts *either* marketing activity in the United States *or* maintains a stock of inventory from which it fills orders. In determining whether a foreign person conducts business activities in the United States, it appears that the United States marketing efforts of its employees will be imputed to that foreign person.

If a foreign person ships inventory to a United States-based dependent *or* independent agent on a consignment basis, such shipments, coupled with the sales efforts of the agent, will mean that the foreign person will be engaged in a domestic trade or business. In a consignment arrangement, the foreign seller ships its products to a United States sales agent who then markets the products to customers. During this marketing period, although the sales agent has possession of the products, title to those products remains with the foreign seller. Thus, the foreign seller will be viewed as maintaining a stock of inventory in the United States. As earlier stated, ownership by a foreign person of physical inventory in the United States together with *any* regular and continuous sales activity (even activity conducted by an independent agent) generally means that the foreign person will be engaged in a United States trade or business.

Notwithstanding the above analysis, it is possible for a foreign person to engage in some ancillary activities within the United States without being considered to be engaged in a domestic trade or business. For example, where the United States office of a foreign corporation maintained United States investments and performed certain tasks ancillary to *two* sales of inventory by the foreign corporation's home office, the Tax Court held that the foreign corporation was *not* engaged in a United States trade or business, commenting that "the real business of petitioner, the 'doing of what [it] was principally organized to do in order to realize a profit' was the sale in Scotland of manufactured goods and the collection of income from investments." The domestic office delivered yarn to a United States customer and collected payment therefor. In the other sale, the domestic office "handled the paperwork." In neither sale did the domestic office actually solicit the customer. In both cases, the sale was made between the home office and the United States customer, with the domestic office handling only routine clerical or follow-up duties.

The Tax Court reasoned that, since this core activity was exclusively conducted outside the United States and only clerical activity was conducted within the United States, the clerical activity alone was insufficient to give rise to trade or business status regardless of how substantial or continuous such ministerial functions happened to be. It thus appears that a foreign person may domestically perform bookkeeping and other ministerial functions without risking trade or business status, so long as that person does not actively solicit orders in the United States.

§ 9.08 Purchasing Activity

A foreign person should not be viewed as being engaged in a United States trade or business simply because it purchases products in the United States for sale. Such a rule would seriously impede domestic exports. This rule holds true regardless of the level of purchases or the sophistication of the foreign person's export activities. For instance, a foreign person should not be considered to be engaged in a trade or business even if it maintains a substantial fleet of ships or trucks with which to transport the purchased products outside of the United States.

§ 9.09 Representative Office Activity

Many foreign corporations have established "representative offices" in the United States. The activities of a pure representative office and its United States tax treatment will not be considered to be engaged in a trade or business for purposes of the Code.

This result seems entirely consistent with the common-law definitions of a trade or business. In order for a foreign person to be engaged in a domestic trade or business, that person must engage in activities in the United States which are closely related to the derivation of profit. Properly conducted, a representative office merely gathers and disperses general information. It does *not* solicit business or participate meaningfully in any specific profit-motivated transaction. Such ancillary activities (arguably devoid of profit motive) should therefore not amount to the conduct of a trade or business.

The Tax Court has held that a foreign corporation was *not* engaged in a United States trade or business, commenting that "the real business of petitioner, the 'doing of what [it] was principally organized to do in order to realize a profit' was the sale in Scotland of manufactured goods and the collection of income from investments." Since this core activity was exclusively conducted outside the United States and only clerical activity was conducted within the United States, the clerical activity alone was insufficient to give rise to trade or business status regardless of how substantial or continuous such ministerial functions happened to be.

It appears that a foreign person may domestically perform bookkeeping and other ministerial functions without risking trade or business status, so long as that person does not actively solicit orders in the United States. Thus, for example, if a foreign corporation is approached by a United States customer in its home country, concludes in that foreign country a contract for the future shipment of inventory, and thereafter ships the goods to the United States for sale, that foreign corporation should safely be able to use a United States-based employee or agent to collect the payments for such inventory and to provide an accounting of the sale to the home office.

§ 9.10 Partnerships

The trade or business activity of a pass-through entity is generally imputed to its owners. For instance, in the partnership context, under § 875(1) a nonresident alien or foreign corporation is considered to be engaged in a United States trade or business if a partnership of which such person is a member is so engaged. This rule applies regardless of whether the foreign partner is a general or a limited partner.

§ 9.11 Use of Dependent and Independent Agents

In determining whether a foreign person conducts domestic business activities, it seems clear that the domestic marketing efforts of its employees and other United States-based *dependent* agents will be imputed to such person. To be considered a dependent agent, it is not necessary for the United States person or entity to be related or affiliated with the foreign person. Instead, it is sufficient that the United States-based person or entity either acts exclusively (or nearly exclusively) for such foreign person. It is unclear whether the activities of a United States-based independent agent will be imputed to a foreign person in determining whether that foreign person will be engaged in a domestic trade or business.

§ 9.12 Licensees and Lessees

In determining whether a foreign person is engaged in a domestic trade or business, the activities of licensees (where the foreign person has licensed intangible property to a United States person) and of lessees (where the foreign person has rented real or personal property to a United States person) are *not* imputed to the foreign licensor or lessor. In other words, such licensees and lessees are not agents of the foreign person.

In view of the above, an example in the Regulations concludes that a foreign person who licenses patents to United States licensees is not engaged in a trade or business under the facts described therein. Similarly, the Service has ruled that a foreign person who "net leases" domestic real property to an unrelated United States person will not be engaged in a trade or business by virtue of such net lease activity, apparently also on the theory that the activities of the lessee will not be imputed to the foreign lessor.

CHAPTER 9   NONTREATY PERSONS—EXISTENCE OF A TRADE OR BUSINESS   213

PROBLEM 9—NONTREATY PERSONS—EXISTENCE OF A TRADE OR BUSINESS

Code: §§ 864(b)(1), 875(1), 871(d), 897(a)

Regulations: §§ 1.864-2(a) and (b), 1.871-10(a)-(c)

T, an individual, was a citizen and bona fide resident of Saudi Arabia, with which the United States does not have a tax treaty. T is single and is on the cash method, calendar-year method of accounting. T has never been present in the United States. During the year, T owned the following assets:

1. 100 shares of the common stock of X Corporation—a domestic corporation;

2. 100 shares of the common stock of Y Corporation—a foreign corporation;

3. Rental real estate located in Modesto, California;

4. A loan to H, a citizen of the United States currently residing in Bolivia, in the amount of $7,000;

5. Deposit in a Chicago, Illinois bank, $20,000;

6. The rights to a patent created by T;

7. Vacant land held for investment in Oregon; and

8. 50 shares of preferred stock of Z Corporation—a domestic corporation.

During the year, T received the following amounts:

a. Cash payment on the X Corporation stock, $20,000;
b. Cash payment on the Y Corporation stock, $13,000;
c. Rents from the rental property, $10,000 (depreciation and expenses for the year totaled $3,000);
d. Interest on the loan to H, $1,000;
e. Interest on deposit at Chicago, Illinois bank, $2,000;
f. Gain on sale of ten shares of Z Corporation stock, $5,000 and loss on the sale five shares of Z Corporation, $1,000; and
g. Payment pursuant to sale to W Corporation of United States rights to a patent for five percent of net profits from product produced through its use $8,000.

1. Does T have a domestic trade or business from any of above activities?

2. Would T have a domestic trade or business if X Corporation, Y Corporation, or Z Corporation conducted a trade or business in the United States? What if T were a minority shareholder? A significant shareholder? A majority shareholder? The sole shareholder?

3. Would T have a domestic trade or business if X Corporation, Y Corporation, or Z Corporation were general partnerships or limited liability companies rather than corporations? What if T had a minor interest in them? A majority interest? What result if they were limited partnerships and T were a general partner? What if he were a limited partner?

4. What result if T were a model and posed in front of the Washington monument for a single day for $2,000? What if T posed for a week, earning $6,000? What if T's activities lasted four months?

5. Can T elect to have any of his activities treated as the conduct of a domestic trade or business?

6. What result if T sold his vacant land for a gain of $25,000?

Chapter 10
Nontreaty Persons—Trade or Business Income

§ 10.01 Overview of the Taxation of Effectively Connected Income
§ 10.02 Determination of Effectively Connected Income—In General
§ 10.03 Fixed or Determinable Income and Certain Other United States Source Income
§ 10.04 The Asset Use Test
§ 10.05 The Material Factor Test
§ 10.06 All Other United States Source Income
§ 10.07 Effectively Connected Foreign Source Income
Revenue Ruling 75-253, 1975-1 C.B. 203
§ 10.08 Foreign Source Income Attributable to a Domestic Office or Place of Business
§ 10.09 United States Office or Other Fixed Place of Business
§ 10.10 Real Property Income Deemed Effectively Connected
§ 10.11 Allocation and Apportionment of Expenses—In General
§ 10.12 The Allocation Process
§ 10.13 The Apportionment Process
Stemkowski v. Commissioner, 690 F.2d 40 (2d Cir. 1982)
Problem 10

§ 10.01 Overview of the Taxation of Effectively Connected Income

Prior to 1966, if a foreign person was found to be engaged in a domestic trade or business, *all* United States source income was attributed to that business under the so-called "force of attraction" concept. Thus, all domestic source income was subject to United States tax under the graduated tax rates of § 1 or § 11. However,

Congress, eager to stimulate foreign investment in the United States, altered the force of attraction rule to require that income bear an "effective connection" to the taxpayer's business before subjecting that income to tax. Given the high tax rates of the 1980s, the modification ensured that investment/passive income would retain such status and bear a 30 percent tax burden under § 871 or § 881, while "true" business income would be subjected to the graduated rates of § 1 or § 11. This distinction was significant given that graduated rates reached as high as 70 percent for individuals and 48 percent for corporations. This distinction also ensured that a foreign person conducting a domestic trade or business would not confront the disincentive of high tax rates with respect to the nonbusiness investment of his surplus funds.

The current effectively connected income regime essentially equates for tax purposes a foreign person engaged in a domestic trade or business with a United States person conducting a trade or business. All of the income connected with that foreign person's United States trade or business is thus taxed on a net basis at graduated rates. Such parity ensures that a foreign person does not enjoy a competitive advantage in the business arena by bearing a lower tax burden on business income than that borne by domestic persons.

Though the fundamental taxing framework applicable to a foreign person's business income parallels that applicable to domestic persons, the method of computing a foreign person's effectively connected net income ultimately subject to tax is distinct and complex. Generally, the determination of a foreign person's United States effectively connected taxable income follows a three-step sequence. First, the gross effectively connected income derived by the foreign person's United States trade or business must be segregated from any other foreign or domestic source income which is not effectively connected with that business. Next, the foreign person's expenses related to the domestic trade or business must be segregated. Once determined, these expenses must be allocated between effectively connected income and other income. If necessary, those expenses must be further apportioned *within* effectively connected income between United States and foreign source income. The net effectively connected income thereby determined is taxed under the graduated tax rates applicable to domestic corporations or citizens and residents, as the case may be.

§ 10.02 Determination of Effectively Connected Income—In General

The first step in taxing a foreign person engaged in a United States trade or business involves separating the income effectively connected with that business from other income. Effectively connected income encompasses three principal categories of income: (1) fixed or determinable income and capital gain or loss from sources within the United States; (2) all other United States source income; and (3) some foreign source income. Other income may be deemed under various Code provisions to be effectively connected income. For instance, as discussed at Chapter 12, under § 897, gains and losses derived from the disposition of United States real property interests are deemed to be effectively connected with a domestic trade or business. Foreign taxpayers may also elect to treat income derived from certain real property investments as effectively connected income.

§ 10.03 Fixed or Determinable Income and Certain Other United States Source Income

A foreign person who conducts a United States trade or business and receives income items described in § 871(a)(1) or § 881(a), such as dividends, interest, and rents, or who realizes capital gain or loss from United States sources has potentially realized effectively connected income. The effectively connected yardstick of § 864(c)(2) mandates an inquiry into the derivation of a host of income categories: for example, gains from the sale of patents, copyrights, and other intangible assets; and amounts derived from bonds and other indebtedness. Effectively connected income also encompasses United States source interest, dividends, rents, and other fixed or determinable annual or periodical income. Foreign source receipts are *not* taxable under § 864(c)(2).

The determination of whether income is effectively connected with a United States trade or business is specified in the Regulations. These provisions set forth the sole mechanism for segregating domestic source passive income from similarly sourced business income and for distinguishing income derived to meet current business needs from income derived from investments made independent of immediate business concerns. The Regulations establish two tests: one to be applied to foreign sellers or manufacturers dealing with tangible goods in the United States (the "asset use" test) and the other to be used by taxpayers conducting service-intensive businesses or those dealing with the licensing of intangible assets (the "material factor" test).

§ 10.04 The Asset Use Test

Foreign persons engaged in business, e.g., the manufacture or sale of tangible goods, in the United States who concomitantly derive passive income items in the course of that business face the asset use test. This test seeks to distinguish income derived from holding investment assets from income generated by using assets in the day-to-day operation of the business. The asset use test focuses on whether the income is derived from assets used, or held for use, in the conduct of a United States trade or business. This test applies primarily to businesses whose general activities do not directly give rise to the realization of the passive income items.

Three factors are considered in deciding whether an asset is used, or held for use, in a United States business: (1) whether the asset is held for the principal purpose of promoting the *present* conduct of a United States trade or business; (2) whether the asset is acquired and held in the ordinary course of the trade or business; and (3) whether the asset is otherwise held in some direct relationship to the trade or business. If the asset is deemed to be a business asset under one of these standards, all income flowing from its use is effectively connected. The asset's status, is, however, mutable depending on its prospective use.

The Regulations provide that an asset is held in a direct relationship with a business only if it is "held to meet the present needs of that trade or business and not its anticipated future needs." An asset thus represents a business asset if it is held for the *immediate* needs of the business. The Regulations are less than pristine in making this determination. The direct relationship standard presents some difficulty since little guidance is given on the almost metaphysical task of distinguishing present needs from future needs. The Regulations distinguish between assets held to meet current operating needs and those held for such long-range plans as diversification into a new business, foreign expansion, plant replacement, or future business contingencies. Generally, as long as the asset generating § 871(a)(1) or § 881 income is not required for present business needs, investment characterization is likely. However, once that immediate business need arises, the use of that asset will give rise to effectively connected income.

A rebuttable presumption exists that the requisite direct relationship is present for purposes of the asset use test if the asset is acquired with funds generated by the trade or business, the income generated from the asset is reinvested in that trade or business, and United States personnel actively involved in that business exercise significant management and control over the investment of the asset. This presumption can be rebutted if the foreign person can demonstrate that an asset is held to carry out some future business purpose and not to meet present business needs.

§ 10.05 The Material Factor Test

Foreign persons engaged in business, e.g., stock or securities dealing or conducting service-intensive businesses or businesses involving the licensing of intangible assets, in the United States face the material factor test for determining whether § 871(a)(1) or § 881 income is effectively connected with that business. The material factor test looks to whether the activities of the domestic trade or business are a material factor in realizing that passive income. If so, the resulting domestic source income is effectively connected.

Unlike the asset use test, which focuses narrowly on the role of particular income-generating assets in business operations, the material factor test focuses on the more overarching measure of the degree of correlation between the business activities of the foreign person's United States trade or business and the §§ 871 and 881 passive income or capital gains or losses generated. Under this test, such income is effectively connected with the foreign person's domestic trade or business if the United States activities of that business are a material factor in the realization of such items of income, gain, or loss.

The Regulations applying the material factor test suggest that a United States business will not be a material factor in generating income if the core activities incident to shaping the transaction are conducted abroad. For instance, an example set forth in the Regulations reaches this conclusion in a patent licensing context where the license negotiation and consummation occurs abroad by foreign employees and the United States branch plays no role in otherwise arranging for the licenses.

§ 10.06 All Other United States Source Income

The existence of a domestic trade or business has broad tax implications for a foreign person. Under § 864(c)(3), all United States source income, gain, or loss of a foreign person engaged in a domestic trade or business which is not fixed or determinable income, capital gain or loss, or other income described in §§ 871 and 881 is per se considered effectively connected with that domestic trade or business. This catch-all category thus encompasses gain from the sale of inventory and most compensation derived from the performance of services in the United States. It also ensnares all other domestic source income which is not truly derived from a United States trade or business, yet is sufficiently unique in character to fall outside of the "fixed or determinable" category of §§ 871(a)(1)(A) and 881(a)(1). The scope of this no person's land is a matter of considerable uncertainty.

One consequence of conducting a domestic trade or business is that income generated from direct sales of inventory from a *foreign* office will be treated as effectively connected income. For instance, § 864(c)(3) captures income generated from direct domestic sales of inventory by a foreign office even though such sales bypass the foreign person's United States operations altogether. Assume that X is a foreign person who, through the activities of a domestic agent, is engaged in the business of selling refrigerators. These sales give rise to domestic source income in the United States. Assume further that X conducts a foreign business and maintains an inventory of refrigerators in his or her foreign domicile. X occasionally makes some direct mail order sales of these refrigerators directly to customers in the United States without relying on his or her United States agent. X's income from United States refrigerator sales by operation of § 864(c)(3) is considered effectively connected with a domestic trade or business and will thus be taxed at graduated rates notwithstanding the lack of any tangible link between that income and X's United States business.

The same effectively connected classification ensues even if the inventory subject to direct sale by the foreign office is wholly unrelated to the inventory sold through the foreign person's United States trade or business. For example, assume that F, a foreign corporation, sells automobiles and farming equipment. F derives domestic source income from the sale of automobiles through a United States showroom. In the same taxable year, F also derives a United States source gain from a single sale of farming equipment in the United States in which F's domestic personnel played no role. F would not be regarded as engaged in a domestic trade or business if its isolated sale of farming equipment was its only United States contact. However, since F is already engaged in a domestic trade or business by virtue of its automobile showroom, its gain from the sale of the farming equipment, albeit of a different nature, will likewise be classified as effectively connected income.

§ 10.07 Effectively Connected Foreign Source Income

The final category of effectively connected income (and loss) encompasses certain items of foreign source income. Generally, income, gain, or loss from sources *without* the United States is not considered effectively connected with a domestic trade or business. Even though a domestic trade or business exists through the requisite sales activity, if the foreign corporation through the source rules ensures that the income has a foreign source, it will not be subjected to United States taxation. However, limited exceptions are provided under which the income will be treated as effectively connected if it is one of three types of specified income having a significant genesis in domestic business activities and if it is attributable to the corporation's office or other fixed place of business within the United States. The specified types of income are:

1. Rents, royalties, or gains from intangible property;
2. Dividends, interest, or gains from the sale of stock or securities; and
3. Income from the sale of personal property inventory items.

The first category of targeted foreign source income includes rents and royalties received for the use outside of the United States of patents, copyrights, and other intangible assets, including gain or loss on the sale of such property, if such income is derived in the active conduct of a domestic trade or business. Whether income is so derived turns on the facts and circumstances of each case. Such income is ensnared to prevent the offshore transfer of intangible assets having a substantial United States business nexus.

The second category of effectively connected foreign source income encompasses dividends, interest, and gains or losses from the sale of stock or securities realized by foreign persons engaged in the active conduct of a domestic banking, financing, or similar business. This category also includes such income derived by a foreign corporation whose principal business is trading in stocks or securities for its own account. The Regulations make clear that incidental investment activity is beyond the reach of this provision.

The third category of effectively connected foreign source income consists of income, gain, or loss derived from sales abroad of tangible inventory property or other property held primarily for sale to customers in the ordinary course of business through the foreign person's domestic office or fixed place of business. However, such income will *not* be treated as effectively connected income if the property is sold or exchanged for use, consumption, or disposition outside of the United States *and* the taxpayer's foreign office or fixed place of business materially participated in such sale. Material participation includes essential steps such as soliciting, negotiating, and performing correlative services related to the sale. If these criteria are met, the sales activity is truly "foreign" activity and, thus, properly without the scope of the domestic taxing net.

In line with this philosophy, the Regulations appear to contemplate a scenario in which the domestic office handles the essential steps involved in the sale, namely soliciting, negotiating, etc., before the income realized from such efforts is treated as effectively connected. The Regulations, however, do not attribute income from a sale to a United States office if that office performs only incidental, ministerial functions related to the sale. Conversely, income derived from foreign sales of inventory will be deemed effectively connected income if such sales occur "through the office or fixed place of business which the [foreign person] has in the United States" regardless of the destination in which such property is used, consumed, or disposed of. This presumption clearly implies that if a sale is handled "through" a domestic office, a foreign office could not have materially participated in that sale.

Much of the force of this provision was undercut with the enactment of § 865(e)(2). That provision classifies inventory or other gain attributable to an office or fixed place of business in the United States as United States source income. As a consequence, gain arising from these transactions generally will constitute effectively connected income under § 864(c)(3) rather than § 864(c)(4). Like § 864(c)(4)(B)(iii), such income is *not* decisively classified as United States source income if the inventory is sold for foreign use, disposition, or consumption *and* a foreign office or fixed place of business materially participated in the sale.

Revenue Ruling 75-253
1975-1 C.B. 203

Advice has been requested whether foreign source interest income received by the taxpayer, under the circumstances described below, is effectively connected with the conduct of a trade or business within the United States under section 864(c)(4). . . .

The taxpayer, a foreign subsidiary of a United States commercial bank, is incorporated in country M, and is in the business of making loans to organizations doing business in less developed countries. The taxpayer has offices in country M and in the United States. The taxpayer's United States office handles the negotiation and acquisition of the securities involved in the loan transactions. The United States office presents interest coupons for payment and presents all securities for payment at maturity. It maintains complete photocopy files of the taxpayer's outstanding loans as well as records indicating dates of maturity of and interest payments on the securities. The only business activities of the taxpayer's office in country M, which had a skeleton staff, consisted of receiving and storing the original securities and giving pro forma approval of the loans.

Section 864(c)(4) . . . provides, in part, that interest income from sources without the United States shall be treated as effectively connected with the conduct of a trade or business within the United States by a foreign corporation if such corporation has an office or other fixed place of business within the United States to which such income is attributable and such income is derived in the active conduct of banking, financing, or similar business within the United States.

Section 1.864-5(a) of the Income Tax Regulations provides, in part, that foreign source income realized by a foreign corporation engaged in a trade or business in the United States shall be treated as effectively connected with such trade or business only if the foreign corporation has in the United States an office or other fixed place of business to which such income is attributable in accordance with section 1.864-6.

Section 1.864-6(b)(2)(ii)(*b*) . . . provides, in part, that the determination as to whether foreign source interest income derived by a foreign corporation in the active conduct of a banking, financing, or similar business in the United States shall be treated as effectively connected with the active conduct of that business, shall be made by applying the principles of paragraph (c)(5)(ii) of section 1.864-4.

Section 1.864-4(c)(5)(ii) . . . states, in part, that United States source interest income derived by a foreign corporation in the active conduct of a banking, financing, or similar business in the United States shall be treated as effectively connected with the conduct of that business only if the securities giving rise to such interest income are attributable to the United States office through which such business is carried on and were acquired in a certain manner or consist of certain types of securities.

Section 1.864-4(c)(5)(iii)(*a*)(*2*) . . . states, in part, that for the purposes of section 1.864-4(c)(5)(ii) a security shall be deemed to be attributable to a

United States office only if such security is or was held in the United States by or for such office and recorded on its books or records as having been purchased or acquired by such office or for its account.

The reference to the principles of section 1.864-4(c)(5)(ii) . . . in section 1.864-6(b)(2)(ii)(*b*) does not mean that the provisions of section 1.864-4(c)(5)(iii)(*a*)(2) will determine whether foreign source income is effectively connected with a United States banking, financing, or similar business. Section 1.864-4(c)(5)(iii)(*a*)(2) provides a standard for determining whether United States source interest income received by foreign banks of financing companies through the efforts of their United States offices will be taxed a flat rate under section 881 of the Code or at graduated rates under section 882 in order to enable such taxpayers to conduct business within the United States with some certainty as to the tax consequences of their activities.

However, in the case of foreign source interest income earned by foreign banks or financing companies in the United States, the question is not whether such interest is to be taxed at ordinary or flat rates, but whether said interest is to be taxed by the United States at all. Therefore, section 1.864-4(c)(5)(iii)(*a*)(2) applies only in the case of United States source income that is to be treated as effectively connected with a United States banking, financing, or similar business with the result that foreign source income (interest, dividends, etc.) may be effectively connected with the active conduct of a United States banking, financing, or similar business despite the wording of section 1.864-4(c)(5)(iii)(*a*)(2). A foreign corporation cannot, for example, avoid the taxation of effectively connected foreign source income simply by holding securities outside the United States.

In the instant case, the taxpayer is engaged in the active conduct of a banking, financing, or similar business in the United States within the meaning of section 864(c)(4) of the Code. Moreover, since the taxpayer's United States office performed all the significant tasks relating to the negotiation and acquisition of the securities, with the sole exception of storage of the securities, the interest income derived from the securities is attributable to the taxpayer's United States office within the meaning of the regulations under section 864.

Accordingly, foreign source interest income derived by the taxpayer from the securities is effectively connected with the conduct of a trade or business within the United States under section 864(c)(4). . . .

§ 10.08 Foreign Source Income Attributable to a Domestic Office or Place of Business

Foreign source income will be linked to a domestic trade or business only if it is "attributable to" the foreign person's United States office or other fixed place of business and is realized in the ordinary course of the business conducted at that office. This rule is intended to ensnare "only income which has its economic genesis in the United States." Thus, income will *not* be attributable to a United States office or fixed place of business unless that establishment was a material factor in the realization of that income. A United States office will not satisfy this standard unless it provides "a significant contribution to the production of that income" and its activities are an "essential economic element in the production of income."

To be effectively connected, the income must have been derived in the ordinary course of the domestic business and must be properly allocable to the domestic business. The Regulations state that if a United States office is a material factor in the realization of income, *all* such income, gain, or loss is considered allocable *in its entirety* to that office. The only limitation on this pseudo-allocation rule is that, with respect to the sale of inventory through a United States office, the amount attributed to that office cannot exceed what would have been brought into the taxing net had the sale been sourced to the United States under §§ 861 through 863.

If foreign sellers of inventory and other tangible property can prove that the property was sold for use, consumption, or disposition outside of the United States and that a foreign office materially participated in a sale, it is irrelevant if a domestic office also played a significant role. To determine whether a foreign office participated materially in a sale, the activities of that office must be scrutinized to determine if it performed significant services necessary for the consummation of the sale. The provision of these services must not have been the subject of a separate agreement outside of the sales contract between the buyer and seller. As with domestic offices, soliciting and negotiating are clearly significant services. In such a case, none of the foreign source sales income will be subject to United States taxation. For example, the Regulations provide that the receipt of a sales order by a United States office or fixed place of business will result in that locale being deemed a material factor in the realization of that income "except where the sales order is received unsolicited and that office is not held out to potential customers as the place to which such sales orders should be sent."

Effectively connected income does not include income from property sold for use, consumption, or disposition outside of the United States. If an individual sells property to an unrelated person, the country of ultimate use will generally be considered the country of destination of that property. If at the time of the sale, the taxpayer knew or should have known that the property probably would not be used in that country of destination, the onus rests upon the taxpayer to determine the true country of ultimate use. Without such proof, the United States is presumed to be that country. However, a taxpayer who sells property to a person whose principal business consists of selling from inventory to retail customers at foreign retail outlets may, in the interest of efficiency, presume that the property will be used abroad.

§ 10.09 United States Office or Other Fixed Place of Business

Foreign source income will not be deemed effectively connected to a domestic trade or business unless that income is attributable to an office or other fixed place of business in the United States. While this requirement entails a facts-and-circumstances determination, an office or fixed place of business is generally a place, site, structure, or other fixed facility through which a foreign person engages in business. The term includes a wide variety of geographic locales—factories, stores and other sales outlets, workshops, mines, quarries, and other places of natural resource extraction. The facility need not be continuously used by the foreign person or his agent to be so classified. If the facility happens to be another related or unrelated person's office or place of business, sporadic use of that office should not cause that office or fixed place of business to be imputed to the taxpayer-user.

Special rules are provided with regard to the offices in the United States of various agents employed by the foreign person. Agents are classified as either independent or dependent agents. The office of a general commission agent, broker, or other *independent* agent will not be considered an office of the foreign principal when that agent acts solely within the ordinary course of his business in that capacity. Because of this carte blanche status, however, the Regulations intone that the prima facie independent status of that agent will be closely scrutinized. Thus, if an agent acts exclusively, or almost exclusively, for a particular foreign principal or if both principal and agent are controlled by the same interests, independent agent status may be threatened.

Generally, the office of a *dependent* agent will also be disregarded unless the agent has the authority to negotiate and conclude contracts in the name of the foreign principal and regularly exercises that authority *or* has a stock of merchandise belonging to the foreign person from which orders are regularly filled. In other words, the agent's business will not be imputed to its principal unless the agent stands in the principal's stead in terms of conducting business. A special rule applies to dependent agents who are also employees. If employee-agents regularly carry on the business of their employer in the ordinary course of their duties in a United States fixed facility, that fixed facility will be imputed to their foreign employer-principal. This result ensues regardless of the scope of the employee's authority to contract or fill orders on behalf of the foreign principal.

§ 10.10 Real Property Income Deemed Effectively Connected

The Code contains two special provisions whereby income related to domestic real property interests may be deemed effectively connected for United States tax purposes, either automatically or as a result of an election by the taxpayer. First, under § 897, gain or loss derived by a foreign person from a sale or other disposition of a United States real property interest is generally deemed to be effectively connected with the conduct of a domestic trade or business. The practical effect of this rule is to expose that gain to United States tax.

Similarly, §§ 871(d) and 882(d) permit foreign persons deriving rents or other income from United States real property to elect to treat all such income as effectively connected income. This election enables foreign persons to reduce their United States tax liability as this effectively connected real property income may be reduced by properly allocated and apportioned deductions.

§ 10.11 Allocation and Apportionment of Expenses—In General

Given the business genesis underlying the effectively connected concept, it is only proper that the foreign person be entitled to offset that income with the expenses incurred to earn such income. Thus, once the taxpayer ascertains the amount of effectively connected gross income, the extent to which deductions against that income are permitted must be determined.

As a general rule, nonresident alien individuals and foreign corporations not engaged in a United States trade or business are *not* entitled to deductions and are taxed on a gross basis on certain types of typically investment income. If such foreign persons are engaged in a United States trade or business, however, they may deduct expenses but only to the extent that those expenses relate to income effectively connected with that domestic business. Thus, if a foreign person is engaged in a domestic trade or business and is also engaged in some other activity (such as investment activity or foreign activity), that person must allocate expenses between income derived from its United States trade or business and income earned from its other activities.

As regards a foreign taxpayer, the Service generally wishes to allocate expenses *away from* the United States. For instance, if a Spanish taxpayer has both Spanish and United States activity, the Service prefers to allocate deductions to Spanish operations and away from domestic operations in order to maximize the effectively connected income subject to United States tax. Obviously, the Spanish individual prefers the opposite result.

The complex and cumbersome procedures for the allocation of deductions are set forth in § 1.861-8 of the Regulations. Basically, the Regulations prescribe a two-tiered method to accomplish this task; the two distinct tiers being, first, "allocation" and then, if necessary, "apportionment." The allocation process is the threshold determination which focuses on whether an expense is directly related to a particular class of gross income. In effect, the task of allocating deductions involves matching those deductions with the gross income to which they most directly relate. Once deductions are matched with a particular class of gross income, the composition of that particular class of gross income must be analyzed to determine whether it is comprised solely of United States source income (a "residual grouping"), solely foreign source income (a "statutory grouping"), or some combination of both. As the term and procedure suggest, the apportionment of allocated deductions within a class of gross income is required only in the last scenario. When apportionment is required, the deduction already allocated to that mixed-source class of gross income under the first-tier allocation procedure is, in effect, further divided between the foreign source income and United States source income comprising that class of gross income.

These complicated maneuvers are perhaps best illustrated by the example of a domestic accounting firm performing services in both the United Kingdom and the United States. The firm's headquarters is in the United States, and it has a branch office abroad staffed by resident members. In the course of its operations, the firm will derive United States and foreign source income from the rendition of services and possibly interest income from both jurisdictions from short-term investment of excess cash reserves. Expenses include those for personnel, rent, utilities, and the like.

Expenses directly related to the rendition of services, namely salaries, rent, etc., are allocable to the class of gross income derived from services. Some expenses, such as supervisory or general and administrative expense, are not definitely related to any class of income and are thus most likely allocated to *all* classes of gross income. As the two presumed classes of gross income (i.e., income from services and interest income) are comprised of both foreign and United States source gross income, allocated expenses must further be apportioned between those two types of income.

§ 10.12 The Allocation Process

The allocation process essentially entails matching deductions to the category of gross income to which those deductions most factually relate. As a general rule, a deduction is allocated to the gross income category to which such deduction is "definitely related." A deduction is definitely related to a class of gross income if it is incurred as a result of, or incident to, an activity or in connection with property from which such class of gross income is derived.

Classes of gross income to which deductions are allocated are *not* predetermined. The Regulations provide that the gross income to which a specific deduction is definitely related is referred to as a class of gross income. As opposed to first delineating certain classes of gross income to which deductions should be allocated, in somewhat of an undefined chicken-or-the-egg fashion, the class of gross income to which deductions are allocated is driven and defined by the nature of the deduction being allocated. However, some guidance is contained in the Regulations which provide that a class of gross income may consist of one or more items (or subdivisions thereof) of the gross income categories enumerated in § 61. For instance, deductions for real estate taxes on a rental property would directly relate to the rents class of gross income.

To compound the ambiguity permeating this Regulation and, in particular, the directly related standard, it is entirely possible under the Regulations that a deduction may not bear a definite relationship to *any* particular class of gross income. In such a case, the deduction is treated as definitely related and allocable to *all* of a taxpayer's gross income. For example, such an expense could be certain general and administrative salaries for top level management that cannot be traced to a given class of income.

Such unmatched expenses, by definition, bypass the allocation process, but are ratably apportioned between the statutory groupings (i.e., foreign and United States source gross income) comprising the taxpayer's gross income. For example, if the corporation's gross income was $1,000,000, consisting of $600,000 foreign source gross income and $400,000 United States gross income, 60 percent of the managerial salaries would be apportioned to foreign source income and 40 percent to United States source income.

The allocation process marches along despite the fact that no gross income has been received or accrued within the relevant class of gross income. Moreover, allocation is appropriate even though the deduction to be allocated exceeds the amount of income in the gross income class.

§ 10.13   The Apportionment Process

The process of apportioning deductions occurs within a class of gross income and matches deductions with the foreign or United States source income to which they are related. The apportionment of deductions is crucial in many varied settings. For foreign taxpayers, the apportionment process bears on distinguishing effectively connected gross income from other gross income.

For these purposes, once a deduction has been allocated to a class of gross income, the source of the gross income item(s) comprising that class must be determined. If the class consists exclusively of foreign source (or effectively connected) income (the statutory grouping) or exclusively of United States source (or non-effectively connected) income (the residual grouping), the taxpayer fortunately may end its analysis after the allocation process is completed. The deduction is allocated in its entirety to the income in the statutory or residual grouping, whichever is appropriate.

Taxpayers analyzing deductions which bear no direct relationship to *any* gross income are also fortunate from a computational vantage point. Such expenses bypass the initial allocation process and are merely apportioned on a ratable basis between groupings.

If the class of gross income to which a deduction has been allocated is comprised of *both* United States and foreign source income (or effectively connected and non-effectively connected income), that deduction must be apportioned between those two groupings of income. The Regulations nebulously direct that the apportionment process be accomplished in a fact-based manner which "reflects to a reasonably close extent the factual relationship" between the deduction and the gross income grouping. Examples of bases and factors which may be considered in making this factual determination include comparisons of sales, gross receipts, cost of goods sold, profit contributions, expenses and intangible costs incurred in generating the activity, and gross income. These possible apportionment bases are by no means exclusive. This open-ended list of bases, coupled with the malleable "factual relationship" standard, renders the apportionment process ripe for tax planning.

Stemkowski v. Commissioner
United States Court of Appeals, Second Circuit
690 F.2d 40 (1982)

OAKES, CIRCUIT JUDGE:

This supposed test case involves the taxability of a Canadian citizen who formerly played professional hockey for the New York Rangers of the National Hockey League (NHL). As a nonresident alien, Stemkowski was subject to United States tax on that portion of his income connected with his performance of services in this country, and entitled to deduct expenditures relating to such United States income. . . . We affirm in part, and reverse and remand in part.

The . . . major issues on appeal are:

. . . .

2. Whether the Tax Court correctly held that taxpayer was not entitled to deduct certain off-season physical conditioning expenses claimed as ordinary and necessary business expenses.
3. Whether the Tax Court correctly held that taxpayer was not entitled to various other deductions for what he claimed were ordinary and necessary business expenses, including those for newspapers, magazines, telephone, television, "promotional" activities, and gifts to trainers.
4. Whether the Tax Court correctly held that taxpayer was not entitled to deduct sales taxes because they were not connected with the conduct of his trade or business within the United States, or to deduct amounts withheld from his salary to pay premiums on disability insurance. . . .

DISCUSSION

. . . .

2. Off-Season Physical Conditioning Expenses

Stemkowski claims deductions for his off-season expenses on golf, bowling, tennis, running, swimming, and using a YMCA and a health club, as business expenses under I.R.C. § 162, on the theory that they were necessary to meet an obligation in the NHL contract to keep in good physical condition throughout the year. The Tax Court reasoned, however, that off-season conditioning was related only to arriving fit at training camp and therefore held that Stemkowski's conditioning expenses were nondeductible because allocable to income earned in Canada. This holding is clearly erroneous. Off-season conditioning contributes not only to the fitness required of players on the first day of training camp under Paragraph 2(a) of the contract but also to the fitness required throughout the regular season under Paragraph 2(b) of the contract. Thus, Stemkowski's off-season conditioning expenses were at least in part connected to United States income.

Because of its erroneous reasoning the Tax Court did not reach the question, on which both sides presented evidence, whether Stemkowski's off-season conditioning expenses were deductible under § 162 as ordinary and necessary for business, or were nondeductible under § 262 as for personal fun and relaxation. Not everything that is done to develop one's body, even if one is a professional athlete, is necessarily for business. For a hockey player, weight-lifting, jogging, bicycling, and other exercises to strengthen and coordinate the body may well be at the business end of the spectrum, because these activities may contribute directly to professional hockey playing ability. Golf, tennis, squash, or bowling, however, at least for a hockey player, may well be at the fun-and-relaxation end of the spectrum, especially in light of Stemkowski's testimony that he played golf to relax, played tennis and squash for fun, and bowled with a girlfriend.

There is no general rule that can be laid down in connection with such expenses, and we remand to the Tax Court to make a factual determination, on the basis of its familiarity with the record and the demeanor of the witnesses, as to which of these expenses were deductible. We remand also for allocation of the off-season conditioning expenses between Canadian and United States source income. With respect to some of the claimed conditioning expenses, e.g., club membership, the Tax Court will also need to determine whether the taxpayer has satisfied the substantiation requirements of § 274.

3. Miscellaneous Business Expenses

Stemkowski also sought to deduct as business expenses the costs of magazines and newspapers in which he read hockey news; the costs of "promotional" activities such as entertaining fans, team members, and media people, purchasing hockey tickets for friends, having his hair styled, and answering fan mail; the tips he paid his trainers; and some of the costs of maintaining a telephone and television. The Tax Court disallowed these deductions on the erroneous ground that they were not required by the employer. While a requirement by an employer that an employee make an expenditure may be one factor weighing in favor of the employee's right to a deduction, it is not a prerequisite for the deduction. Section 162(a) requires only that the expense be a necessary and ordinary expense paid or incurred during the taxable year in carrying on a trade or business. For all expenses except those for hockey publications and for fan mail, Stemkowski either failed to establish deductibility, or failed to meet the substantial requirements of § 274(d), which applies to travel expenses, expenditures on activities or facilities generally considered for entertainment, amusement, or recreation, or gift expenses.

The purchase of general newspapers is personal and cannot be deducted. Because Stemkowski's claimed purchase of hockey journals might be deductible as relating to his work, however, and because no substantiation under § 274(d) is required for such expenses, we remand for a determination whether Stemkowski's "hockey news" deduction meets the "ordinary and necessary" business expense standard of § 162. . . .

4. Sales Tax and Disability Insurance Deductions

Only three types of expenses not related to income from a trade or business in the United States are allowed as deductions to nonresident aliens under § 873(b): casualty or theft losses; charitable contributions; and personal exemption(s). A nonresident alien's United States sales taxes are not deductible unless shown to be business related. Stemkowski failed to make this showing; for example, taxpayer's sales taxes were not shown to be business related, he specifically deducted the sales tax on wedding ring purchases, and these expenses are not otherwise deductible under § 873(b). Disability insurance premiums, even for hockey players, are personal and not business expenses. Thus the Tax Court properly disallowed Stemkowski's sales tax and disability insurance deductions. . . .

PROBLEM 10—NONTREATY PERSONS— TRADE OR BUSINESS INCOME

Code: §§ 864(c)(1)-(4), 871(d), 873

Regulations: § 1.871-10(a)-(c)

T, an individual, was a citizen and bona fide resident of Saudi Arabia, which has not entered a tax treaty with the United States. T is single and is on the cash method, calendar-year method of accounting. T has never been present in the United States. During the year, T owned the following assets:

1. 100 shares of the common stock of X Corporation—a domestic corporation;
2. 100 shares of the common stock of Y Corporation—a foreign corporation;
3. Rental real estate located in Modesto, California;
4. A loan to H, a citizen of the United States currently residing in Bolivia, in the amount of $7,000;
5. Deposit in a Chicago, Illinois bank, $20,000;
6. The rights to a patent created by T;
7. Vacant land held for investment in Oregon; and
8. 50 shares of preferred stock of Z Corporation—a domestic corporation.

During the year, T received the following amounts:

a. Cash payment on the X Corporation stock, $20,000—domestic source;
b. Cash payment on the Y Corporation, $13,000—$5,200 domestic source, $7,800 foreign source;
c. Rents from the rental property, $10,000—domestic source;
d. Interest on the loan to H, $1,000—foreign source;
e. Interest on deposit at Chicago, Illinois bank, $2,000—domestic source;
f. Gain on sale of ten shares of Z Corporation stock, $5,000—foreign source; and
g. Payment pursuant to sale to W Corporation of United States rights to a patent for five percent of net profits from product produced through its use, $8,000—domestic source.

T's expenses for the year included:

a. Depreciation and expenses with respect to the United States rental property, $3,000;
b. Loss on the sale of five shares of Z Corporation stock in the United States, $1,000; and
c. Medical expenses, $4,500.

1. Suppose T's activities in connection with his United States rental real estate constitute engaging in a trade or business.

    a. What is T's tax liability for the year?
    b. What if T also conducts a wine business located in Saudi Arabia (not a United States trade or business) and in response to solicitations sells occasional cases of wine to United States purchasers with title passing within the United States?
    c. What result if T's $20,000 deposit at the Chicago, Illinois bank are rental deposits which were moved into the checking account when balances became minimal?
    d. What result if T sells depreciable personal property (e.g., a computer) which had been used at its rental office?

2. What is T's taxable United States income for the year and his tax liability assuming that none of the activities constitutes a trade or business but that T makes an election under § 871(d)?

    a. What is his taxable income and his tax liability for such a year?
    b. What if T also conducts a wine business located in Saudi Arabia (not a United States trade or business) and in response to solicitations sells occasional cases of wine to United States purchasers with title passing within the United States?
    c. What result if T's $20,000 deposit at the Chicago, Illinois bank are rental deposits which were moved into the checking account when balances became minimal?

Chapter 11
Nontreaty Persons—Inventory Income; Branch Profits Tax

§ 11.01 Sales of Inventory Property
§ 11.02 Section 863(b)—Source Rules for Taxable Income
§ 11.03 Production and Sale of Inventory Property Involving a Foreign Jurisdiction
§ 11.04 Branch Profits Tax—In General
§ 11.05 Branch Profits Tax on the Dividend Equivalent Amount
§ 11.06 Special Rules for Year of Termination of United States Trade or Business
§ 11.07 Secondary Withholding Tax and Branch Profits Tax
  Problem 11

§ 11.01 Sales of Inventory Property

The inventory source rules generally focus on the jurisdiction in which title passes. Under § 861(a)(6), income derived from the purchase of inventory property *outside* the United States and its sale *within* the United States is United States source income. Section 862(a)(6) supplies its converse: if inventory property is purchased *within* the United States and sold *outside* it, the income so derived is foreign source. Thus, the purchase of inventory in France by a Greek national and its sale in the United States with title passing to the buyer domestically will generate United States source income. A similar transaction with a purchase in the United States and title passing in France yields foreign source income.

Curiously, neither the Code nor the Regulations specifically addresses the source issue when inventory property is *both* purchased and sold domestically or when inventory property is *both* purchased and sold in a foreign country. It is clear, however, that the situs of sale controls in those cases as well. Thus, in the above hypotheticals, a purchase in France with title passing on the sale in France produces foreign source income, while a purchase in the United States with title passing on the sale in the United States generates United States source income.

A sale takes place "at the time when, and the place where, the rights, title, and interest of the seller in the property are transferred to the buyer." This passage of title issue is not peculiar to tax law. Rather, it is a question of local commercial law.

A major distinction exists between purchase-and-sale income and production-and-sale income. When dealing with purchase-and-sale income, no income is allocated to the purchase—only the sale is deemed responsible for generating the income. Thus, all income derived from the sale has its source where the sale took place. In production-and-sale situations, discussed below, some of the income is seen as a result of production activity and thus income does not stem from the sale alone. Consequently, the source of the income is split according to specified rules.

Special rules are provided for sales of personal property, including inventory, through offices or other fixed places of business. Section 865(e)(2) applies to nonresidents and extends to inventory as well as to all other types of personal property. Thus, for nonresidents, the source rules of § 861(a)(6) and the title passage rules for inventory are not applicable. The focus of § 865(e)(2) is on the existence of a United States office or fixed place of business and whether the income derived from sales of inventory or other property is attributable to that office. If both tests are met under the principles and Regulations of § 864(c)(5), United States source income arises. Thus, under § 865(e)(2), a Spanish resident with only a domestic business that sells inventory with title passing in either Spain or the United States will have United States source income if the income is attributable to the nonresident's local business. Similarly, sales of other assets, including depreciable property, goodwill, and intangible assets, bearing the requisite nexus to the domestic business generate Untied States source gains as well.

Section 865(e)(2)(B) engrafts a further exception which will preclude United States source if a foreign office materially participated in the transaction and the use or consumption of the property is outside the United States. Thus, in the above example, if the Spanish resident also possesses a Madrid office which materially participated in the sale of the inventory to a United States purchaser, forcign source income would arise provided the property is destined for a location outside of the United States. It appears that § 865(e)(2) has emasculated the effectively connected rule of

§ 864(c)(4)(B)(iii), since that section only applies to foreign source income and, under the rules of § 865(e)(2), all such transactions will have a United States source.

§ 11.02 Section 863(b)—Source Rules for Taxable Income

Section 863(b) provides additional source rules but, interestingly, offers them while masquerading as an apportionment device rather than a straightforward source rule statute. Section 863(b) comes into play only when it is shown under other Code sections, Rulings, or, paradoxically, under § 863(b) itself that the taxpayer has had gross income from both foreign and United States sources. Furthermore, as a prerequisite to the application of § 863(b), the taxpayer must have had a specified type of income including production and sale of inventory property (involving a foreign jurisdiction).

Once these two conditions have been met, the taxpayer is generally allowed to compute manufacturing income, for example, by apportioning the gross income into foreign and United States sources as described in the Regulations and then subtracting allocable manufacturing expenses. Thus, § 863(b) is perhaps best seen as a taxable income source rule, i.e., an apportionment device which may override both the normal source rules of §§ 861 through 863(a) as well as the basic scheme of relating expenses to income through § 61 income classification (rather than § 863 activity) envisioned in § 1.861-8 of the Regulations.

Section 863(b) differs from the gross income source rules in that the latter statutes (with the exception of some types of dividend, interest, and services income) are "all or nothing" rules under which all income stemming from a transaction is considered to possess either a United States or a foreign source. Section 863(b), on the other hand, splits or allocates income: some income is treated as foreign source, other as United States source. Thus, major distinctions may arise between the tax consequences of the purchase and sale of inventory and the production and sale of inventory.

Additionally, § 863(b) allocations may be based upon an individual's own records if application for such treatment is made to the Service with proof that the taxpayer has, in good faith and unaffected by tax considerations, regularly employed an accounting procedure which more clearly reflects income source than that described in the Regulations. If this weighty standard is not met, the method described in the Regulations must be used.

§ 11.03 Production and Sale of Inventory Property Involving a Foreign Jurisdiction

The most significant class of § 863 taxable income is that from the sale of exchange of personal property (inventory) produced (in whole or in part) within the United States and sold or exchanged in a foreign jurisdiction or produced without the United States and sold or exchanged domestically. This income is considered partly from United States and partly from foreign sources because the income is attributable to both the production activity and the sales activity which have occurred in two separate jurisdictions. The Regulations specify two methods of source apportionment: the independent factory or production price method or an alternative method (the "50/50 method").

The first method may be elected by a manufacturing operation that sells its goods to independent distributors and also transfers that product to its own distributing branch which is located in a country other than the one of production. In such a case, the distributing branch is treated as having paid to the manufacturing branch the same price as was paid by the independent distributors. For foreign producers, the difference between this fictional payment and the basis for the product is foreign source, while the difference between that payment and the payment actually received by the distributing branch is domestic source.

Under the second method, manufacturing gross income is divided into two halves. One half is allocated on the basis of property value—that portion of the sales price which represents the ratio of United States property to worldwide property owned by the taxpayer will be domestic source. The remaining half is apportioned through a ratio of United States gross sales to worldwide gross sales. Thereafter, deductions are allocated on a pro rata basis regardless of whether they relate primarily or exclusively to the production or sale component of the transaction.

As earlier mentioned, a third permissible method of source determination is permitted by application to the Service to base the return on the taxpayer's books of account. This method is quite likely to be onerous in terms of the burden of proof necessary to sustain it.

§ 11.04 Branch Profits Tax—In General

Foreign corporations engaged in United States trade or business are subject to a branch profits tax. The tax is designed to parallel the United States tax treatment of foreign corporations doing business through a branch with the tax treatment of operating domestically through a United States subsidiary. In the latter case, the subsidiary is subject to corporate-level tax on worldwide income plus a withholding tax on dividends repatriated to its foreign owners. In the former case, the foreign corporation is subject only to United States taxation on effectively connected income and dividends are taxable to its shareholders only if the United States effectively connected earnings constitute more than 25 percent of its worldwide earnings. The branch profits taxes impose on corporations doing business in the United States through an unincorporated form an additional tax of 30 percent that simulates the additional withholding tax imposed on earnings repatriated by a United States subsidiary. The branch profits taxes are imposed under § 884 in addition to the regular corporate income tax on income attributable to a domestic trade or business.

The branch profits tax equals 30 percent (or a lower treaty rate, if applicable) of a foreign corporation's "dividend equivalent amount." The dividend equivalent amount generally represents the foreign corporation's current earnings and profits from a domestic trade or business as adjusted for net increases and decreases in "United States net equity." The dividend equivalent amount is essentially the amount available for repatriation (i.e., the amount that would be treated as a dividend). This tax is a substitute for the 30 percent withholding tax which would be imposed on dividends repatriated by a United States subsidiary to its foreign owners.

§ 11.05 Branch Profits Tax on the Dividend Equivalent Amount

Under § 884(a), a foreign corporation is subject to a 30 percent tax (or a lower tax treaty rate, if applicable) on its annual dividend equivalent amount. The intent of the legislation is to impose a 30 percent tax on the annual effectively connected earnings of a foreign corporation which are not reinvested in the assets of a domestic trade or business and thus are repatriated to shareholders in some fashion. The dividend equivalent amount, the measurement base for the tax, is equal to the foreign corporation's current effectively connected earnings and profits adjusted for increases or decreases in its United States net equity. A foreign corporation's United States net equity is determined by reducing, but not below zero, the amount of money and the adjusted basis of its effectively connected assets (United States assets) by its effectively connected liabilities (United States liabilities).

The computation of the dividend equivalent amount and the concept of United States net equity is best illustrated by an example. As the starting point for computing the dividend equivalent amount, the normal annual determination of earnings and profits is made. The reliance on earnings and profits as a computational base is logical as it measures the base of earnings available for distribution as a dividend which § 884 is designed to reach. For example, if a newly formed foreign corporation has $500 of effectively connected earnings and profits from the conduct of its domestic trade or business in Year 1, its Year 1 dividend equivalent amount begins at $500.

The branch profits tax is avoided if these earnings remain in the United States (i.e., United States net equity increases) since the abusive removal of earnings without tax has not occurred. Thus, if the foreign corporation's United States net equity increases during its taxable year, the corporation's effectively connected earnings and profits and thus its taxable base is reduced (but not below zero) by the amount of reinvestment in the United States. In the above example, if $500 is invested in United States property, the dividend equivalent amount would be zero in Year 1, properly ensuring that the branch profits tax does not apply when United States earnings have merely been reinvested in a domestic trade or business rather than repatriated.

Conversely, if the foreign corporation's net equity decreases during the taxable year, thereby signaling the targeted withdrawal of the corporation's investment of earnings in the United States, its effectively connected earnings and profits are *increased* by the amount of the reduction. This repatriation represents the appropriate juncture at which to impose tax. Thus, in the preceding example, if in Year 2 the corporation withdrew $150 and had no effectively connected earnings for the year, the $150 decrease in net equity appropriately increases the dividend equivalent amount and the branch profits tax base. Thus, a 30 percent tax would be imposed on the $150 withdrawal.

Any such increase in the dividend equivalent amount, however, cannot exceed the foreign corporation's accumulated effectively connected earnings and profits (i.e., the excess of the corporation's aggregate earnings and profits derived from its domestic trade or business over its aggregate dividend equivalent amounts as determined for prior years). In the above example, if the corporation withdrew $700, it should not give rise to a dividend equivalent amount of $700 since such a tax base would exceed the corporation's domestic earnings component (to date, $500). Thus, broadly speaking, a foreign corporation which has never derived any earnings and profits from a United States trade or business should not be liable for the § 884(a) tax.

The branch taxes are not without limitation. Investment earnings of foreign enterprises are immune from § 884. Moreover, significant business earnings unaccompanied by withdrawals are temporarily immune from the branch taxes. Earnings of foreign individuals are not subject to § 884 as the tax is imposed only on foreign corporations.

§ 11.06 Special Rules for Year of Termination of United States Trade or Business

One of the broad purposes of the § 884(a) branch profits tax in the case of a foreign corporation is to accelerate the payment of the United States withholding tax that would be imposed on a comparable dividend by a domestic corporation of its after-tax earnings to a foreign shareholder. Under current law, no withholding tax is generally imposed on a *liquidating* distribution by a domestic corporation to a foreign shareholder. In such a case, the distribution typically generates a capital gain, rather than a dividend, and such amounts are generally exempt from taxation. Effectively connected earnings and profits that have been exempt from the § 884(a) branch profits tax will not be subject to the branch profits tax when actually distributed by the foreign corporation if the "complete termination" exception is met.

In the interest of parity underlying the branch profits taxes, a foreign corporation will not be subject to the § 884(a) branch profits tax for the taxable year in which it completely terminates all of its United States trades or businesses. A foreign corporation is deemed to completely terminate all of its domestic trades or businesses for any taxable year if the corporation has no United States assets. A termination does not occur unless the corporation's shareholders adopt an irrevocable resolution to completely liquidate and dissolve the corporation and, before the close of the succeeding taxable year, all of its domestic assets are either distributed, used to satisfy liabilities, or otherwise cease to be United States assets. Moreover, neither the corporation nor any related corporation can directly or indirectly use any of the assets of the terminated trades or businesses or property attributable to the assets or the effectively connected earnings and profits for three years after the year of termination. The corporation also cannot have any effectively connected income for three years after the year of termination.

§ 11.07 Secondary Withholding Tax and Branch Profits Tax

One of the basic purposes of the § 884(a) branch profits tax is to accelerate in the case of a foreign corporation the United States withholding tax that would be imposed on a dividend paid by a domestic corporation to a foreign shareholder. Thus, it follows that if a foreign corporation is subject to the § 884(a) branch profits tax, no withholding tax is imposed on any dividends *actually* paid by that foreign corporation out of its earnings and profits for that year. This exemption is generally proper since the tax on such a repatriated dividend has already been levied and collected under § 884(a). Additionally, it must be remembered that the enactment of the branch profits tax is applicable to *all* foreign corporations deriving income from a domestic trade or business, including those whose earnings when repatriated possess a domestic source. Without this treatment, such earnings would be subject to a triple, rather than an intended double, tax—once as received by the shareholder under § 871 or § 881 and twice by the corporation under §§ 882 and 884.

CHAPTER 11   INVENTORY INCOME; BRANCH PROFITS TAX   245

PROBLEM 11—NONTREATY PERSONS— INVENTORY INCOME; BRANCH PROFITS TAX

Code: §§ 881(a), (c), and (d), 882(a) and (c), 884(a)-(c), 865(e)(2)

Regulations: §§ 1.864-6 and 1.864-7; 1.863-3

F Corporation was organized under the laws of Brazil, which has not entered a tax treaty with the United States. Its principal business activity consists of the purchase and sale of rugs and tapestries from Guatemala. F's office facilities are located in Brazil and its sales are made in the United States. All sales were shipped with beneficial title and risk of loss passing in Brazil. Orders for F's goods were solicited by traveling salesman operating out of the home office on a commission basis. Purchase orders were sent to the Brazilian office where they were accepted and filled from inventory warehoused in Brazil. F maintained no inventory, plant, office, or other facilities in the United States.

1. What is F's tax obligation to the United States?

2. Assume that the contracts in 1. were made with beneficial title passing in the United States.

3. Assume in 1. that F had a United States office or other fixed place of business.

   a. Assume that the United States office after acquiring the property sells it to Canadian customers.
   b. Assume that the United States office after acquiring the property sells it to Australian customers who were solicited by the Brazilian office.

4. Assume that F itself manufactured the goods and sold the items to United States customers with beneficial title passing in Brazil.

5. What result in 4. if F's sales were made with beneficial title passing in the United States?

6. Assume in 4. that, instead of the above distribution system, F maintained a branch office located in leased office space in Chicago. F's American branch maintained a leased warehouse for storage of its stock. Title to the purchased goods would pass to American customers in Brazil under the purchase contracts. The United States salesmen operated out of its Chicago office,

but all orders had to be accepted in Brazil. What is F's tax obligation to the United States?

7. Under 1.-6., is F responsible for the branch profits tax of § 884? What result if F under 1.-6. distributes a dividend to its foreign shareholders?

Chapter 12
Nontreaty Persons—United States Real Property Interests

§ 12.01 Background

§ 12.02 Tax Consequences of Treating Income as Effectively Connected to a United States Trade or Business
Revenue Ruling 90-37, 1990-1 C.B. 141

§ 12.03 Direct Investment in United States Real Property

§ 12.04 United States Real Property Interests

§ 12.05 Dispositions

§ 12.06 Indirect Investment—Interests Held Through Domestic Corporations

§ 12.07 United States Real Property Holding Companies

§ 12.08 Indirect Investment—Interests Held Through Foreign Corporations

§ 12.09 Coordination of § 897 with Nonrecognition Rules
Revenue Ruling 84-160, 1984-2 C.B. 125

Problem 12

§ 12.01 Background

In order to prevent the tax-free disposition of United States real property by foreign investors and to put domestic and foreign investors on an equal tax footing, Congress enacted § 897. Thereunder, gain or loss from the disposition of a "United States real property interest" by a foreign investor is treated as if the gain or loss were effectively connected with a United States trade or business. The amount of gain or loss realized on such a disposition is determined under § 1001 and is recognized for tax purposes unless one of the § 897 nonrecognition exceptions applies to shield it from taxation. The practical effect of this rule is to expose such gain to United States tax at graduated tax rates.

This characterization of the gain controls even if the foreign person's domestic activities do not constitute an actual trade or business and even if the gain is not effectively connected to a domestic trade or business under the principles of § 864(c). Moreover, the nonresident need not satisfy a physical presence test to be subject to tax.

While the statutory reach of § 897 is broad and all-encompassing with regard to *direct* investment in United States realty, as regards *indirect* investment (i.e., the formation by foreign persons of a foreign or domestic corporation through which to invest in United States realty), significant distinctions exist. Depending upon whether a United States or a foreign holding company is employed, certain transfers are exempt from the coverage of § 897.

While § 897 as originally drafted blocked numerous tax-avoidance techniques, some of its provisions became redundant with the passage of corporate tax reform in 1986. Though the corporate reform was not addressed specifically to the international area, the effect of many of its amendments was to curtail some of the circumvention techniques previously available to foreign investors without reference to § 897.

§ 12.02 Tax Consequences of Treating Income as Effectively Connected to a United States Trade or Business

The gain or loss of a foreign taxpayer from the disposition of a United States real property interest is deemed to be effectively connected to a domestic trade or business. As such, absent a special nonrecognition exception, the gain will be taxed at the graduated rates of § 1 for nonresident individuals and at the graduated rates of § 11 for foreign corporations. The effectively connected tag also means that deductions attributable to the gain may be taken.

If a foreign person has gain from the disposition of a United States real property interest, that gain is considered effectively connected to a domestic trade or business under § 871(b)(1) or § 882(a)(1). For nonresident alien individuals, § 871(b) generally provides that effectively connected income is taxed at the rates provided in § 1. Section 897(a)(2)(A) modifies § 871(b) by providing for a minimum tax. This floor ensures that a significant tax will be levied, even if the gain is fragmented over several years. For such amounts, the benefits of the graduated rates under § 1 are denied.

Revenue Ruling 90-37
1990-1 C.B. 141

ISSUE

Does the agreement between the United States and Argentina described below exempt gain from the disposition of U.S. real property interests from the tax imposed by section 897 of the Internal Revenue Code?

FACTS

X, a U.S. Branch of an Argentine corporation, is engaged in the international operation of ships and aircraft through its offices in the U.S. In 1988, X disposed of real property that it had used in its business in a transaction in which X realized gain. The property is a U.S. real property interest within the meaning of section 897(c) of the Code.

LAW AND ANALYSIS

Section 872(b) and 883(a) of the Code exclude from the gross income of a nonresident alien individual and of a foreign corporation, respectively, income derived from the operation of ships, aircraft, and certain railroad rolling stock if the foreign country in which such individual is a resident or such corporation is organized grants an equivalent exemption to U.S. individuals and corporations. The excluded income is exempt from United States taxation under subtitle A of the Code.

These provisions . . . are intended to prevent the double taxation of shipping income of individuals or corporations that operate internationally and to eliminate the difficulties associated with determining the sources of income so earned. Reciprocal exemption may be provided by the exchange of notes through formal diplomatic channels. In addition, countries enacting laws similar to the provisions of sections 872(b) and 883(a) may be treated as granting an equivalent exemption.

The legislative history of sections 872(b) and 883(a) . . . reflects the intent of Congress to exempt from U.S. taxation the shipping profits generated by the international transport of goods and passengers. These provisions were not intended to exempt investment or other non-shipping business income derived by shipping enterprises.

Section 897(a) of the Code requires foreign persons to take into account gain or loss from the disposition of a U.S. real property interest under section 871 in the case of nonresident alien individuals, or under section 882 in the case of foreign corporations, as if the gain or loss were effectively connected with the conduct of a trade or business by the foreign person within the United States. A U.S. real property interest is defined, in general, as an interest in real property in the United States or the U.S. Virgin Islands, or an interest in a domestic corporation that is a U.S. real property holding corporation within the meaning of section of 897(c)(2). Gain from the disposition of a U.S. real property interest taxable under section 897 is not exempted by sections 872(b) and 883(a). . . .

HOLDING

Gain realized by X from the disposition of a U.S. real property interest is not exempted . . . from U.S. taxation under section 897 of the Code. Thus, amounts realized that are taxable pursuant to section 897 are not exempt from United States taxation. . . .

§ 12.03 Direct Investment in United States Real Property

Section 897(a) provides that gain or loss derived by a foreign person from the sale or other disposition of a United States real property interest is treated as effectively connected with a domestic trade or business. Various modes of investment are available through which foreign taxpayers may acquire United States real property interests—direct investment by the taxpayer or indirect investment through the property holdings of a foreign or United States corporation. The simplest case, a disposition of a direct investment in property actually and directly owned by the taxpayer, is clearly subject to tax under § 897(a). A nonresident individual or a foreign corporation that disposes of such a direct property interest is subject to United States taxation. Therefore, in the direct investment setting, two critical definitional issues are encountered—(1) the determination of whether a United States real property interest is involved and (2) whether a disposition of that interest has occurred.

§ 12.04 United States Real Property Interests

The statutory prerequisite for the application of § 897 is a disposition of a United States real property interest. Under § 897(c), this term generally is defined as any interest in real property located in the United States and any interest (other than an interest solely as a creditor) in any United States real property holding corporation. Thus, the term includes both direct and indirect investment via outright ownership, co-ownership, options, and leaseholds.

United States real property interest includes not only land, but also any unsevered natural products, improvements, and any personal property associated with the use of land. It also includes leaseholds of land and improvements and options to acquire such land or leaseholds. In keeping with the legislative purpose, the term is particularly broad and far reaching. Local law definitions are not controlling. Furthermore, the term "improvements" is liberally construed so that buildings, permanent structures, and the structural components thereof are subject to § 897.

Associated personal property encompassed by the term results in a significant expansion of the statute's reach to include personalty. Such property is limited to four basic categories of tangible property, among them property used predominantly in the improvement of real property, for example, razing equipment used to improve or construct real property; furniture, appliances, and personalty used in common areas of apartments, hotels, motels, dorms, residences, or other permanent structures offering lodging for consideration; and property used predominantly in the rental of furnished office and other work space, including office equipment and furniture used by the lessor to provide rental space. However, such property does not constitute a United States real property interest if it is disposed of more than one year before or more than one year after the disposition of the realty with which it is associated or, if within those time periods, separate dispositions of the personalty and realty are made to unrelated taxpayers.

While the definition of a real property interest is broadly focused and easily determined as regards tangible property, if intangible interests were not included in the term as well, circumvention techniques could be easily employed. For example, instead of an outright sale of domestic realty, a foreign investor might employ an installment sale and shortly thereafter liquidate its investment by disposing of the installment obligation to a third party. If the latter transfer were not subject to § 897, the legislation would be nothing more than a "paper tiger." To foreclose such opportunities, the Regulations extend the statute's coverage to include various intangible ownership interests.

As a general theme under § 897, interests held solely as a creditor are immune from its reach. The Regulations note, however, that an interest in a shared appreciation mortgage is, under certain circumstances, an interest other than one held solely as a creditor. A mortgage generally runs afoul of § 897 to the extent it has an equity feature (e.g., participation in appreciation).

Options and related executory interests likewise constitute an interest in real property unless that interest is derived by the holder in his capacity solely as a creditor. A security interest or possessory interest as a lender does not alone represent an interest in real property. Likewise, an interest other than a creditor's interest does not arise simply via an entitlement to fees or commissions for arranging the sale, financing, purchase, or lease of a property interest. If that fee is tied to subsequent occurrences, however, such as appreciation or profit realized upon a later disposition, the broker will find itself entangled in § 897.

§ 12.05 Dispositions

The Regulations provide that a disposition of a United States real property interest is "any transfer that would constitute a disposition by the transferor for any purpose of the Internal Revenue Code and regulations thereunder." By defining disposition broadly, § 897 forecloses the tax benefits derived from a host of efforts to sever ownership. Thus, an outright sale of property, its transfer in satisfaction of a claim, or any other taxable transfer will constitute a disposition. Similarly, nonrecognition transfers which produce as a corollary taxable gain, such as the receipt of boot in a like-kind exchange or, with regard to a gift, the relief of a liability in excess of the taxpayer's basis in the property, should constitute a disposition. Moreover, certain transactions which would normally be afforded nonrecognition treatment under the Code may trigger § 897 recharacterization.

More difficult questions arise with respect to less traditional types of transfers—gifts, bequests, nontaxable transfers to partnerships and corporations, and like-kind exchanges. As a general rule, nonrecognition transactions are respected so long as the real property interest received in the exchange similarly carries the § 897 taint upon its disposition.

However, in those cases not specifically addressed by § 897, the resolution of the issue of whether such a transfer constitutes a disposition should turn on an analysis of the policy behind the enactment of § 897. As long as the transfer does not remove the property from the taxing jurisdiction of the United States or generate an increased basis which would shield a portion of the gain from domestic taxation upon a subsequent disposition, it generally should not constitute a disposition for purposes of § 897. Consequently, a gift of a United States real property interest should be exempt from § 897 as the property's basis will transfer to the donee. The donee, even if a nonresident with no United States activity, will itself be subject to tax under § 897 upon a subsequent disposition of the property. Such an interpretive approach is consistent with § 897(e) which conditions any otherwise available nonrecognition treatment upon the continued application of § 897 to the property received in the nonrecognition event.

§ 12.06 Indirect Investment—Interests Held Through Domestic Corporations

Indirect investment through domestic corporations is also targeted by § 897. In keeping with the statutory purpose, the interposition of a United States corporation between the foreign taxpayer and a United States real property interest will not insulate the foreign investor from the application of § 897. In fact, in such settings, the Service may enjoy additional benefits: (1) taxation at the corporate level upon the domestic corporation's sale of the property, and (2) taxation at the shareholder level upon the shareholder's sale of the shares in the corporation if the sale of the corporate stock precedes the corporation's sale of the property.

Gain from the sale by a foreign person of shares in a United States corporation will be taxed under § 897 if that corporation has at *any time* within the past five years (or, if shorter, the taxpayer's holding period) been a "United States real property holding company." This determination is predicated upon the extent of the corporation's investment in United States real property interests. This treatment generally will ensue regardless of the foreign shareholder's percentage ownership in the corporation and regardless of whether he disposes of all or only a portion of his holdings. Thus, a one percent foreign shareholder in a domestic real property holding company will be ensnared by § 897.

The focus of the indirect investment provisions is on any interest *other than an interest solely as creditor* in a United States real property holding company. The obvious exclusions from creditor interests are stock, options, shared appreciation interests, and partnership interests.

However, the Regulations address in detail numerous other interests which are classified as other than an interest solely as a creditor and which are thus taxed under § 897 upon disposition.

§ 12.07 United States Real Property Holding Companies

A foreign investor who sells shares in a United States real property holding company must pay tax. Section 897 applies *only* to the sale or other disposition of an interest in a United States corporation which is a United States real property holding company. A United States real property holding company is any *domestic* corporation whose fair market value of its United States real property interests equals or exceeds 50 percent of the value of all of its combined foreign and domestic real property interests and business assets.

The statute does not perceive corporate ownership as potentially circumventive if that ownership is publicly traded and thus is theoretically immune from the abuses more readily available to shareholders in a closely held entity. Regardless of the mix of corporate assets and valuation standards, if the stock of a corporation is publicly traded, it will not constitute an interest in a real property holding company unless the shareholder owns more than five percent of the stock.

In determining whether a domestic corporation is a United States real property holding company, holdings by that domestic corporation in other entities and other corporations are taken into account. If the United States corporation owns an interest in a partnership, whether foreign or domestic, it is treated as holding directly its proportionate share of that entity's assets. For example, if Corporation A owns a ten percent interest in a foreign partnership, its ten percent interest in *all* of the assets of the foreign partnership is calculated and combined with the assets it owns directly in determining whether Corporation A meets the 50 percent test for real property holding company status.

If the United States corporation owns an interest in another corporation, whether domestic or foreign, different imputation rules apply depending upon the degree of ownership. If the corporation owns a controlling interest of 50 percent or more of the value of the stock of another corporation, an imputation rule similar to that applicable to other entities applies to attribute a proportionate share of the subsidiary's assets to the parent corporation. Thus, if Corporation B owns a 60 percent interest in a foreign or domestic corporation, its 60 percent interest in *all* of the assets of the foreign or domestic subsidiary is determined and combined with the assets it owns directly in determining whether Corporation B meets the 50 percent test for United States real property holding company status.

Alternatively, if a United States corporation owns less than a controlling interest in another corporation, whether domestic or foreign, the attribution of assets becomes an all-or-nothing proposition. In such a case, the sole issue is whether the shares in the domestic or foreign subsidiary corporation constitute a United States real property interest. If so, the value of the entire interest is considered a real property interest in the determination of whether the investing corporation is a United States real property holding company. If not, none of the interest is so considered. However, in determining whether the stock of a noncontrolled foreign or domestic subsidiary is a real property interest, the status of the subsidiary must be assessed to ascertain whether that subsidiary is itself a real property holding company. For these limited purposes, the determination is made with respect to the subsidiary regardless of whether it is a domestic or foreign corporation.

The statutory valuation process of § 897(c)(2), notwithstanding the administrative leniency that reduces the number of dates on which a determination must be made, would be a laborious task involving a cadre of appraisers. Consequently, the Regulations construct an alternative test under which the fair market value of the assets is presumed to be less than the 50 percent standard if, on the relevant determination date, the total book value of the United States real property interests is 25 percent or less of the book value of the aggregate realty and business assets.

In examining whether a corporation has been a United States real property holding company during the statutory testing period, the Service looks to the shorter of the period during which the foreign investor held the shares or the five-year period ending on the date of disposition of the shares. Thus, a corporation will be classified as a United States real property holding company if it had the requisite level of United States real property interests on any of the applicable determination dates during the shorter of those periods. For example, if a corporation was a United States real property holding company during Year 1 but was not so classified from Year 2-Year 6, a shareholder who acquired his shares in Year 3 and sold them in Year 6 would not be subject to § 897. However, shareholders who acquired their shares in Year 1 and who disposed of them in Year 6 would be taxed under § 897. In the latter circumstance, sage counsel would have advised the shareholders that patience is its own reward. A delay of the sale to Year 7 would prove beneficial, since the holding company taint disappears with the expiration of the five-year holding period.

However, even if the corporation was a United States real property holding company at some point during the measurement period, a foreign taxpayer will not be taxed on the disposition of his shares in that entity if, on the date of disposition, the corporation did not hold any United States real property interests and all of such interests previously held were disposed of during the applicable period in (1) fully taxable transactions in which the full amount of any realized gain was recognized, or (2) if the property ceased to be a United States real property interest by virtue of the application of this cleansing rule. Thus, in the above examples, if the corporation had disposed of all of its real property interests in a taxable sale on June 15, Year 4 *and* had not acquired *any* additional interests thereafter, none of its shareholders would be subject to § 897 upon their post-June 15, Year 4 disposition of those shares.

§ 12.08 Indirect Investment—Interests Held Through Foreign Corporations

Before the enactment of § 897, indirect investment in domestic real property via a foreign corporation was the principal technique employed by foreign persons for investing in United States realty. A direct disposition by the foreign corporation at a time when it did not have a United States trade or business via the use of an installment sale or a sale in the context of a corporate liquidation was not taxed. An indirect disposition via a shareholder sale of the shares of a foreign corporation holding an interest in real property, even if the entity was engaged in a United States trade or business, likewise yielded immunity from tax provided the shareholder was neither engaged in a domestic trade or business himself nor present in the United States for more than one-half of the year.

Section 897 now provides particularized rules to preclude some of the tax planning techniques previously used involving foreign corporations. Regardless of the treatment of the shareholder upon the disposition of his shares, gain or loss is recognized upon direct dispositions of the property by the foreign corporation, namely sales and exchanges. Thus, on the whole, parity is achieved in the treatment of both foreign and domestic corporations as regards their direct holding and disposition of real property interests. However, in contrast to the gain recognition imposed by § 897 on foreign shareholders on the sale of their stock in a domestic corporation having significant holdings of domestic real property, no gain or loss is recognized under § 897 when a foreign shareholder disposes of his shares in a *foreign* corporation having significant holdings of domestic real property.

Because the foreign corporation continues to hold the domestic real property interest and thus will be taxable under § 897 upon its disposition of that property, the overall policy concerns of the United States taxing authorities apparently are protected. Nevertheless, foreign shareholders in a foreign corporation holding a United States real property interest enjoy greater latitude in the disposition of their ownership interests (which are not subject to § 897) than do similarly situated foreign taxpayers whose investment vehicle is a domestic corporation (which are subject to § 897). The distinction in tax treatment between these two vehicles most likely stems from enforcement and detection difficulties particular to foreign corporations.

§ 12.09 Coordination of § 897 with Nonrecognition Rules

Nonrecognition provisions apply to exchanges of United States real property interests by foreign taxpayers only to the extent prescribed by the Regulations. They generally apply "only in the case of an exchange of a United States real property interest for an interest the sale of which would be subject to taxation under this chapter." Thus, deferral of tax is permitted, but a complete exemption from taxation is not. The statute cedes to the Regulations the responsibility of specifying which nonrecognition events will qualify and which will not.

In the domestic-to-foreign arena, the focus of the Regulations is typically on efforts to move United States real property interests outside of the United States taxing net. Thus, a transfer of domestic realty by a nonresident individual to his wholly owned domestic corporation, an otherwise qualifying § 351 nonrecognition event, would be entitled to nonrecognition treatment provided the stock of the corporation is properly classified *after* the transfer as a property interest which continues to carry a § 897 taxable taint. In such transfers, the taxable gain is preserved if the transferee corporation is a United States real property holding corporation. Under such conditions, a subsequent disposition of the stock would be subject to § 897. Accordingly, § 897(e) will not override the general nonrecognition bestowed on the transfer by § 351 since the stock of the domestic corporation received in the exchange continues to carry potential United States tax liability under § 897. If instead the transfer is made to a *foreign* corporation, nonrecognition is not available as the stock of the foreign corporation received in the exchange cannot be a United States real property interest through which the § 897 taint is preserved.

As a further safeguard, Congress amended the like-kind exchange provisions which typically afford nonrecognition treatment and provided that the exchange of United States real property for foreign real property (and vice versa) is not a qualifying exchange of like-kind property. Thus, such an exchange is a taxable event.

Revenue Ruling 84-160
1984-2 C.B. 125

ISSUE

Whether section 897(e) of the Internal Revenue Code permits nonrecognition of tax in the fact situation set forth below.

FACTS

FX is a corporation organized under the laws of a foreign country (FC), which does not have an income tax treaty with the United States. FX holds 100 percent of the stock of corporation S, a domestic corporation. S is engaged in real estate development and has determined that it constitutes a U.S. real property holding corporation as defined in section 897(c)(2) of the Code. Therefore, the stock of S constitutes a U.S. real property interest pursuant to section 897(c)(1). For business purposes FX wishes to interpose a holding company between itself and S. Therefore, on December 1, 1984, in a transaction qualifying for nonrecognition under section 351, FX transfers all of the shares of S to H, a corporation newly organized in the United States, solely in exchange for the stock of H. Because the shares of S are the only assets of H, H constitutes a U.S. real property holding corporation as defined in section 897(c)(2).

LAW AND ANALYSIS

Under section 897(a) of the Code, a foreign corporation's gain or loss from the disposition of a U.S. real property interest is treated as if the foreign corporation were engaged in a trade or business within the United States and as if the gain or loss were effectively connected with the trade or business. . . .

Section 897(e) of the Code provides that except to the extent otherwise provided in section 897(d) and section 897(e)(2), any nonrecognition provision shall apply for purposes of section 897 to a transaction only in the case of an exchange of a United States real property interest for an interest the sale of which would be subject to taxation under this chapter, i.e., chapter 1 of the Code. Section 897(e)(2) provides that the Secretary shall prescribe regulations (which are necessary or appropriate to prevent the avoidance of Federal income taxes) providing the extent to which nonrecognition provisions shall, and shall not, apply for purposes of section 897, and the extent to which the transfers of property in reorganization and changes in interest in, or distributions from, a partnership, trust, or estate, shall be treated as sales of property at fair market value. Section 897(e)(3) defines the term "nonrecognition provision" as meaning any provision of this title, i.e., the Internal Revenue Code, for not recognizing gain or loss.

Section 897(e) of the Code provides that any nonrecognition provision shall apply for purposes of this section to a transaction only in the case of an exchange of a United States real property interest for an interest the sale of which would be subject to taxation under chapter 1 of the Code.

This provision is intended to preserve otherwise available nonrecognition in cases where it is clear that gain inherent in a U.S. real property interest will remain subject to U.S. taxation. In the present case, FX has exchanged, in a transaction qualifying for nonrecognition under section 351, one U.S. real property interest for another U.S. real property interest, the sale of which will be clearly subject to U.S. taxation. Therefore, FX is entitled to receive nonrecognition treatment pursuant to section 897(e) of the Code.

HOLDING

In accordance with section 897(e) of the Code, in the above fact situation, the nonrecognition provision will apply for purposes of section 897. . . .

PROBLEM 12—NONTREATY PERSONS—
UNITED STATES REAL PROPERTY INTERESTS

Code: §§ 897(a)-(c)(4)(A), 897(e); 1031(h)

Regulations: §§ 1.897-1(b)(1)-(4)(ii)(A), 1.897-1(d)(1) and (2), 1.897-2(a)-(c)(1), 1.897-6T(a)(1)-(3)

T, an individual, was a citizen and resident of Argentina, which has not entered a tax treaty with the United States. T has never been present in the United States. During the year, T owned the following assets:

   a. 100 shares of the common stock of X Corporation—a domestic corporation;
   b. 100 shares of the common stock of Y Corporation—a foreign corporation;
   c. Rental real estate located in Modesto, California. T's activities in this connection do not constitute engaging in a domestic trade or business; and
   d. Vacant land held as an investment located in Oregon.

1. Suppose that T had a $13,000 gain on the sale of the vacant land. What if it were sold on an installment basis payable over ten years?

2. Suppose that T exchanged the vacant land for vacant land in Ireland.

3. What if T contributed the vacant land to Z Corporation, a domestic corporation, in return for all of its stock?

4. What result in 3. if T in the next taxable year sells the Z Corporation stock for a gain of $20,000?

5. What result in 3. if T contributed the vacant land to Q Corporation, a foreign corporation, in return for all of its stock?

6. T buys stock in W Corporation, a domestic corporation, the exclusive holdings of which are United States real property.

   a. What result on the sale of the stock four years later for a gain of $5,000?
   b. What if in a. T had purchased a ten-year debenture rather than stock?
   c. What if W was publicly traded?
   d. What result if W's real estate holdings comprised only 30 percent of its asset base on the date of sale?

CHAPTER 12   NONTREATY PERSONS—UNITED STATES REAL PROPERTY   261

    e.   What result in d. if T sold his stock ten years after its purchase?

7.   Assume that Y Corporation held exclusively real property located in the United States.

    a.   What result upon its sale of such property?
    b.   What result on the sale of its stock by its foreign person shareholders?

Chapter 13

Foreign Personal Holding Companies

§ 13.01 Foreign Personal Holding Companies

§ 13.02 The Gross Income Test

§ 13.03 Foreign Personal Holding Company Income

§ 13.04 Stock Ownership Test

§ 13.05 Deemed Dividend of Undistributed Foreign Personal Holding Company Income

§ 13.06 Undistributed Foreign Personal Holding Company Income

§ 13.07 The Dividends-Paid Deduction

§ 13.08 Deemed Dividends and the Indirect Foreign Tax Credit Revenue Ruling 74-59, 1974-1 C.B. 183

§ 13.09 Shareholders Required to Include the Deemed Dividend in Income

Problem 13

§ 13.01   Foreign Personal Holding Companies

The Foreign Personal Holding Company (FPHC) provisions of §§ 551-558 prevent the deferral of United States tax on certain categories of typically passive income of a foreign corporation. These provisions force the inclusion of that income in the gross income of the FPHC's United States owners. The statutory imputation is limited to owners of those closely held foreign corporations deriving passive or investment income from domestic and foreign sources. The imputation mechanism prevents these shareholders from sheltering their worldwide investment income from United States taxation by interposing a foreign corporation between themselves and passive income-generating assets.

The effect of FPHC status on United States shareholders is that each domestic shareholder must include in gross income his or her pro rata share of the corporation's undistributed foreign personal holding company income as if the corporation had actually distributed a dividend to that shareholder. The imputed dividend is included in the shareholder's income for the taxable year which ends with or during the FPHC's taxable year.

To constitute a FPHC, two requirements must be met that focus on the income derived by the corporation and its ownership structure. A foreign corporation constitutes a FPHC if at least 60 percent (or 50 percent in certain subsequent years) of its gross income for the taxable year is foreign personal holding company income *and* more than 50 percent of the voting power or value of the corporation's stock is owned at any time during the taxable year by five or fewer United States individuals.

§ 13.02 The Gross Income Test

As a general rule, a foreign corporation constitutes a FPHC if at least 60 percent of its gross income for the taxable year is foreign personal holding company income. Thus, broadly speaking, a newly formed foreign corporation (or a foreign corporation which has never been a FPHC) will not be a FPHC unless at least 60 percent of its gross income is comprised of foreign personal holding company income. In applying this gross income test, both the corporation's gross income as well as its foreign personal holding company income must be scrutinized. Once computed, it is a simple matter to determine the percentage of gross income comprised by the tainted or forbidden income and to compare this percentage with the requisite statutory gross income percentage.

Once a corporation is classified as a FPHC, however, the gross income percentage requirement is modified. In subsequent taxable years, only 50 percent or more of the corporation's gross income need be foreign personal holding company income for such status to continue. The 50 percent threshold continues for subsequent taxable years until *either* the corporation ceases to be a FPHC by virtue of failing the ownership requirement for an entire taxable year or by failing the 50 percent standard for three consecutive taxable years. Although the statute is more generous to start-up or new FPHCs, once the FPHC label has attached to an entity, it is difficult for that label to be stripped away.

For example, assume that F Corporation was a FPHC for the first time in Year 1. For Years 2-4, with no change in its shareholders, F had foreign personal holding company income representing 35 percent, 51 percent, and 30 percent of its gross income. Thus, F was a FPHC for Year 1 and Year 3, but not for Year 2 and Year 4. Assume further that F Corporation has foreign personal holding company income for Year 5 and Year 6 equal to 37 percent and 20 percent, respectively, of its gross income. F has three consecutive taxable years (Year 4, Year 5, and Year 6) in which less than 50 percent of its gross income was foreign personal holding company income. Thus, after Year 6, before F can be classified as a FPHC again, the 60 percent gross income requirement must be met.

The foreign corporation's measure of gross income is not limited solely to domestic source gross income or income related to a domestic trade or business. Rather, to parallel the tax treatment applicable to the corporation's domestic shareholders, gross income broadly encompasses the corporation's worldwide gross income even if derived from foreign sources and even if unrelated to a domestic trade or business.

§ 13.03   Foreign Personal Holding Company Income

Foreign personal holding company income includes seven broad categories of typically passive or investment gross income from both foreign and domestic sources. Some of the categories of foreign personal holding company income, and any related loss limitations, are enumerated and explained below.

In many instances, special rules apply to prevent the inclusion of losses in the foreign personal holding company income calculation. If not for such rules, a foreign corporation could conceivably escape FPHC status by merely "cherry-picking" certain devalued stock or other investments in order to trigger inherent losses. Any economic loss on such planned, or even deliberately rigged, transactions would be more than offset by the avoidance of imputed ordinary income to the shareholders.

One broad category of foreign personal holding company income consists of gross income from dividends, interest, and certain royalties. "Dividends" include traditional dividends and deemed dividends from lower-tier FPHC subsidiaries. This latter inclusion enhances the likelihood that *both* foreign corporations will be deemed FPHCs.

"Interest" includes any taxable interest received for the use of money loaned. Discount income from factoring is treated as interest for FPHC purposes.

"Royalties" include mineral, oil, and gas royalties, as well as those payments (other than rents) derived from the privilege of using intangible assets. However, royalties generated from the corporation's active business of licensing computer software are generally excluded from foreign personal holding company income.

Foreign personal holding company income generally includes net nondealer gains from the sale or exchange of stock or securities. The amount of such gain included is the *excess* of all such gains includable in gross income over all deductible losses from the sale or exchange of stock or securities. Any excess loss cannot be used in isolation to reduce other categories of foreign personal holding company income nor can such income reflect any capital loss carryover under § 1212.

Amounts received under certain contracts in which the corporation is to furnish personal services, as well as amounts received from the sale or other disposition of such contracts, constitute foreign personal holding company income. This category includes amounts received only from those contracts in which either a person besides the corporation has the right to designate, or the contract specifies, the individual who will perform the services. Moreover, at some time during the taxable year, the designated or anticipated performer of such services must own directly or indirectly at least 25 percent of the value of the contracting corporation's stock. If the contract additionally requires the performance of important and essential services by other persons, the contract is bifurcated to include in foreign personal holding company income only that portion of the contract income attributable to the services of the 25 percent shareholder. The inclusion of such income prevents the escape of what would otherwise constitute income from services of the shareholder performer via the use of a foreign corporation.

Compensation received by a foreign corporation for the use of corporate property by a shareholder owning directly or indirectly at least 25 percent of the value of the recipient corporation constitutes foreign personal holding company income. This inclusion results regardless of the form of the arrangement and regardless of the form of payment or the identity of the payor.

"Rents" include compensation, however designated, received for the use of property other than any amounts included under the preceding category. Such amounts constitute foreign personal holding company income unless they comprise at least 50 percent of the corporation's gross income. The effect of the 50 percent threshold is that a foreign corporation which derives its primary source of income from rental activity will fail the gross income test and avoid FPHC status. The assumption driving this result is that an *active* rental business is being conducted.

§ 13.04 Stock Ownership Test

The stock ownership test is satisfied if more than 50 percent of the total voting power *or* value of the stock of the foreign corporation is owned by five or fewer individuals who are United States citizens or residents (the "United States group"). This stock ownership test is driven by the notion that such individuals effectively control the dividend stream of the corporation. As the stock ownership test is satisfied if the requisite ownership is present at any time during the taxable year, no matter how briefly, every change in the corporate stock structure must be closely assessed.

The determination of whether stock is directly or indirectly owned by the requisite five or fewer individuals is governed by constructive stock ownership rules. These attribution rules are designed to maximize stock ownership. In essence, the effect of these provisions is to constructively place all of the foreign corporation's stock in the hands of individuals. If an individual has family or business ties with other shareholders, stock owned by these related individuals or entities is constructively placed in the hands of that individual.

Various categories of constructive ownership are set forth as to when stock owned, directly or indirectly, by one person is deemed to be owned by another. Two of these categories address: (1) stock not owned by an individual; and (2) stock owned by family members and partners.

The first attribution rule targets entity ownership of stock. The rule directs that stock owned, directly or indirectly, by or for a corporation or a partnership is considered owned proportionately by its shareholders and partners. For example, A and B, two equal partners of a partnership owning 100 percent of the outstanding stock of M Corporation which in turn owns 100 percent of the stock of N Corporation, are considered equal owners by attribution from the partnership of all of the outstanding stock of both M and N Corporation. The entity attribution rule thus effectively disassembles the entity structure, placing ownership in the hands of the *individual* owners of that entity, and precludes entity inclusion in a United States group.

The second attribution rule focuses exclusively on family and business relationships, attributing to an individual ownership of stock owned, directly or indirectly, by or for certain family members or the individual's partners. "Family" for purposes of this attribution rule is limited to the individual's siblings, spouse, ancestors, and lineal descendants. The family and partner attribution rule applies for purposes of the stock ownership test only if the effect of the rule is to qualify the corporation as a FPHC or to make certain income items includable as foreign personal holding company income.

Two special limitations apply to limit the family or partner attribution of stock owned by nonresident individuals and foreign persons to United States citizens or residents. First, family attribution of stock owned by a nonresident individual to a United States family member is prohibited unless such family member is a spouse or owns stock in the corporation (either directly or by application of the nonfamily attribution rules). Similarly, attribution of stock owned by a foreign person to a United States *individual* partner is prohibited unless that partner owns stock in the corporation (either directly or by nonpartner attribution).

Stock constructively owned by attribution from an entity is considered as actually owned for purposes of both reapplication of the entity attribution rule to another and for the application of the family/partner attribution rule. This multiple attribution provision causes stock held by an entity to be constructively carried through any imaginable chain of entities until ownership rests in the hands of individuals. Once accomplished, this provision further attributes stock so placed to family members and partners.

The multiple attribution scheme is not boundless. Stock constructively owned by a family member or partner pursuant to the family/partner attribution rules is *not* considered as actually owned by that individual for purposes of reapplying that rule to make another the constructive owner of that stock. Thus, double attribution of stock owned by a related individual will not occur. For example, a father's stock attributed to a daughter will not be reattributed to the daughter's husband.

Once the constructive ownership rules have been applied, the composition of the resultant group of individual shareholders is scrutinized. The stock ownership requirement is applied to determine whether a majority of the voting power or the value of the stock of the corporation is owned by five or fewer United States citizens or residents (i.e., to determine whether a United States group exists). The United States group may be comprised, by operation of the attribution rules, of individuals possessing constructive ownership, as opposed to or in addition to, actual ownership. If the stock ownership and gross income tests are satisfied, the corporation is deemed to be a FPHC and its undistributed foreign personal holding company income is imputed to its United States shareholders.

§ 13.05 Deemed Dividend of Undistributed Foreign Personal Holding Company Income

Once a foreign corporation has been classified as a FPHC, its domestic shareholders must include in gross income as a dividend a portion of the corporation's undistributed foreign personal holding company income. Each domestic shareholder must include his pro rata share of the corporation's undistributed foreign personal holding company income as if the corporation had actually distributed a dividend to that shareholder. Thus, only that portion of the deemed distribution constituting a dividend under § 316 should be taxable. The imputed dividend is included in the shareholder's income for the taxable year which ends with or during the FPHC's taxable year.

A United States shareholder is entitled to an increase in the basis of the FPHC stock commensurate with the amount of the imputed dividend. This adjustment parallels the result which would have occurred if the shareholder had actually received a dividend followed by a contribution of that dividend to the capital of the corporation. The adjustment likewise ensures that the shareholders will not again be taxed on the subsequent distribution of FPHC income. To avoid double taxation upon actual distribution, the FPHC also makes a correlative reduction to its earnings and profits for the amount imputed to the shareholders. It further increases its capital accounts by the amount of the dividend deemed reinvested by its shareholders.

Although the definition of a FPHC requires closely-held United States *individual* ownership of a foreign corporation, the deemed dividend treatment applies to domestic corporate shareholders, other domestic entity shareholders, and domestic individual shareholders who are not members of the United States group. Additionally, in some cases, income may be imputed to a United States person even though no actual ownership exists.

Domestic shareholders of the FPHC are taxed on all of the corporation's income subject to the modifications discussed below. Although passive income forces the classification, the FPHC provisions also impact business income. For example, assume that foreign Corporation X satisfies the gross income and stock ownership requirements. Corporation X is owned equally by four United States citizens. If Corporation X has undistributed foreign personal holding company income of $100,000, each shareholder must include $25,000 of such income in his or her gross income. Corporation X would reduce its earnings and profits by $100,000 and increase its paid-in capital account by $100,000. Each shareholder would increase his or her basis in Corporation X stock by $25,000. This result would hold true even if one of the shareholders was a domestic corporation. If one of the shareholders of Corporation X was a foreign corporation that itself was not a FPHC and was wholly owned by one of the United States citizens, the foreign corporation's stock in the FPHC would be treated as owned by the United States citizen and the tax consequences would be imputed to him or her.

§ 13.06 Undistributed Foreign Personal Holding Company Income

The concepts of undistributed foreign personal holding company income and foreign personal holding company income are wholly distinct. Undistributed foreign personal holding company income subject to the deemed dividend provisions is more broadly defined as the corporation's worldwide taxable income, adjusted for certain expenses and taxes, less a deduction for dividends paid by the FPHC during the taxable year. The base of this formula, taxable income, closely resembles the taxable income of any domestic corporation subject to a few adjustments peculiar to this provision. The adjustments to taxable income are intended to eliminate attempts to artificially minimize the amount of foreign personal holding company income. In essence, this reflects the statute's mission to approximate, via the computation of undistributed foreign personal holding company income, the amount of corporate funds actually available for distribution. An adjustment is allowed for federal income taxes accrued during the taxable year and for income taxes paid to foreign countries.

Certain deductions allocable to the maintenance and operation of property are permitted in the computation of undistributed foreign personal holding company income. However, the deductible trade or business expenses and related depreciation may not exceed the amount of rent or other compensation received for the use of the property. This cap on expenses is not applicable if the shareholder establishes that the rent received was the maximum obtainable, the property was held in the course of a bona fide business carried on for profit, and the property was either held with a reasonable expectation of profit or was essential to the operation of the business.

§ 13.07 The Dividends-Paid Deduction

Once taxable income is adjusted, undistributed foreign personal holding company income is determined by subtracting the dividends-paid deduction from adjusted taxable income. The dividends-paid deduction is consistent with the rationale behind the FPHC provisions. The offense targeted by the statute is not merely the use of a foreign corporation or the derivation of passive income thereby, but rather the ability to structure the entity and its investments to escape current United States taxation. The payment of dividends thus precludes the targeted deferral or escape from taxation. Accordingly, the dividends-paid deduction appropriately reduces the base upon which the FPHC tax is levied.

The dividends-paid deduction, inter alia, includes the dividends paid during the taxable year and the consent dividends for the taxable year. The term "dividend" for purposes of the deduction includes any distribution of cash or other property to shareholders by the corporation out of current and accumulated earnings and profits. Distributions of undistributed foreign personal holding company income to *corporate* shareholders in complete liquidation of a FPHC are also considered dividends for purposes of the deduction, as are certain dividend distributions of corporate obligations.

In determining the dividends-paid deduction, a foreign corporation may treat as a current year dividend any properly designated dividend paid after the close of the taxable year prior to the fifteenth day of the third month following the close of the taxable year. The relation-back of such dividends is permitted only if the distribution is made to the shareholder of record on the last day of the corporation's year.

A special exclusion exists for consent dividends declared shortly after the close of the FPHC's taxable year. A consent dividend is a hypothetical distribution which the owner of consent stock expressly agrees to treat as a dividend. The effect of the consent dividend on the individual shareholder is very similar to the overall deemed dividend result under the FPHC provisions. Thus, the deferral abuse is similarly foreclosed. The shareholder is considered to have received a cash dividend for the amount consented to on the last day of the corporation's taxable year. The shareholder is then deemed to immediately make a capital contribution to the corporation in the amount of the consent dividend, resulting in a commensurate basis increase in the consent stock.

§ 13.08 Deemed Dividends and the Indirect Foreign Tax Credit

Section 902 entitles domestic corporate shareholders owning ten percent or more of a foreign corporation to claim an indirect credit for foreign income taxes paid by the foreign corporation with respect to a dividend distribution. The Service has ruled, however, that the domestic corporate shareholder of a FPHC is *not* entitled to a § 902 indirect credit for those foreign taxes paid by a FPHC with respect to the income comprising the deemed dividend. The Service based its conclusion on the legislative history of the FPHC provisions which suggested that such indirect credits should not be available. This result is arguably inconsistent with the plain language of the statute which unequivocally treats the FPHC distribution as a dividend.

In contrast, the Service has ruled that consent dividends made by FPHCs to United States corporate shareholders *do* entitle such shareholders to the indirect credit. A consent dividend may be made after the close of the distributing corporation's taxable year, but it must be made on or before the extended due date of the distributor's tax return. Thus, where United States corporate shareholders meet the ownership requirements, a premium is placed upon promptly identifying the relevant foreign corporation payor as a FPHC so that a timely consent dividend election may be made to preserve the shareholder's entitlement to the indirect credit.

Revenue Ruling 74-59
1974-1 C.B. 183

Advice has been requested whether a dividend received by a foreign personal holding company and included in the gross income of its United States parent corporation as undistributed foreign personal holding company income will be treated as a dividend received by the United States parent corporation for purposes of the foreign tax credit provision of section 902 of the Internal Revenue Code of 1954.

P, a domestic corporation, is the sole shareholder of Y, a holding company organized under the laws of Canada. During the current taxable year Y's wholly-owned Canadian subsidiary S made a dividend distribution to Y from its accumulated earnings and profits. No dividends were paid to P. During the year in question Y was a foreign personal holding company within the meaning of section 552(a) of the Code.

Section 551 of the Code provides the manner and extent that undistributed foreign personal holding company income shall be included in the gross income of a domestic corporation which is a shareholder in such foreign personal holding company.

Section 551(b) of the Code provides, in part and in effect, that in the case of a foreign personal holding company controlled for the entire taxable year by a United States group each United States shareholder shall include in his gross income, as a dividend, the amount he would have received as a dividend if on the last day of its taxable year there had been distributed by the company, and received by the shareholder, the undistributed foreign personal holding company income of the company for the taxable year.

Section 556(a) of the Code provides that the term "undistributed foreign personal holding company income" means the taxable income (including dividends received) of a foreign personal holding company, with certain adjustments, minus the dividends paid deduction. Among the adjustments provided in section 556(b) is a deduction for Federal income and excess profits taxes, and income, war profits, and excess profits taxes of foreign countries and possessions of the United States (to the extent not allowable as a deduction under section 275(a)(4)).

Section 561 of the Code provides, in part, that the deduction for dividends paid includes the dividends paid during the taxable year and the consent dividends for the taxable year (determined under section 565).

Section 565(a) of the Code provides, in general, that if any person owns consent stock (as defined in section 565(f)(1)) in a corporation on the last day of the taxable year of such corporation, and such person agrees, in a consent filed with the return of such corporation, to treat as a dividend the amount specified in such consent, the amount so specified shall constitute a consent dividend for the purpose of section 561.

Section 565(c)(1) and (2) of the Code provides that the amount of a consent dividend shall be considered, for the purpose of subtitle A of the Code, (1) as distributed in money by the corporation to the shareholder on the last day of the taxable year of the corporation, and (2) as contributed to the capital of the corporation by the shareholder on such day.

Section 902(a) of the Code provides, in general, that a domestic corporation that owns at least 10 percent of the voting stock of a foreign corporation from which it receives dividends in any taxable year that were paid out of accumulated profits shall be deemed to have paid a certain portion of any creditable income tax paid or deemed to have been paid by such foreign corporation to any foreign country or to any possession of the United States on or with respect to such accumulated profits. . . .

The foreign personal holding company provisions, originally enacted as part fo the Revenue Act of 1937, were based on proposals of the Joint Committee on Tax Evasion and Avoidance . . . that the United States shareholders of foreign personal holding companies should have gross income as if they had received a hypothetical dividend. However, the Report also specifically recommended at page 18 as follows:

> The American shareholders should not be allowed any credit against their Federal income taxes for foreign income taxes, if any, paid by the foreign personal holding company in respect to the undistributed adjusted net income returned by them.

. . . Congress enacted the Joint Committees' proposals without substantial alteration.

Accordingly, it is held that the dividend paid to Y by its subsidiary S which constitutes undistributed foreign personal holding company incomes includible in the gross income of P under section 551 of the Code will not be considered a dividend received by P for purposes of the allowance of a foreign tax credit under section 902. However, where a consent dividend is utilized by a domestic corporate shareholder and a foreign personal holding company the consent dividend will be considered a dividend received for purposes of the allowance of a foreign tax credit under section 902.

§ 13.09 Shareholders Required to Include the Deemed Dividend in Income

For purposes of determining whether a United States group exists under the FPHC stock ownership test, the stock ownership attribution rules apply. However, for purposes of determining which United States shareholder is required to include a deemed dividend in income, different ownership rules apply. For instance, assume that X is a domestic corporation which is a United States shareholder in a FPHC on the last day of its taxable year. X is required to include the imputed foreign personal holding company income in its gross income even though X was not a member of the United States ownership group comprised of five or fewer domestic *individuals*. Thus, the realm of United States persons potentially subject to imputation is a considerably broader universe than those persons considered for purposes of determining FPHC status.

For deemed dividend purposes, United States shareholders, including individuals, corporations and partnerships *directly* owning stock in a FPHC must include in gross income their proportionate share of the corporation's undistributed foreign personal holding company income. Inclusion is typically based on the shareholder's actual, not constructive, ownership. Thus, a shareholder with actual ownership of one percent and constructive ownership of 25 percent will have only one percent of the FPHC's undistributed foreign personal holding company income imputed to him or her.

However, one constructive ownership scenario applies in the imputation context under which a FPHC deemed dividend is included in the gross income of certain *indirect* FPHC shareholders. Specifically, stock of a FPHC owned by United States persons through a foreign partnership or through a foreign corporation which is *not* itself a FPHC is deemed proportionately owned by its partners or shareholders. These rules prevent the avoidance of the imputation via the interposition of foreign entities between the FPHC and its United States shareholders.

PROBLEM 13—FOREIGN PERSONAL HOLDING COMPANIES

Code: §§ 551-556, 561, 563(c), 565

Regulations: §§ 1.551-2, 1.551-5, 1.556-2(a)

A, B, C, D, E, F, G, and H, unrelated United States citizens, form Z Corporation in the Cayman Islands, which does not have a corporate income tax. A contributes $37,000 and B-H each contribute $9,000 in cash to Z in return for stock. Z Corporation purchases various stocks and bonds with these funds and also opens a travel agency. During the year, Z received the following income: $40,000 in dividends, $35,000 in interest, $30,000 from the travel business. Expenses for the year totaled $5,000.

1. What result to A-H?

2. What if Z Corporation pays $15,000 in foreign taxes and A is a United States corporation with two United States citizen shareholders, W and Y?

3. What if E is a foreign corporation with two United States citizen shareholders, O and P?

4. What result in 1. if Z Corporation pays a dividend of $1,000 each to the shareholders B-H and $4,100 to A on December 15? What if the dividend is paid on February 15 of the next year? What if the dividend is paid on May 15 of the next year?

Chapter 14
Controlled Foreign Corporations

§ 14.01 The Advantages of Tax Deferral

§ 14.02 The Intent Behind, and Overview of, the Controlled Foreign Corporation Provisions

§ 14.03 The United States Ownership Standard for Purposes of Controlled Foreign Corporation Status

§ 14.04 Amount of Imputed Income; Determining Ownership for Purposes of Income Inclusion

§ 14.05 Section 951 Inclusion and Computation: Subpart F Income and Earnings Invested in United States Property

§ 14.06 Subpart F Income; Foreign Base Company Income

§ 14.07 Foreign Personal Holding Company Income
Revenue Ruling 82-209, 1982-2 C.B. 157

§ 14.08 Foreign Base Company Sales Income—In General

§ 14.09 Exempted Manufacturing and Same-Country Activities

§ 14.10 Foreign Base Company Services Income

§ 14.11 Allocation of Deductions to Base Company Income: Rules and Limitations

§ 14.12 Special Exceptions to Foreign Base Company Income

§ 14.13 Basis Adjustments

§ 14.14 Exclusions from Gross Income—Previously Taxed Earnings and Profits

§ 14.15 Controlled Foreign Corporation Interaction with the Foreign Tax Credit—§ 902 Implications

§ 14.16 Disposal of Stock of Controlled Foreign Corporations—§ 1248

§ 14.17 Shareholders and Transactions Subject to § 1248

§ 14.18 General Limitation on Amount of Gain Recaptured
Problem 14

§ 14.01 The Advantages of Tax Deferral

The prime advantage of insulating income from United States taxation within a foreign corporation is the opportunity afforded domestic shareholders to defer tax on corporate income. So long as the corporate income remains safely within the confines of the foreign corporation, absent some deemed distribution device, the shareholder is not taxed on such income until it is repatriated via direct distributions (dividends) or indirectly on the disposition or exchange of their ownership interest (stock sales, redemptions, or corporate liquidations).

The shareholder's ability to defer tax liability often generates significant economic benefits. This is particularly true in the case of domestic shareholders investing or conducting business through a foreign corporation. The foreign corporation becomes a virtual Pandora's box for domestic shareholders, replete with tempting tax benefits. By lodging income in a foreign corporation, the corporation may enjoy a lower statutory or tax treaty rate on its earnings while avoiding the traditional double taxation of corporate earnings. In addition, by playing the waiting game, the shareholder may convert stockpiled ordinary income "dividends" into preferentially taxed capital gains upon disposition of his ownership interest—a desirable result given recent tax rate increases. Moreover, and perhaps most importantly, the domestic shareholders may economically benefit from the time value of deferral by reinvesting the deferred tax liability and generating additional earnings.

This panoply of potential benefits is not, however, boundless. The income of the foreign corporation may be subjected to tax in the jurisdiction of its formation or income source. However, judicious selection of such contact countries can minimize the corporation's foreign tax liability. Furthermore, the rate structure of the country of organization may yield substantial tax savings. There are a number of tax havens which apply exceptionally low tax rates or a complete tax exemption to corporations formed within them. This funneling of income away from the United States and into tax havens has not unexpectedly attracted significant attention from Congress.

§ 14.02 The Intent Behind, and Overview of, the Controlled Foreign Corporation Provisions

Congress enacted the Controlled Foreign Corporation (CFC) provisions in an attempt to remedy these deficiencies and to curb an outflow of United States investment. The CFC provisions attempt to attribute both business and passive income to its domestic owners and thus are broader than the previously enacted Foreign Personal Holding Company provisions, discussed in Chapter 13. They are designed to curb the meld of tax haven and deferral abuses. Albeit powerful, the CFC legislation is not a plenary solution, as numerous foreign corporations owned by United States shareholders fall outside of its reach. Furthermore, a number of planning techniques are available to avoid CFC status.

In order to thwart the benefits of deferral, the Code imposes on certain United States-owned foreign corporations the status of a Controlled Foreign Corporation. If a CFC exists, United States shareholders are subject to current taxation, inter alia, on their proportionate share of: (1) the CFC's Subpart F income and (2) the CFC's investment in United States property.

Subpart F income essentially embraces items which are ripe for tax haven abuses and are readily moveable between jurisdictions, thereby preventing the use of a foreign corporation as a tax-avoidance alter ego for direct shareholder investment. It includes foreign base company income (divided into five categories—personal holding company income and income from shipping, oil, services, and sales). The shareholder is also subject to imputation of those CFC earnings invested in domestic assets, thereby capturing what are in effect earnings repatriated to the United States. The sum of these income categories is imputed to the CFC's United States shareholders, subject to tax at ordinary income rates even though such income has not been received.

The CFC shareholders are entitled to corresponding basis adjustments to their CFC stock for the income imputation. This mechanism prevents double taxation of income upon the subsequent disposition of a shareholder's equity interest. Additionally, the statute provides tracing rules for actual distributions to avoid the double taxation of income previously imputed to the shareholder.

Finally, if the CFC provisions do not capture such income during the shareholder's ownership tenure, § 1248 ensures that the shareholder upon disposition of the stock in the CFC is not spared an ordinary income inclusion. That provision converts capital gain realized on the disposition to ordinary income if untaxed CFC earnings have accumulated.

§ 14.03 The United States Ownership Standard for Purposes of Controlled Foreign Corporation Status

The legislative focus of the CFC provisions is on closely-held corporations controlled by a small nucleus of domestic taxpayers. A foreign corporation is a CFC for a given taxable year if greater than 50 percent of the voting power *or* value of its stock is owned, directly or indirectly, on *any day of the taxable year* by "United States shareholders." CFC income is imputed only to the CFC's United States shareholders. A United States shareholder is any United States person holding, directly or indirectly, at least ten percent of the corporation's voting power.

Section 958 sets forth two indirect ownership schemes to attribute ownership of the stock of a foreign corporation. First, the constructive ownership rules of § 318 apply by incorporation to determine whether a domestic person holds the required ten percent ownership interest necessary for classification of that person as a United States shareholder. These rules ensure that the United States owners of a foreign corporation cannot circumvent CFC status by judiciously distributing corporate ownership among and between related individuals. Second, ownership attribution rules apply with respect to foreign entities for the limited purpose of determining the pro rata share of imputed CFC income of a United States shareholder. For purposes of determining the shareholder's pro rata share of CFC income, stock ownership includes direct ownership as well as indirect ownership by attribution on a proportionate basis from other foreign entities. Stock owned by or for foreign corporations, partnerships, trusts, or estates is considered proportionately owned by its shareholders, partners, or beneficiaries.

CFC status is not imposed on a corporation unless United States shareholders own the requisite more than 50 percent of voting power or value of the foreign corporation. Under a surprisingly narrow definition, a shareholder is not a United States shareholder unless the shareholder owns at least ten percent of the voting power of the foreign corporation. Thus, despite 100 percent *aggregate* domestic ownership, if 11 *unrelated* United States citizens each own roughly 9.09 percent of a foreign corporation, that corporation is *not* a CFC. Furthermore, CFC status is avoided if a United States citizen owns 50 percent of the vote and value of a foreign corporation, but other unrelated United States citizens own less than ten percent each of the remaining stock.

The Regulations adopt a substance-over-form approach in determining whether the greater than 50 percent United States ownership requirement exists. The Regulations employ a facts-and-circumstances analysis of the voting structure, intoning that:

> Any arrangement to shift formal voting power away from United States shareholders of a foreign corporation will not be given effect if in reality voting power is retained. The mere ownership of stock entitled to vote does not by itself mean that the shareholder owning such stock has the voting power of such.

This vague standard, though difficult to pin down, is a functional necessity given the possible range of formal and informal control arrangements that could be employed to circumvent the CFC regime. The requisite level of voting power is found in all cases where United States shareholders have the power to elect, appoint, or replace a majority of the board of directors (or comparable governing body). Even if the shareholders lack authority to appoint a majority of the foreign corporation's board, the corporation will be a CFC if its board (or equivalent thereof) must be appointed by a majority vote of the shareholders and United States persons own a majority of shares.

Attempts at manipulating ownership interests through weighted voting, cumulative voting, irrevocable proxies, or special issue veto power may have special significance in determining whether the ownership standard is met.

It is significant to note that CFC status arises if the United States ownership threshold is met on *any* day of the taxable year. Thus, a corporation may well not be a CFC throughout most of the year. A year-end shift of ownership via a sale or a redemption of a foreign shareholder's stock may result in the requisite ownership by United States shareholders for any day during the taxable year.

However, it is possible for CFC status to be imposed on a corporation *without* forcing an imputation of the corporation's income to its United States shareholders. CFC income is imputed to those shareholders only if the foreign corporation constitutes a CFC for an uninterrupted period of 30 days or more during the taxable year.

§ 14.04 Amount of Imputed Income; Determining Ownership for Purposes of Income Inclusion

The starting point in ascertaining whether domestic shareholders of a foreign corporation will suffer adverse tax consequences is a determination of CFC status. However, CFC designation does not dictate that all corporate income must be imputed or that every domestic shareholder will necessarily be taxed. Instead, the statute specifies a number of limitations as to which, if any, shareholders will be taxed and the extent of that taxation.

The domestic shareholder's pro rata share of various income categories will be included in its gross income if the following conditions are met:

1. The corporation constitutes a CFC for an uninterrupted period of 30 days or more during the taxable year;
2. The shareholder is a United States person at any time during the taxable year and owned either directly, or indirectly through a foreign entity, at least ten percent of the total voting power of all classes of stock; and
3. The United States shareholder owns stock in the foreign corporation on the last day of such taxable year on which the corporation is a CFC.

Though designed to mirror a repatriation of earnings, the statute does not expressly deem the income inclusion to be a "dividend."

Under the first standard, a corporation experiencing frequent shifts in stock ownership may be a CFC for a majority of the year without any income being imputed to its shareholders. For example, a foreign corporation could theoretically be a CFC for 29 consecutive days of each of the 12 months of its taxable year, yet its shareholders are spared an income imputation so long as the corporation is not labeled as a CFC for any consecutive *30*-day period.

The laxity of the third standard (i.e., ownership on the *last* day of the year) enables shareholders who dispose of their stock during the year to escape income imputation. For instance, assume a corporation is a CFC for its entire taxable year. B remains a 12 percent United States shareholder until one month prior to the end of such year. If B disposes of all of his stock in the CFC at that point, B escapes the income imputation by not holding CFC shares at year-end. Nevertheless, as discussed below, § 1248 may apply to the gain, thereby producing, in part, something of a similar result.

Conversely, shareholders with reduced holdings may be surprised by an income imputation under this standard. Under the definition of United States shareholder, CFC income may be imputed to individuals who on the last day of the taxable year own less than ten percent of the corporate voting power, but who, at some earlier point in the year, satisfied the ten percent standard. For instance, if B in the prior example merely reduced his stock ownership from 12 percent to nine percent by year end, B would still suffer some income imputation.

Once the prerequisites for imputation have been met, certain categories of CFC income must be imputed to its United States shareholders. This amount is computed solely by reference to the percentage of stock which the stockholder owns directly and to stock deemed "actually owned" by the shareholder under a limited attribution rule from a foreign entity.

The constructive ownership provisions are determinative of whether the shareholder is a United States shareholder for purposes of imputing an income inclusion. They are not, however, determinative of the amount of the imputation. Only the shareholder's direct ownership and indirect ownership via the limited entity attribution rules of § 958(b) bear on the amount of his "pro rata share."

§ 14.05 Section 951 Inclusion and Computation; Subpart F Income and Earnings Invested in United States Property

The amount of CFC income imputed to United States shareholders is comprised of specified categories of income. Such shareholders must include, inter alia, in income: the sum of the shareholder's pro rata share of the CFC's Subpart F income; and the shareholder's attributed portion of the CFC's investment in United States property. The first category captures income perceived to be amenable to tax haven deflection. The latter category targets directly the CFC-cloaked investments of United States shareholders and indirect repatriation.

The taxpayer's pro rata share of Subpart F income is the portion of the hypothetical income available for inclusion which would have been distributed to that shareholder on the last day of the taxable year that the corporation was a CFC. The shareholder's share is quite properly reduced by any dividends actually paid during the year. The intention of the CFC provisions is to prevent the retention of earnings in foreign jurisdictions. If distributions were made during the taxable year, shareholders should not be penalized by a forced income inclusion, since the actual distributions would be subject to United States tax.

United States shareholders are required to include in income their share of the CFC's increase in earnings invested in United States property as determined under § 956. This inclusion targets indirect repatriation of CFC earnings cloaked in United States property investments. Conflicting policy notions underpin this category—on the one hand, domestic investment is something to be encouraged by Congress; at the same time, domestic investment by a CFC is damning evidence that it is being used primarily as a tax avoidance device by its United States shareholders.

§ 14.06 Subpart F Income; Foreign Base Company Income

The most expansive category of imputed CFC income requires the shareholder to include his pro rata share of the CFC's Subpart F income. Subpart F income includes foreign passive income as well as certain foreign business income which is readily moveable between jurisdictions and is generally subject to comparatively lower foreign tax rates. These tax-favored features make such income a hallmark of the targeted use of foreign corporations by domestic shareholders and accordingly have caused it to be the focal point of the CFC antideferral regime.

To prevent the use of foreign tax havens to reduce the tax liability of domestic corporations, the Subpart F provisions capture foreign base company income. This category of inclusion generally targets those situations where a domestic parent establishes a foreign "base company" subsidiary in a low-tax jurisdiction in order to avoid United States taxation on certain types of income. Foreign base company income is a broad measure, comprised of categories of readily moveable income, the most significant of which are: (1) foreign personal holding company income, (2) foreign base company sales income, and (3) foreign base company services income.

§ 14.07 Foreign Personal Holding Company Income

The foreign personal holding company income category targets primarily passive income. Foreign personal holding company income under the CFC provisions, while mirroring the passive income categories of a Foreign Personal Holding Company, has a markedly wider reach.

The statute provides several exclusions from foreign personal holding company income, generally encompassing items of income which, inherently or under the facts and circumstances of their receipt, are not the type of moveable, tax haven income marked for inclusion as Subpart F income. For instance, rents and royalties derived in the active conduct of a CFC's trade or business from unrelated parties are not deemed to be foreign personal holding company income. The determination of whether rents or royalties are so derived is generally made on a facts-and-circumstances basis.

If a corporation constitutes both a Foreign Personal Holding Company and a CFC, the CFC provisions trump with respect to any amount imputable under § 951(a). Thus, shareholders of that entity will not be spared the resulting income imputation under the CFC provisions. Some corporations which have successfully avoided Foreign Personal Holding Company status through stock ownership or gross income manipulation may be ensnared by the more inclusive CFC provisions.

Revenue Ruling 82-209
1982-2 C.B. 157

ISSUES

1. Whether interest income derived from the making of a single loan by a controlled foreign corporation is excluded from foreign personal holding company income under section 954(c)(3)(B) of the Internal Revenue Code if the corporation qualifies in Montserrat as a "class B" bank?

2. Whether such foreign corporation can avoid the foreign personal holding company provisions under the "banking" exception provided in section 552(b)(2) of the Code?

FACTS

Situation 1.

In 1981, Bank BK was established in Montserrat as a "class B" bank. A class B bank is defined under Montserrat law as a bank that exclusively carries on business outside of Montserrat. BK has outstanding one class of stock which is owned equally by 10 United States persons. Thus, BK is a controlled foreign corporation within the meaning of section 957(a) of the Code. During 1981, BK's sole activity consisted of the making of a loan to an unrelated United States person. BK realized interest income from the loan. No distributions were made during the taxable year to the shareholders of BK.

BK has no fixed business address from which banking services are provided to the public. The only indication of BK's presence in Montserrat is that BK receives its mail at the office of a local agent, who only performs certain administrative functions. BK does not have any facilities to receive deposits nor provide trust services. BK receives no requests from the public to provide financing of any sort.

Situation 2.

Assume the facts are the same as in Situation 1, except that the stock of BK is owned by three individuals. Two of the individuals are United

States citizens who own 50 percent and 5 percent of the stock, respectively. The remaining individual is a nonresident alien who owns 45 percent of the stock. Thus, BK is a foreign personal holding company within the meaning of section 552(a) of the Code.

LAW AND ANALYSIS

Section 954(a)(1) of the Code provides that the term "foreign base company income" includes the foreign personal holding company income for the taxable year as determined under section 954(c). Section 954(c)(1) of the Code provides that the term "foreign personal holding company income" means the foreign personal holding company income as defined in section 553, with certain modifications and adjustments.

Section 553(a)(1) of the Code provides that the term "foreign personal holding company income" includes that portion of the gross income that consists of interest.

Section 954(c)(3)(B) of the Code provides that, for purposes of subsection (c)(1), foreign personal holding company income does not include interest derived in the conduct of a banking, financing, or similar business.

Section 1.954-2(d)(2)(ii) of the Income Tax Regulations defines a banking, financing, or similar business as a business the activities of which consist of one or more of the following activities carried on in transactions with persons situated within or without the United States:

(A) Receiving deposits of money from the public;
(B) Making personal, mortgage, industrial, or other loans to the public;
(C) Purchasing, selling, discounting, or negotiating for the public on a regular basis, notes, drafts, checks, bills of exchange, acceptances, or other evidences of indebtedness;
(D) Issuing letters of credit to the public and negotiating drafts drawn thereunder;
(E) Providing trust services for the public;
(F) Financing foreign exchange transactions for the public; or
(G) Purchasing stock, debt obligations, or other securities from an issuer or holder with a view to the public distribution thereof; or offering or selling stock, debt obligations, or other securities for an issuer or holder in connection with the public distribution thereof, or participating in any such undertaking.

Section 1.954-2(d)(2)(ii) of the regulations also provides that although the fact that the controlled foreign corporation is subjected to the banking and credit laws of a foreign country shall be taken into account in determining whether it is engaged in the conduct of a banking, financing, or similar business in that country, the character of the business actually carried on during the taxable year shall determine whether it is conducting a banking, financing, or similar business.

Section 552(b)(2) of the Code excludes from the definition of foreign personal holding company any corporation organized and doing business under the banking and credit laws of a foreign country if it is established to the satisfaction of the Secretary that such corporation is not formed or availed of for the purpose of evading or avoiding United States income tax which would otherwise be imposed upon its shareholders.

Section 1.552-4(b) of the regulations provides that an application for certification under section 552(b)(2) of the Code may be submitted by the taxpayer to the Commissioner of Internal Revenue. The application must explain the extent of the corporation's business in receiving deposits and making loans and discounts and similar banking and credit operations. The taxpayer shall also provide a statement as to the extent of the operations other than such banking and credit operations and any other facts or information the corporation may wish to submit to show that it was not formed or availed of for the purpose of evading or avoiding the United States income taxes which would otherwise be imposed on its shareholders.

Situation 1: The fact that BK is subject to the banking laws of Montserrat is not determinative of whether BK is conducting a banking, financing, or similar business. The character of the business actually carried on during the taxable year shall determine whether BK is conducting a banking, financing, or similar business.

BK entered into a single transaction, the making of one loan. BK received no deposits, made no other loans or discounts, nor conducted any banking activities with the public. Therefore, under the above mentioned circumstances, BK is not considered to be engaged in a banking business.

Situation 2: Under section 552(b)(2) of the Code, the question of whether BK is doing business as a bank depends upon the facts and circumstances. During 1981, BK entered into a single transaction, the making of one loan. Therefore, under the aforementioned circumstances, BK is not considered to be doing business as a bank and will not receive the certification required under this section in order to be classified as a corporation that is not a foreign personal holding company.

HOLDINGS

1. In Situation 1, BK does not qualify for the exclusion from foreign personal holding company income under section 954(c)(3)(B) of the Code for banks. The interest income realized by BK is included in the foreign base company income of BK under section 954(a)(1).

2. In Situation 2, BK does not qualify for the exception under section 552(b)(2) of the Code provided for banks and is subject to the rules applicable to a foreign personal holding company defined in section 552(a).

§ 14.08 Foreign Base Company Sales Income—In General

The second category of foreign base company income is comprised of that income attributable to sales of personal property. This category of Subpart F income has its genesis in the practice by United States corporations of establishing foreign subsidiaries in base countries with low tax rates and distributing goods through these subsidiaries to a third corporation, usually foreign, or to the ultimate consumer. For example, if X, a domestic manufacturer, sells directly to its foreign customers, it is subject to tax on the profits earned from such sales at United States tax rates. By establishing subsidiary B in a low-tax jurisdiction to purchase goods from X and sell those goods to X's foreign customers, X lodges a portion of such profits indefinitely in the low-tax foreign jurisdiction. In essence, the foreign base company merely serves as a conduit for the sale of the parent company's goods to consumers outside of the base country.

This layering mechanism permitted business profits to be indefinitely lodged in the foreign sales entity, thereby deferring United States taxation on such profits until they were repatriated to the domestic parent. The Subpart F provisions mandate deemed distributions to domestic shareholders on account of certain CFC sales activity.

For income to constitute foreign base company sales income, four requirements must be met:

1. The subject purchase or sale must be to, from, or on behalf of, a related party;
2. The transaction must involve personal property;
3. The purchase or sale must be for use or destination outside the base company jurisdiction; and
4. The personal property must be manufactured or produced outside of the CFC's country of incorporation.

A "related person" for purposes of this provision includes all entities and individuals owning, directly or indirectly, more than 50 percent of the CFC's stock. It also includes any entity controlled by the CFC or controlled by the same persons as the CFC.

§ 14.09 Exempted Manufacturing and Same-Country Activities

The inclusion of foreign base company sales income is aimed at the use of a foreign sales entity to funnel the sales of products from a domestic parent or other foreign sources to purchasers outside of that base country. Accordingly, foreign base company income does not include income derived from the purchase and sale of personal property manufactured by the CFC or property purchased within the jurisdiction in which the CFC is incorporated. The Regulations provide elaborate rules for making this determination which are keyed to whether the CFC manufactured the property at issue.

There are obvious difficulties in determining the amount of manufacturing efforts required by the base company to take the transaction out of the statute's reach. The regulatory scheme insists on either complete manufacture by the CFC or a "substantial transformation of the property." This substantial transformation occurs, most obviously, when the resulting product sold is not the product purchased (e.g., significant conversion activity occurs). The Regulations cite as examples such processes as the conversion of wood pulp into paper, steel into bolts and screws, and raw fish into canned fish. This analysis is undoubtedly more qualitative than quantitative and thus it suffers from an obvious lack of predictability.

More uncertainty arises as to the necessary degree of manufacturing when the property sold is comprised of purchased component parts. Two basic tests arise for determining whether a foreign company utilizing component parts is the sort of devilish sales entity the statute will prosecute: first, a general test of facts and circumstances, and second, an overriding 20 percent cost of goods sold test.

Under the first test, if purchased property is utilized as a component part in personal property which is ultimately sold (such as engines purchased in the manufacture of airplanes or automobiles), the integration activity is deemed to constitute manufacturing if it is substantial in degree. In no case, however, do such incidental manufacturing activities as packaging, repackaging, labeling, or minor assembly rise to the requisite level of manufacturing activities necessary to claim the exclusion. This test is generally one of facts and circumstances, seemingly generously applied by the courts.

The second test represents a significant safe harbor rule for manufacturing involving component parts. No foreign base company sales income arises if 20 percent or more of the total costs of goods sold is comprised of direct labor and overhead incurred by the CFC in converting the purchased item into the finished product.

If the foreign entity is branded a sales organization, as opposed to a manufacturer, income is imputed back to the CFC shareholders. The formula employed in determining the imputation focuses on the manufactured components' country of origin, sales of the finished product outside of the CFC's jurisdiction, and a determination of whether the parties to whom the property is sold, or from whom components were purchased, are related or unrelated.

§ 14.10 Foreign Base Company Services Income

Another category of foreign base income is comprised of foreign base company services income. This category prevents foreign manufacturers from deflecting to low-tax jurisdictions income derived from certain services performed on their behalf. The primary concern of this category was the formation of service subsidiaries in low-tax jurisdictions. The rendition of services for a related party performed outside of the CFC's country of incorporation constitutes foreign base company services income. The nominal classification of the payment is irrelevant; targeted income may be in the form of compensation, fees, commissions, or otherwise. Services are similarly broadly defined and include technical, managerial, engineering, architectural, skilled, industrial, commercial, or other services.

Income from services targeted as foreign base company services income are divided into four broad categories in the Regulations: (1) services paid for by the person related to the CFC; (2) services which the related person is obligated to perform; (3) services which were a condition of a related-party sale of property; and (4) services to which a related person gave "substantial assistance." Assistance is broadly defined to include direction, supervision, know-how, financial assistance, or provision of materials. Assistance is substantial if it is either a principal element in producing the services income or exceeds 50 percent of the cost of the performed services. Financial assistance and the provision of supplies or materials are deemed assistance for purposes of this test only to the extent that the CFC pays less than an arm's-length charge for such use or purchase.

Certain services are specifically exempted from the reach of Subpart F. For instance, services wholly performed within the CFC's country of incorporation are exempted. As distinguished from postsale, maintenance-type service, income from services related to the sale of property manufactured by the CFC is excluded if such services are rendered prior to the sale or are specifically related to the sale of that product. Services performed pursuant to certain guarantees are also not includable within this category.

§ 14.11 Allocation of Deductions to Base Company Income: Rules and Limitations

Once the aggregate CFC foreign base company income has been computed, it is reduced by "properly allocable" deductions. Such deductions are allocated under the Regulations in a fashion that parallels the allocation and apportionment scheme applicable for purposes of computing the foreign tax credit limitation. Deductions are logically allocated to the gross base company income category to which they directly relate. If no such relationship exists, a next-best rule is triggered, i.e., ratably apportioning deductions among all gross income categories. The allocation process is limited in that it cannot create a "loss" with respect to a given category of base company income.

A special rule applies, however, if the CFC's foreign base company income exceeds 70 percent of its gross income. In such a case, *all* of the CFC's gross income is treated as foreign base company income. It thus follows that all of the CFC's deductions may be offset against gross foreign base company income.

§ 14.12 Special Exceptions to Foreign Base Company Income

After the computational dust settles, the fact that a CFC has foreign base company income by no means automatically warrants its inclusion in Subpart F income. On the other hand, an excessive amount of foreign base company income can poison the CFC's gross income, recasting all of its income as Subpart F income.

Three special provisions dictate the extent of the inclusion of base company income and hence the amount of Subpart F income attributable to United States shareholders. Under these special rules, foreign base company income may be completely erased or become a lethal all-inclusive concept.

If gross foreign base company income is less than the lesser of five percent of the CFC's gross income or $1,000,000, a de minimis rule shields *all* of the gross income from classification as foreign base company (or insurance) income. For example, if A Corporation, a CFC, has gross income of $4,000,000 and gross foreign base company income of $100,000, A's adjusted foreign base company income is deemed to equal zero.

In sharp contrast, the derivation of gross foreign base company income in excess of 70 percent of the CFC's gross income results in foreign base company classification of *all* corporate gross income. If, in the above example, A Corporation had gross income of $4,000,000 and gross foreign base company income of $3,000,000, A would be deemed to have realized $4,000,000 in foreign base company income.

As the foreign base company provisions are geared toward discouraging the use of tax haven base companies to avoid domestic taxes, Congress has properly crafted an elective exception to exclude from Subpart F foreign base company income which does not enjoy a significantly lower foreign tax rate. Under this high-taxed income exception, any item of income subject to an effective tax rate exceeding 90 percent of the maximum § 11 corporate tax rate (i.e., currently 31.5 percent (35% x 90%)) will not constitute foreign base company income regardless of its genesis.

§ 14.13 Basis Adjustments

As the United States shareholders of a CFC are paying tax on a hypothetical, rather than an actual, distribution, it is necessary to have a device to prevent double taxation. The Code provides for an increase in a shareholder's basis of each share of CFC stock or other property by the amount of the income inclusion.

The upward basis adjustment ensures that a sale of the stock prior to receipt of actual distributions will not lead to double taxation. The basis adjustment operates to reduce the gain recognized on the ultimate sale of the stock. Thus, income imputed serves to reduce taxable gain and the attendant tax liability on the subsequent disposition of the CFC stock.

Conversely, to preserve the taxable nature of certain CFC imputations, the Code also specifies circumstances under which a United States shareholder must *decrease* its basis in stock or other property giving rise to imputed income. Since a CFC retains its corporate characteristics notwithstanding the imputation of income provisions, a protective device is required to ensure that earnings imputed to a shareholder will not again be taxed upon actual distribution. In order to prevent such onerous treatment, the Code mandates that distributions of previously includable income be excluded from gross income. When the untaxed distribution is made, a concomitant basis reduction must ensue given that the danger of double taxation has already been averted by means of the income exclusion.

§ 14.14 Exclusions from Gross Income— Previously Taxed Earnings and Profits

The CFC provisions impute income to United States shareholders even though no actual distribution of such income to those owners has transpired. In view of the hypothetical foundations of these provisions, if, after the imputation of income, a distribution of dividends from the CFC actually occurs, a mechanism is necessary to ensure that distributions representing earnings which have previously been imputed to the CFC shareholder are not again taxed.

Section 959 supplies this mechanism. In situations where particular earnings and profits have been subjected to imputation, it provides that such earnings and profits (and the distributions from them) are thereafter insulated from taxation (i.e., the dividend income represented by these earnings and profits will not be taxed). This income exclusion is predicated on the notion that Congress has already taken its pound of flesh from the shareholder and has prevented the untoward harboring of what would otherwise be tax-free income in the CFC. As such earnings have already been taxed, the exclusion shields those earnings from a second layer of taxation upon actual distribution. Another exclusion applies to those earnings and profits attributable to imputed amounts which have been reinvested by the CFC in United States property. Amounts imputed from investment in United States property are excludable to the extent such earnings are attributable to income derived from the other categories of imputed income.

As it is possible for actual and constructive distributions to occur during the same year, priority rules respecting such distributions have been enacted. Section 959 invokes the normal ordering rules of § 316—distributions are deemed to come first from current earnings and profits to the extent thereof and thereafter from accumulated earnings and profits. This priority scheme is preferential to taxpayers. Through it, previously taxed income is deemed distributed to shareholders first. Until distributions exceed the amount of previously taxed income, actual distributions will not be taxable as dividends to the shareholder.

§ 14.15 Controlled Foreign Corporation Interaction with the Foreign Tax Credit—§ 902 Implications

As it is possible for a CFC to be owned by a United States corporation, the issue arises as to the availability of the § 902 deemed paid foreign tax credit. If CFC shareholders were taxed only on actual distributions, then the normal rules for determining the availability of the deemed paid credit would suffice. However, as CFC shareholders may be taxed on both distributed and undistributed amounts, special rules are required to prevent either total denial of such credits (on the constructive and actual distribution) or the doubling of credit benefits.

Section 960 specifies rules under which the foreign tax credit may be available for such corporate shareholders. These rules effectively parallel the § 902 deemed paid dividend provisions. The operative event in the CFC context is the imputation of income rather than an actual distribution. Section 960 provides that a domestic corporation is deemed to have paid a portion of the CFC's foreign income taxes, determined under § 902, as if the corporation had received a dividend. After such a determination, CFC shareholders must also gross-up their incomes to account for the amount of foreign taxes deemed paid. Thus, for tax credit purposes, the corporate shareholder is treated as if an actual distribution had been made.

It is possible for a CFC to distribute amounts to its shareholders in a year in which income is imputed. These actual distributions are tested to ascertain whether they are includable in income. In most cases, corporate shareholders will have taken advantage of the deemed paid credit in a prior year and should not be entitled to another credit for the same earnings. Therefore, any foreign taxes paid or deemed paid by the CFC in connection with the earnings attributable to any distribution which is excluded from gross income cannot trigger the § 902 credit. Conversely, if foreign taxes not deemed paid in prior years are attributable to a distribution excludable under § 959(a), that distribution is treated as a dividend so as to qualify such taxes for the § 902 credit.

§ 14.16 Disposal of Stock of Controlled Foreign Corporations—§ 1248

As previously discussed, a United States shareholder's ownership of a ten percent or greater interest in a CFC can lead to inclusion of specified income in that taxpayer's gross income. However, the remainder of the CFC's income may be accumulated by the corporation without adverse consequences. If such accumulated income is not distributed to the United States shareholders, domestic taxation can be deferred. If no additional legislative safeguards were in place, the controlling shareholders could cash-out their investment upon a subsequent sale of stock in the CFC at a profit which would be favorably taxed at capital gains rates. Despite the fact that part of such gain represents the accumulated earnings which would have been taxed to the shareholder as ordinary income dividends, the shareholder would be able to simply convert such amounts from ordinary income to capital gain. While this occurs with respect to domestic corporations as well, the distinction is that the domestic corporation would have been taxed on the income as earned while the foreign corporation would have avoided taxation.

To prevent repatriation of such earnings without direct taxation, Congress enacted § 1248. Upon certain dispositions of CFC stock, the legislation recaptures a portion of the gain representing the previously deferred earnings as a *dividend* subject to ordinary income treatment. The taxpayer secures foreign source dividend characterization, and a § 902 credit may attach to that dividend.

§ 14.17 Shareholders and Transactions Subject to § 1248

The net of § 1248 is not so wide that the gain from every disposition of CFC stock is recaptured. Recapture affects only the gain realized by United States persons who own or owned, directly or indirectly, stock representing ten percent or more of the CFC's voting power at any time during the five-year period ending on the date of the subject transaction. The foreign corporation must have been a CFC for some portion of that ownership period, but not necessarily on the date of disposition or exchange. The voting interests in question may be owned either directly, indirectly, or constructively and need not be so owned at the time of the sale or liquidation. It is sufficient that the required percentage of the voting interest was owned at *any time* during the previous five years. Thus, the simplest, though lengthy, method of avoiding the effects of § 1248 is to wait the requisite five-year period after a loss of CFC status before disposing of the stock.

§ 14.18 General Limitation on Amount of Gain Recaptured

Section 1248 limits the amount of gain characterized as dividend income. The gain is includable as a dividend to the extent of the CFC's earnings and profits attributable to the owner's disposed shareholdings which: (1) were accumulated in the CFC's taxable years during which the United States shareholder held the CFC stock and (2) were accumulated during those ownership periods of the taxpayer during which the foreign corporation was a CFC. For instance, assume that D, a United States citizen, acquired his stock in C, a CFC, on January 1, Year 1 for $60,000. On December 31, Year 4, he sells that stock to B for $130,000. C's accumulated earnings and profits attributable to D's ownership period were $20,000. Of the $70,000 gain realized by D, only $20,000 would be subject to characterization under § 1248.

Should gain exist in excess of this amount, it retains its character—generally, capital gain. Thus, in the above example, the $50,000 of remaining gain would retain its capital gain character.

Since § 1248 applies only to gains, any loss recognized on such transactions will be characterized under other sections, typically as capital in nature.

Corporations, which no longer enjoy a capital gain preference, may affirmatively seek out § 1248 recharacterization. Section 1248 generates foreign source income which may carry § 902 deemed paid foreign tax credit benefits.

PROBLEM 14—CONTROLLED FOREIGN CORPORATIONS

Code: §§ 951, 952(a), 954(a)-(d), 957, 958, 959(a), 960(a), 961, 1248(a), (c), (d)

Regulations: §§ 1.954-1(a)-(d), 1.954-2(a)-(c), 1.1248-1

1. W, X, Y, and Z, unrelated United States citizens, form Q Corporation in the Cayman Islands, which does not have a corporate income tax. Each contributes $25,000 in cash to Q Corporation in return for stock. Q Corporation purchases various stocks and bonds with these funds and also opens a travel agency. During the year, Q Corporation received the following income; $40,000 in dividends, $35,000 in interest, $80,000 from the travel business. Expenses for the year totaled $5,000. What result to W-Z?

2. A, a United States citizen, and P, a domestic corporation wholly-owned by A, form F, a corporation under Argentine law, on January 1, with a contribution of $5,000 each in return for 50 shares of common stock. F Corporation purchases equipment in the United States from independent parties and sells it to independent parties in other Latin American countries. F Corporation makes $100,000 of net income from sales. Foreign income taxes of $30,000 are paid by F Corporation on its income.

   a. What are the United States tax consequences for A, P Corporation and F Corporation?
   b. Suppose F Corporation purchased all of its equipment from P Corporation. What consequences for A, P Corporation, and F Corporation?
   c. What result in b. if an unrelated shareholder D owned eight percent of the stock of F Corporation and A and P Corporation owned 46 percent each?
   d. Suppose F Corporation makes the same $100,000 of income and pays the same $30,000 of foreign taxes each year from Year 1-Year 5. On January 1, Year 6, A sells his shares to M, an unrelated Argentine citizen, for $400,000. What consequences to A?
   e. What result in d. if an unrelated shareholder D owned eight percent of the stock of F Corporation and A and P Corporation owned 46 percent each and D sells his shares?

3. A, a United States citizen, and P, a domestic corporation wholly-owned by A, form F, a corporation under Argentine law, on January 1, with a contribution of $5,000 each in return for 50

shares of common stock. F Corporation purchases equipment in the United States from P Corporation and sells it to independent parties in Argentina and other Latin American countries. F Corporation makes $50,000 of net income from sales in other Latin American countries and $100,000 of net income from sales in Argentina. No foreign income taxes are paid by F Corporation on its income.

a. What consequences for A, P Corporation, and F Corporation?

b. What result in a. if an unrelated shareholder D owned eight percent of the stock of F Corporation and A and P Corporation owned 46 percent each?

c. Suppose F Corporation makes the same $150,000 of income from Year 1-Year 5. On January 1, Year 6, A sells his shares to M, an unrelated Argentina citizen, for $400,000. What consequences to A?

d. What result in c. if an unrelated shareholder D owned eight percent of the stock of F Corporation and A and P Corporation owned 46 percent each and D sells his shares?

Chapter 15

International Taxation and Tax Policy

§ 15.01 Report of Treasury Department, Selected Tax Policy Implications of Global Electronic Commerce (November 21, 1996)

**Selected Tax Policy Implications of Global Electronic Commerce
Department of the Treasury Office of Tax Policy
November 1996**

This paper provides an introduction to certain federal income tax policy and administration issues presented by developments in communications technology and electronic commerce. This paper is a discussion document, designed to elicit views on the issues presented as well as suggestions as to solutions for new problems. This paper is neither intended, nor should be taken as an expression of the legal or policy views of the United States Government, including the Department of the Treasury and the Internal Revenue Service. In addition, no inference is intended as to current law. . . .

TABLE OF CONTENTS

Section I: Introduction

Executive Summary
    1.   Introduction

Section II: Technical Background

    2.   An Overview of the Global Information Infrastructure or "Information Superhighway"
    3.   The World Wide Web and Electronic Commerce
    4.   Security and Encryption
    5.   Payment Mechanisms

Section III: Tax Policy and Administration Issues

    6.   Tax Policy and Administration Issues: General Considerations
    7.   Substantive Tax Law Issues
    8.   Tax Administration and Compliance Issues
    9.   Conclusion

EXECUTIVE SUMMARY

New information and communications technologies such as the Internet are creating exciting opportunities for workers, consumers, and businesses. Information, services, and money may now be instantaneously transferred anywhere in the world. Firms are increasing their imports and exports of goods, services, and information as the costs associated with participating in global markets plummet, and they are forming closer relationships with suppliers and customers around the world. New markets and market mechanisms are emerging. Consumers can choose from a much broader range of goods and services, and "intelligent agent" software will soon give consumers an unprecedented ability to hunt for bargains.

These new technologies, particularly communications technologies including the Internet, have effectively eliminated national borders on the information highway. As a result, cross-border transactions may run the risk that countries will claim inconsistent taxing jurisdictions, and that taxpayers will be subject to quixotic taxation. If these technologies are to achieve their maximum potential, rules that provide certainty and prevent double taxation are required.

In order to ensure that these new technologies not be impeded, the development of substantive tax policy and administration in this area should be guided by the principle of neutrality. Neutrality rejects the imposition of new or additional taxes on electronic transactions and instead simply requires that the tax system treat similar income equally, regardless of whether it is earned through electronic means or through existing channels of commerce.

A major substantive issue raised by these new technologies is identifying the country or countries which have the jurisdiction to tax such income. It is necessary to clarify how existing concepts apply to persons engaged in electronic commerce. In addition, transactions in cyberspace will likely accelerate the current trend to de-emphasize traditional concepts of source-based taxation, increasing the importance of residence-based taxation.

Another major category of issues involves the classification of income arising from transactions in digitized information, such as computer programs, books, music, or images. The distinction between royalty, sale of goods, and services income must be refined in light of the ease of transmitting and reproducing digitized information.

In the area of tax administration and compliance, electronic commerce may create new variations on old issues as well as new categories of issues. The major compliance issue posed by electronic commerce is the extent to which electronic money is analogous to cash and thus creates the potential for anonymous and untraceable transactions. Another significant category of issues involves identifying parties to communications and transactions utilizing these new technologies and verifying records when transactions are conducted electronically. However, developments in the science of encryption and related technologies may lead to systems that verify the identity of persons online and ensure the veracity of electronic documents.

Treasury invites comments on the issues raised by this paper as well as any other issues relating to electronic commerce....

1. INTRODUCTION

It is by now a well-worn cliche to say that we live in an era of rapid technological and social change. Technologies and businesses that were unknown a few years ago are now widespread. Most recently, the explosive growth of telecommunications technology, sometimes referred to as the "Global Information Infrastructure," or the "Information Superhighway" which includes the Internet, has enabled people to communicate and exchange information on an unprecedented scale. These technologies present tremendous opportunities to enrich all of our lives in so many ways, many of which we are likely not to have envisioned. As President Clinton has said, "The day is coming when every home will be connected to it, and it will be just as normal a part of our life as a telephone and a television. It's becoming our new town square, changing the way we relate to one another, the way we send mail, the way we hear news, the way we play."

These new technologies bring with them social changes and new ways of doing business. Services are an ever-growing sector of the economy. Modern telecommunications allow information, services, and money to be instantaneously transferred anywhere in the world. Some have even speculated that the traditional corporation could itself become obsolete in certain cases as "virtual corporations" bring together varying groups of consultants and independent contractors on a project-by-project basis.

These technological advances may put particular pressure on the principles governing the taxation of transnational transactions. It is the very nature of these developments that they tend to blur national borders and the source and character of income. Consequently, significant issues often arise regarding how the income arising from transnational transactions utilizing these technologies should be treated under current rules. As a result, it is possible that countries will claim inconsistent taxing jurisdiction, with the attendant possibility that taxpayers will be subject to international double taxation. If these technologies are to achieve their maximum potential, this must be avoided. Our overall tax policy goal in this area should emulate policy in other areas—maintain neutrality, fairness and simplicity—a policy which serves to encourage all desirable economic activity new and old.

These technological developments dictate that the Internal Revenue Code and generally accepted principles of international tax policy be reexamined. It is in all parties' interests to study the potential issues now, seek public comment, and develop rules that accommodate evolving technologies and ways of doing business.

This paper is meant to be a step in this process of reexamination. It is neither a treatise on taxation of technology nor a blueprint for future changes. Instead, the purpose of this paper is to stimulate public discussion by raising issues that currently exist or seem likely to arise. This paper is intended to encourage interested taxpayers, practitioners, academics, and others to comment on the issues identified herein and other similar tax issues that they believe require resolution.

The modernization process of which this paper is an early step will proceed on many fronts. Some of the issues identified in this paper can be resolved through the administrative process. It is possible that other issues can be resolved only through amendments to the Internal Revenue Code. Treasury will work with the Ways and Means Committee, the Finance Committee, and the Joint Committee on Taxation to study the statutory changes that may be required. Finally, it may also be necessary to reach an international consensus on certain issues. Treasury will be involved with the work of groups such as the Organization for Economic Cooperation and Development and with our treaty partners, to establish international standards to deal with these emerging issues.

Treasury intends that the goal of this process is to develop a framework for analysis that will not impede electronic commerce. The solutions that emerge should be sufficiently general and flexible in order to deal with developments in technology and ways of doing business that are currently unforeseen. In most cases, this will require that existing principles be adapted and reinterpreted in the context of developments in technology. In extreme cases, it may be necessary to develop new concepts.

The nature of the Global Information Infrastructure obviously has ramifications beyond taxation, including national security, copyright, privacy, security, financial trading systems, and even economic measurement. These issues are outside the scope of this paper, although the Office of Tax Policy and the Internal Revenue Service intend to coordinate their work with other branches of the Treasury Department and the United States government.

2. AN OVERVIEW OF THE GLOBAL INFORMATION INFRASTRUCTURE OR "INFORMATION SUPERHIGHWAY"

2.1. The Information Superhighway. The Information Superhighway or Global Information Infrastructure is not a single computer network or means of communication but instead refers to the convergence of previously separate communications and computing systems into an interoperable, global network of networks. Eventually, this superhighway may transmit a wide spectrum of information, films, programs, and services into every business and household, incorporating voice telephony and cable television. This trend is driven in part by the fact that the cost of communications is falling quickly. The Information Superhighway permits its users to send and receive information around the world, at relatively low cost.

2.2. Convergence of technologies. The distinct communications systems that will converge to form the Information Superhighway include telephone systems, cable and satellite communications, and computer networks. This convergence has been in part driven by two major technological changes. In telecommunications, transmission has evolved from copper wire, which has a relatively limited data transmission capacity, to fiber optic cable, which has virtually limitless capacity. This increased capacity makes it practical to rapidly transmit large amounts of information such as videos or x-rays. The second technological development is "digitization," the conversion of text, sound, images, video and other content into a common digital format. Any type of information, including cash equivalents, which can be digitized can be transmitted electronically.

2.3. Communications revolution is more than the Internet. Although the Internet, which is discussed below, is the best known aspect of the communications revolution, the Internet is only an example of these developments. Many companies now operate extensive internal corporate networks, or "intranets," and certain transactions, such as in the financial services sector, are likely to occur on private networks for security reasons. For tax considerations, it is generally immaterial whether parties communicate over the Internet or over a private, proprietary network, such as an online service or over an intra corporate network. It is also necessary to keep in mind that the communications revolution is the result of a number of technological and economic developments, such as relatively inexpensive computers and telecommunications services and the growth of the service sector. The growth of the service sector plays an important role because developments in communications allow services to be instantaneously transmitted around the world. As a result, services frequently no longer need to be produced at the place where they are consumed. As developments in communications facilitate international trade in services, there may be increasing pressure on the international tax rules that apply to such services.

2.4. The Internet. The most widely publicized part of the information superhighway is the Internet. While originally a system connecting governmental and academic institutions, the Internet has expanded beyond its initial participants [into a] "world-wide network with user estimates ranging from 30-60 million, and growing rapidly. The Internet has been described as a world-wide network of networks with gateways linking organizations in North and South America, Europe, the Pacific Basin and other countries. . . . The organizations are administratively independent from one another. There is no central, worldwide, technical control point. Yet, working together, these organizations have created what to a user seems to be a virtual network that spans the globe."

The Internet has no central computer or organizational structure. "Far from being a hub with spokes, the Internet is more like a spider's web, with many ways of getting from point A to point B." What links the Internet together and allows its many disparate parts to communicate is the "TCP/IP" protocol (Transmission Control Protocol/Internet Protocol), which is simply a means of specifying how data is broken up in "packets" and assigned addresses to be transferred over the Internet. It allows computers to communicate regardless of differences in hardware and software, or communications technology.

Instead of a central computer, the Internet uses hundreds of thousands of computers called "routers." Routers are like postal substations; they make decisions about how to route "packets" of data just like a postal substation decides how to route envelopes containing mail. Each router does not need a connection to every other one. Instead, packets of data are sent in the right general direction, using the best route available at the time, until they finally arrive at their destination. In fact, the individual packets making up a single message may end up taking different routes, to be recombined when they reach their destination.

The packets are transmitted over existing telephone networks. However, since the Internet is not tied to any communications technology, Internet traffic can also travel over cable TV systems, satellite links, or fiber optic cables.

3. THE WORLD WIDE WEB AND ELECTRONIC COMMERCE

3.1. Background.

3.1.1. The World Wide Web. The World Wide Web ("WWW" or "Web") is one of the fastest growing applications of the Internet. What distinguishes the Web from other components of the Internet is that it is a multimedia, hypertext system. Unlike other Internet services, the Web blends text, images, video and audio instead of displaying simple text. Web documents are hypertext documents that can contain links to other documents which can be accessed by "clicking" on these links. In fact, the links could be to any other "WWW" document on any Internet server anywhere in the world. Accessing the Web requires a browser program. The browser reads information accessed from the Web and presents it to the user in a standard format. Internet search tools allow users to locate Web pages containing the desired information.

3.1.2. Web pages and Web sites. A company's or individual's collected Web documents are usually referred to as a "Web site." A uniform addressing system allows users around the world to access information on any Web site. The information is stored in the form of Web documents and pages on central computers called servers. The location of a server is irrelevant since it can be accessed by users around the world.

3.1.3. Exponential growth of the Web. Some indication of the speed at which the World Wide Web has developed is given by the fact that it was invented in 1989. Graphical browser programs, which made the Web easy to use and thus accessible to a wide audience, were only invented in

1993. By 1996, it was estimated that there were over 250,000 commercial Web sites and a substantial number of major companies, and countless small ones, have invested in a presence on the Web.

3.1.4. Technical barriers. Two factors that will be critical to the growth of electronic commerce are bandwidth and improved payment mechanisms. Bandwidth refers to the speed at which data can be transferred over the system. Currently, at the transfer speeds available to most consumers, it would take about two days to transfer the entire contents of a music CD across the Internet. With higher speed connections likely to occur in a few years, transfer time is likely to be drastically reduced, to about 10-15 minutes. Payment is also of course a critical factor. There is an emerging consensus that electronic money . . . will accelerate the growth of electronic commerce. If payments can be made by a mouse click on an "electronic wallet" instead of transmitting credit card numbers, commerce is likely to grow.

3.2. Electronic Commerce.

3.2.1. Generally. "Electronic commerce is the ability to perform transactions involving the exchange of goods or services between two or more parties using electronic tools and techniques." The growth of electronic commerce will be driven in part by the fact that two of the present economy's important products are software and recorded entertainment (both films and music) which are particularly well suited to being distributed through computer networks.

3.2.2. Retailing and wholesaling. Web pages are now supplementing paper catalogs for many mail order companies and wholesalers. These Web pages are similar to pages from a paper catalog, displaying images of the goods and product information. Links to the vendor's inventory control system can make it possible to verify whether the requested goods are in stock. For example, one such Web site is a bookseller that allows customers to search a database of over one million books, searching by either subject or name. It is open twenty-four hours a day and has customers in over 60 countries. This Web site does not merely allow customers to select and order books but also recommends related titles and will automatically notify customers when a desired book is published.

3.2.3. Computer software. Computer software, which is created and used in digital form, can be sold and delivered electronically. Software may be transferred directly from the seller's computer to the purchaser's computer without the need to deliver a floppy disk or CD-ROM. One such electronic software vendor allows customers to select software, which is transmitted and downloaded in encrypted format. Customers then enter credit card information, which is verified over a private network via a toll-free number. After authorization, a key that unlocks the software is sent to the customer. Alternatively, the cost of the software may be charged to a pre-existing account.

3.2.4. Photographs. Photographs can be purchased over the Internet, and customers can select varying rights to utilize the photograph. For example, stock photo agencies maintain large selections of photographs on a wide range of topics, which are licensed to publishers and advertising agencies who need a photograph on a given subject. Some stock photograph agencies have established Web sites which allow customers to purchase and download digitized images.

The price is based on the customer's intended use of the photograph. For example, one such arrangement involves five, successively more expensive categories, beginning with consumers who intended to make only personal use of an image, such as a student illustrating a term paper, and increasing to commercial customers who might want to distribute an unlimited number of copies.

3.2.5. On-line information. Electronic research databases are in widespread use. Services such as Lexis-Nexis and Dialog have created vast computerized databases of reference information, such as legal materials or newspaper and magazine articles. Customers can access these databases and locate the desired information, which can be either read on-screen or printed. The distinction between on-line research services and books is now being blurred. Many publications, primarily reference works, are now being created and distributed in digital form, generally via CD-ROMs. In addition, once information has been digitized, it can also be transferred electronically. Some encyclopedias, for example, are now available either on CD-ROM or through an on-line service. With a sufficiently fast modem connection, a user might be indifferent as to whether she were accessing a CD-ROM on her desktop computer or a mainframe computer located at a distance. However, the latter, which can be easily and regularly updated, can make time-sensitive databases much more valuable than traditional "hard copies" or even CD-ROMs. In the future, the distinction between information stored on a desktop computer and information retrieved from a network will become increasing blurred as desktop software adopts Web style interfaces which will seamlessly integrate desktop and Web functions.

3.2.6. Services. Services will be a fast-growing area of electronic commerce. For example, at least one accounting firm is currently offering consulting services electronically. For a yearly fee, subscribers can obtain a password to visit the firm's Web site, where they can search a database of information and monitor relevant news. Subscribers can also submit questions, which are then routed to appropriate advisers from the firm's tax, accounting and management consulting divisions.

3.2.7. Health Care. Health care is also an area in which services can be provided electronically. Fiber optic telephone links can now transmit high quality medical images to distant specialists in minutes. For example, at the Massachusetts General Hospital, "a team of 70 radiologists has X-rays wired from their own telemedicine center in Riyadh, Saudi Arabia."

3.2.8. Videoconferencing. Videoconferencing also creates expanded opportunities for distant persons to collaborate. Currently, videoconferencing is primarily used by large businesses because it requires expensive, dedicated equipment, but it is becoming more widespread. For example, videoconferencing is being used by rural residents to obtain access to urban specialists. It is also being used by coaches to train athletes and by employers to interview job applicants. Videoconferencing is expected to become more widespread with the introduction of inexpensive desktop video cameras that can be connected to a personal computer, coupled with higher speed Internet connections.

3.2.9. Gambling. Although Internet gambling may be illegal in the United States, Internet casinos have been established offshore. These Internet casinos operate through Web sites which are virtual replicas of casinos offering electronic slot machines, black jack, poker and roulette. Customers pay for their wagers either by credit card or by establishing an account with a bank associated with the casino and winnings are credited to either the credit card or bank account. In the future, gamblers will presumably be able to place their bets using electronic money.

3.2.10. Stock trading. Some stockbrokerages and mutual fund companies have Web sites which allow customers to trade securities electronically, including stocks, bonds, mutual funds, options, futures, and commodities. Customers can access information regarding stock prices and company research and after researching the desired stock, an investor can enter an order on-line, specifying the stock, the number of shares and the price. Orders placed at the market price are routinely completed and confirmed in less than a minute. The trade is confirmed electronically and sometimes by mail as well. At present, trades are still settled conventionally, although electronic money could be used in the future. In addition to trading in the secondary market, securities are now being offered on-line.

3.2.11. Global dealing. "Global dealing" refers to the capacity of financial intermediaries, mainly banks and securities firms, to execute customers' orders and to take proprietary positions in financial products in markets around the world and around the clock. For security reasons, global dealing is conducted over private networks, instead of the Internet, although as discussed above, the means of communication is not relevant for tax purposes. Global dealing is impossible without modern computer and communications technology, which allow orders to be transmitted around the world and a firm's trading position to be continually transferred to locations where markets are open.

3.2.12. Offshore banking and incorporation. Some Web sites now offer offshore incorporation and banking services with the capacity for payment by credit card. Customers complete questionnaires on their computer, specifying the company name, desired jurisdiction, number of shares, etc., and this information is transmitted to a service company, which prepares and files the necessary forms. Although individuals and companies have always been able to create offshore corporations and open offshore bank accounts, these developments make it easier and less expensive to do so.

4. SECURITY AND ENCRYPTION

4.1. Security requirements for an open system. Security issues pose a particular problem for Internet commerce because the Internet is an "open" and inherently non-secure public system designed to facilitate information exchange. Therefore, the security that is required for practical Internet commerce requires that security procedures be applied at the level of individual commercial transactions instead of being applied to the network as a whole. This involves the encryption of transmissions, which is the first line of defense against interception, duplication, and alteration of a confidential message, whether the message represents an electronic payment or a text. Developments of systems requiring security on the Internet generally rely on "public key" encryption. In addition to keeping the contents of a message secret, these encryption procedures may also be used to create a "digital signature" which can enable the recipient of the message to independently verify the identity of the sender.

4.2. Public key encryption. Public key encryption, which is based on complex formulae involving certain mathematical properties of large prime numbers, is intended to allow someone to send a secure communication to a person with whom they have never met, or previously communicated. If they operate as intended, public key encryption techniques may play an important role in tax administration of electronic commerce transactions.

Public key cryptosystems involve two related complementary strings of numbers called keys, a publicly revealed key and a secret key (also frequently called a private key). Each key unlocks the code that the other key makes. Knowing a person's public key does not help you deduce the corresponding secret key. The public key can be published and widely disseminated across a communications network.

Anyone can use a recipient's public key to encrypt a message to that person, and that recipient uses her own corresponding secret key to decrypt that message. No one but the recipient can decrypt it, because no one else has access to that secret key. Not even the person who encrypted the message can decrypt it. Message authentication is also provided. The sender's own secret key can be used to encrypt a message, thereby creating a digital signature. Alternatively, the sender could use a separate key solely for the purpose of creating his digital signature. The recipient can check the validity of this digital signature by using the sender's public key to "decrypt" it. This proves that the sender was the true originator of the message, and that the message has not been subsequently altered by anyone else, because the sender alone possesses the secret key that made that signature. It is not practically possible to forge a digitally signed message and the sender cannot later disavow his signature.

These two processes can be combined to provide both privacy and authentication by first signing a message with the sender's secret key, then encrypting the signed message with the recipient's public key. The recipient reverses these steps by first decrypting the message with her own secret key, then checking the enclosed signature with the sender's public key. These steps are done automatically by the recipient's software.

5. PAYMENT MECHANISMS

5.1. Introduction. At present, a large portion of the money supply already exists in "digital" form, as bank account balances and other book entries with financial institutions, and is transferred in digital form through wire transfers. Physical tokens or paper instruments are no longer utilized for large-dollar payments in financial or foreign exchange transactions and roughly 90 percent of financial transactions, by value, are now conducted electronically. Conventional consumer transactions are also occurring electronically as the use of automatic teller machine cards in retail outlets continues to grow.

Electronic money, which is the focus of this chapter, involves consumer use of electronic payment systems that may partially displace cash, checks, and credit cards, which constitute about 90 percent, by volume, of financial transactions. These electronic payment systems have the potential to create new forms of money in which value is represented in digital form. "Electronic money" encompasses a wide range of products, which are all still under development. However, electronic money systems share certain similar features and an understanding of these general features is a necessary step in developing means to integrate these new payment systems into our system of tax administration and compliance.

5.2. Electronic debit and electronic credit. An electronic debit system is a payment system based on funds stored in a deposit account with a financial institution and subject to electronic payment orders to transfer funds from one account to another. An existing example of such a system is the use of automatic teller machine cards used at point of sale terminals. However, emerging electronic debit systems allow consumers to use an electronic checkbook, which can be either a hardware device or a software program, to generate unique check identifiers, maintain a check register, and create a digital signature. The electronic checks are sent via e-mail over the Internet from the payor to the payee, who uses a digital signature for endorsement and forwards it for deposit. Thus, consumers and retailers can gather, transmit, and deposit electronic checks into their accounts without physically going to a bank. If the electronic check is drawn on a bank account, it is cleared and settled through the banking system similar to a paper check.

Electronic credit systems use conventional credit card numbers to make payments over the Internet. Consumers transmit their credit card details to merchants, generally in encrypted form, who process transactions using the existing credit card payment infrastructure. In some cases third parties are used to approve and execute payments in order to eliminate the need to send a credit card number over the Internet.

Electronic debit and electronic credit systems should not raise any fundamental tax policy or administration issues because they essentially represent new ways of executing traditional bank or credit card transactions. Since an independent third party maintains records of the identity of the parties to a transaction and the amounts involved, these transactions are fully auditable. Moreover, unlike the electronic money systems described below, they do not involve new payment systems.

5.3. Electronic money. Electronic money involves tokens of value expressed in digital form, in the same sense that a casino chip is a token of value expressed in physical form. In contrast, the electronic debit and credit card systems described above are the functional equivalent of conventional check and credit card transactions and do not involve the creation of new tokens of value. The digital form of electronic money allows it to be processed inexpensively and instantaneously transferred around the world. All electronic money systems function as payment systems or payment system components and all depend upon application of high-speed communication and information analysis. Although no commonly accepted general definition of electronic money exists, some generalizations can be made.

- All purport to permit their users, in some environment, to move funds electronically.
- All rely upon advanced information technology to store, transmit, and receive representations of value.
- All depend upon modern developments in the science of encryption to provide security and upon public communications networks.
- All are possible only because of the reduced costs and economies of scale that technological advances create.
- All at some point, at least at present, require "loading" from funds held within the financial system.

The loading of funds involves the exchange of cash or deposits for digital value backed by an issuer. This could occur, for example, at an ATM, where a consumer loads a smart card with electronic cash and has a bank account debited for the same amount, or over the Internet by downloading electronic money onto a PC hard drive.

5.4. Distinctions between electronic money systems. Electronic money systems differ in a number of basic ways. The primary differences include:

 (i) the identity of the issuer;
 (ii) whether transactions are fully accounted for by the issuer;
 (iii) whether value resides in a ledger with a third party or on a storage device belonging to the consumer; and
 (iv) the means of accessing and transferring value.

These distinctions are discussed in more detail below. They are important because the way in which any particular electronic money system implements these distinctions will be the primary factors in determining how the system should fit into our system of tax administration and compliance and the concerns that the system poses for our system of tax administration and compliance.

5.5. Identity of the issuer. One distinction among electronic money systems is the identity of the issuer or sponsor. At present, electronic money can be issued by either a bank, a nonbank financial services company, or a non-financial company.

5.6. Whether transactions are fully accounted for by the issuer. The second distinction is whether electronic money transactions are fully accounted for by the issuer. There are both accounted and unaccounted systems. In an accounted system, the e-money issuer maintains a complete or partial audit trail of transactions, and can identify the person to whom the electronic money is issued as well as the people and businesses receiving the electronic money as it flows through the economy. In an unaccounted system, the e-money is issued and passes through the economy without a transaction trail. Unaccounted e-money may operate much like paper currency, moving through the economy anonymously.

There are advantages and disadvantages to both accounted and unaccounted electronic systems and they are likely to operate in tandem. Unaccounted systems may pose risks to the issuer because there are no records to rectify any problems that might arise. However, consumers may not feel comfortable using accounted electronic money for some transactions which they can currently conduct anonymously with cash. In addition an accounted system may impose costs on merchants and e-money issuers that would be passed on to consumers. These costs may be excessive relative to the benefits that consumers receive if electronic money is used for only small value transactions. In contrast, consumers may prefer accounted systems when they wish to have an independent record of the transaction.

5.7. Where the value resides. The third important distinction is whether the electronic money is stored on a ledger maintained by a third party ("notational electronic money") or is stored on a token which is maintained by the consumer ("token electronic money"). A notational electronic money system stores value as a notation in the ledger of a third party and is exchanged by subtracting amounts from one entry and adding it to another. The third party serves as an off-site control point which verifies and authorizes transactions. Token electronic money is represented by value stored on a "smart card," computer disk drive, or other storage device and the value is directly exchanged between payor and payee like currency.

5.8. Card vs. PC. Finally, a distinction can be drawn between PC-based systems and card-based systems. In PC-based systems, value is transferred to and held in a personal computer and transferred electronically from one computer to another. The PC acts as both a storehouse of value and a device to access that value.

PC-based systems usually:

- enable payment to be made by either clicking on virtual notes and coins appearing on the screen or by typing in an amount;
- are fully integrated with Web browser software to facilitate impulse buying while browsing the Internet;
- show the user's existing balance; and
- affirm transaction completion and maintain a running balance.

In contrast, card-based systems employ so-called "smart-cards" which are plastic cards containing microchips which can process and store any type of digital information, including electronic cash. Customers load value onto their cards from their bank accounts by using automated teller machines or specially equipped telephones in their homes, and eventually, over the Internet. In order to utilize the stored value a separate access device is needed which might be included in a vending machine or attached to a cash register. Similar to the farecards used on many subway systems, the stored-value card is inserted into the access device which debits value from the card and transfers the value to the merchant's account. Card-based systems also differ from PC-based systems in that PC-based systems are designed to be used remotely, whereas card-based systems are designed for face-to-face commerce in retail transactions. This is not a rigid distinction because a PC or telephone could be used as an access device for a smart-card, which would enable the card to be used remotely.

Smart card systems can be further distinguished based by whether they are "open" or "closed" systems. In a "closed" system there is generally only one card issuer and one vendor that accepts the card for payments; usually the issuer and the accepting vendor are the same entity. Common examples of closed systems are public transportation farecards, prepaid telephone cards, and prepaid copier cards. In contrast, open systems involve single or multiple issuers which provide cards that can be used with multiple vendors. Card-based systems can also permit personal transfers of value between individuals, rather than just commercial transactions, provided that the individuals have the appropriate equipment.

5.9. Example of a PC-based system. One PC-based system, for example, permits customers to purchase electronic money from a bank, generally by debiting an existing bank account. As consumers browse various Web sites which sell goods and services, their electronic money software is active in the background. The program senses when payment is required and pops up a dialog box that prompts the buyer to approve the transaction. The software removes the digital "coins" from the buyer's hard disk and transfers the serial numbers representing the electronic money to the seller's computer. The seller's computer contacts the issuing bank, which verifies that the serial numbers representing the electronic money have not been used and notifies the seller that the electronic money is valid. At that point, the seller sends the electronic goods to buyer. The seller will eventually deposit the electronic money in a bank.

In the context of the analytical framework discussed above, such a system is a nonbank, token, unaccounted, PC-based system. Although the electronic money was issued by a bank, it is a nonbank system because a bank is not required. It is a token system because the strings of numbers representing "digital coins" are stored on the customer's computer, not a central ledger. Finally, it is an unaccounted system because the issuer does not maintain any records of how the electronic money is used until it is presented for conversion into conventional funds.

6. TAX POLICY AND ADMINISTRATION ISSUES: GENERAL CONSIDERATIONS

6.1. General. Any consideration of the substantive tax policy, and tax administration and compliance issues that arise in this area must be guided by basic tax policy principles and must also take into account the technical and scientific characteristics of the Global Information Infrastructure, including the Internet.

6.2. Neutrality. A fundamental guiding principle should be neutrality. Neutrality requires that the tax system treat economically similar income equally, regardless of whether earned through electronic means or through more conventional channels of commerce. Ideally, tax rules would not affect economic choices about the structure of markets and commercial activities. This will ensure that market forces alone determine the success or failure of new commercial methods. The best means by which neutrality can be achieved is through an approach which adopts and adapts existing principles—in lieu of imposing new or additional taxes.

Recent technological developments may appear to be radical innovations primarily because they have evolved within a relatively short period of time. However, careful examination may very well reveal that few, if any, of these emerging issues will be so intractable that their resolution will not be found using existing principles, appropriately adjusted.

6.3. Impact of technical features of the Internet. The policies and rules governing the taxation of electronic commerce cannot be developed without an understanding of the underlying technical features. Although chapter three presented a sampling of current means of electronic commerce, the basic technical structure of the Internet has some important implications for tax policy and administration. These aspects are restated here.

6.3.1. Radically decentralized; no central control. The Internet has no physical location. Users of the Internet have no control and in general no knowledge of the path traveled by the information they seek or publish. Many participants in the system are administrators or intermediaries who have no control over what type of information travels over their computers; rather they offer interconnectivity which enables the system to operate. In practical terms, it would therefore be difficult to monitor or prevent transmissions of information or electronic cash across the Internet. From a technical perspective, in principle and generally in practice, it makes no difference whether the information or electronic money sought to be transmitted are within one jurisdiction or between several, as the Internet pays little or no regard to national boundaries.

6.3.2. Disintermediation. In general, tax compliance is facilitated by identifying key "taxing points": for example, reporting requirements can be imposed on financial institutions which are easy to identify. In contrast, one of the great commercial advantages of electronic commerce is that it often eliminates the need for intermediating institutions.

6.3.3. Weak correspondence between computer domain name and reality. The pieces of an Internet address (or "domain-style name") tell you who is responsible for maintaining that name. It may not tell you anything about the computer corresponding to the actual Internet address, or even where that machine is located. Even if an e-mail address is clearly associated with a certain person and computer, that person and her computer could be located anywhere in the world. This makes it difficult to determine a person's location and identity, which is often important for tax purposes.

6.3.4. Lack of central control/Registration. It is not difficult to introduce a new computer to the Internet. Registration requirements are not difficult to satisfy, and there is little to prevent transfer of the site to new controllers. In general, proof of identity requirements for Internet use are very weak.

6.3.5. Auditability/Remote control. Untraceable use of an Internet site, with the permission of the site's controllers, is quite easy to arrange. For example, if Anne, who lives in Australia, is running a commercial site on the Internet for U.S. customers, using a computer located in Canada, Anne can control the Canadian computer from Australia through a series of computer programs which can be configured to leave no audit trail. Moreover, if the need arises, operations can be shifted to somewhere else on the Internet.

6.3.6. Detection of contents. Since all electronic communication consists of streams of binary digits, it is difficult, if not impossible, to determine the contents until converted. At present, a personal letter appears indistinguishable from a message transmitting electronic money. Even if the nature of the contents is determined, the use of encryption could preclude comprehension.

7. SUBSTANTIVE TAX LAW ISSUES

7.1. Introduction.

7.1.1. General. This section discusses the impact of electronic commerce on substantive principles of taxation. Current tax concepts, such as the U.S. trade or business, permanent establishment, and source of income concepts, were developed in a different technological era. However, the principle of neutrality between physical and electronic commerce requires that existing principles of taxation be adapted to electronic commerce, taking into account the borderless world of cyberspace. An advantage of an approach based on existing principles, in addition to neutrality, is that such an approach is suitable for adaptation as an international standard. Existing principles are, in broad outline, common to most countries' tax laws.

7.1.2. Bases for taxation. The United States taxes income on the basis of both the source of the income and the residence of the person earning that income. U.S. source income is subject to tax when earned by foreign persons as is the worldwide income of U.S. citizens, residents, and corporations. Although U.S. persons are subject to net basis taxation on their worldwide income, the foreign tax credit provisions avoid double taxation of foreign source income. Our international tax treaty network, while attempting to minimize taxation at source, also protects against double taxation.

7.1.3. Source of income. Source of income concepts play a central role in international taxation since the country of source generally has a right to tax income and residence countries generally avoid double taxation through either a credit system or an exemption system. Source of income principles are generally similar worldwide. In general, the source of income is located where the economic activities creating the income occur. For example, income derived from the use of intellectual property has its source in the location where the intellectual property is utilized. Compensation for labor or personal services has its source in the location where the labor or personal services are performed. Furthermore, residence-based source rules have been adopted for certain types of income such as capital gains and swap income because the country of residence represents the location where the economic activity that produces the income occurs. Generally, the nature of an item of income is important for determining source because the source of income flows from its nature.

7.1.4. Role of tax treaties. The United States currently has comprehensive income tax treaties with 48 countries. The rules embodied in these tax treaties generally give the residence country an unlimited right to tax income while limiting or eliminating the source country's right to tax. One of the most important concepts in tax treaties is that of a "permanent establishment." Source countries tend to give up their source-based taxing rights over business profits if they are not attributable to a "permanent establishment" or "fixed base" in their jurisdiction. Treaties generally limit the rate of taxation at source that can be applied to interest, dividends, and royalties paid to a resident of a treaty partner.

7.1.5. The ascendancy of residence-based taxation. The United States, as do most countries, asserts jurisdiction to tax based on principles of both source and residence. If double taxation is to be avoided, however, one principle must yield to the other. Therefore, through tax treaties, countries tend to restrict their source-based taxing rights with respect to foreign taxpayers in order to exercise more fully their residence-based taxing rights. This occurs in a number of ways. The permanent establishment concept represents a preference for residence-based taxation by setting an appropriate threshold for source-based taxation of active business income. By setting a threshold, in most cases it is not necessary to identify the source of active business income and the income is only subject to tax in the country of residence. In the case of interest, dividends, and royalties, the income is still potentially subject to source-based taxation but in many cases is effectively subject to only residence-based taxation because of a nil rate of withholding. The country of residence also agrees to take appropriate steps to ameliorate any possible double taxation resulting from the limited source-based taxation.

The growth of new communications technologies and electronic commerce will likely require that principles of residence-based taxation assume even greater importance. In the world of cyberspace, it is often difficult, if not impossible, to apply traditional source concepts to link an item of income with a specific geographical location. Therefore, source based taxation could lose its rationale and be rendered obsolete by electronic commerce. By contrast, almost all taxpayers are resident somewhere. An individual is almost always a citizen or resident of a given country and, at least under U.S. law, all corporations must be established under the laws of a given jurisdiction. However, a review of current residency definitions and taxation rules may be appropriate.

In situations where traditional source concepts have already been rendered too difficult to apply effectively, the residence of the taxpayer has been the most likely means to identify the jurisdiction where the economic activities that created the income took place, and thus the jurisdiction that should have the primary right to tax such income. For example, . . . Congress adopted residence-based sourcing rules for sales of noninventory property. This reflected Congress' belief "that source rules for sales of personal property should generally reflect the location of the economic activity generating the income, taking into account the jurisdiction in which those activities are performed." In the case of certain sales of personal property, the residence of the seller was thought to best represent the location where the underlying economic activity occurred. Similar rules were adopted for certain space and ocean activities. Therefore, United States tax policy has already recognized that as traditional source principles lose their significance, residence-based taxation can step in and take their place. This trend will be accelerated by developments in electronic commerce where principles of residence-based taxation will also play a major role.

7.2. U.S. Trade or Business and Permanent Establishment.

7.2.1. Taxation of non-resident aliens and foreign corporations.
Non-resident aliens and foreign corporations are generally only subject to tax on their U.S. source income, including income derived from the performance of personal services in the United States, and certain foreign source income that is attributable to a U.S. trade or business. Unless a treaty applies, non-resident aliens and foreign corporations are taxed at ordinary graduated rates on their net income effectively connected with a trade or business in the United States, and are taxed at a flat rate on the gross amount of their U.S. source "fixed or determinable annual or periodical gains, profits and income." A U.S. trade or business includes the performance of personal services within the United States. Therefore being engaged in a trade or business in the United States is a threshold requirement for the taxation of active business income earned by foreign persons.

7.2.1.1. "In the United States."
In many cases, it is clear that a foreign person is engaged in a trade or business but it is not clear whether they are so engaged "in the United States." However, a foreign person not physically present in the United States who merely solicits orders from within the United States only through advertising and then sends tangible goods to the United States in satisfaction of the orders is unlikely to be engaged in a trade or business in the United States even though such a person is clearly engaged in a trade or business. A person who is not directly engaged in a U.S. trade or business may nevertheless be deemed to be engaged in a U.S. trade or business as the result of the activities of an agent.

7.2.2. Impact of tax treaties: Permanent establishment concept.
Tax treaties adopt a different and generally higher threshold for source basis taxation of active income. U.S. source active income ("business profits") of non-resident aliens and foreign corporations who are entitled to benefits under a U.S. income tax treaty is only subject to U.S. tax if the income is attributable to a permanent establishment located in the United States. A permanent establishment is a fixed place of business through which the business of an enterprise is wholly or partly carried on. "[I]t has come to be accepted in international fiscal matters that until an enterprise of one State sets up a permanent establishment in another State it should not properly be regarded as participating in the economic life of that other State to such an extent that it comes within the jurisdiction of that other State's taxing rights." Therefore, a foreign person who is entitled to benefits under a tax treaty with the United States will not be subject to U.S. tax on the income arising from a trade or business in the United States if the income is not attributable to a permanent establishment in the United States.

7.2.3. U.S. tax jurisdiction in the context of electronic commerce.

7.2.3.1. U.S. trade or business.
The concept of a U.S. trade or business was developed in the context of conventional types of commerce, which generally are conducted through identifiable physical locations. Electronic

commerce, on the other hand, may be conducted without regard to national boundaries and may dissolve the link between an income-producing activity and a specific location. From a certain perspective, electronic commerce doesn't seem to occur in any physical location but instead takes place in the nebulous world of "cyberspace." Persons engaged in electronic commerce could be located anywhere in the world and their customers will be ignorant of, or indifferent to, their location. Indeed, this is an important advantage of electronic commerce in that it gives small businesses the potential to reach customers all over the world.

Electronic commerce permits a foreign person to engage in extensive transactions with U.S. customers without entering the United States. Although such a person is clearly engaged in a trade or business, questions will arise as to whether he is engaged in a trade or business in the United States or has a permanent establishment in the United States. Therefore, it is necessary to clarify the application of the U.S. trade or business and permanent establishment concepts to persons engaged in electronic commerce. In developing principles to classify these activities, it will be important to consider the extent to which electronic commerce simply represents an extension of current means of doing business, the tax consequences of which are understood. For example, to the extent that the activities of a person engaged in electronic commerce are equivalent to the mere solicitation of orders from U.S. customers, without any other U.S. activity, it may not be appropriate to treat such activities as a U.S. trade or business. It will also be necessary to consider whether it is appropriate or practical to treat foreign persons engaged in electronic commerce with U.S. customers as being engaged in a U.S. trade or business if they are physically located outside the United States.

Another example is the treatment of foreign persons who maintain or utilize a computer server in the United States. Computer servers can be located anywhere in the world and their users are indifferent to their location. It is possible that such a server, or similar equipment, is not a sufficiently significant element in the creation of certain types of income to be taken into account for purposes of determining whether a U.S. trade or business exists. It is also possible that if the existence of a U.S.-based server is taken into account for this purpose, foreign persons will simply utilize servers located outside the United States since the server's location is irrelevant.

Finally, consideration may also be given to the role other activities should play in determining whether a U.S. trade or business exists. For example, it may ultimately be decided that a foreign person who operates a computerized research service through computers located outside of the United States might not be engaged in a U.S. trade or business unless other U.S. situs activities exist. However, U.S.-based individuals engaged in providing marketing and support services for a foreign-based provider of computerized research may create a U.S. trade or business for the foreign person even if the computer servers and other activities are located outside the United States.

7.2.4. Permanent establishment. To the extent that a foreign person is not engaged in a U.S. trade or business, then the absence of a permanent establishment is irrelevant since the United States will not tax that person's active business income. However, some persons entitled to benefits under a U.S. income tax treaty will not be subject to U.S. tax due to the lack of a permanent establishment, notwithstanding the fact that they may be engaged in a U.S. trade or business. A U.S. permanent establishment generally requires a fixed place of business in the United States although a permanent establishment can also arise by imputation from the activities of an agent. Therefore, persons engaged in electronic commerce may not have a U.S. permanent establishment because they do not have a fixed place of business in the United States, unless a permanent establishment is created by imputation. . . .

Telecommunications or computer equipment owned or used by a foreign person engaged in electronic commerce raises a question as to whether this equipment could constitute a fixed place of business of the foreign person in the United States, taking into account that there would not necessarily be any employees present. It will be necessary to consider whether a foreign person who owns or utilizes a computer server located in the United States should be deemed to have a U.S. permanent establishment. Again, it is useful to review the treatment of existing, traditional commercial activities and consider whether any existing exclusions from permanent establishment treatment should apply in this situation. For example, a permanent establishment generally does not include "the use of facilities solely for the purpose of storage, display, or delivery of goods or merchandise . . . ." For a business which sells information instead of goods, a computer server might be considered the equivalent of a warehouse. Examination and interpretation of the permanent establishment concept in the context of electronic commerce may well result in an extension of the policies and the resulting exceptions to electronic commerce.

7.2.5. U.S. trade or business or permanent establishment by imputation: Telecommunications and Internet service providers. A U.S. trade or business or permanent establishment can also arise by imputation from an agent's activities. Agency issues arise from the relationship between a foreign person and a computer online service or telecommunications service provider. Even if a person engaged in electronic commerce does not maintain a computer server or similar equipment in the United States, issues of U.S. trade or business or permanent establishment would also arise. In most cases, information will be transmitted to the customer's computer through telephone lines. For example, a foreign person who operated a computerized research service might contract with a U.S. telecommunications company to provide local dial access service so that the foreign person's U.S. customers can access its computerized databases. Alternatively, the U.S. customers might access the foreign information seller's Web site using a U.S.-based Internet service provider. Presumably, the foreign person's relationship with a local telecommunications service provider is such that the telecommunications service provider would not even be considered an agent of the foreign person. Even if an agency relationship were deemed to exist, the service provider would likely be considered an independent agent, with the result that a U.S. trade or business or permanent establishment would not arise. Nevertheless, it may be necessary to further clarify the applicable principles in this area and seek to create an international consensus on this issue.

7.2.6. Taxation of telecommunications service providers. The principles used to determine whether a person is engaged in a U.S. trade or business or maintains a U.S. permanent establishment might differ if the person is primarily engaged in providing telecommunications services, in contrast to a business which is primarily engaged in selling goods or services for whom the telecommunications services are merely incidental. A distinction is generally recognized between activities that "contribute to the productivity of the enterprise" and activities that involve the "actual realization of profits." In the case of a foreign telecommunications service provider, the operation of a computer server in the United States or the sale of computing services and Internet access to U.S. and foreign customers is clearly integral to the realization of its profits, in contrast to the case of a foreign person who is primarily engaged in selling data which is stored on a U.S.-based server.

7.3. Digitized Information: Classification of Income.

7.3.1. Transactions in digitized information. Any type of information that can be digitized, such as computer programs, books, music, or images, can be transferred electronically. For example, a U.S. person could, via the Internet, communicate with a computer located in a foreign country and download a computer program or digitized image or video in exchange for a fee. The purchaser's rights in the information transferred could vary depending on the contract between the parties.

The purchaser of a digitized image could obtain the right to use a single copy of the image, the right to reproduce ten copies of the image for use in a corporate report, the right to reproduce the image for use in an academic work that is expected to have a limited press run, or the right to reproduce the image in a mass-circulation magazine. Depending on the facts and circumstances, some of these transactions may be viewed as the equivalent of the purchase of a physical copy or copies of the photograph, which would probably not subject the seller to U.S. taxation, while other of these transactions would result in royalty income because they involve payments for the use of or the privilege of using copyrights or similar property in the United States, which could be taxable in the United States.

Technological developments have necessitated a reexamination of existing income classification principles in light of the ease of perfectly reproducing and disseminating digitized information. Classifying transactions involving digitized information may require a more complex analysis that disregards the form of the transaction—without regard to whether tangible property is involved—in favor of an analysis of the rights transferred. This is necessary to ensure neutrality between the taxation of transactions in digitized information and transactions in traditional forms of information, such as hard copy books and movies, so that decisions regarding the form in which information is distributed are not affected by tax considerations.

7.3.2. Classification of income issues. Information that can be digitized is generally protected by copyright law. Payments made for the use of or for the privilege of using copyrights are considered royalties. Similarly the U.S. Model Tax Convention defines "royalties" as "payments of any kind received as consideration for the use of, or the right to use, any copyright of literary, artistic or scientific work including cinematograph films . . . ." It is not always clear how this definition applies to the sale of digitized information. Yet, it is clear that some of these transactions, such as the electronic purchase of computer programs, are merely substitutes for conventional transactions involving physical objects.

Digitized information also presents unique issues because it can be perfectly reproduced, often by the purchaser. Although someone desiring to purchase ten copies of a bound book will generally purchase ten copies from a publisher, someone wishing to purchase ten copies of an electronic book may simply purchase one copy and acquire the right to make nine additional copies. This transaction might literally be considered to create royalty income, at least in part, since the right to make reproductions is a right reserved to the copyright holder and by allowing a third party to make reproductions, the payment is, at least in part, in consideration for the use of the copyright. However, this transaction may also be viewed as merely a substitute for the purchase of ten copies from the publisher in which the purchaser has undertaken to make the copies, a process which would not be feasible were the information not digitized. Therefore, it is necessary to apply the definition of "royalties" in a manner that takes into account the unique characteristics of digitized information. . . .

7.3.4. Definition of services income. Digitized information may also further complicate existing difficulties in defining services income, as distinguished from sales of goods income or royalties. This distinction is important for purposes of determining the source of income, and for the application of various Code provisions including the Subpart F rules. Under Subpart F, the definition of foreign base company sales income differs from the definition of foreign base company services income. Therefore, whether a transaction is deemed to result in sale of goods income, as distinguished from services income, may affect whether such income will be Subpart F income that will be subject to current tax.

The distinction between services income and other types of income is a pervasive issue throughout the Code. For example, in many cases, the distinction between service contracts and other arrangements is unclear. Although many commercial transactions involve elements of both the provision of tangible property and the performance of services, these transactions are generally classified in accordance with their predominant characteristic. For example, a transaction involving the performance of professional services may result in the provision of a letter or other document. The aspect of the transaction consisting of the provision of the tangible property is treated as incidental to the performance of the services. In contrast, if a retail establishment sells a suit to a customer but agrees to make slight alterations as part of the purchase price, the performance of services would be viewed as an integral part of a transaction consisting of the sale of goods. . . .

A further example of where new technologies will blur these distinctions involve transactions in digitized information over the Internet. For example, a reference work, such as an encyclopedia, would previously have been sold only as a set of bound volumes and the sale of the bound volumes would have resulted in sale of goods income, notwithstanding the fact that the cost of printing and binding represented only a fraction of the encyclopedia's value. Now, instead of purchasing a bound volume, a potential purchaser might be able to choose between a set of CD-ROMs and a computer on-line service through which the encyclopedia's content can be accessed. If the customer has a sufficiently fast modem connection, there may be little practical difference between accessing the on-line service and the CD-ROMs on the customer's personal computer. The sale of the CD-ROMs may result in sale of goods income while the classification of the income arising from the on-line service is not clear. The on-line service may result in services income although in some circumstances it could be characterized as a means of distributing copies of copyrighted works. However, a distinction between sales of goods and services income may still be appropriate in this area taking into account the frequency at which the on-line service will be updated and the fact that the user of the online service must continue to make periodic payments, as contrasted with the fact that the purchaser of the CD-ROM may acquire the right to use the disk in perpetuity for a single payment. It will be necessary to consider the principles to be applied in these situations that will best implement the policy behind the underlying Code provisions.

7.3.5. Effect on Controlled Foreign Corporation rules. The ability of taxpayers to electronically sell digitized information and services may have an effect on existing rules regarding the controlled foreign corporation provisions of Subpart F. Subpart F limits the use of tax deferral through controlled foreign corporations (CFCs) by currently taxing certain types of highly mobile income to the CFC's "United States shareholders." If CFCs can engage in extensive commerce in information and services through Web sites or computer networks located in a tax haven, it may become increasingly difficult to enforce Subpart F. Some persons engaged in electronic commerce may already be locating their businesses offshore. . . . [T]his presents enforcement problems because it may be difficult to verify the identity of the taxpayer to whom foreign base company sales income accrues and the amount of such income. It may be necessary to revise Subpart F or the regulations thereunder to take these new types of transactions into account.

7.4. Source of Services Income.

7.4.1. Geographic basis. Income derived from the performance of labor or personal services only constitutes U.S. source income if the person performing the services is physically present in the United States. This is also a generally accepted international principle. This requirement is based on the view that there is generally an independent, substantial significance to the location where the person rendering the services is located with the result that it is reasonable for that country to tax such services. This concept is also relevant for purposes of Subpart F since foreign base company services income only includes services which "are performed outside the country under the laws of which the controlled foreign corporation is organized." As travel and communications have become more efficient and less expensive, the relationship between the service provider's location and the service consumer's location has weakened. For example, it is now possible for physicians to remotely diagnose certain diseases through telecommunications links and videoconferencing has eliminated the need for many face-to-face meetings.

7.4.2. Role of existing concepts. These technological developments are generally extensions of existing communications devices. For example, a video conference is likely to be a substitute for a conference telephone call. Although these communications developments may pose some base erosion potential since service providers will find it easier to relocate to low-tax jurisdictions, it may be the case that the base erosion potential is not so significant as to require review of the current general principles of residence-based taxation applicable to services. In devising rules to source this type of income, it may also be necessary to consider the relationship between the service-provider's physical location and other potential indicia of source, such as the location of a computer server or communications link. Furthermore, to the extent the source of this income is becoming both less meaningful and increasingly difficult to determine, residence-based taxation should necessarily play a larger role.

7.5. Global Services: Allocation of Income and Expenses.

7.5.1. Global collaboration. The foregoing section discussed the problem of determining the source of income derived from the performance of services. A related issue arises from increases in global collaboration arising from modern telecommunications. One example is global dealing. As discussed above, global dealing refers to the capacity of financial intermediaries, mainly banks and securities firms, to execute customers' orders and to take propriety positions in financial products in markets around the world and around the clock. Global dealing could not take place without modern computers and communications, which permit a firm's trading position to be transferred around the world as markets open and close. Similarly, certain scientific and engineering projects are now being worked on twenty-four hours a day as laboratories in one region electronically hand-off the project at the end of the day to a laboratory where the day is beginning. This type of global collaboration is expected to increase.

7.5.2. General principles of allocation. Global collaboration is not a new concept. When goods are manufactured in one country and marketed and distributed in another, the overall transaction could be characterized as global collaboration in the sale of goods. Global collaboration requires transfer pricing and source of income principles, to correctly allocate the resulting income between the countries involved. Current transfer pricing principles are focused on global collaboration in the manufacture and sale of goods and the creation and transfer of intangibles. The cost sharing regulations under section 482 apply to allocate the results of certain global research and development efforts, but only when intangibles are created.

By contrast, global dealing income has been allocated through case-by-case negotiations between the competent authorities involved, although a guidance project on global dealing is currently developing rules of general application. As the ways in which companies collaborate globally to provide services continue to grow, it may be appropriate to consider the creation of general principles for the arm's length allocation of broader categories of services income based on each situation's particular facts. These rules could be implemented through Treasury Regulations and international consensus. To the extent that capital is not a material income-producing factor in this situation, it would be expected that the place where the component services were performed would be of primary importance in allocating such income. . . .

9. CONCLUSION

As the communications revolution continues to sweep through the world economy, tax principles and systems of tax administration will have to adapt. This paper represents an attempt to further that process. It is not intended to resolve the tax policy and administration issues posed by the communications revolution but is intended to identify and assess some of these issues. Certain issues may initially appear to be so complex that they cannot be dealt with by existing principles. Further study is likely to result in the conclusion that one or more existing principles are more flexible than they may seem and they remain relevant notwithstanding technological developments. However, some of these technological developments, such as the potential growth of extensive anonymous transactions involving electronic cash, do raise certain existing administration and compliance issues to new levels of concern.

Treasury looks forward to receiving comments from, and working with taxpayers and their advisors, including both tax law specialists and computer technology specialists, academics, and foreign tax policy makers and administrators, to better understand these technologies and develop rational and enforceable tax rules. This can play an important role in fostering the growth of these technologies and transactions. Clear and rational principles will ensure that the tax law will not be an impediment to the growth of these exciting technologies that have such a great potential to improve our lives. . . .